# New Poets of the American West

*~An anthology of poets from eleven Western states~*

**Many Voices Press**
*Flathead Valley Community College*

**Cover Painting:** AM Stockhill

**Cover Design:** Sally Johnson

**Many Voices Press** is a nonprofit press from Flathead Valley Community College. Donations are tax-deductible. We depend on the generosity of people like you.

For more information about our books:

Lowell Jaeger, Editor
Many Voices Press
Flathead Valley Community College
777 Grandview Drive
Kalispell, Montana 59901
(406) 756-3822
ljaeger@fvcc.edu

*New Poets of the American West*
First Edition

Softbound
ISBN — 978-0-9795185-4-6

© 2010 Many Voices Press

Cataloging-in-Publication data on file at the Library of Congress.
Library of Congress Control Number 2010924070

Created, produced, and designed in the United States.
Printed in the United States.

## Special Thanks to:

James Soular
Sally Johnson
Holly Schaffer (University of Arizona Press)
Hannah Mae Bissell
Sinda Puryer
Robert O'Neil
Copper Canyon Press
New Directions Publishing Corporation
Shaun Griffin
Amy Jaeger
Margaret Smith
Lisa Simon
Jason Neal
Margaret Kingsland
Kathy Hughes
Flathead Valley Community College
Barclay Agency
Robert Blesse (Black Rock Press)
Fran Morrow (Nevada Arts Council)
Simon Ortiz
Guy Lebeda (Utah Arts Council)
Ken Egan (Humanities Montana)
Kim Anderson (Humanities Montana)
Arlynn Fishbaugh (Montana Arts Council)
Aaron Anstett
Allen Weltzien
Brady Harrison
James Kraft

## About the Cover Artist:

AM Stockhill is a working artist/illustrator specializing in richly-textured painting surfaces, and warm, earth-inspired colors. The popular *Horse* series presents the essence of the horse's strength, beauty, passion and power. AM's Earth series responds both to the peace and the fury of nature. Mixed-media work extends into the abstract and non-representational worlds as well. To learn more about AM Stockhill and view her paintings, visit www.amstockhill.com.

~ Two poets in *New Poets of the American West*, Will Inman and Bill Cowee, and
translator Sophie Mays have passed away since we began this project ~
We shall miss their voices in the choir.

# Table of Contents

**Colorado**

~ for Bernadine Tomasik ~

(1940—1996)

# Editor's Note: In This Spirit I Gathered These Poems

There are all kinds of poets and all kinds of poems. Of course. And so much talk about which poets and poems are praise-worthy and which are not so worthy. With or without our critical theories and analytical studies of differing styles, let's hope the worthy voices—of any style, every style—find appreciative ears.

As a reader, I'm most pleased by poems made from the stuff of this world, the nuts and bolts of our daily existence. Erin Fristad's "Advice to Female Deckhands," for instance, is such a poem. She tells us, "You must keep the kettle on the stove full / and the juice jug and two gallons of milk in the fridge." She fills the poem with real objects, real people, real experience. The poem convinces me that this woman knows what she's talking about, and sure enough her bio on the same page says she's worked as a deckhand for years. But I wouldn't need the bio; the details in the poem echo with hard-earned experience. Only someone who has truly been there, done that, could know such things.

> You will learn
> to ignore the other crew members sitting
> at the galley table reading. You must know
> how to create a corral in rough weather,
> so pots of soup don't end up dripping
> down the firewall behind the stove. You will need
> bungee cords to keep the cast iron skillet from sliding.
> These cords melt if they touch the stovetop.
> Keep a squeeze container of Aloe Vera gel
> under the galley sink for the burns
> on your hands and forearms.

These are the specifics of a female deckhand's daily routine. Through the poet's careful selection of detail, she has earned my attention. She's credible. I'm assured, as a reader, that this poet has something of importance to tell me, something beyond easy platitudes, armchair philosophies, or just pretty words.

These details, these specifics, spark my imagination. As I read the poem, I can "see" in my "mind's eye" what the poet is talking about. I've never been a deckhand, but this poem is my opportunity to experience at least a piece of a deckhand's duties and concerns. Laurence Perrine, author of the old-but-always-reliable text, *Sound and Sense*, says a poem is the "re-creation of experience." A poem can project a little movie in the reader's mind; for a couple pages, I walk in the poet's shoes, stand before the galley stove, as she re-creates her experience for me. Her words are like a camera lens, feeding images to the reader. It's no small trick to make images with words, mere black and white marks on the page. It's an Olympic challenge to select just the right images—grab readers and carry them forward—word by word, line by line, stanza by stanza, through the poem.

"Advice to Female Deckhands" is firmly engaged in the real world, a poem with a high "reality quotient." The poem resists simplifying, prettifying, or romanticizing the nitty-gritty complexities of the deckhand's reality. Conversely, the poem resists sensationalizing the hardships of the job.

> The stove will blow out on windy days
> when you're exhausted,
> your skin stinging with jelly fish.
> The crew will say they're not hungry on these days
> but when you slide behind the Cape, it will be flat
> calm and all of you will be starving.

The fire in the stove has blown out, the cook is exhausted and miserable with jelly fish stings. The same crew who sat idle at the galley table while the cook struggled with her duties in the first stanza, now claim they're not hungry anyway, as much of a compassionate gesture as they can muster, but a compassionate gesture nonetheless. The poem stays true to the complexities of real human interaction, in which none of us are all good or all bad, and all of us are full of surprises.

As a poet, I feel I walk through my life with a split consciousness. Part of me is engaged in the here and now, doing what I do, like everyone else. Poets live ordinary lives. Another part of me hovers somewhere above, watching, witnessing. The engaged part of me is focused on the particulars of my days; the witness part takes a broader perspective, sees the big picture. It's usually the witness part of me speaking in my poems. In Erin Fristad's poem, as in so many other poems to which I'm attracted, I hear the poet's witness speaking.

> . . . turn off the fuel source
> by flipping a breaker in the engine room.
> You don't have time for ear protection. Get down there
> and back before someone hollers for you on deck.
> Passing the engine, watch the straps on your raingear,
> your ponytail, where you put your hands.

The action is in the present, immediate, and so close at hand only the particulars will come into focus, as it is for most of us, most days. That's the engaged part of the poet. Meanwhile, the perspective of the poem, or "voice," is the poet's witness speaking, that part of the poet's consciousness that suspects these seemingly petty details add up to matters of larger significance.

This larger significance is revealed in the final two stanzas of the poem, where a third consciousness opens its eye, widens the poet's eye, and the reader's, too. Most poets will tell you, if asked, that they have little to no preconceived notion of a poem when they begin scratching out the first few lines. This "third consciousness" has something to do with language itself. In the act of writing things down, the writer discovers things, comes to new realizations and surprising conclusions. It's a pleasurable experience to let language carry you forward into new vistas, a thrill to have connected with a "consciousness" larger than your own. Maybe this is Jung's "collective unconscious." Maybe not. In the fourth stanza of "Advice to Female Deckhands," a third consciousness rips the poem from the poet's control, and surprising things happen. The speaker of the poem is still the experienced female deckhand giving us advice: "When cooking, remember all odors from the galley / drift directly into the wheelhouse. Fish sauce / smells like dirty tennis shoes." These lines trigger something powerful, and suddenly the poem leaps to its larger significance.

>                                 Once she smells this,
> the skipper's daughter will refuse to eat anything
> she suspects has fish sauce. As a woman and cook
> you will be expected to have a special bond with the skipper's daughter
> and you will . . . .
>                        When she cries
> put your arm around her, kiss her
> on the top of the head and let her cry.
> Allow her to use your cell phone to call friends
> in exchange for making salads, pots of coffee,
> washing lunch dishes, carrying groceries to the boat.
> Develop sign language for communicating
> when she stands in the galley door
> peering out at you on deck.

It's impossible to know for certain, but I suspect the mention of tennis shoes conjures the skipper's daughter into the poem. A surprising turn. The poem is about the daughter now, and the female deckhand's esteem for this young girl. "This isn't what I intended," the poet tells us.

> I set out to give you advice for taking care
> of yourself, now it's about taking care of a girl
> you're related to by circumstance.

No, it's not at all what the poet intended; the poem has swerved in a new direction, and the poet lets it go there. That's the pleasurable, unpredictable outcome of letting language, or a "third consciousness," take over. Now the poem is about things bigger than the details of the poet's experience, however vivid and captivating those details are. The poem is first of all about working on a fishing boat, and second of all about specific challenges a female deckhand must overcome. As soon as the skipper's daughter comes into focus, the poem is poking at truths bigger than what it is to be a female deckhand; the poem wants to illuminate an important question about womanhood. What is it in a woman, the poem asks, that is instinctually nurturing? The poem knows it's an unanswerable question. The poem ends, "You'll notice a hum / more penetrating than the engine." That "hum" is the unknowable, instinctual drive each of us has glimpsed, especially under pressure, a deep-seated something in our blood that defines who we are.

Yes, poems with an embedded narrative animated by fresh images of real world experience win me over as a reader, and you will find I've chosen, as editor, many similar poems for this anthology. There are other kinds of poems here, too. In poetry, there are lots of strategies to catch a reader. What matters most, in the end, is that the reader is rewarded for his or her efforts in reading through the poem. This was my final criterion in pasting these poems, page by page, to build *New Poets of the American West*. I've discussed Erin Fristad's poem in particular to open a path for readers who are new to poetry—a humble lesson in how to read a poem. It's my fondest hope that many readers who are unfamiliar with poetry will open these pages and discover a lasting appreciation for the wonders of words. Over nearly three decades, I've taught poetry courses and workshops to audiences of all descriptions, beginners especially, and I know with certainty that people who claim they can't understand poetry, can indeed. It's a matter of exposure, I think. Most people haven't sat with a poem long enough to get to know one. We are busy people, more likely to spend our lives stacking bricks and mixing mortar than we are inclined to fortify our hearts and minds. Maybe in this culture it's a poet's job to slow people down from all this "doing" and get them thinking about what it is they are doing and why they are doing it.

So, let's slow down a moment, and let's look again at "Advice to Female Deckhands" from another slant. Consider the poem as artifact. Try reading the poem as if we are archeologists on a dig. We've just unearthed this message, dusted it off, and determined the marks are in a language still decipherable. What can the words reveal about the person who wrote them? What can we learn about this person's world? The poem was written by a woman. It's a poem about work, about being a deckhand on a fishing boat, about stoves, bungee cords, and deck buckets. This culture values equipment and technologies and the knowledge to use them. In this culture, both men and women labor, at times side-by-side. Although the woman in the poem is expected to do difficult and often dangerous work, her status in the labor force is nonetheless subservient to the men. A male-dominated society? At times, the poet is exhausted and miserable, but she takes pride in her competence and in her ability to cope with adversity. The men rely on the woman to prepare their food, and in other ways, she takes care of them. Gender roles are in some instances clearly defined in this culture and in other instances not so clearly defined. Could this have been an era in which gender roles were shifting? We know this poet lived in the American Pacific Northwest. Is her experience typical of other women's experience in that region at that time in history?

On the basis of one poem alone, as archeologists, we haven't enough evidence to conclude anything. All we can do is surmise. Of course. But what if we continued to dig and found a whole trunk full of poems, or its equivalent—an anthology, *New Poets of the American West*, containing over 250 poets, 450 poems? Now we might glean a more articulate and reliable sense of what life was like for these people, these residents of Western America in the early twenty-first century. How did they live? What were their ambitions, their dreams, their hopes, their fears? What were their causes and concerns? What was their relationship to the environment in which they lived? Were their lives in this particular region any different from the lives of Americans in other regions of the nation? How similar were their lives to what we know of their ancestors? How dissimilar? Were they a settled or mobile people, or both? Do they identify themselves as Westerners, as Americans? Or something else? Is this a diverse and inclusive society? Or not? Which topics captured these poets' imaginations, and why? Why did these people write anything at all?

Now we share our artifact, this anthology, with our neighbor the historian. She reads the manuscript, asks her own particular set of questions, and contributes her knowledge of history to our examination of these poems. We show the book to a sociologist; he considers the poems from yet another point of reference, and he contributes what he knows. Our friend the psychologist reads the manuscript and wants to get into these poets' heads. A famous political scientist declares the poems both support and refute evidence that twenty-first century Americans had lost the vigor of their predecessors and that the American political system of this era was sliding into decline. Inevitably, the literature scholars get their hands on the anthology and . . . well . . . they squint through bifocals at the poems and go on and on in various and contradictory directions, evaluating and analyzing, questioning and researching, each according to his genetic predisposition, a loquacious crowd, all generally enjoying themselves. As a result of our bringing these poems to light, lots of people are talking, studying, reflecting, sharing, debating, writing, revising established views, and refining scholarly texts. And, best of all, people who never read poems before are reading poems.

Lots of possibilities. The world moves forward in big ways and in small ways. *New Poets of the American West* is not an artifact, not yet. It's a chorus of many voices, all of them contemporary, living in this day. Many of these poets are teachers. Why is that? Others are deckhands, ranchers, bus drivers, social workers, doctors, bookstore owners, farmers, painters, dancers, bartenders, human rights activists, administrators, lawn-keepers, musicians, rodeo riders, hitchhikers, factory workers, translators, community service volunteers, truck drivers, miners, event coordinators, dam builders, trail guides, river guides, prison inmates, housecleaners, fishermen, cooks, engineers, firefighters, and newspaper reporters. Why do we label ourselves this way?

Some of these poets are Navajo, Hopi, Assiniboine, Souix, Crow, Salish, Colville, Pueblo, Piute, Yakama, and Cree. Some are Asian American, some are African American. Some are gay, and some are lesbian. Some write in Spanish, some in the language of their tribe. What do these markers signify?

All of the poets in this anthology are living in or are identified with one of the eleven states from the Continental Divide to the Pacific Ocean. Why these boundaries? The West has been mapped in many different ways, some maps including everything west of the Mississippi, some maps excluding the I-5 corridor through Washington, Oregon, and California. What about the western providences of Canada? What about Mexico? So much of what is now the American West was once Mexico. Why an anthology of Western poets at all? What do boundaries mean? Are they more than imaginary lines, arbitrary demarcations? From the moon the land masses on Earth have no lines drawn across them.

I haven't a better answer to these questions other than that, intuitively, this anthology seems like a worthy project, an opportunity to document who we are in this particular place at this particular time. Collected here are poems about horse racing, mining, trash collecting,

4

nuclear testing, firefighting, border crossings, buffalo hunting, surfing, logging, and sifting flour. In these pages you will read about gang violence, rock climbing, elk skinning, grave blasting, apple-heifers, and a Hollywood suicide. In your "mind's eye," you will meet a simple-minded girl who gets run over by a bull, two mothers watching a bear menacingly nosing toward unsuspecting children, and children who "have yet to be toilet trained out of their souls." You will visit flea markets, military bases, internment camps, reservations, funerals, weddings, rodeos, nursing homes, national parks, backyard barbecues, prisons, forests, meadows, rivers, and mountain tops. You will learn to "reach into the sacred womb, / grasp a placid hoof / and coax life toward this certain moment." You'll teach poetry to third graders, converse with hitchhikers, lament for an incarcerated brother "trying to fill the holes in his soul / with Camel cigarettes / and crude tattoos." You will sit at the kitchen table where perhaps the world will end "while we are laughing and crying, eating of the last sweet bite." In the short time each of us has in this world, here's your chance to experience life widely and to reflect on your experiences deeply.

And why the "new" in *New Poets of the American West*? Many of the poets here have been publishing for decades. Some are Pulitzer Prize winners, McArthur Fellows, state and national poet laureates. By "new," I'm simply meaning that these are new poets to readers who haven't read these poems, and that includes most of the population of this region, this nation, this world. Why do people shy away from poetry? How can we change that? A poet and friend of mine lamented, "I could drop my books from an airplane, and no one would stoop to pick them up." Why is that? Some poetry aficionados argue that efforts to increase readership are wasted energy; people in general, they say, are too thick-headed to appreciate the gifts poetry can offer. I don't feel this way at all. At the back of this anthology is an extensive list of books by the poets herein. Dear reader, if you are smitten by the words of particular poets in this anthology, go to this list, buy these books. If it does happen one day that poetry books fall from the sky, let's gather up armloads and carry them to our neighbors, door-to-door.

These are also new poets in that they are living now, and now is "new" at least as often as now is pretty much the same as it's been all along. Fundamentally, maybe human nature hasn't changed since God invented grapefruit. Are we evolving? Are we devolving? How can we begin to reflect on these things unless we sit still a moment and listen closely to who we are in the moment at hand? Poems tell us who we are as individuals, as societies, as a species. "Poetry is news that stays news," said Idaho poet Ezra Pound.

*New Poets of the American West* is the creation of an all volunteer staff at Many Voices Press, a nonprofit entity of Flathead Valley Community College. Let's give loud applause to spirit of volunteerism, and to these volunteers especially, who have labored in service to the literary arts, connecting writers with readers, working together to improve the quality of our lives.

This anthology is dedicated to Bernadine Tomasik, my eighth grade English teacher. I sat in the back row. One day in class I was scribbling bawdy parodies to Beatles lyrics, and Miss Tomasik caught me at it. My face flushed and my heart raced as she lifted my notebook. I was certain she'd read aloud what I'd written and humiliate me. She put her hand on my shoulder, returned my notebook, looked me in the eye and said, "Mmmm. A budding poet." She lifted me up, rather than put me down. I showed her everything I wrote from then on. Decades later, after the publication of my first book, she sent a card, saying simply, "I'm proud of you." In Bernadine Tomasik, I saw how books can open one's heart as well as one's mind.

In this spirit, I gathered these poems.


Lowell Jaeger, Editor
Many Voices Press

# Introduction: Many Voices, Many Wests

You now hold in hand—to borrow that phrase of intimacy Walt Whitman employed when addressing his readers—a remarkably vast, diverse, and searching anthology of contemporary Western American poetry. Comprising the work of poets from eleven Western states, this collection features some of the latest work of such well-known and celebrated writers as Sandra Alcosser, Sherman Alexie, Jimmy Santiago Baca, Marilyn Chin, Joy Harjo, Garrett Hongo, Philip Levine, Alberto Ríos, Pattiann Rogers, and Robert Wrigley, and recent work of such emergent talents as Sherwin Bitsui, Karen An-hwei Lee, Melinda Palacio, Mandy Smoker, Miles Waggener, Joe Wilkins, Erin Fristad, and Kathleen Flenniken. Languages offered in this collection include English, Navajo, Salish, Assiniboin, Dakota, and Spanish. Readers will encounter the work of poets from places as different (and the same) as, say, Los Angeles and Encampment, Wyoming, or Boulder and Port Townsend, Washington. As the sheer vastness of the American West promises a diversity of places and experiences, the intricacies and complexities of the languages, cultures, histories, religions, values, and desires of Westerners suggest a staggering, kaleidoscopic array of voices and perspectives: we hear from Native Americans and first-generation immigrants, from ranchlanders and megaopolites, from poet-teachers and street-poets. In fact, the West is so big, and home to such diversity that the deeper one reads in this anthology, the more voices and world views one encounters, the more textures of thought, emotion, and language one discovers, the less we may find ourselves able to speak of a single, stable something called the American West. Rather, we may find ourselves living in (or reading into) not one West, but many.

If the pleasure of reading, savoring, and making sense of the poems falls to the reader (and her or his community of interlocutors), my job in this introduction is to offer some literary, cultural, and historical contexts for reading and interpreting the superabundance of poetic riches that follow and, along the way, to explain what I mean by the phrase, "many Wests." In the first instance, we'll do our best to throw away such abiding, yet possibly threadbare and monolithic, notions as the "frontier" and "the American character," and the equally worn-out (and racist), yet oddly persistent, notion of writers as either "palefaces" or "redskins," and to offer in their stead some of the latest thinking in Western Studies. In the place of such a reductive, Manichean vision of writers, and of a diversity-defying, essentialist take on American identity, we'll find an unfixable plurality of poets, experiences, imaginations, and identities; in the place of a singular West, we'll find an array of critical terms competing to describe the not-quite-reducible-to-one-another Wests we seem to live in now: the New West, the Postwest, the Rhizomatic West, and more. To put the matter plainly (and no doubt polemically): as the poets in this collection amply demonstrate, we live (no matter how much people like the authors of Arizona's SB1070 may wish to say who counts and who does not) at a time of rich diversity and plurality, and no one person or group of people speak for the West, can name and thereby fix (for everyone else) a spirit or essential nature of the West, can claim perfect knowledge of what the West means, has meant, or may mean. Readers will find many visions of the West in these poems, and the implication seems clear: nobody owns the West (though a few, like Ted Turner and Archie Emmerson, own sizeable chunks). We live in a dazzling, ever-shifting, enlivening multiplicity of linguistic, cultural, historical, political, economic, ethnic, gender, natural, geographical, intellectual, and emotional states that cannot be added together or perfectly reconciled to make a whole, singular, fixed West.

## I. Out with the Old . . .

As Clyde A. Milner II tells us, Frederick Jackson Turner first delivered his famous essay, "The Significance of the Frontier in American History," "on an especially warm July evening in 1893": "he gave the final talk at the last session on the second day of the World's Congress of Historians and Historical Students organized as part of the Columbian Exposition in Chicago. His audience did not respond with any enthusiasm, but four other speakers had preceded him. So it was a long meeting after a very hot day, yet Turner's essay would not be forgotten" (3). While Turner's audience might have been dozing at the time, the historian's arguments had and continue to have—as countless historians and literary scholars have noted—a profound influence on how many Americans viewed and continue to view both the American West and that imagined something, the "American identity." In his address, Turner asserted not only "that the advance of the frontier has meant a steady movement away from the influence of Europe, a steady growth of independence on American lines" (28), but also that the American "character" was forged largely west of the Mississippi:

> The result is that to the frontier the American intellect owes its striking characteristics. That coarseness and strength combined with acuteness and inquisitiveness, that practical, inventive turn of mind, quick to find expedients, that masterful grasp of material things, lacking in the artistic but powerful to effect great ends, that restless, nervous energy, that dominant individualist, working for good or evil, and withal that buoyancy and exuberance which comes with freedom,—these are traits of the frontier, or traits called out elsewhere because of the existence of the frontier. (47)

For Turner (as for Teddy Roosevelt writing a few years later in essays such as "The Strenuous Life" [1899]), there was not only an essential national identity—Americans were rough and tumble, ready and able, and so on—but it was also a product of westwarding, of Euro-American expansion across the continent. And, if Americans were like that, then the West and Westerners were—to adapt a phrase from Wallace Stegner—even more so.[1]

Although we might pause at this point and acknowledge that kicking old Fred Turner has been sport for historians and scholars for years and that there's perhaps no reason to kick him again, as David Mogen, Mark Busby, and Paul Bryant, among others, point out, however much we might want to condemn and dismiss Turner's notions as essentialist, masculinist, ethnocentric, and so on, his ideas persist and have become part of American mythology and the American literary tradition. In the introduction to their collection, *The Frontier Experience and the American Dream: Essays on American Literature* (1989), Mogen, Busby, and Bryant argue "that understanding the dialectical and dialogical nature of this literary tradition will help open up the literary canon, by revealing how different regions, ethnic groups, classes, and genders have adapted frontier archetypes and enriched the American Dream, giving it new patterns and meanings" (4-5). Although we might quibble with the phrase "American Dream" as too singular and monolithic in itself, the editors rightly suggest that American, and perhaps particularly Western, writers come up against, argue with, critique, seek to ignore, and in countless different ways engage Turner's ideas and claims whether they want to or not. Reject him however much one might, he and the constellation of ideas associated with his famous essay seem almost as much a part of the West as beetle-infested pine trees, drought, and strip-malls. One challenge, therefore, for readers of the present volume is to read our poets with at least a half-closed eye on the old paradigms of the West and to ask how each—in any measure—explores, negates, ignores, or thinks around or past them. And although this risks re-inscribing Turner once again (and forever?) into anything anyone can say about the West and its writing, it also encourages us to think historically, to confront the clear limitations and biases of Turner's Euro-centric thinking, yet at the same time to acknowledge the stories of any number of immigrant families (and their descendants) that now populate the West and to examine the effects poets can achieve by taking up elements of the old paradigms.

We can see some of this if we turn briefly (and by way of example) to just one of the many engaging and exceptional poems in our collection that evoke, in some measure, the immigrant experience of the West. In Krista Benjamin's "Letter from My Ancestors," we encounter new Americans who undertook some of the hard labor of rationalizing the West in the U.S. economy, but who, if they could see from the grave our world and our lives, might view us with some detachment and irony—and appreciation. The poem opens with a collective voice that sounds rather like the rough and tumble Americans Turner described:

> We wouldn't write this,
> wouldn't even think of it. We are working
> people without time on our hands. In the old country,
>
> we milk cows or deliver the mail or leave,
> scattering to South Africa, Connecticut, Missouri,
> and finally, California for the Gold Rush—

For Benjamin's ancestors, the idea of time to write poetry seems like an extravagance—they had (and here the poet addresses one of the most Western of all American themes) to work and to think hard while taking advantage of whatever opportunities might have presented themselves: "Morris comes / later, after the earthquake, finds two irons / and a board in the rubble of San Francisco." Intent upon making a life for himself, Morris realizes that "plenty of prostitutes need their dresses pressed," and he goes on to open "a haberdashery and marry / Sadie." Although the collective voice registers some bemusement over the difference between living lives and writing about them—"we all have stories, yes, but we're not thinking / stories. We have work to do, and a dozen children"—it also takes pride in their accomplishments. Their steadfastness has helped to create "the luxury of time" for subsequent generations to be able to reflect on the lives of their ancestors—and thereby to create art. Tough, yet wry, the poem nicely plays upon the old tropes in order to take the long view, and to appreciate the difficulties and challenges of the diasporic experience.

Moving on from Turner, another set of ideas that we might wish to throw away (and in this case, absolutely once and for all), but that unfortunately seems to remain with us, can be found in the persistence of Philip Rahv's essay, "Paleface and Redskin," first published in *The Kenyon Review* in 1939. Rahv possesses a Manichean turn of mind, and he writes that "viewed historically, American writers appear to group themselves around two polar types" (251) and that "the typical American writer has so far shown himself incapable of escaping the blight of one-sidedness: of achieving that mature control which permits the balance of impulse with sensitiveness, of natural power with ideological depth" (253). He labels the two types of male writers—he mentions Dickinson on the last page of the essay—as "palefaces" and "redskins" and finds that "the differences between the two types define themselves in every sphere" (251). On the one hand, then, Rahv offers for our consideration the palefaces, the patricians and urbanites of American life. Here, he means "highbrow" writers such as Henry James and Nathaniel Hawthorne: "At his highest level the paleface moves in an exquisite moral atmosphere; at his lowest he is genteel, snobbish, and pedantic" (252). The redskins, on the other hand, hail from the plebian classes and glory in their "lowbrow" Americanness: "In giving expression to the vitality and to the aspirations of the people, the redskin is at his best; but at his worst he is a vulgar anti-intellectual, combining aggression with conformity and reverting to the crudest forms of frontier psychology" (252). Among the redskins Rahv numbers Mark Twain and Walt Whitman, and his description of the redskins not only shows the persistence of Turnerisms into at least the mid-twentieth century but also suggests why his dichotomy may be a nagging problem for contemporary Westerners, particularly Western poets.

Rahv goes on to include several of the Moderns among the redskins—in fact, he rather remarkably lumps William Faulkner and Ernest Hemingway together with James Fenimore Cooper and Theodore Dreiser[2]—and his reference to the "frontier" implies a ready-made split that a number of scholars and commentators have taken up: why not call Eastern writers (who must, apparently by their proximity to any number of universities and colleges, cities and towns, and the relatively gentle terrains on the other side of the Mississippi, be generally intellectual and well-mannered) the palefaces and Western writers (who live in the rugged, vast open spaces of the plains or deserts or coasts and who, even if they live in cities, occasionally speak in full sentences, and have earned degrees, seem much more rough and tumble) the redskins?

Even though such sweeping, binary thinking ought to appear incredible, and therefore easily dismissible, a couple of recent instances demonstrate the persistence of Rahv's implicit assertion. In an August 20, 2008, entry in the *New York Times'* "Paper Cuts: A Blog About Books," for example, Barry Gewen cites a public disagreement between novelist Walter Kirn and critic James Wood and concludes that

> Kirn's review of Wood demonstrates that the Rahvian dichotomy is alive and well—or if not well, at least energetically festering. Indeed, maybe it wasn't even necessary to read the review to know this. Maybe all one really needed to know was that Paleface Wood writes his criticism out of Cambridge, Mass., and that Redskin Kirn writes from—where else?—some place in Montana. (3)

In "Cowboys and Immigrants," an article in the May 2009 issue of *Smithsonian* magazine, Lance Morrow also evokes Rahv's binary model and locates within it a distinctive geographical split: asserting that "two dueling archetypes dominated 20th century American politics," and asking, "Is it time for them to be reconciled?," he offers, on the one hand, Ellis Island as a locus of imported, intellectualized, feminized European energies; on the other, he cites the Western states and the frontier as the wellspring of American masculinity and the propensity to solve matters with a pistol. As he remarks, "Barack Obama's victory represented, among other things, a repudiation of the Frontier style of Bush and Dick Cheney, in favor of an agenda arising from the Ellis Island point of view, with its emphasis on collective social interests, such as health care and the environment" (3).

If Rahv's distinction between Westerners and Easterners, and therefore between Western and Eastern writers, remains almost as alive and vibrant as Turner's frontier thesis—no doubt we all rely on any number of shorthands and have too many things to do and places to go to rethink the immense catalogues of commonplaces that infiltrate and order our lives and perceptions—we must nevertheless wholly reject his model. In the first place, the model relies on old and hateful racist categories—unless I am much mistaken, isn't "redskin" analogous to the very worst racial epithets? In the second, we shouldn't prejudice—with such a dated and reductive idea— our reading of any writer: the richness of imagery, language, music, and more in these poems invite all sorts of responses and engagements, draw upon any number of cultures, histories, and experiences, and to assume that Western writers must be flinty, tough, and terse will be to miss far too much, perhaps everything. In the third—and unless I am much mistaken again—any number of Western poets are women. And people of color, and folks of non-normative sexual identities and practices, border crossers, multi-linguists, cultural and ethnic hybridists, and more. As a Westerner, and if I had a six-gun (or any gun at all), I'd shoot the eyes out of Rahv's binary—I see, however, that leaving old behaviors and ideas behind does not come easy. Nevertheless, we forge ahead.

## II. And in with the New?

Over the past couple of decades in Western Studies—that hybrid discipline of history and cultural and literary studies—scholars have attempted not only to rethink models of Western historicity (including, and perhaps especially, Turner's thesis) but also to come up with new terms and concepts to describe life as it has been and is currently being lived in the American West. Influenced by work in Native American Studies, Ethnic Studies, Regional Studies, Gender Studies, Philosophy, and more, Western historians and literary scholars have studied and investigated everything from notions of authenticity in the West to the lasting appeal of the Western as a genre, from the importance of nature in Western literature to the impact of transnational corporations and global media on representations of the West, and from the importance (or lack of importance) of place in the West to the history of internment, racial profiling, deportation, and more. Although the historical, cultural, political, economic, and literary contexts for approaching the poems in this collection seem almost numberless, we'll take up two recent models that seek to describe the contemporary West: the New West and the Rhizomatic West.

First, then, a journey from the Old West to the New West, and as with many journeys, we'll begin with a map. In my office at work, beside my desk, I have taped a particular map of the West to the wall so that I can not only regularly consult it while researching, writing, and prepping for classes, but also so that I can remind myself of the vast energies and violences that went into creating the territory that we now refer to as the American West: I lifted this map, "Western Territorial Expansion, 1803-1959," from *The Oxford History of the American West* (1994), and it very clearly dates and graphically represents major land acquisitions and takings. In the first instance, and beginning on the western bank of the Mississippi, it maps the Louisiana Purchase (1803), that immense swath of mid-continent reaching from the Gulf of Mexico to as far north as what is now the province of Alberta and as far west as what is now part of the boundary between Montana and Idaho. Then, we see in 1818 that Great Britain ceded sizeable parts of what are now Minnesota and North Dakota to the U.S. in exchange for a strip of the Montana territory above the 49th parallel. In 1845, the Texas Annexation; in 1846, the division of the Oregon country between the U.S. and Great Britain; in 1848, the Mexican Cession that brought what would become Utah, Arizona, Nevada, California, and parts of Wyoming, Colorado and New Mexico under U.S. control; in 1853, the Gadsden Purchase, that pruning saw-shaped cut of what was to become the southern reaches of New Mexico and Arizona; in 1867, the Alaska Purchase; and, in 1898, the Hawai'i Annexation.

All of this deep history lies in the background to, and often resonates in, the poems in this collection. The histories of European imperialism and American Manifest Destiny form part and particle of the Old West, and the ghosts and revenants of the Indian Wars, the war with Mexico, and the "settling" of the West with its concomitant displacement and disenfranchisement of Native Americans and Mexicans and its importation (and subsequent exploitation) of Asian laborers, move through these pages. The Old West was, for many, many people, a very Hobbesian realm, and the challenge of bringing that history forward as one reads falls squarely on each of us.

If the hard history of the Old West can be found explicitly or in traces in the work of our poets, readers must also keep in mind that other "Old West" that lives in the minds of many Americans and that writers sometimes play with or against or in countless other ways seek to engage or negate: the mythic, even clichéd Old West, the Old West that comes to us in movies and on television. This is the West of cowboys and Indians, sheriffs, gunslingers, corrupt ranchers, trappers, railroad barons, brides going West, homesteaders, and copper mines under a big sky. This is the usually handsome and masculine West of John Wayne and Clint Eastwood, and, more recently, of Kevin Costner and Val Kilmer (as the wryest of all Doc Hollidays). This is the glamorized, unreal, mostly happy endings (depending upon your point of view, of course) West of *Gunsmoke* and *Bonanza* (if not *Deadwood*), of *Little House on the Prairie* and its countless sequels, spin-offs, and imitators, of what Melody Graulich succinctly calls the "mythic Anglo-Saxon pioneer West" (xii). If you own a television (or any number of the new toys dreamt-up in Palo Alto or Seattle) or have seen ads for dude ranches and "ghost" towns with shoot-outs at high noon, or visited such strange, happy places as Knott's Berry Farm, Wild Bill's Western Diner Extravaganza, and the Covered Wagon Motel located along Buena Park's "Entertainment Corridor,"[3] then you, like any number of our poets, perhaps feel the imaginative, cultural weight of this sometimes remarkable and entertaining (and perhaps almost always pernicious) Old West. Just as we might keep Turner's paradigms in mind while reading—in order to judge, among other things, how far the new work has come in reimaging the West—we might also keep alive some of the vast repertoire of manufactured images, tropes, and characters in order to see, in another way, not only how deep in the dust our contemporary poets have left the representations of the mythic Old West but also how they might very well enjoy, mock, or in some other way take up or recast the old material.

In contrast, perhaps, to the Old West, we now have the New West. In an exceptional essay on *The Virginian*, Owen Wister's famous, ur-Western, Susan Kollin offers one of the best (and nicely ironic) portraits of the New West, and I quote it here at length:

> Ex-urbanite telecommuters dwell in one-acre ranchettes featuring *Sunset* magazine front-room vistas. Small-town food co-ops offer organic bison to their health-conscious middle-class consumers [. . .]. Satellite dishes connecting the rural West to the global community and sports utility vehicles delivering weekend recreationists to ski resorts grace the yards and driveways of gated communities and subdivisions alike. Ralph Lauren-clad professionals and New Age enthusiasts join forces to prevent the building of yet one more Wal-Mart or strip mall in their communities. Snowmobilers, skiers, mountain bikers, and out-of-state tourists clash with each other over trail use and other outdoor etiquette in national and state parks. (234)

This passage expertly delineates some of the politics, people, and things of the New West, and even as we instantly—and perhaps bemusedly—recognize the yuppification of the West, Kollin also reminds us that such portraits constitute, at least in part, a new mythology that not only obscures the diversity of lives and peoples in the contemporary West but that also obfuscates the connections—both imaginative and material—between the Old and New Wests.

As Kollin argues,

> problems arise in discussing the emergence of this New West, primarily because the concept risks establishing a radical break between 'old' and 'new,' between the identity of the region and the shape and contour of the region as it seemingly once was. A dichotomy between old and new, for instance, threatens to overlook the ways in which the New West might not be so new after all. (235)

If, as Kollin points out, mining, ranching, and logging have given way to high-tech and service industries, and if the ranch, small town, and mid-sized city have given way to corporate farms, endless suburbs, and such booming multi-cities as Las Vegas, Sea-Tac, and Los Angeles, the economic and demographic shifts in the New West have their roots in the Old West. More, and crucially for our purposes here, Kollin suggests that as readers of Western writing, not only do we have to attend equally to the well-entrenched mythologies of the past and the emergent mythologies of the present, but also (and particularly) to the very material conditions at play in any region or corner of the West. We may live in the New West, but to read the poems in this collection well, one needs not only to read the poems against the old and new narratives but against and with the myriad conditions on the ground (and in the air and water) of the Western states. And, perhaps above all, one might be suspicious of the term, New West, altogether; as Kollin remarks,

> All these regional changes [such as industrialization, urbanization, migration, and immigration] may lead us to wonder whether contemporary discussions of the New West are merely the lamentations of a late-twentieth-century white middle-class populace now finding itself displaced, strangely located in much the same position as the American Indians who, a century earlier, were themselves removed from and dispossessed of their ancestral homes. (236)

If one of the Wests we may now live in has been dubbed the New West, Neil Campbell offers a different sort of West, the Rhizomatic West. Campbell, one of the leading scholars of Western and American Studies, and working from the University of Derby in the United

Kingdom, builds upon the work of such influential French philosophers and literary theorists as Jacques Derrida, Roland Barthes, and particularly Gilles Deleuze and Félix Guattari, and argues not only that Turner momentarily acknowledged and then promptly ignored, in his famous essay, "the multiplicities and mobilities of the prismatic West" (7), but that the West must be understood, especially in our age of transnational, global media, as far too complex and fluid to be neatly summed up or encapsulated. Rather than a stable, bounded, essential place or idea, the American West must be understood as a place of shifting hybridities and constantly reformulating identities, as a place of motion and movement across all sorts of imagined and real borders. Taking Deleuze and Guattari's notion of the rhizome, or a plant that has no single, dominant, or central root or stalk, but that runs in all directions and cannot be traced back to an origin, Campbell rejects Turner's essentialist and masculinist formulations (and any formulations like them), and asserts that

> in these metaphors of mobility, spatiality, and outsideness, of going 'off the map' via encounters and reinventions, Deleuze offers a process and approach I wish to apply, in varying ways, to understanding the overcoded West not as a single region but as a mutating multiplicity, a 'way of departing from the compartmentalization of knowledge, yet without recourse to an organic unity (Romantic nostalgia for its loss).' (9)

For Campbell, our understandings of the West come not only from American and Western American writing, art, films, and more, but from all over, from Europe and Mexico and Australia—from anywhere anyone comments on, writes about, imagines or re-imagines "westness." In short, we cannot speak of a Western (or American) identity or fix the meanings of the West; rather, we live in a West of constantly fluctuating and reformulating identities, a West of multiple, ever-changing, unstable meanings.

We can see some of this if we turn briefly to one of the poems in our anthology. In "Names," for example, Teresa Chuc Dowell evokes the complexities and uncertainties of finding one's self at the multitudinous intersections of cultures, religions, languages, experiences, desires, and more. As she remarks in the opening (and observe how the poem gains mass as it cascades down the page in free verse couplets), "I am tired of having five different names; / Having to change them when I enter / A new country or take on a new life. My / First name is my truest, I suppose, but I / Never use it and nobody calls me by this Vietnamese / Name though it is on my birth certificate—." By means of a fine auditory and visual image, she sounds her name: "Tue My Chuc. It makes the sound of a twang of a / String pulled." But her parents call her "Ah Wai," and her name in Cantonese is "Chuc Mei Wai." After she moves to the U.S., she tells us, she became "Teresa My Chuc, then Teresa Mei Chuc." After her first marriage: "Teresa Chuc Prokopiev"; after her second, "Teresa Chuc Dowell." With these few details, the poet evokes the astonishing movement of people and languages in our time, our West. If I have barely scratched the surface of Dowell's exemplary poem, we can nevertheless perhaps see in her work something of the multiplicity and complexity of the rhizomatic West.

For readers of this anthology, Campbell's model should raise any number of productive questions: Do any of the poets present a similar, rhizomatic vision of the West? What multiplicities, borders, routes, mobilities, and identities come into play in this collection? Do the poems, taken collectively, support the notion of a Rhizomatic (or Old or New) West, or can we abstract something rather more solid and singular? Is the East also rhizomatic? The South? Or is there something about life in the booming West that distinguishes it as particularly fluid and fungible when compared to other regions of the country? More, we can ask: Does such a model help or hinder your reading of individual poems? Do you buy the model? Do you also buy Kollin's description and critique of the New West? Are there other, better ways to see or describe the contemporary West and the complexity of life in the West?

If our journey thus far has carried us from the Old West to the New West, and from the

New West to the Rhizomatic West, we can perhaps now take the next logical step and say that we have or live in not one West, but many Wests, Wests that cannot be reconciled to one another, but that must remain provisional, overlapping, intersecting, never quite lining up or coalescing. If, as Campbell's theorizing suggests, we cannot pin the contemporary West down to one essential meaning, cannot fix anything like an essential Western identity or character, then we have, instead, many meanings, many identities, and we cannot—if such a thing were possible—ever arrest the mutability and fluidity of life in the West to fix a definition, even for a moment. We have, all at once, the Old West in the New West, the Rhizomatic West in the Old West, and so on in any number of fluctuating and unstable permutations and combinations. Call it—with emphasis on the lower case—the whirlwind wests. And, rather remarkably, this unfixability might even apply to the geography of the West, to the very land itself.

### III.  Point Roberts

With the spirit of Campbell's fluid, destabilizing model in mind, I would like to pose a seemingly innocent question: geographically speaking, what lands and territories do we mean when we say "the American West"?

The answer, of course, may depend upon whom you ask.

As odd as it might seem, for example, the editors of *Atlas of the New West: Portrait of a Changing Region* (1997) do not include most of California—or, indeed, any of the Pacific Coast or the Great Plains—in their portrait of the West. As Michael F. Logan asks, rather incredulously, at the beginning of his review of the atlas, "What do Dallas, Los Angeles, Omaha, and Seattle have in common? All are situated outside the New West, according to the creators of the *Atlas of the New West*" (192).  Although we don't have the space here to go into the editors' rationale, their tactical decisions clearly demonstrate at least some measure of the arbitrariness that can be associated with defining, at any given time, for any given reasons, a region. What's more, though my logic may differ from theirs, I generally don't think of California as being part of the American West, either. Rather, I think of it as its own thing, something like its own country; population- and wealth-wise, it rivals Spain and Italy, and outdoes any number of other nations. In a similar manner, I often think of Texas as being outside the West: it has its own histories and cultures, and the Lone Star seems to invite us to take it as a state apart. Or, perhaps we could give west Texas to the West, and east Texas to the South, but then what to do with south Texas?

If we might exclude California and at least parts of Texas, what about Point Roberts, Washington (and other anomalies like it)?

Point Roberts, for those who may not have heard of it, can be found in the Pacific Northwest—or is it the lower mainland of British Columbia?—a bit of land that juts out, modestly, into Georgia Strait. Although the point lies dead west of Blaine, directly across Boundary Bay, a person can't reach it by land from the U.S.; instead, from Blaine, to get to Point Roberts, you have to cross the border at White Rock, B.C., and then follow the signs for the Tsawwassen Ferry, at last diverting south to cross the border, again, and thereby reach this pocket-sized piece of America. As the geological and political fates would have it, Point Roberts lies south of the 49$^{th}$ parallel, and so belongs to the U.S. although it is landlocked from the rest of Washington State. But borders are borders, and lines of latitude cannot be trifled with, and so we find an orphan, dangling into the water just south of greater Vancouver.

Neither an island nor part of the continental U.S., what, then, is Point Roberts, and could we say that rather than being part of the American West, it is, rather, its own thing? Could we call it an itch, a nagging oddity at the back of the brain? And what if, say, Walt Whitman had been born and raised in Port Roberts; would we then call him a Western poet? An American poet? An Amer-Canadian poet since, after all, he would have done most of his shopping and wandering in Vancouver rather than New York?

If we count the notion of excluding California, Texas, and Point Roberts from the West as mere nonsense, the issue does not really become less vexing since we also have other lines and territories to decide about. Taking our cue from the editors of the new atlas, how many (and which) of the plains states should we count in the West? For example, the ghost of Teddy Roosevelt doubtlessly would be distressed if we did not include the Dakotas in the West, and many Americans might also include Nebraska and Kansas, but what about Oklahoma? Or what if we went back to the Louisiana Purchase and took everything west of the Mississippi as the West; we might include Missouri, but Arkansas and Louisiana wouldn't count, being part of the South, and then what to do about the lands north of Lake Itasca, Minnesota, the headwater of the great river?

And what about Alaska? And Hawai'i? And, if we kept heading west, what about Guam or the Commonwealth of the Mariana Islands?

For my own part—and to keep peace with the editor of the current volume—I completely understand taking our eleven states as the American West, but if, legitimately, one could see the West in a number of greater or lesser configurations, then we can say that just as the meaning of the West cannot be fixed, neither can its territories or boundaries. In that sense, we may very literally have many Wests.

## IV. Does Place (or Region) Matter?

I raised this question in the introduction to a collection of critical essays on Montana literature, and I ask it here, once more, for the simple reason that it remains an abiding issue in Western Studies.[4] In *Reading the West* (1996), for example, Michael Kowalewski argues that readers and scholars must always consider "region" in the study of literature:

> Finding region an important factor in literary studies is still often seen as the equivalent of being an overenthusiastic salesman with a special marketing territory. Regionalism, it seems, is often next to boosterism, a puffing of 'merely' local talent—a kind of literary chamber of commerce juxtaposed to the three national congressional houses of race, class, and gender. (8)

For Kowalewski, as for such poets in our collection as Marvin Bell, Vic Charlo, Roger Dunsmore, Carol Moldaw, Venaya Yazzie, and many more, few things seem to matter more than place, than a sense of belonging to or coming from a place, of inhabiting a place, taking emotional and psychological possession of it, and naming it home. For many scholars and poets, place impacts consciousness, works its way into the body and the folds of the mind, and in turn finds expression in myriad ways in such products of consciousness and being as thought, art, and poetry. As Kowalewski reminds us, as readers we must always take into consideration how place or region find expression in a literary work, and we can ask any number of questions about how a poet seems to feel about place, about the past, present, and future of a particular place, and about the things and people she or he knows or encounters in that place.

Although some scholars and writers foreground matters of place and region, others see place not as a force in people's lives but rather as a realm onto which to project desire and constructed meanings. For some, in other words, place does not have anything like an essential or vibrant quality or nature; but rather it serves as just one more thing that people, for their own reasons (and whether those reasons be conscious or unconscious, good or bad, and so on), understand however they want to understand. In an odd way, in this view, place does not matter, or matters only to the degree it matters to the beholder; region does not really exist, or exists only to the degree that we say it does. Place and region are just things we make up for our convenience and in an effort to satisfy any number of desires that we cannot otherwise satisfy.

We can find this rather cynical (at least to my mind) and provocative (in the sense of perhaps trying to upset folks and their deepest convictions) in the commentary of no less a literary light (and sometime Westerner) than the Pulitzer Prize-winning author, Richard Ford. In interviews, Ford—"Ah," you say, "a novelist. That explains it! No poet would ever make such a silly—and patently wrong—claim!"—has said that mountains, rivers, coast lines, forests, plains, and more, constitute screens or tabula rasa onto which we project our wants and needs; they have no presence of their own, or if they do, we can't detect or know it and instead view them in ways that suit us:

I shouldn't say I have *no* relationship with landscape. But . . . saying I miss Montana is just expressing a feeling of need of mine in terms of place, likewise saying Mississippi is my home. I could express that need differently, but for some reason, something like instinct, I express it in terms of place, landscape.

This is [why] I so strongly resist the notion of regionalism—in literature, in defining culture. My life has simply shown me that we're more in the same boat wherever we are, and that recognizing that fact might enable us to adapt to our situations more successfully. (qtd. in Dobozy 3; Morris 109)

As Tamas Dobozy writes of this passage, for Ford "region, rather than determining literature or culture—rather than forming the basis of the need that in turn articulates it—becomes, instead, not antecedent but ancillary to need. Region is simply one of the many options for voicing desire" (3). Although, as I say, I find Ford's articulations somewhat cynical and designed to provoke, at the same time I cannot quite deny his analysis: don't we project our desires outward all the time, onto people and things—and place? Do we really know, say, what an arroyo is or means? a mountain? a river? a ranch? a city? For our purposes, we once more (I hope) have found the basis for some engaging questions to consider as we read the poems: Does place (or region) matter? Why or why not? If it does, in what way or ways? If it doesn't, where does that leave the poet? us? What sort of world, after all, do we live in? If region doesn't really exist, is there such a thing as a Western poet? Western poetry?

## V. Commonsense

For a good part of this introduction, I have drawn on works and models that seek to unfix our notions of what sort of place the West may be, to unsettle—if possible—our sense of what the West means in terms of American histories, cultures, and literatures. At the same time, to read our poets, and to read them well, we don't necessarily need recourse to the latest theories in Western Studies. We can always step back from any array of arguments and counter-arguments and re-pose the basic questions. For one, even if we live in a multiplicity of Wests, can we still speak of such a being as a poet of the American West(s)? Absolutely. To be a poet of the American West, all one needs is to live in the West (however one may draw the lines), or self-identify as a Western poet, or explore in her or his work, at least in some measure, the histories, cultures, languages, mythologies, desires, and more, of the West and the peoples living in or journeying through the West. Could a poet, residing in, say, Bangor, Maine (or, perhaps, Vladivostok, Saigon, or Brisbane), be a poet of the contemporary American Wests? Why not? We live in a mobile, global world, and I don't believe any badges of authenticity or resident papers are required in order to write about whatever interests or compels us. Could a person who never lived in the West, or traveled to the West, be a Western poet? Probably. Why seek to limit the power of the imagination and language?

We can also re-ask, upon taking a step back, are there Western themes, Western meanings? Sure: many; a multitude. But whatever they are, they probably have something to do with life as it has been lived, is lived, might be lived, or ought to be lived in the West. In a region so vast (and yet so difficult to pin down), so complex, so fluid, so changing, why, any more than we would seek to limit anyone's imagination and gifts for language, thought, and emotion, would we seek to limit what can be said or thought about a poem or an anthology of poems? The poems may be "set" in the West, and be about life in the West, and may sound any number of Western themes, paradigms, or images, but they are also about so much more that their westness may be only part (or even a small part) of their achievement and interest. Revel, ye readers, in these poems! And, even as you might take into consideration the histories, paradigms, mythologies, and theories set forth in this introduction, the most important thing is to turn the page and, in a word, enjoy.

Brady Harrison, Professor
Department of English
University of Montana

16

Notes:

I would like to thank Jill Bergman, Rick Canning, and Ashby Kinch for discussing the geography of the American West with me.

i. In fact, I'm playing on Clyde A. Milner II's play on Stegner's infamous remark about California being America, only more so. As Milner remarks, "the West is America only more so" ("Introduction" 3)

ii. Today, scholars who casually linked Moderns such as Hemingway and Faulkner with a writer of literary Naturalism like Dreiser and a Romantic like Cooper would have, as the saying goes, some explaining to do.

iii For more on Buena Park, see Hsuan L. Hsu's "Authentic Re-Creations: Ideology, Practice, and Regional History along Buena Park's Entertainment Corridor" in True West: Authenticity and the American West. Eds. William R. Handley and Nathaniel Lewis. Lincoln: U of Nebraska P, 2004. 304-27.

iv. See All Our Stories Are Here xvi-xviii and 1-51.

# Works Cited

Busby, Mark, David Mogen, and Paul Bryant. "Introduction: Frontier Writing as a 'Great Tradition' of American Literature." The Frontier Experience and the American Dream:Essays on American Literature. Eds. David Mogen, Mark Busby, and Paul Bryant. College Station: Texas A & M UP, 1989). 3-12.

Campbell, Neil. The Rhizomatic West:Representing the American West in a Transnational, Global, Media Age. Lincoln: U of Nebraska P, 2008.

Dobozy, Tamas. "Burning Montana: Richard Ford's Wildlife and Regional Crisis." All Our Stories Are Here: Critical Perspectives on Montana Literature. Ed. Brady Harrison. Lincoln: U of Nebraska P, 2009. 3-20.

Gewen, Barry. "Paleface v. Redskin." Paper Cuts: A Blog About Books. New York Times. Aug. 20, 2008. http://papercuts.blogs.nytimes.com/2008/08/20/paleface-v-redskin/

Graulich, Melody. "Introduction." Reading The Virginian in the New West. Eds. Melody Graulich and Stephen Tatum. Lincoln: U of Nebraska, P, 2003. xi-xix.

Kowalewski, Michael. "Introduction." Reading the West: New Essays on the Literature of the American West. Ed. Michael Kowalewski. Cambridge: Cambridge UP, 1996. 1-18.

Kollin, Susan. "Wister and the 'New West.'" Reading The Virginian in the New West. Eds. Melody Graulich and Stephen Tatum. Lincoln: U of Nebraska, P, 2003. 233-54.

Logan, Michael F. "Review of Atlas of the New West:Portrait of a Changing Region." Great Plains Research: A Journal of Natural and Social Sciences. 8.1 (1998): 192-94.

Milner II, Clyde A. "Introduction: America Only More So." The Oxford History of the American West. Eds. Clyde A. Milner II, Carol A. O'Connor, and Martha A. Sandweiss. New York: Oxford UP, 1994. 1-7.

Morris, Gregory L. Interview with Richard Ford. "Richard Ford." Talking Up a Storm: Voices of the New West. Ed. Gregory L. Morris. Lincoln: U of Nebraska P, 1994. 102-29.

Morrow, Lance. "Cowboys and Immigrants." Smithsonian May (2009): 1-3. http://www.smithsonianmag.com/people-places/Presence-of-Mind-Cowboys-and-Immigrants.html?c =y&page=3

Rahv, Philip. "Paleface and Redskin." The Kenyon Review. 1.3 (1939): 251-56.

Turner, Frederick Jackson. "The Significance of the Frontier in American History." Frederick Jackson Turner: Wisconsin's Historian of the Frontier. Ed. Martin Ridge. Madison: State Historical Society of Wisconsin, 1986. 26-47.

# Arizona

**Dick Bakken** (Bisbee, AZ) grew up in Spokane, Washington, where he began publishing his writing at age eleven, started the first literary magazine of West Valley High School with his sophomore English teacher and a classmate, and published nationally in the same sci-fi magazine printing reviews by youths Roger Ebert and Clarence Major. As a Teaching Assistant graduate candidate at Washington State University, he was the first allowed a creative MA thesis in English there, a volume of his poetry.

### Going into Moonlight

I didn't intend
to walk the old road

at midnight
but there I was, surprised

to see my faint shadow
on the dirt. I looked up to that

open moon coming down through
all the mist. A few more steps and there

lay my shadow across a jack rabbit
dead on the road.

I whispered
and reached and there waited

my shadow beneath
as I lifted from the earth the jack by those

silver ears. From beyond
the silhouetted hills, lightning

kept on washing up.
I love

that I couldn't
hear the night wings that passed before

my upturned throat. Only the muffled
roll of thunder far

from the other
side. I swung the jack

high away
into darkness while the next flashes

outlined us. And when I stepped forward, night
misting my face, the shadow

came with me.

## (excerpted from: *Flood Song*)

Alarm clocks, eagle plumes,
a moth's unblinking eye
hover from left to right,
in the shrinking room
where the children huddle
        nibbling orange crusts
        from diesel-soaked butterfly wings.

Their dimmed faces—hollowed-out with spoons—
are then folded over lightbulbs
and placed diagonally alongside the freeway
to fill the ear with the clacking of lab mice
swirling toward final light
        in rain buckets shipwrecked
                on turtle shells near the turnpike.

The meeting hall of their bodies
        piled on lawns
        caked with dying birds cooing at them
            remains landlocked inside the naming of:
                *them, those, not like us . . .*

———

I sensed the knife in your past,
its sharp edge shanked from the canyon stream—
a silver trickle between the book jacket,
*nihizaad* peeled open inside a diabetic mouth.

The waters of my clans
flash flooded—
I fell from the white of its eyes—
our fathers had no children to name their own
no baby's cry to place between argument and arguments.

The commercial flashed a blue path
across the lakes of our veins
the bluest glint, a rock in the ear
told our tongues entwined,

that I was reaching for the corn field inside you,
that I was longing to outlive this compass
pointing toward my skull
gauzed inside this long terrible whisper

damp in a desert canyon,
white-washed by the ache of fog lights
reaching to unravel        my combed hair.

**Sherwin Bitsui** (White Cone, AZ) was raised on the Navajo Reservation and currently lives in Tucson. He is Diné of the Todich'ii'nii (Bitter Water Clan), born for the Tl'izilani (Many Goats Clan). Bitsui has received the 2000 Individual Poet Grant from the Witter Bynner Foundation for Poetry, the 1999 Truman Capote Creative Writing Fellowship, a Lannan Foundation Marfa Residency and, a 2006 Whiting Writers' Award. His books of poems are *Shapeshift* (University of Arizona Press, 2003) and *Flood Song* (Copper Canyon Press, 2009).

**Jefferson Carter** (Tucson, AZ) retired from community college teaching so he could devote more time to poetry and to his other passion, attending quarter horse races all over the state. For him, horse racing offers the perfect combination: gambling and beauty. It also provides him with a subject for his poetry. His eighth collection of poems is *My Kind of Animal* (Chax Press, 2010). He also volunteers with Sky Island Alliance, a local environmental organization.

## Match Race

*—for Joey*

I'm not slogging through the mud
of the pecan grove, my Doc Martens
sinking like wooden clogs into
the foreground of a landscape
by Bruegel. I'm not walking beside
the big gelding that just won
by a head, costing me 60 dollars.
I'm not at the match races,
hearing the 5-piece Norteño band
& glancing at my 20-dollar bills
poking out of the breast pocket
of Joey's pearl-button shirt.
I'm in yoga, hearing the instructor
say be here in your body,
not your past. I blame
Wordsworth, who wouldn't hold
a mirror up to nature, who wrote
poetry is the spontaneous overflow
of powerful feelings recollected
in tranquility. I touch the heaving
bay flank beside me, admire
the curve of hock & fetlock, slow
my breathing to match the nearby
beating of that huge heart.


## A Centaur

For laughs,
I imitate a horse,
lowering my bare shoulder
into the sand
of the arroyo, my wife
watching from above
& our son inside the blue backpack
watching while I roll, kicking
my hooves & neighing, husband
turned centaur, father
as some big animal.
The boy laughs
because his mother's laughing
& I lurch to my feet, shaking,
blowing through my nostrils,
feeling foolish,
but what's a family for?
Climbing back up,
I smell creosote & sage
& I understand the Greeks
who carried in their armor
a bag of spices
that smelled like home.

## Wyoming Miners

When someone asks us
Where we are from
We smile and say
We're from under Wyoming
The land of our fathers
And their fathers too
It's in our blood
The earth within us
We're not happy in the sunshine
We spend our days and nights in tunnels
Where darkness is our friend
The gophers and prairie dogs
Live above us
In tunnels of their own
Sometimes they don't understand
The sounds down below
In the winter when they sleep
They dream of metal monsters
Digging in the earth below
When spring comes
Sometimes they are awakened early
By the sound of fireworks
Before the Fourth of July
We work the earth
Like the farmer works the surface
Following the steps
Our fathers took
They walk in our shadows
Protecting us from the sun

**Virgil Chabre** (Mesa, AZ) was born and raised in Rock Springs, Wyoming, and graduated from the University of Wyoming. He worked for over twenty years in a Trona Mine in Wyoming, spending some time 1,600 feet below the ground. He moved to Arizona in 1997 and teaches at a junior high school.

**David Chorlton** (Phoenix, AZ) grew up in England, spent several years in Vienna, and moved to Phoenix in 1978, where he began writing poems about the desert and its wildlife. One such poem was included in an anthology of art and poetry published by the British Museum, entitled *Birds*. He is the recipient of the Ronald Wardall Poetry Prize for his chapbook, *The Lost River* (Rain Mountain Press, 2008).

## Everyday Opera

The trash collector's aria is a shock
so early in the morning
and the day's first chorus rises
from a hundred bus stops
where the waiting has become a test
of patience equal
to the heroine's whose status
in the kingdom is awaiting resolution.
Dressed as help in a sleek resort
she changes endless sheets and washes
time from her hands
hoping it will pass as quickly as her next
duet, the one she sings with the gardener
about homesickness. Inmates
at the city jail
gather in ensemble, but sing so low
and quietly nobody hears their dull complaint.
A man without a home
performs arioso outside
a strip mall where his feet
move loosely as his voice
and passers-by all hide their faces
in a cloud of shame
until the coloratura shines
through the gloom
and a shower of coins descends from
the clouds. Suddenly the traffic
that had stalled
is moving freely and the men
soliciting for work smile and sing
bel canto to impress, but wait; by way
of response comes the basso profundo
from the local police
and the men exit, stage left and stage right.
Decked in jewels, the diva
emerges from a limousine, declining
to perform, but standing long
enough to be envied by the cheaply clad
whose leitmotiv each day is work
in service of the king
they have never seen. Their miseries
begin sotto voce
but rise when the ballet dancers arrive
at a parking lot where the order
is given to clear away all cars
to make space for dancing and they dance
and the voices gain in power and
the libretto is abandoned
for one, glorious finale before
the curtain is drawn and nobody knows
which side of it is reality.

**Blue**

During last night's blue moon
the Great Matter and Original Mind
were as close as your skin.
In the pre-dawn dark you ate muskmelon
and the color of the taste lit up the mind.
The first finch awoke and the moon
descended into its mountain burial.


**René Char II**

What are these legitimate fruits
of daring?
The natural brain bruises of mental
somersaults.
On a bet to sleep naked
out in the snow.
To push your forefingers into your ears
until they meet the brain
To climb backwards into the heavens because
we poets live in reverse.
It is too late to seduce the heroine
in my stories.
How can enough be enough
when it isn't?
The Great Mother has no ears and hallelujah
is the most impossible word in the language.
I can only say it to birds, fish, and dogs.

**Jim Harrison** (Somewhere, AZ) is the author of over thirty books of poetry, non-fiction, and fiction, including *Legends of the Fall* (Delta, 1980). His most recent books are *In Search of Small Gods* (Copper Canyon Press, 2009) and *The Farmer's Daughter* (Grove Press, 2009). A member of the American Academy of Arts and Letters and winner of a Guggenheim Fellowship, he has had work published in twenty-seven languages. Harrison now divides his time between Montana and the Mexican border of Arizona.

## Love

Love is raw as freshly cut meat,
mean as a beetle on the track of dung.
It is the Celtic dog that ate its tail in a dream.
It chooses us as a blizzard chooses a mountain.
It's seven knocks on the door you pray not to answer.
The boy followed the girl to school eating his heart
with each step. He wished to dance with her
beside a lake, the wind showing the leaves'
silvery undersides. She held the moist bouquet
of wild violets he picked against her neck.
She wore the sun like her skin
but beneath her blood was black as soil.
At the grave of her dog in the woods
she told him to please go away forever.


## Larson's Holstein Bull

Death waits inside us for a door to open.
Death is patient as a dead cat.
Death is a doorknob made of flesh.
Death is that angelic farm girl
gored by the bull on her way home
from school, crossing the pasture
for a shortcut.  In the seventh grade
she couldn't read or write.  She wasn't a virgin.
She was "simple minded" we all said.
It was May, a time of lilacs and shooting stars.
She's lived in memory for sixty years.
Death steals everything except our stories.

## That Wild Chance of Living (2001)

> *Death in us goes on*
> *testing the wild*
> *chance of living.*
> —Denise Levertov

This morning we hear the air
of Los Alamos is uranium-
laced. Harmless amounts,
a reporter reports. Wind
tests the currents as we drive
past, chancing to live here
and not there: As in Salgado's
"Human Migrations," light-
filled photos of all the places
where death has gone on and
on of good people on good
days, as Lakota and Apache
once said, to die, riding
to fight the whites, that history

flawing the tranquil town surface
with ghosts, spirits, sounds from
another time's *real* we can sense.
*I called the angels by name*,
H.D. wrote of the Blitz—
*Uriel, Annael, Angel of Death,*
*Angel of Peace.* At the Saint
Geronimo (*Michael*) dances
lightning flickered in the distance.
A young Coyote whirled from the circle
of Clowns to climb the tall pole
raised in the pueblo's center,
a flag caught on his belt
like an irreverent loincloth.

On top the pole, the dancer
slowly turned, holding
the flag whipping in wind rising
as rain came. *Did you know each one*
*of our nation's symbols is from war?*
my friend whispered. Thunder
clouds hid Taos Mountain,
the crowd humming when sun broke

       through and two
spectral arches       irradiant color—

       struck above the
eye watching       the war begin

**Cynthia Hogue** (Phoenix, AZ) is author of seven collections of poetry and co-editor of *Innovative Women Poets: An Anthology of Contemporary Poetry and Interviews* (University of Iowa Press, 2006). She has received Fulbright, National Endowment for the Arts, and National Endowment for the Humanities fellowships. In 2003, she joined the Department of English at Arizona State University as the Maxine and Jonathan Marshall Chair in Modern and Contemporary Poetry.

**Will Inman** (Tucson, AZ) co-founded and edited the literary journals *Kauri* and *New Kauri*. After years in North Carolina and New York City, he moved to Tucson, where he led writing workshops in many venues, including homeless shelters and prisons. Will is author of numerous chapbooks as well as the collections *I Read You Green*, *Mother* (Howling Dog Press, 2008) and *Surfings: Selected Poems of Will Inman* (Howling Dog Press, 2005). Archives of his works are in collections at Duke University and the University of North Carolina Wilmington.

### The Bones that Humans Lacked

Savants declared proof that Humankind
were created distinct from lesser mammals
existed in the lack of intermaxillary
bone in the human skull.
                            Goethe, whose
vision intuited that all life is interconnected,
searched a skull for the bone he knew
had to be there.
                            He found it. (Yet, aha!
what lower beast could also have found it?)


### given names

i make poems with young children
in classrooms
first, they tell me their names
one by one they pull the sounds out of
their mouths, each name a petal
torn from a different flower and,
from a few, thorns
from secret hurts, yes,
listening to their voices, i
read their eyes,
naked with wanting to know
they're special, how they
give their names, self words, soul words,
strips of flesh torn from inner skins
hungry for connection

they're all beautiful, even the fat ones,
even those with pinched faces, with broken
eyereaches, their energies
surge down that hidden lake among them,
waves to and fro—whisperings, small cries,
giggles, quick movements, turnings,
eager answers    interruptions    lovelooks
No-o-o-o! they cry together
Ye-e-e-sss! they call as one
but one or two will yell No!
when the others shout Yes!
they laugh. they know what they mean.
something from their eyes
conspires with mine when they're
mischievous and ornery. we
laugh about it.

they have yet to be toilet trained
out of their souls

## mesquite   mother   territory

aluminum cans are not always easy to retrieve
from under mesquite trees, the branches of which
tend to drag the ground: they wear thorns and
grow in knotty thickets. i poke my stick in
at a can under the dragging limbs, the can
bounces off a stem and caroms closer to the trunk.
i have to find a way in through branches to
reach the can with fingers that by now are
scratched and bleeding from thorns. mesquites
belong to a tribe often beaten in battles with
cattlemen and utility people who lay gas lines
and string wires, but the mesquite tribe has
never surrendered and still considers desert its
own mother territory. mesquites grow along the
chainlink fence between me and neighbors on both
sides, but it's not my land they're marking—
where they grow is theirs. sometimes i trim
their bottom limbs, but that doesn't bother them;
they still send roots as far as they need to for
water, and they still drop sticky bean pods on
my pick-up's windshield. i do find a lot of cans
under mesquites along the gas line and bleed some
getting them, but i don't resent the trees or even
their thorns. they're my only real firsthand
connection with indigenous souls, they remind me
i'm not a conqueror, only a temporary pestilence.
mesquites outnumber me and my kind, and they have
plenty of time. unless and until we decide to
get our aluminum and other ores with something
noisier than a stick. then, well, even mesquites . . .

## To Catch the Truth

Truth
must be played with patience, fish
at the end of a line.
Play and ply, pull
and let line out, then in,
till
bringing in the catch, you find
the hook set fast
in your own jaws

**James Jay** (Flagstaff, AZ) has taught poetry in prisons, public schools, and at Northern Arizona University. Between stints as a bookseller, surveyor, furniture mover, and wildland firefighter, he authored a weekly column for *FlagLive*, served as Executive Director of the Northern Arizona Book Festival, and owned a bar with his wife, Alyson. He received an MFA from the University of Montana and an MA in Literature from Northern Arizona University.

## Mars Hill

*—for Alyson*

That night-hike up Mars
Hill, a flask of John Powers going
down fast, my finger brushing
your hand on the exchange,
big full moon, and light-rain
that morphed to sheets
of snow as we climbed
to the log where we found
ourselves a seat.
           You leaning in
to kiss me, me too scared to go
first, wet lips, snow drenched
faces and heads, followed by the firm hold
of hands as we leapt back down
the trail like
           Jack & Jill: the tale revised
as if by dumb angels who scribbled sweet,
naïve edits with no flair
for drama; simply stupid enough
to wish to help; who worked
the soles of our feet to keep us
from falling familiarly down; who erased twisted
ankles; who brushed aside sticks, stones;
kept our shoes tied; our strides in step.
The angels whose pens are filled
with the ink of surviving
           so many
falls before, the dumb angels
that earned the calluses that guide
us; the light of stars caught
in the scars of their barely visible cheeks!

## Two Parts Hydrogen, One Part Oxygen

Driving down the Hohokam Expressway I wonder:
Hohokams didn't want this—metal buildings, dry
palm trees, a run over dog, gun shots.

The Salt River Project is full of water currently
in litigation between Arizona, Native American
tribes, developers. Yesterday a young Mexican boy
drowned in the canal, he only wanted to swim—cool
down from the 105 degree day. Today, the Hohokams
are gone, only the water and the few fragments of
stone watch over . . .

A quail with its outlined eyes. A bowman with a
quiver full of arrows. The sun, a disk, an eye watching
earth. The cornstalk with its perfect shadow. A bird
at the water's edge. Flute players and dancers play in
the blowing wind. Antelopes made from sticks and
bark strips.

Green, green, green into the desert, more unnatural
green. Grow more green aliens—golf courses.
Concrete waterways based off Hohokam design
pump water into swimming chlorine pools and
elaborate fountains in central Phoenix, the rain gods
abused. Concrete waterways based off Hohokam
design pump water to the Palo Verde Nuclear Power
Plant. Water is cubic and feet—bought and sold—
two parts hydrogen, one part oxygen now lights
all of Las Vegas. There is no more water for corn,
avocados, melons . . .

No, this isn't what they wanted. They wanted the
water to tell their story . . .

Perhaps this is what the water would say today:

A Tohono O'odham boy sitting under a Palo Verde,
watching a roadrunner chase a dragonfly. He's tired
from swimming in the river with his brown dog all
afternoon. After eating a sweet green melon, he
throws the rinds at the curious antelopes grazing
nearby on wild wheat stems.

**Hershman John** (Phoenix, AZ) is both poet and fiction writer. He received his BA in English and MFA in Creative Writing from Arizona State University. He is a faculty member at Phoenix College. His first collection of poems is *I Swallow Turquoise for Courage* (University of Arizona Press, 2007).

**Jane Miller** (Tucson, AZ) is author of eight collections of poetry, including *The Greater Leisures* (Doubleday, 1983), a National Poetry Series Selection, and *August Zero* (Copper Canyon, 1993), winner of the Western States Book Award. She is a recipient of the Lila Wallace-Reader's Digest Award and fellowships from the National Endowment for the Arts and the John Simon Guggenheim Memorial Foundation. She has taught at the University of Iowa Writers' Workshop, Goddard College, and the University of Arizona, where she has served as writing program director.

### xii  (excerpted from *Midnights*)

The walk of friendship is littered. There's Robin's memory, I follow, of her mother, a nurse, looking terribly older in her graying uniform, and there's Robin's first husband, divorced long ago and living in a distant city, gliding by in the mental picture she draws for me of his white Mercedes. We gringas can barely make him out behind darkened windows and dark glasses. She recognizes the cock of his head; yes, she says definitively, That's him, Jane, do you see him? I see him for her, even though I'm crying and can't see anything. Yes, there he is, I say. That's his tan, lined face. We pass by actual, undocumented

workers digging holes and putting in yet one more drip system to monitor the timing for those of us of Tucson's foothills who need to water the indigenous cacti and illegal Meyer lemon trees and illegal California olives that we transport into Arizona, and, in the case of those of us trying to replicate lives from the other North American coast, grasses and roses. Here is Robin; she disapproves of anyone, with papers or without, working for her. Obediently, she's picked up an empty twelve-pack from the street. I admire her; it's as if she's walking her dead dog.

She tells her famous story, at the end of which are important syllables. The nouns and the verbs, the signatures of acts of betrayal and denial that parted the husband from the wife, and the wife from the husband, smolder in the dry air of the hill we climb. They trail off the trail, off the tail end of my own thoughts, *cheater, liar,*

up, up, shortness of breath, little muscles gripping tight the vessels of the heart. The words of Robin's story several years old still burning. *Which is hotter, the heat of the day or the char of a love story?* I ask my friend;

I am remembering the day I asked. I turn and press her arm. She presses mine, says, Keats, my man, I know you are suffering. Have I earned the disreputable honor of crossing one of Robin's lines? She has promised to be honest, but now she is comparing my psychodrama to a great man's deadly tuberculosis. Or, she's joking. The fact that I don't know is not pleasant.

Camino del Sueño / (Street of Dreams), 7 a.m.

## The Half-Life of Memory

It's as toxic as any nuclear mountain,
though it's a mountain that comes to you.
It's not out there beside some wasted stretch
of Nevada 50 or among the radioactive rabbits
on the high plains of eastern Washington
where tumbleweeds choke the fences
and little rodent deaths foul the wells.

You are the soldier it was tested on,
the shadow vaporized onto the wall.
Take off your goggles, your safe
white suit, ignore the Geiger's jittering.
To look back is to risk becoming salt
like the lining of subconscious dumps
half a mile beneath southern New Mexico.

Memory's waning anticipates yours.
It decays before your bags are even packed,
was last seen traveling toward the vanishing point
of a half-lived life. A mirror with degraded silver,
you see through it but not back.
It is spent fuel, seems benign and clean,
sweet-talks you into thinking exposure won't burn.

But even showers of alkaline regret
can't prevent contamination.
You don't have enough years to wait it out,
enough concrete to contain it.

**Jim Natal** (Prescott, AZ) is author of *Memory and Rain* (Red Hen Press, 2009) and two previous poetry collections, *In the Bee Trees* (Archer Books, 2000) and *Talking Back to the Rocks* (Archer Books, 2003). The co-founder of Conflux Press, his work has appeared in many journals and anthologies. He teaches creative writing at Yavapai College, where he also serves as series director for The Literary Southwest.

**Sean Nevin** (Tempe, AZ) teaches at Arizona State University, where he directs the Young Writer's Program and is Assistant Director of The Virginia G. Piper Center for Creative Writing. His poems have won the Robinson Jeffers Tor House Prize for Poetry and The Alsop Review Poetry Prize, and he is the recipient of fellowships in poetry from the National Endowment for the Arts and the Arizona Commission on the Arts.

### The Carpenter Bee

Black and polished
with light, it treads the air
beneath the arched soffits
of our house, where

this morning I smeared,
with a clean metal blade,
a dollop of putty
over the bullet-sized hole
it bored into the wood.

I watched, for an hour
that bee, tap-tap-tapping
like the severed tip
of a cane groping
after what was lost, and

like that, I saw again
the frostbitten toe
the medics let thaw,
then amputated as I slept
through a gauze

of morphine. The charred
and inconsolable knuckle
that would, for years, try,
each night in my dreams,
to come home from the war.

### Wildfire Triptych

> Fire burns: that is the first law.
> —William Carlos Williams

#### I. What the Smoke Brings

For two full days the sirens
realized their high notes
in the quivering saucers
stacked inside cupboards,
and an exodus of field deer
cropped the blooming gladioli
down to a stubble.

The wind grew jaundiced,
carried with it a sacrament
of wood ash to the tongue's
sour root, left me raw-throated
and quiet in the car's backseat.

It was a sad evening all day
and the deer, like refugees,
plodded the centers of streets.

I spelled with my finger
the words: wash me in soot
on the hood of my father's
Coupe DeVille, as I watched
a six-point buck pause,

then spill a small cache of shit
like polished beads, unstrung
and falling through the yellow
air of the Sears parking lot.

## II. Roof Dancer

If the winds swung east
my father would climb
the wooden ladder,

a pail of water weeping
from one hand, and wait
for the first stars to fall.

He'd stamp and douse
the cinders where they'd land
all night. This secret dancing

made weather inside our rooms:
thunder through the bones
of the house, a flurry of snow

descending from the rafters.

### III.  Variations on Sleep

1.
To sleep that night was to travel
   a great distance by train,
      to drag from iron wheels

the crushed chassis of a Ford
   a mile down the tracks, that,
      and a clean rooster tail of sparks

to set the punk-capped cattails blazing.

2.
To sleep that night was to sing
   trainsong falsetto: the lucid song
      of metal gouging metal,

to hear the storm windows rattle
   like teeth in the skull, to know
      fire and the dark brother of fire

careening unhinged.

3.
To sleep that night was to work
   worm gears and pistons
      swing shift through the night,

to watch flame carve,
   like a greased machine,
      the hillside, to wheeze

and shimmy oiled phone poles,
   to cleave the roofline
      like a dawn sun, stalled

and dilating above a field.

4.
To sleep that night was to detonate
   floorboards in dream, to stoke
      the locomotive's blast furnace:

fire-belly barreling through
   the interior, the dried creek beds,
      the bleached crackle of scrub grass

sprouting, at once, into flame.

5.
To sleep that night was to arrive
       a refugee in a foreign station,
             to avert my eyes and vanish

into the unmapped countryside,
the still-smoldering landscape.


## Losing Solomon

> *We estimate a man by how much he remembers.*
> —Ralph Waldo Emerson


Things seem to take on a sudden shimmer
before vanishing: the polished black loafers
he wore yesterday, the reason for climbing
the stairs, even the names of his own children

are swallowed like spent stars against the dark
vault of memory. Today the toaster gives up
its silver purpose in his hands, becomes a radio,
an old Philco blaring a ball game from the '40s
with Jackie Robinson squaring up to the plate.

For now, it's simple; he thinks he is young again,
maybe nineteen, alone in a kitchen. He is staring
through his own reflection in the luster and hoping
against hope that Robinson will clear the bases
with a ball knocked so far over the stadium wall
it becomes a pigeon winging up into the brilliance.

And perhaps, in one last act of alchemy,
as Jackie sails around third, he will transform
everything, even the strange and forgotten face
glaring back from the chrome, into something
familiar, something Solomon could know as his own.

**Simon J. Ortiz** (Tempe, AZ), is a native of New Mexico, where he grew up at Deetseyaamah, a rural village in the Acoma Pueblo community. He is a poet, fiction and creative non-fiction writer, essayist, and Professor of Indigenous Literature and American Indian Studies at Arizona State University. He is author of *Woven Stone* (University of Arizona Press, 1992), *From Sand Creek* (Thunder's Mouth Press, 1981), *Out There Somewhere, After and Before the Lightning* (University of Arizona Press, 1994), and many other books. Over a span of forty years, his work and life have focused on Indigenous decolonization and liberation. He is the father of three children—Raho, Rainy, Sara—and a grandfather of eight.

## just phoenix

just phoenix
actually tempe
is where i live
but when people ask me
where i live
i say tempe
so i don't have to say
i'm from phoenix

just phoenix
where the airport is
a destination a place
to land safely enough
since my life has seen
so many edges i'm shy
now and then to land
so it's okay if phoenix
is the airport i land at
and not where i live

just phoenix
and for now comparatively
i have to say it's more open
land space time choice
than manhattan ny where
for two days i've been at
cooper union where i talked
last night plus sang a song
singing i felt especially strong
not worried about forgetting
words timing and breath
since i had it written down
and i didn't have to worry
what next and what now

just phoenix
this time not albuquerque nm
like one time headed there
and didn't have the loot
to buy a ticket all the way there
and only made it to reno nv
so hitched-walked rest of way to nm
there is there somewhere there
so here i go now on flight
online on time and on the way
even if "there" is just phoenix
where i know i'll be there
tonight at 8:30 okay alright
good guess and good news

## Spring

I was bedded down in the attic
my breath visible in the light
of a kerosene lantern
I lay under the roof's slant
counting the nails that pointed
from both sides to the middle
and listened to the bears hooting
on the ridge behind the house
while I imagined the next morning
we would walk down the dirt road
break the skin of ice off the spring
splash our faces with water so cold it hurt
and if grandfather's old logging horses
were down from the woods
we'd go on to the meadow
then walk back with grandmother telling stories
that would be impossible to believe now
but seemed then to be entirely logical and true
there was one about bears
coming into the yard to attack the goat
and being chased away by my grandparents
in their night clothes
yelling and banging cooking pots with spoons
I shivered and fell asleep to that sound
to dream what I can't remember now
I woke late that next morning
to the sound of water dripping
the frost on the roof nails beginning to thaw

**Michael Rattee** (Tucson, AZ) works as a software engineer, developing web applications for use in education. He is author of *Michael Rattee Greatest Hits: 1976—2006* (Pudding House, 2007). He co-edited, with David Ray, *Surfings: Selected Poems of Will Inman* (Howling Dog Press, 2006).

**David Ray** (Tucson, AZ) is author of *When* (Howling Dog Press, 2007) and *After Tagore: Poems Inspired by Rabindranath Tagore* (Nirala Editions, 2008). His book *Music of Time: Selected & New Poems* (Backwaters Press, 2006) offers work from fifteen previous volumes. Other titles include *The Death of Sardanapalus and Other Poems of the Iraq Wars* (Howling Dog Press, 2004) and a memoir, *The Endless Search* (Soft Skull Press, 2003).

## The Sleepers

*Bodies of two illegal migrants were found this morning on the Southern Pacific tracks.*
—*Tucson Citizen*

What they have endured, making it north
from deep in the belly of Mexico,
would make a great novel, picaresque,
the two companions trembling with hope.

After many perils they make it across
the border, manage to survive the desert,
search squads, spotlights, police dogs,
helicopters, klieg lights, and armed vigilantes.

But there is a great weariness after such
a journey, and rest is essential. Exhausted,
they lie down between rails, safe from
the hazards of snakes and scorpions.

The rotten rail ties called sleepers are like
slats of a bed, their frayed surface soft as flannel,
and perfume of the creosote is familiar,
like brush growing along *barrancas* back home.

If the last breath is inhaled in the new land
it mingles with pollen from home, and scent
of smog joins toxins acquired in the past
as if there has been no border at all to dispute.

As the two lie down in the night between tracks
they dream of how soon they will pick oranges
or lay tiles, trim trees and clip hedges. But a train
not expected is sometimes the one that arrives.

## Illegals

An X-ray of a truck, a million bananas
at least, row upon row—
and huddled within a few chosen spaces—
God knows how they breathed—
are a few dozen human creatures
packed in as tight as the bananas.

They show up on the film as white
forms sitting stiff and upright
as on choir benches—pale ghosts,
diagnostic as TB or cancer. They
don't have a chance or a prayer
of success in their quest. With such
humble devotion many a saint
earned his time on the calendar.

In the front of this toy-like two-
dimensional truck the engine shows up
like a dark heart, and the gas tanks
appear like lungs. Viable creatures
are the bananas, unwilted, kept bright
by a misting of poison. The dead
souls are a cargo impounded.

The truck was heading North.
The drivers never know anything.
Americans eat the bright yellow bananas.

## Arizona Satori

Why should the old man
not feel young again
when he stops to consult

for fifty minutes or so
the great saguaro standing
tall—300 years of wisdom

speaking with silence,
sending no bill, keeping no
illegible records, having

no license at all on the wall?

## The White Buffalo

The long-predicted miracle took place
upon a winter's morning, and by the time
the white buffalo was weaned enough

to munch her hay, the tourists came,
held nightly vigil with candles glowing,
their prayers in chorus to expedite

the day this wondrous calf would bestow
blessings on one and all. She munched
her hay and took no notice as campfires

burned throughout the night and faces
glowed with bliss and hope, the chanting
endless, along with drums and dancing.

Some came in wheelchairs, some with canes.
In half an hour many got all and more
than prayed for. Props of old despair were tossed

aside until a field filled up with piles of crutches
and prosthetic trash. The TV crews flew in
from Rome and Paris, and had a tower

been raised it could have been named Babel—
for many tongues were heard babbling
breathy wonder, along with guesses just how soon

the white buffalo would turn into a maiden
clad in soft white deerskin. Over the horizon
she would dance to put an end to all the evils

prophesied, their horrors fading like bad dreams.
There'd be no more hurricanes or earthquakes,
wars or murders, nor floods to rival Noah's.

We too should have rushed off on our pilgrimage,
for as our luck would have it—or destiny, or karma—
and like the tow hair on our children—

the pristine fur turned dark. The buffalo grew up.

## These Days

Yesterday the postman left
a white square box—tape over
the severe, sans-serif typed address,
no names, no stamps, no clues.
I shook it gently, set it down
in the yard, bright against rainy
green weeds. An error? A prank?
A surprise un-birthday gift?
The postman did not know
how it passed without stamps.
He called his supervisor.
"These days…" he suggested.

The police asked if we have any enemies.
I wanted to say "We're Friends"
but thought he might not understand.
"These days" means wariness,
white vans, protective shields,
x-rays, geiger counters.
We did not think this box
would blow out our windows.
But "these days," they all said.

Thick gloves picked up the box,
shook it lightly, as I had. Would
a butterfly fly out of this smooth cocoon?
Would a lotus open into the sun?
But no, the cut sheets of white coated
paper found inside were blank, no clues.
Crumpled glossy travel ads
made packing. No code to be broken.

Today the postman knocks
and hands me another package,
this one wrapped in coarse paper
and tied with string.  Loud black
ink has danced its way here
from Kathmandu, declaring itself
to be a book of poems, hidden runes
of metaphor to escape detection.
"Stamps are on the back,"
the postman tells me.
"This time I checked.
These days I have to check."

**Judy Ray** (Tucson, AZ) is author of *To Fly Without Wings: Poems* (Helicon Nine Editions, 2009), her third published collection. Her chapbooks include *Fishing in Green Waters* (Cervena Barva, 2006), *Sleeping in the Larder: Poems of a Sussex Childhood* (Van Zora, 2005), and *Judy Ray Greatest Hits 1974—2008* (Pudding House, 2008). In Tucson, Judy volunteers as a teacher of English as a Second Language to adults in the community.

**Alberto Ríos** (Chandler, AZ) is author of *The Smallest Muscle in the Human Body* (Copper Canyon Press, 2002), a National Book Award finalist. His book *The Theater of Night* (Copper Canyon Press, 2006) received the 2007 PEN/Beyond Margins Award. He has also authored short story collections and a memoir, *Capirotada* (University of New Mexico Press, 1999), about growing up in Nogales, Arizona, on the Mexican border. Regents' Professor and Katharine C. Turner Chair in English, Ríos has taught at Arizona State University for twenty-seven years.

## Border Lines

*A weight carried by two*
*Weighs only half as much.*

The world on a map looks like the drawing of a cow
In a butcher's shop, all those lines showing
Where to cut.

That drawing of the cow is also a jigsaw puzzle,
Showing just as much how very well
All the strange parts fit together.

Which way we look at the drawing
Makes all the difference.
We seem to live in a world of maps:

But in truth we live in a world made
Not of paper and ink but of people.
Those lines are our lives. Together,

Let us turn the map until we see clearly:
The border is what joins us,
Not what separates us.

## Líneas Fronterizas

*Un peso cargado por dos*
*No pesa más que la mitad.*

El mundo en un mapa parece el dibujo de una vaca
En la carnicería, todas esas líneas mostrando
Dónde cortar.

Ese dibujo de la vaca es también un rompecabezas,
Mostrando cómo caben muy bien juntas
Todas las piezas extrañas.

La manera en que miramos el dibujo
Nos hace ver la diferencia.
Parecemos vivir en un mundo de mapas:

Pero en verdad vivimos en un mundo hecho
No de papel ni de tinta sino de gente.
Esas líneas son nuestras vidas.  Juntos,

Demos vuelta al mapa hasta que veamos claramente:
La frontera es lo que nos une,
No lo que nos separa.

## Rabbits and Fire

Everything's been said
But one last thing about the desert,
And it's awful: during brushfires in the Sonoran desert,
Brushfires which happen before the monsoon and in the great,
Deep, wide, and smothering heat of the hottest months,
The longest months,
The hypnotic, immeasurable lulls of August and July—
During these summer fires, jackrabbits,
Jackrabbits and everything else
That lives in the brush of the rolling hills,
But jackrabbits especially,
Jackrabbits can get caught in the flames,
No matter how fast and big and strong and sleek they are.
And when they're caught,
Cornered in and against the thick
Trunks and thin spines of the cactus,
When they can't back up any more,
When they can't move, the flame—
It touches them,
And their hair catches fire.
Of course they run away from the flame,
Finding movement even when there is none to be found,
Jumping big and high over the wave of fire or backing
Even harder through the impenetrable
Tangle of hardened saguaro
And prickly pear and cholla and barrel,
But whichever way they find,
What happens is what happens—they catch on fire,
And then bring the fire with them when they run.
They don't know they're on fire at first,
Running so fast as to make the fire
Shoot like rocket engines and smoke behind them,
But then the rabbits tire,
And the fire catches up,
Stuck onto them like the needles of the cactus,
Which at first must be what they think they feel on their skins.
They've felt this before, every rabbit.
But this time the feeling keeps on.
And of course, they ignite the brush and dried weeds
All over again, making more fire, all around them.
I'm sorry for the rabbits.
And I'm sorry for us
To know this.

## Refugio's Hair

In the old days of our family
My grandmother was a young woman
Whose hair was as long as the river.
She lived with her sisters on the ranch
La Calera, the land of the lime,
And her days were happy.

But her uncle Carlos lived there too
Carlos whose soul had the edge of a knife.
One day to teach her to ride a horse
He made her climb on the fastest one
Bare-back, and sit there
As he held its long face in his arms.

And then he did the unspeakable deed
For which he would always be remembered.
He called for the handsome baby Pirrín
And he placed the child in her arms.
With that picture of a Madonna on horseback
He slapped the shank of the horse's rear leg.

The horse did what a horse must
Racing full toward the bright horizon.
But first he ran under the *álamo* trees
To rid his back of this unfair weight,
This woman full of tears
And this baby full of love.

When they reached the trees and went under
Her hair which had trailed her
Equal in its magnificence to the tail of the horse
That hair rose up, and flew into the branches
As if it were a thousand arms
All of them trying to save her.

The horse ran off and left her
The baby still in her arms,
The two of them hanging from her hair.
The baby looked only at her
And did not cry, so steady was her cradle.
Her sisters came running to save them.

But the hair would not let go.
From its fear it held on, and had to be cut
All of it, from her head.
From that day on my grandmother
Wore her hair short, like a scream
But it was long like a river in her sleep.

## Mi Biblioteca Pública

En este lugar nos hemos rodeado
Con nosotros mismos: Bienvenido, pero cuidase
También. Somos risa y orilla, somos
Amplios y agudos, pan y pimienta.

En esta vecindad de libros, en este
Edificio hecho de palabras, esta biblioteca,
Nuestros brazos son estantes:
En ellos, soportamos todo.

*Si nos lastimamos uno al otro,*
        *Déjelo que sea un acto de la imaginación.*
*Si nos curamos uno al otro,*
        *Déjelo que sea un acto de pasión.*

## My Public Library

In this place we have surrounded ourselves
With ourselves: Welcome, but be wary too.
We are laughter and edge, we are
Broad and sharp, bread and pepper.

In this neighborhood of books, in this
Building made of words, this library,
Our arms are shelves:
In them, we hold all things.

*If we hurt each other,*
        *Let it be an act of the imagination.*
*If we heal each other,*
        *Let it be an act of passion.*

**Rebecca Seiferle** (Tucson, AZ) was awarded a Lannan Literary Fellowship in 2004. Her poetry collections have won the Grub Street Poetry Prize, the Western States Book Award, the Hemley and Bogin Awards, the Writer's Exchange Award, and the National Writers' Union Prize. She has translated two books by Cesar Vallejo, most recently *The Black Heralds* (Copper Canyon Press, 2003). Seiferle founded the online poetry journal *The Drunken Boat* and teaches at The Art Center Design College in Tucson.

### Ghost Riders in the Sky

You can no longer say where the photo was taken;
it resembles so many Western landscapes: the sun
going down in the flare of its own glory, the ship
sailing off in flames. Yet you know the figure
that is lost, that is always lost, is your brother,
his purposeful saunter of one lamed
like any failed god or hero, fate's mediocre
toe lost to a bicycle chain, his heel caught
in his mother's grip, who bent over and scooped
up his wounded foot in her apron. Yet still who managed
to stride, to stroll, in the too-large hand-me-down
boots on his feet, though the toes curled up, and
all the kids laughed at his Rumplestiltkin-curly-toes.
He would not take the boots off, but clamped them
on, striding into the playground, already caught
in the haze of the golden dream of being, beyond
ridicule, beyond pain, beyond any hope of rescue.
He kept on striding away, though his spine was bent
and his vertebrae shattered, though he ached from the fury
of unnamed horses and uprooted posts flying
through the air and nailing him in the back, from punches
thrown in parking lots, from barbed wire unrolling
its private range in scars along his arms;
he always got up and strolled away, as he did
the last day he put down his chaps
and his lariat, hung his leather skin and left
his life hanging neatly like an abandoned flag upon the railings,
as one who went armed, who went forth, who faced
himself at the edge of the water and fell beneath his own hand,
and even in death, his eyes have that look, honed
beyond any horizon, trying to pierce that godforsaken golden haze.

## Apache Tears

In the rock bins of my childhood, every tourist stop
sold Apache tears—obsidian drops, smooth and velvety
in the hand, obdurate, until, held up to the light,
each became a smoky being, a cloud pregnant
with rain in that desert—making a story of the beauty
of grief out of a tribe of Apache (really no more than
an extended family) who were trapped at the edge
of the cliff (by the Mexicans some said, others
the U.S. cavalry), who all leapt to their deaths
rather than being taken captive, and the tears
they shed before dying turned to wild stones
at the base of the cliff. I don't know how many
tears I bought and lost; a galaxy of black stars
in those bins, and yet each time, I looked through
that landside of sorrow, thinking if I found
the right one and held it up to the light,
I could see entirely through it. If it's ever possible
to see *through* human suffering: beyond knowing
in any climate and any time, there are those who are turned to stone.

**Leslie Marmon Silko** (Tucson, AZ) grew up at Laguna Pueblo, where her father and family still reside. She now lives in the Tucson Mountains with a number of parrots and dogs. She is author of novels *Ceremony* (Penguin, 1988), *Almanac of the Dead* (Penguin, 1992), and *Gardens in the Dunes* (Simon & Schuster, 2000). She received a fellowship from the John D. and Catherine T. McArthur Foundation. Her memoirs of walks in the hills, rattlesnakes, and rain clouds are recounted in *The Turquoise Ledge* (Viking, 2010).

## How to Hunt Buffalo

Think what you are about to do, think how precious all life is,
how difficult the struggle is, for all of us born into this world. Think
how much the mother loves her little ones and how they love her.
None of us wants to die, though we all must change and return to
Mother Earth.

Prepare months in advance. Prepare by visiting the old folks who
fed you and held you in their arms. Visit the old man who used to walk
you across the highway after school. Prepare by helping others who have
been in trouble, who have no place to live, who are sick and lonely, help
your brothers and sisters, see to them first. Find those who shiver because
they are cold without coats or boots. Remember them, the hungry
              and the cold
when you go to ask the Buffalo People to make a gift to us.

Practice with your hunting bow or rifle so your aim is accurate,
so the buffalo will not suffer.

You will go to ask them to give you one of their family, you will ask
              for a buffalo's life.
The buffalo agrees to come home with the hunter; if we fail to act
              with respect, the
buffalo will not come. It is not for yourself that you go—not for you,
              or your glory, or your
big-shot reputation. Your heart must be humble, otherwise you won't see
              even one.

Walk alone on the plain. Look at the beauty all around you as if this
              is the last time
you will ever see it. Smell the wind, the sweet grass and sage,
smell the promise of rain. Take a deep breath.
All beings wish only to go on as they are, to be left in peace.
Remember the color of the sky and the luminous light at the edges
              of the clouds.

Now sing the song that rises into your chest and throat. Stand on
              the plain
and sing from your heart. Don't prepare a song ahead of time—
              begin the song only
after you are alone there. Sing the sorrow that we are born to die;
              someday we all will
be food for poor hungry creatures. The life we nourish carries us inside it
              so there is no
end. Sing this song, sing it patiently, sing it and wait.

You may have to stand all day long in the bright sun, singing.
You may get thirsty and tired, but you must not stop singing if you want
    the buffalo
to come give you one of their own.
Even after you think it is hopeless, and you no longer believe the buffalo
    will come,
still you must sing your heart out. Even when your throat is tight with
    disappointment
because they have not come, still you must stand there and sing.
Sing patiently, sing hopelessly, sing and wait.

They appear suddenly when the sun is low in the west. At first you are
    not sure if
they are approaching or moving away from you. You see only a few
    buffalo but soon
others join them. The buffalo walk calmly but you see they are alert;
    they are listening
to your song as they move closer now. Big buffalo bulls form a circle
    around you; they
are watching you. Still you must sing, though now you feel uneasy. The
    darkening sky is
immense and you are so much smaller than the buffalo. Alone here, no
    bow and arrow
or hunting rifle can save you if the buffalo decide to trample you. Still
    you must sing—
sing your own fear now, sing your own regret as the sun drops below the
    horizon.

Then one buffalo steps out of the herd, away from the others. The buffalo
    stands and
looks at you. The eyes of this buffalo are calm. You glance around and
    notice the other
buffalo have begun to move away, leaving him to stand alone. They turn
    and walk
slowly across the prairie; in the twilight they seem to dissolve into
    shadow.

You have imagined this moment for a long time—you have prepared
    yourself—
you have practiced with your rifle so the first shot is accurate, so the
    buffalo does not
suffer. Now whisper, "Thank you my brother, we cherish you."

**Laurel Speer** (Tucson, AZ) has lived in Tucson for the last thirty-nine years, where she enjoys good films, live theater, proximity to the University of Arizona, and bookstores galore. She has published poetry in small press and university literary magazines since 1963. She also authored a column of literary opinion in *Small Press Review* for sixteen years, as well as editing and writing for two review magazines.

### Buffalo Stones

To help digestion, the buffalo swallows small stones
that sit in one of its two stomachs. We can imagine
these tumbling like pennies in a dryer, only hidden.
When the stones are found, they're round and polished.
But first the buffalo must go down, be picked clean.
Then only through bones will the stones show through.
Imagine millions of them winking in grass and sod
during the late carnage. So many there couldn't be
enough kids in dungarees with pockets to pick them up
for good luck. So many they'd become commonplace
as shells on sand after a high and violent tide.
And as we all know, the commonplace doesn't astonish.

### Candyman

I meet my first husband in the desert. This isn't
the beautiful, complicated desert of animals, plants,
hillocks and varieties of green. This is the flat,
desolate stretch off I-10. He gestures for me to get
in the car. He's imperious, elegant, well-dressed.
His hair is styled and he's finally found out what
to do about those hangnails.

I have a little water left in my canteen. It's warm
and metallic. The canteen inside its holder bangs
against my hip and dangles at an awkward angle
from the metal eyelets of the web belt on which
it's hooked. Very boss, very rakish, death-defying
and childish. But I do not get into that car.

## After Noon in Yootó

The Santa Fe afternoon is warm and bright.
The dogs are delirious to be outdoors; they prance about, panting loudly.
"Simmer down, guys," I say.
They don't have to wear jackets today.
Once my husband said they were embarrassed to wear jackets.
"I never saw a dog embarrassed," I said. He just smiled.

A few months ago on another warm afternoon,
my mother sat on the comfortable old couch in the front of the woodstove.
The stove is in the center of the house and the room is dim and cool.

After straightening the kitchen, I sat beside her.
"Uh," I said, leaning against her, meaning "tell me stories,"
or "tell me what's going on."
"T'áá 'ákódí. That's all," she said. We both laughed.

I adjusted the pillow behind her head as she leaned back.
I slipped my hand into hers and leaned against her.
Her hands are warm and thin.
Unlike mine, she has slim, elegant fingers.
She patted my hand and we were silent.

We were alone in the quiet house.
Across the road, a cow bellowed and somewhere by the wash,
dogs were barking playfully. One sounded like a puppy.
Here in the living room, we rested closing our eyes.
Then she said, with her eyes still closed, "Let's sing."
So I started a song and she joined in. I sang close to her so she could hear.
We sang several songs, then she started one and I was quiet.
"I don't know that one," I said after she raised her head and looked at me.
"You do," she said. "One time I heard you singing it."
She kept on singing and after a while, I got it and we finished.

"Whaa," she said, like she was tired.
She fell asleep. I kept holding her hand and leaning on her.
I wanted to sleep, but couldn't.
It seemed like there was too much going on,
but it was just she and I sitting together on a late summer afternoon.
Her cat, Kitty Baá, jumped on the couch and stretched out beside us.
It seemed that Kitty Bah and Mom always napped at the same time.

Today in Yootó, there's snow on the highest peaks
of the Sangre De Cristos—the mountains of the Blood of Christ.
The bright snow is startling against the deep blue sky.

It's warm enough to use the screen door;
the afternoon sun slants into the kitchen in thin lines.
The dogs sleep on the warm tile squares.

It's mid-October in Yootó where beads of clear, cold water
form an ancient necklace that encircles the Sangre De Cristos.

**Luci Tapahonso** (Tucson, AZ) is Professor of American Indian Studies and English at the University of Arizona. She is author of three children's books and six books of poetry. The Native Writers Circle of the Americas named Tapahonso the 1999 "Storyteller of the Year." She served as Grand Marshal for the Northern Navajo Fair Parade in 1991 and 1999 in her home community of Shiprock, New Mexico.

**Miles Waggener** (Phoenix, AZ) describes the Phoenix of his youth as an "ever-widening grid of strip malls, mini-marts, and storage units . . . a proving ground for runaway business scams, xenophobia, and sports teams named after animals that its citizens would kill if they actually encountered them in the wild: coyotes, rattlers, and diamondbacks." His collection of poems, *Phoenix Suites* (The Word Works, 2002), won the Washington Prize. He teaches in the Writer's Workshop of the University of Nebraska at Omaha.

## Direction

Here are landmarks
   and if you should find
      the magician's tomb
   the Sinagua built
in the maze
   of cinder cones and scrub
      keep quiet about it.
   Skeletons and talismans
are in boxes in Washington.
    Only you would want to know
      the way to a robbed grave.
   Find a slow chain
of rail cars pushing on
   beyond withering
      tennis courts and follow
   clattering shadows
and graffiti
   through town
      past curio shops
   live bait and ammo
the Napa Auto
   the Mormon church
     and reach
   a frontage road.
Take it as far east
   as you can—power
      lines humming overhead
   ponderosas and junipers
dwindling to salt bush—
   until the sun ends
     and a gas lamp appears
   in the clouded window
of a derelict school bus.
   The man selling
     ersatz Kachina dolls
   will tell you
he is your last landmark.

## Canister and Turkey Vulture

You don't bug the cops
but you fly like a feather-minded bullet
fasten the updraft
pivot the jet.
You are the in between
the so far as
the as to.
You note every missing shingle
every drop of vapor
everything that stands between the oh so obvious
and the almost can't imagine.

Peck the eyes out of the sun.
Cannot see you.
Throw away air.
Pound the dust with your demanding wings.
Promise that water and seed and enough claw and straw
will mark your rolling
will scrape the sky
keep it from falling.

Promises Promises
Who knew the sky so heavy?
Who knew speed
could catch light's comeuppance?
Who knew together they would sag,
ruffle, catch and molt?

**Nicole Walker** (Flagstaff, AZ) is author of *This Noisy Egg* (Barrow Street Press, 2010). Her poetry and creative nonfiction have appeared in *Ploughshares, North American Review, Bellingham Review, Fence, Iowa Review, Fourth Genre, Ninth Letter,* and *Crazyhorse,* among others. She is the recipient of a fellowship from the National Endowment for the Arts. A graduate of the University of Utah's doctoral program, she is now an assistant professor of poetry and creative nonfiction at Northern Arizona University.

# California

**Kim Addonizio** (Oakland, CA) is author of *Ordinary Genius: A Guide for the Poet Within* (W.W. Norton, 2009) and *Lucifer at the Starlite* (W.W. Norton, 2009). Addonizio has also published two novels, four previous poetry collections, and a book of stories. Her awards include a Guggenheim and two National Endowment for the Arts fellowships. Addonizio moved to the San Francisco Bay Area in 1976 and now lives in Oakland, where she teaches privately.

## Yes

Do you sometimes drink alone?
Have you ever woken up the next morning
after a night of heavy drinking?
Does your cat wander through the house
meowing inconsolably,
despite having fresh food and water?
Hunger, thirst, friendship, love.
Green Bee, Russian Quaalude, Redheaded Slut:
IEDs on the supply route to pleasure.
There's a gala in your hypothalamus,
helium balloons rising to the rafters,
the fizzy ricochet of laughter.
There's a stumblebum in your cerebellum.
That empty feeling crawling toward you—
should you kill it with a wadded paper towel
or trap it in a jar and shake it out
and send it flying into the grass?
Is your head full of frozen tamales
and a vodka bottle curled on its side?
How do you get through the interminable evenings?
Are they really interminable?
Have you considered the alternative?
Now get out of your car,
stand by the side of the road
and take a step. Now recite
"The Waste Land," backwards,
beginning with that sexy Sanskrit word.

## In the Evening,

according to the Psalms, we are cut down
and withereth like the grass, so on my birthday
I got up early and put on my suit. *Psst!*
*Look at this, it will change your life*, the man said,
motioning us toward his store.
A long time ago I was pulled from the place
I cleaned with a soapy washcloth the other day,
bathing her in her narrow bed
by the light of the big-screen TV.
All her underwear was dirty. In the evening
there will be canned chili and Cheez-Its,
there will be falling and femoral fractures.
There will be someone you know
but  can't quite  remember,
and an underpaid stranger
hoisting you into a wheelchair
you could race down the hall like a chariot,
crashing into your retromingent neighbors.
In the store window was a big dusty bottle
with a schooner inside it
made of bottle caps. Many, many bottle caps.
On my birthday, my mother tried
to navigate to her bathroom.
I took a voyage and tried
to lose sight of the shore
and to ignore the god-sized beings
looking down on me,
their baffled faces,
their troubled expressions of hope.

**William Archila** (Los Angeles, CA) earned an MFA in poetry from the University of Oregon. His poems have been published in *The Georgia Review, AGNI, Poetry International, The Los Angeles Review, Poet Lore, Poetry Daily,* and *Notre Dame Review.* His first collection of poems, *The Art of Exile,* won the Emerging Writer Fellowship Award from the Writer's Center.

## Blinking Lights

At a crossing gate, I hear the whistle
then the rumble, wheels popping and grinding

shaking the bed of gravel, the pile of dirt
holding up the roadway. Suddenly, clank and roar,

one hundred tons of iron
race down the line like a long

black river rushing through the city,
a shot of smoke cutting the sky.

I remember the plug run I rode as a boy
with the windows down, wind swollen with rain,

hills stepping aside. My grandmother in a flower dress
sat beside me, no apron, no basket full of hens.

She brought coffee, French bread stuffed
with black beans, cream and avocado. We watched

tin huts and their trail of smoke,
stray dogs rambling along the rails,

country girls, clay pitchers, baskets of fruit
perched on their heads. Here, for the first time

I see how they live in the mountains,
running across coffee fields, scurrying like ants

they crawl into the cracks of the earth
as the sun goes down, lurk in their shadow.

Everything's red up front in the cab, coals
with a core of glowing fire.

No sound comes from the engine driving on
beyond the green bay, stacked

logs chained to its flat beds,
pushing into the failing light.

I gaze at a shack—broken roof, jagged
holes. A shirtless man

stands in the doorway getting smaller,
smaller as the train pulls away.

**Ellen Bass** (Santa Cruz, CA) is author of *The Human Line* (Copper Canyon Press, 2007) and *Mules of Love* (BOA, 2002). Her poems have been published in *The Atlantic Monthly, The Sun, The New Republic, The Kenyon Review*, and *American Poetry Review*. She is also co-author of *The Courage to Heal* (Harper, 2008). She teaches at Pacific University and at writing workshops in the United States and Europe.

## Gate C22

At gate C22 in the Portland airport
a man in a broad-band leather hat kissed
a woman arriving from Orange County.
They kissed and kissed and kissed. Long after
the other passengers clicked the handles of their carry-ons
and wheeled briskly toward short-term parking,
the couple stood there, arms wrapped around each other
like he'd just staggered off the boat at Ellis Island,
like she'd been released at last from ICU, snapped
out of a coma, survived bone cancer, made it down
from Annapurna in only the clothes she was wearing.


Neither of them was young. His beard was gray.
She carried a few extra pounds you could imagine
her saying she had to lose. But they kissed lavish
kisses like the ocean in the early morning,
the way it gathers and swells, sucking
each rock under, swallowing it
again and again. We were all watching—
passengers waiting for the delayed flight
to San Jose, the stewardesses, the pilots,
the aproned woman icing Cinnabons, the man selling
sunglasses. We couldn't look away. We could
taste the kisses crushed in our mouths.


But the best part was his face. When he drew back
and looked at her, his smile soft with wonder, almost
as though he were a mother still open from giving birth,
as your mother must have looked at you, no matter
what happened after—if she beat you or left you or
you're lonely now—you once lay there, the vernix
not yet wiped off, and someone gazed at you
as if you were the first sunrise seen from the Earth.
The whole wing of the airport hushed,
all of us trying to slip into that woman's middle-aged body,
her plaid Bermuda shorts, sleeveless blouse, glasses,
little gold hoop earrings, tilting our heads up.

### Women Walking

"I'm fat and I'm old and I'm going to die," Dorianne says
as we're taking our after dinner walk on the grounds of the Esalen Institute
which are gorgeous, but not very big, so we tromp back and forth
up the back entrance road, past the parked cars and the compost pile
where we turn around and start back again.


Dorianne's smoking American Spirits
with an Indian in a feathered headdress on the pale green box,
packaged to make you feel they're organic, connected to the native tradition,
bits of tobacco in a soft leather pouch offered to the gods
to ward off something—maybe the exact thing she's feeling now.


We're crossing over the arched wooden bridge, the river running under us
past a round redwood meditation hall neither of us has ever entered.
"I took a shower," she says, "and as I was drying I looked in the mirror.
Wouldn't it be enough to be just fat or just old or dying?"
We're passing through the garden now.


There's a virtual wall of sunflowers, each magnificent
full seeded head fringed with yellow flames,
and on the wide lawn ahead the yoga class unfurls their arms toward the sun.
The aroma of whole wheat bread baking mixes with the scent of salt and kelp.
I say, " I've gained back the weight I lost, I've got my pot belly again.


Last week I asked Janet how much it mattered on a scale of one to ten.
She said seven. I thought she'd say two, or maybe three at most.
So I waited a few days and broached it again.
'Maybe I'll cut out desserts,' I ventured, but she was reading about hive death
and raids on illegal aliens and lacing up her boots to go to work."


We're headed toward the baths. You're not allowed to smoke
past the bench halfway down, so Dorianne grinds her cigarette into the dirt
and shreds it as we stride along. When we get to the bottom of the incline,
we can smell the sulphurous fumes, the hot bliss I now connect with sinking
into those stone tubs, but we turn right around and head back up.

There are so many things to feel bad about, just in our two families alone,
but we don't talk about them now. I've cried so much this past year,
I just can't cry anymore. We're crossing the bridge again.
Someone has planted succulents along the edge of a stump
like a ribbon of green petaled roses. Dorianne lights another cigarette

with a Bic she slips from her pocket. "I stole this," she says, "from the 7/11."
"Oh," I say, "do you do that a lot?" She takes out a smaller Bic.
"This one I bought. My hair looks terrible, even though I washed it."
"I read," I tell her, "the average woman has 12.5 miles of hair."
"We get nervous with silence," she says.

"Mostly we talk just to reassure each other."
"Yea," I say, "I'm not going to eat you. Don't eat me."
Dorianne slips her hand through my arm. There's not a star visible in the sky.
The fog's come in so thick we can barely see the tops of the cypress.

We've passed the compost again and are headed back down.
"Do you want to soak in the baths?" I ask. "No," she says,
"Joe's been down there already and he'll be back soon."
We're standing outside her door. She says, "To me, your belly is only a two."
"Probably not even that," I say and kiss her and go to my room.

## Ode to Dr. Ladd's Black Slit Skirt

Praise to the little girl whose grandmother taught her to embroider,
slip the tip of the needle through the taut cloth and scallop the clouds,
fasten the feathers to blue bird wings.

And praise to the student who gulped muddy coffee
and memorized maps of muscles, puzzle of bones,
slid tendons through their shafts, curling and uncurling
each finger of the corpse like a deft puppeteer.

When I got to the ER Janet lay there, the morphine
not strong enough to winch up the pain.
Her arm looked like a carcass where a lion had fed.

Praise Dr. Ladd pulling green scrubs over her head
and gathering her long hair under a cap.

All the days we drove up to Stanford and waited for hours
in the room with the ugly orange carpet
thumbing through tarnished pages of National Geographic,
wondering what Dr. Ladd would be wearing,
until we heard the strike of her high heels on the hallway linoleum,
distinctive as the first notes of Beethoven's fifth.

Praise her hands that lifted Janet's hand, her fingertips brushing
over the gnarled scars, flesh lumped like redwood burl.

Praise her for getting up early to outline her eyelids,
slick her lips. And praise to her blouses, the silk creamy
as icing on a cake, the generous buttons open
like windows in summer. And praise

her bracelets coiled gold and her wide leather belts
encircling her waist like two strong hands about to lift her.
Praise to her earrings, little tinkling tambourines
and her perfume that braced us like a dry martini.

But most of all, praise to her slim black skirt
with the slit up the front so that when she sat down
and crossed her legs, the two panels parted like the Red Sea
and we were seized by the curve of her calves,
the faceted shine of her knees sheathed in sheer black mesh,
a riff of diamonds rippling up her thighs.

## Off Shore

*—for Mark Jarman*

Fifteen and what was there to do? The world so flat and slow,
Arthur Godfrey and Andre Kostelanetz still somewhere
on the radio? So I'd charge out on my Honda trail bike
to the beach and check the swell, the disposition of the tide,
see if the breeze was blowing off shore, holding
the wide waves up.
              From under a friend's beach-front porch
I'd haul out my dinged-up board and wax it down,
scratch through the soup to waves lined up and pealing
perfectly left to right at Sharks, Mirarmar, or Fernald Point.

Holy Days of Obligation—public school kids sweating it out
till 3:00—we had the best breaks to ourselves. And sometimes,
like palpable grace, the translucent sets steamed through
shoulder-high and sprayed spindrift back against the sky
as I took the drop and trimmed it up, nose-riding to shoot the curl,
then back pedaling as if walking on coals to kick out
before the shore break and the crunch.
                    Was there nothing
clear but that compulsion to climb out of myself onto the air
into that surging life and green whorl we cut through
but would not think beyond, numb and knee paddling
for the next outside set, the overhead walls tunneling
into the world and wholly apart from it?
                   What light
this now throws on every other thing is almost lost—
like me then, it was only what it was, burning wholly
at any cost on its own elemental terms. To step out
beyond the scene leaves me in my stiff, un-soaring bones
and short of breath, when what I want is the cheap grace
of a body that breaks through space smoothly as the sun,
my mind clear as water, with its unconscious message quick
to my heart and lungs to breathe.
               Even in February,
my legs gone grey as ice, I caught the rip-tide out
and slotted in, cranked a bottom turn and, grabbing a rail,
ripped through the tumbling trough to hang five pearling
forward off the board, careless and coming up easily
as a cork for the only reason that I was, and knew it there—
the salt and sea water chorusing in my blood and every
singing molecule of my skin.

**Christopher Buckley** (Lompoc, CA) is author of seventeen books of poetry, including *Rolling the Bones* (University of Tampa Press, 2010), winner of the Tampa Review Prize. Other books include *Modern History: Prose Poems 1987–2007* (Tupelo Press, 2008) and *Bear Flag Republic: Prose Poems & Poetics from California*, edited with Gary Young (Alcatraz Editions, 2008). He was a Guggenheim Fellow in Poetry and has received two National Endowment for the Arts Fellowships. He teaches creative writing at the University of California Riverside.

Back up the hills at dusk,
the roads were empty, and there was next to nowhere
then to go. There was a Hi-Fi and my stack of 45's;
there were hundreds of dollars and a year or more
between me and a car.
                    Each morning, fog burning
off the oaks and pines, and I'd kick-start my bike
with some Stratocaster surf tracks still pumping
like quick sets of waves over a reef in my mind,
and make the early run to find the break,
the glassy tubes—my life calmly racing out
in front of me, wind clearing the frothy light—
most everything still before me there in 1963, and
everywhere in the world I had to be was there.


## Wine

*I like to drink wine more than I used to—*
*Anyway, I'm drinking more . . .*
                    —Don Corleone


        All day, the twine crisscrossing my heart—
the way you'd tie up brown paper parcels
in the '50s for the post—tightens
by degrees . . . but at last, in our lawn chairs,
in the late afternoon shade of the pine,
the first glass—a bruise-dark Tempranillo
or black Umbrian, complex, big-bodied—
loosens the knot and lets me breathe out
into the sky, far enough away
from the world to love
the honey suckle swimming up
the stem of the air, the pink foxgloves
aligned like tiny Venetian cups.
                    Each sip
calms my blood like wind quitting
over a pond, the light trickling down
the plum leaves, the ruby shimmering
of the hummingbird's throat.
                    I look west
        over the haze of foothills, and I am on a terrace
above a small estate, its vineyards stretching
into an amber dust, off to the horizon
where I can feel the few clouds stationed there—
going red against the sun, sweet as Sangiovese—
lifting lightly from my chest.

## Oracular

*"It is all a Tree." —Thomas Carlyle*

By making things rare, we create an elite:
in the Sudan, how a chicken
is poisoned for divination.

Jung's dream of the wings of a house—
I misread as a house with wings—
"the distorted notions of invisible things."

Let us speak of what we haven't seen,
the light that fills the room or
page on which words float like clouds.

How conscience gets extinguished
with threadbare slogans.
Let us now praise embryonic growth,

One thousand poems about the same cathedral,
fixations and ruses, earth-worn objects
and those who love them.

.

## Garden/ Book

*"Good works . . . are not of this world."*
*—Hannah Arendt*

False start, said the gardener,
as he hurried to establish
this arbor here, that trellis there.

Juniper and jasmine, alyssum
in spring. Can we know
natural laws outside
our own analogies?

*It was like X when I met him:*
the day cloudy, clear, or fair.
Weather as usual, conditions
to note, the apprehending
named in the moment.

But damask roses exist.
And yarrow, more reckless
than its name, will bloom
all fall. Serving its will,
we're willed  into being,
eyes leading us to the words.

**Maxine Chernoff** (Mill Valley, CA) is author of nine books of poems, including *Among the Names* (Apogee Press, 2005) and *The Turning* (Apogee Press, 2008). With Paul Hoover, she edits the journal *New American Writing*. Together they have also translated the *Selected Poems of Friedrich Hölderlin* (Omnidawn Press, 2008). She chairs the Creative Writing Department at San Francisco State University.

**Marilyn Chin** (San Diego, CA) is author of *Revenge of the Mooncake Vixen* (W.W. Norton, 2009), *Rhapsody in Plain Yellow* (W.W. Norton, 2002), and *The Phoenix Gone, the Terrace Empty* (Milkweed Editions, 1994). Her works have become Asian-American classics and are taught all over the world. She teaches at San Diego State University.

## Formosan Elegy

*—For Charles*

You have lived six decades    yet you have lived none
You have loved many    yet you have loved no one
You wedded three wives    but you lie in your cold bed alone
You sired four children    but they cannot forgive you


Knock at emptiness   a house without your love
Strike the pine box    no answer   it's hollow
You planted plums near the gate   but they bear no fruit
You raised herbs in the veranda    they are fresh and savory


I cry for you    but no sound wells up in my throat
I sing for you    but my tears have dried in my gullet
Walk the old dog    give the budgies a warm bath
Cut a tender melon    let it bleed into memory


The robe you washed   hangs like a carcass flayed
The mug you loved    is stained with old coffee
Your toothbrush is silent    grease mums your comb
Something's lost    something's made strong


Around the corner       a new prince yearns to be loved
A fresh turn of phrase    a bad strophe erased
A random image    crafts itself into a poem
A sleepless Taipei night    a mosquito's symphony


Who will cry for you    me and your sister Laurette
Who will cry for you    me and your Algerian sister
You were a rich man    but you held on to your poverty
You were a poor man   who loved gold over dignity


I sit near your body bag    and sing you a last song
I sit near your body bag    and chant your final sutra
What's our place on earth    nada    nada    nada
What's our destiny?   War    grief    maggots    nada


Arms    cheeks   cock   femur   eyelids   nada
Cowl   ox    lamb    vellum    marrow   nada
Vulva    nada   semen   nada   ovum   nada
Eternity    nada    heaven   nada   void   nada

Birth and death in the same blackened womb
Birth and death in the same white body bag
Detach    detach     we enter the world alone
Detach    detach     we leave the world bone lonely


If we can't believe in god     we must believe in love
We must believe in love     we must believe in love
And they zip you up     in your white body bag
White body bag    white   white    body bag


## After Enlightenment, There Is Yam Gruel


When Buddha woke up hungry, the animals offered him their favorite food.

The baby sea lion offered him day old fish bits that her mother regurgitated.

The jackal offered a piece of smelly rotting meat infested with maggots.

The squirrel monkey offered a handful of bruised bananas, veiled with gnats.

The hare was the most selfless of all. She went into the forest and gathered

an armload of wood, lit it on fire and placed herself in the center as sacrifice.

Mrs. Wong, exhausted from long hours at the restaurant, was not impressed

with the feast. She handed Buddha a broom and said, "Old man, sweep the

back porch first, then the filthy hallway," and went to the kitchen and heated

up last night's yam gruel.

**Craig Cotter** (Pasadena, CA) supports himself as a working poet, publishing and giving private writing workshops. His first book of poetry, *The Aroma of Toast* (Black Tie Press, 1989), became an international best seller. His third book, *Chopstix Numbers* (Ahsahta Press, 2002), was written in an underground gay nightclub in West Hollywood and published by Boise State University's Ahsahta Press.

**5/23/96**

maybe i shouldn't bother you
                                        at work—
why.
              it's not a problem.
              good to hear from you.
can i take you out
                          to dinner?


when?
tonight.
what time?
how about 7.
730.
where can i pick you up?
corner of 2nd and vermont.
              there's a subway station there.


a straight mexican couple
in their early 20s
as they walk north
on vermont sidewalk
the male looks at me & smiles—
i think of the restaurant co-workers
of eduardo who
laughed at him
as he took my call.

714.

is this eduardo?
yes.
do you also work at chopstix?
yes.
man laughing
at him in the phone
background.
eduardo's voice
stays serious & focused.

2 latino boys
around his age,
one could be him—
i want him to come alone.
they pass
& are his age
with similar hair cuts
but they are not eduardo.

*

741.
walked to the intersection
& looked in the subway.

man after un-eduardo man
walks by.

now none of them
is his age.
he is apparently 19.
the sun is down
& now there is twilight.

i still glance at the walkers
like initially waiting
for his phone call.
every ring could be him.
now as it gets dark
more walkers could be him.

804.
another one
that could be him.

another one that isn't.

**Carol V. Davis** (Los Angeles, CA) was twice a Fulbright Scholar in Russia. Her work has been read on National Public Radio and Radio Russia. She won the 2007 T.S. Eliot Prize for *Into the Arms of Pushkin: Poems of St. Petersburg* (Truman State University Press, 2002). She teaches at Santa Monica College and was the 2008 Poet-in-Residence at Olivet College, Michigan.

### Entering the Forest

You enter the forest
and it seals itself behind you.
How you find the opening
or where doesn't matter.
Only that you have crossed
an invisible threshold
and your previous life
vanishes imperceptibly
as if it were a snake
shedding, and you had missed
the moment when the old skin
becomes devoid of body and
the new one rustles down a foxhole.
All previous pain you have carried
with you, sewn carefully into secret
chambers, left behind.
The sun filters through the lace
of leaves scattering into dust
a thousand years old.
The giant mushrooms embrace you
with such tenderness no lover
could ever match.
With each step memory fades.
There is no turning back.
The stench of decay is the only
smell you have ever loved,
the moss your only bed,
this life the only one imaginable.

## 710 Ashbury, 1967

*—For Gene Anthony*

The photographer hangs out on Haight Street,
entranced by youths in beads
and braless girls in lace and feathers
who weave flowers in their hair.
He smokes weed with his subjects
and taps his foot to the beat
of Jimi, Janis and the Jefferson Airplane.

He has told his agent not to call him:
"No more dogs, flags, wine labels,
politicians or corporate portraits."
In his office in New York
the agent paces. He's apoplectic,
so many clients waiting.
His guy in San Francisco is a flake—

lugging his camera bag up Ashbury,
where nothing is more important
than Jerry Garcia in his Uncle Sam hat
and Phil Lesh with a golf club.
The photographer rings the bell at 710,
tells the Dead where to stand,
and the world snaps into place.

**Lucille Lang Day** (Oakland, CA) is author of eight poetry collections and chapbooks. She also writes fiction and creative nonfiction, and her work has appeared widely in magazines and anthologies. She earned an MFA in creative writing from San Francisco State University and her Ph.D. in science and mathematics education at University of California Berkeley.

**James DenBoer** (Sacramento, CA) is author of five full-length poetry books, six chapbooks, a scholarly bibliography, and two books of translation. He is the recipient of grants, awards, and prizes from the International Poetry Forum, the National Endowment for the Arts, the National Council on the Arts, the Authors League of America, PEN Center—New York, the Carnegie Fund for Authors, the Katherine Tremaine/Sunshine Fund, and the Walter Pavlich Memorial Poetry Award. He makes a living as a lackadaisical book scout.

## Three Men on Isle Royale

Dying fire at the foot of lean-to.
Wolves are calling, beavers listen
through a chink in the wet logs of their dam.

Cow moose and calf haul themselves on shore,
dripping with black water. The night
is suddenly on us in our sleeping bags,

the stars writing a long scatter of light
over Chickenbone Lake. Last night we stayed up late
under Northern Lights, with coffee

and our one pint of brandy for the week:
Nick the philosopher, Stuart the epidemiologist,
me, whatever I was then.

## Red Wine

The smell of red wine
as lush as raspberries, almost
black in a white thick mug.
The earth gives us this gift;
is it a sin I don't drink anymore,
is it a slap at her grace?

## I Owe My Soul

Few secrets in a little town, kids
brooming sidewalks after school,
fat-tired *Schwinns* slung with bags

of county history we thought was news.
No one felt anonymous, not even
the lean Okie kids from Tuleville

who rode the bus with the rest of us
they hated. The older girls claimed
the long black seat and brayed

gospel songs as the bus filled-up—
but then someone behind me
would always start it to rocking:

erupting with Tennessee Ernie Ford's
"Sixteen Tons." Lyrics you could see
before they got off at the company store,

three dirt streets of clapboard shacks
with broke-down wrecks looking-out
so helplessly that we all sang along.

**John Dofflemyer** (Lemon Cove, CA) and his family represent the fifth generation to graze cows and calves in the Kaweah River watershed of the southern Sierra Nevada range in California. An invitee to the National Cowboy Poetry Gathering since 1989, his *Poems from Dry Creek* (Starhaven, 2008) was selected as the Outstanding Poetry Book for 2008 by the National Cowboy and Western Heritage Museum in Oklahoma City. He is editor of *Dry Crik Review*. He and his wife maintain *Dry Crik Journal*, a weblog of ranch poetry and photographs.

**Teresa Chuc Dowell** (Pasadena, CA) is a high school English teacher, writer, lifelong learner, and mother of three boys. Her poems appear in magazines such as *The National Poetry Review, Poetry Magazine.com, Jack Magazine, Babel Fruit, Miller's Pond, Verse Daily, California English,* and *English Journal*. Teresa has a bachelor's degree in philosophy and is working on an MFA in Creative Writing at Goddard College.

## Names

I am tired of having five different names;
Having to change them when I enter

A new country or take on a new life. My
First name is my truest, I suppose, but I

Never use it and nobody calls me by this Vietnamese
Name though it is on my birth certificate—

Tue My Chuc. It makes the sound of a twang of a
String pulled. My parents tell me my name in Cantonese

is Chuc Mei Wai. Three soft bird chirps and they call
me Ah Wai. Shortly after I moved to the U.S., I became

Teresa My Chuc, then Teresa Mei Chuc. "Teresa" is the sound
Water makes when one is washing one's hands. After my first

Marriage, my name was Teresa Chuc Prokopiev. After my second
Marriage, my name was Teresa Chuc Dowell. Now I am back

To Teresa Mei Chuc, but I want to go way back. Reclaim that name once
given and lost so quickly in its attempt to become someone that would

fit in. Who is Tue My Chuc? I don't really know. I was never really her
and her birthday on March 16, I never celebrate because it's not

my real birthday though it is on my birth certificate. My birthday is on
January 26, really, but I have to pretend that it's on March 16 because my

Mother was late registering me after the war. Or it's in December, the date
Changing every year according to the lunar calendar—this is the one my

Parents celebrate because it's my Chinese birthday.
All these names and birthdays make me dizzy. Sometimes I just don't feel like a

Teresa anymore; Tue (pronounced Twe) isn't so embarrassing. A fruit learns to
Love its juice. Anyways, I'd like to be string . . . resonating. Pulled back tensely
        like a bow

Then reverberate in the arrow's release straight for the heart.

## Aching Knees in Palm Springs

One gray Thursday during winter break,
Albert and I plucked patches of grass
From petunia beds wide as swimming pools
Within a condo complex; one-story stucco blocks
For old men who wipe sweat with dollar bills.
We spent our school vacations in shivers:
Raking, trimming, and mowing frosted yards with Dad.
At the eighth hour of kneeling,
The weight of my knees was too much for me.
For each fistful of grass, I stood up to stretch
And let the cold air sneak under my shirt.
When Dad noticed the weeds slowly filling the can,
He turned to me red-faced, and said,
*You're packing down the dirt, kneel on the lawn*
*And weed the beds from there.* I said,
*I am at least entitled to some circulation . . .*
I kept the truth from slipping past my chapped lips,
How I didn't care about dirt and weeds
From a bourgeois' garden—these few men
I learned about in sociology class—
Who raked in more hundred-dollar bills
Than I did citrus leaves in a day.
I wanted to tell Dad that these men didn't care
If Mexicans spent ten hours—or even a lifetime
Weeding out the same bed the following week.
To only tell him about the hours I felt wasted,
When we could've rested our sore backs on a bed
And drowned in the lake of a much-deserved sleep,
Or sailed through Tierra del Fuego, us standing
On the deck and never bowing, not even to the sun.
Or how he could have learned to read,
And I would finally show him a poem I wrote.
But I didn't. Because I knew what he would say—
*It's the only way to put you through school—this oily sweat.*
I kept my tongue hidden behind my teeth
And watched my brother hunched over, tossing weeds
And years inside a green plastic can without a word.

**John Olivares Espinoza** (San Jose, CA) is a native of Southern California. He studied creative writing at the University of California Riverside and Arizona State University. His first book, *The Date Fruit Elegies* (Bilingual Press, 2008), was a finalist for the 2009 Northern California Book Award in Poetry. He writes and lives in San Jose, California.

**CB Follett** (Sausalito, CA) was awarded the 2001 National Poetry Book Award from Salmon Run Press for her book *At the Turning of the Light* (Salmon Run Press, 2001). She has been nominated for numerous Pushcart Prizes and is the recipient of a grant for poetry from the Marin Arts Council. She was publisher and co-editor of *RUNES: A Review of Poetry*. CB Follett lives in Sausalito, California, perched on a hill between the coastal range and San Francisco Bay, where she serves as the current Poet Laureate of Marin County.

### Early Morning, Yosemite

Like an old matron on her way to market,
the bear came lumbering around the corner
of the cabin, placing her plantigrade paws
*clomp clomp,* first the right legs, then the left,
rumbling as if with lumbago, as if with old stiff knees,

not sniffing the air, not hungry it seemed,
only about her business, and the sun
glistened through her fur as it prickled her back
and all of us stopped dead in our tracks as if
Simon Says said *STOP* and we did.

And across the meadow I saw my small daughter—
her red sweater like a toreador's cape—
sitting on a log with her friend, Julie,
their blond heads close together,
gossiping their four-year-old gossip—
like neighbors over a cup of coffee at the back fence—
and neither noticing the bear approaching,
and me watching uncertain how to handle this
and Julie's mother gripping my arm with her long nails
and the bear walking her slow market lurch
and the girls talking
and the sun blasting the trees
throwing shadows like tall men across the grass
and the bear
only the bear
moving.

## Mystery Rider

*—Limestone Canyon Corrals,*
*Old Irvine Ranch*
*Spring 2005*

The door was busted off the shed.
It looked like everything was gone
that wasn't nailed down, except
way up on a loose board, one
twisted piece of metal hung—

a make-shift bridle, bitless,
with a smooth fence-wire nosepiece
all neatly wrapped with cotton strips.
Someone's bandana? Someone's blouse?
Someone in love with falling off a horse.

The rest of it was a simple thing:
a loop of  plastic baling twine
to quickly shove behind the ears
of a startled horse, grab some mane
and you were up and on the run

yanking on twine reins, I bet.
Was it a dare? Or were you alone
with the last bunch of horses here,
your heart dropping like a stone
at the stock truck's low approaching drone?

**Thea Gavin** (Orange, CA) writes, teaches, and hikes. In the local wildlands of coastal sage scrub and chaparral, Thea leads creative writing rambles as a volunteer naturalist for the Irvine Ranch Conservancy and the Laguna Canyon Foundation. Her MFA in poetry is from Spalding University.

**Dana Gioia** (Los Angeles, CA) is a poet and critic. For six years he served as Chairman of the National Endowment for the Arts. He has published three full-length collections of poetry, including *Interrogations at Noon* (Graywolf Press, 2001), which won the 2002 American Book Award, and three collections of criticism, most notably *Can Poetry Matter?* (Graywolf Press, 1992). He divides his time between Washington, DC, and northern California.

## The Apple Orchard

You won't remember it—the apple orchard
We wandered through one April afternoon,
Climbing the hill behind the empty farm.

A city boy, I'd never seen a grove
Burst in full flower or breathed the bittersweet
Perfume of blossoms mingled with the dust.

A quarter mile of trees in fragrant rows
Arching above us. We walked the aisle,
Alone in spring's ephemeral cathedral.

We had the luck, if you can call it that,
Of having been in love but never lovers—
The bright flame burning, fed by pure desire.

Nothing consumed, such secrets brought to light!
There was a moment when I stood behind you,
Reached out to spin you toward me . . . but I stopped.

What more could I have wanted from that day?
Everything, of course. Perhaps that was the point—
To learn that what we will not grasp is lost.

## To an Old Woman

Come, mother—
      your rebozo trails a black web
      and your hem catches on your heels,
you lean the burden of your years
on shaky cane, and palsied hand pushes
      sweat-grimed pennies on the counter.
Can you still see, old woman,
the darting color-trailed needle of your trade?
      The flowers you embroider
      with three-for-a-dime threads
cannot fade as quickly as the leaves of time.
      What things do you remember?
Your mouth seems to be forever tasting
the residue of nectar-hearted years.
Where are the sons you bore?
      Do they speak only English now
      and say they're Spanish?
One day I know you will not come
and ask for me to pick
the colors you can no longer see.
      I know I'll wait in vain
for your toothless benediction.
      I'll look into the dusty street
      made cool by pigeons' wings
until a dirty child will nudge me and say:
         "Señor, how mach ees thees?"

**Rafael Jesús González** (Berkeley, CA) was born and raised in El Paso/Juárez and writes in Spanish and English. Professor Emeritus of Creative Writing and Literature, his work is published in the United States, Mexico, and abroad. He lives in Berkeley, California, and has received honors from the city for his writing, art, and activism for justice and peace.

## A una anciana

Venga, madre—
        su rebozo arrastra telaraña negra
        y sus enaguas le enredan los tobillos;
apoya el peso de sus años
en trémulo bastón y sus manos temblorosas
        empujan sobre el mostrador centavos sudados.
¿Aún todavía ve, viejecita,
la jara de su aguja arrastrando colores?
        Las flores que borda
        con hilazas de a tres-por-diez
no se marchitan tan pronto como las hojas del tiempo.
        ¿Qué cosas recuerda?
Su boca parece constantemente saborear
los restos de años rellenos de miel.
        ¿Dónde están los hijos que parió?
¿Hablan ahora solamente inglés
y dicen que son hispanos?
        Sé que un día no vendrá
        a pedirme que le escoja
        los matices que ya no puede ver.
Sé que esperaré en vano
        su bendición desdentada.
Miraré hacia la calle polvorienta
refrescada por alas de paloma
hasta que un chiquillo mugroso me jale de la manga
y me pregunte:
                — Señor, how much is this?—

## Out of This Place

They offer me five extra dollars to get a new face
For the benefit of Miss Julie's advanced modeling class.
Weekends I clean offices in Salt Lake City
With Angie and her sister, and now
Miss Julie's second floor modeling school
Is bringing in an expert who can make a girl

Into anyone she wants to be. I sweep up
Wads of wet tissue and cotton, scrub powder
And smears of oily color from white counter tops
And stools, pour drain cleaner down clogged sinks,
And sometimes I have to wrench open
A grease trap, tearing apart slimy gobs of tangled hair

To let clean water run through. I've learned all this
From Angie Romero's sister—how to shine
Mirrors and windows with lemon ammonia
And crumpled newspaper, to lift the darkest
Heel marks from linoleum with a pink
Pearl eraser, and how to cover up

The deepest wood scratches with the perfect shade
Of Shinola. Saturday mornings we move
Through this empty uptown building
Like three spirits, cleaning real estate office, travel agency,
Weight loss clinic, but we all hate the upstairs
Modeling school, its glossy front wall photos, pastel

Dressing rooms lined with neat rows
Of mirrored tables, each with its own glass top,
Ruffled stool and bright white light bulbs marching
Around every mirror. The modeling girls all look alike.
We despise their thin blond bodies and their prom queen
Confidence and the way they leave all their sticky messes

For us to wipe up. After work, when Angie and I
Begin to wonder why Miss Julie has chosen me,
Angie's sister stares at us as if we are idiots,
Pinches my cheeks hard between her dark fingers
And pulls me by my face to the bathroom mirror.
She says: why don't you take a look

At your big blue eyes? On Monday I take the city bus
Uptown. The modeling girls are already sitting
In a tight circle, and someone quietly covers my clothes
With a slick plastic robe, sitting me down in a rolling chair
Directly under the skylight at the center of the room.
The make-over man speaks quickly, and starts

**Corrinne Clegg Hales** (Fresno, CA) is author of four poetry collections, including *Separate Escapes* (Ashland Poetry Press, 2002), winner of the Richard Snyder Poetry Prize. She has received two fellowships from the National Endowment for the Arts and won first place in the *River Styx Poetry Prize* in 2000. She lives in Fresno, California, where she coordinates the MFA Program at California State University, Fresno.

With my hair. First, we've got to cut some shape into it—
He begins lopping off blond handfuls, talking as he cuts.
And she's got to stop teasing it up like those Mexican girls—
We're after an innocent, just-washed look here.
No more hoop earrings or ankle bracelets
Or dangling crosses around your neck, sweetie. Nice girls

Wear a simple pearl, OK?  And I laugh along with the other girls
As he lifts my silver hoops high over his head and drops them
One at a time onto the floor. Winding my hair up in rollers,
He goes to work on my eyebrows, plucking them almost
To nothing, humming and talking about shape
And definition, then smoothing cream after cream

Over my face and throat, saying I should be thankful
For my clear, fair skin. His hands are warm and soft, stroking
The ivory and pink tints onto my face—to build
Cheekbones out of nothing, he tells the class, and I remember
The minister my mother once called to heal me
When I was small and sick, laying his fat hands

On my head and commanding the powers of darkness
To leave my body—commanding my body to make itself
Whole. My features are just too rounded,
The make-over man is saying, kind of Irish looking—
And he isn't sure what to do about the nose. You really want
Either a classic straight line or something cute, pert, slightly turned up

At the end. What we need here, frankly, is a vision
With sharper, more definite lines. He draws precise
And delicate eyebrows, brushes on blue lids and liner,
Lashes, mascara, and lips. Then, pulling the rollers
From my hair, he works fast and close for several minutes,
Causing a hush to fall over the room. Spinning my face

Away from the crowd, he huddles over me, fussing,
Spraying, murmuring as if in prayer, until I am transformed
And he whirls me around to face his class—and the girls all gasp.
This is true. They actually gasp. At that moment I believe
I am beautiful. That roomful of rich girls is applauding
The new me. You see? The man is asking—with a little faith

And work, and a lot of imagination? He turns me around again
To face the mirror. Afterward, I walk around the city
For hours, staring at my bright reflection
In department store windows, smiling at sales girls
And trying on clothes and expensive shoes as if
I might buy them. I've started to imagine the possibility

Of another life. But when I get home,
My mother is still sick, my little brothers spooning
Pork and beans cold from a can, the baby lying wet
On the floor, sucking his sugar water
From a glass bottle without a sound. Over at Angie's house
Everyone is impressed. Her mother smiles, walks all the way

Around me and says I look just like one of those
Regular white girls. Angie whistles and her sister begins to call me
Sandra Dee. You're so cute, Sandra Dee—where's Troy Donahue,
Sandra Dee?  I say it was no big deal—I made
Five easy bucks and got a free haircut. That's all.
But the ground has already shifted

Between us—and all of us know by now
Exactly how this story goes—who'll get a ticket
Out of this place—who'll be left behind.


## Covenant: Atomic Energy Commission, 1950s


While we wait, crouched under our desks
Or in well-stocked basement shelters
For it to fall screaming out of the sky, the atom bomb

Is already sneaking in through the side door, blowing
Like a tumbleweed across the desert, rippling through shirts
And diapers hanging on the line, dusting pickup trucks,

Bicycles, porch swings. We've been expecting
Such unambiguous Russian-made tragedy
That we're not even watching the signs:

The birth of a malformed baby, missing
Arms or eyes or born with its vital organs outside
Of its body; persistent rashes that swell and crack

A roadworker's skin; serial miscarriages; sterility; the endless
Procession of cancers igniting imperceptibly while we sleep
Or eat or put the kids to bed. A woman peels potatoes

And slices them into a casserole with butter and milk;
Her husband wipes grayish-white residue off his car
With a towel, sits on the porch smoking,

Reading the paper, watching the children wrestle
With the dog in the yard, all of them completely unaware
Of the subtle internal explosions taking place. We see

Those slow pink clouds pass over our heads, and we see
The man from AEC chase after them
In his Plymouth Fury, monitoring area and extent

Of exposure. But we feel ground tremors
As reassurance that someone is working hard
To protect us from the climactic nuclear moment

We rehearse for. Nearly a third of a neighbor's
Spring lambs are piled in a heap to be burned—born dead
Or two-headed or missing legs, their wool falling off

In clumps. Children play in fields and trees,
Eating apples, riding horses, scratching their names
In the fine dust coating every flat surface. Nevada

School teachers follow every advised precaution and march
Science classes to a hilltop to watch significant blasts.
Farmers' wives shake white dust from their husbands'

Work clothes and throw them into the washer
With loads of sheets and towels. Fathers come home
From the fields or their jobs at the test site

With unbearable nausea, itching, peculiar blistering
Sunburns; one child has a chronic bloody nose, a mother's teeth
Loosen and fall out. Self-sufficient Utah families grow

Vegetables in the dirt, raise pigs, chickens,
And goats for milk. Their children shake white ashes
Out of oleanders into their hair, calling it desert snow

And wiping it off ripe strawberries before popping them
Into their mouths. Tumors sprout cunningly, and take root
Unnoticed in developing organs, hideous fruit

Demanding a grim and perpetual harvest.
A dairy farmer notices his Geiger counter goes crazy
Not only near rocks and dirt, but near the pile of cow carcasses

He's had to destroy, and it goes strangely silent
When he digs beneath the soil's surface. He tests feed bins,
Water troughs, the milk his children drink.

Five years ago he believed the bomb was God's chosen
Instrument for the salvation of the free world,
And he understands now that he's accepted it

Into his life as absolutely as Jesus.
Death is just part of the deal
We make to be saved.

A thin, religious woman, wearing a bright scarf
To cover her bald head, tells her neighbors
It's the inevitable end to protecting ourselves

By keeping a loaded gun at hand. She's lost her father,
Two stillborn babies, and her own blossoming
Body to the bomb that would deliver us all

From evil. As we obediently duck and cover,
Duck and cover, constantly keeping an eye out for Khruschev
On the six o'clock news, the bomb seeps in

Silently through the bedroom window, settling
On tables and chairs and into our bones; it travels east
With the weather, hovering quietly over neat clusters

Of suburban tract houses and breathing
Its isotope-ridden breath into air ducts of hospitals,
Schools, high-rises. It is delivered

In refrigerated meat trucks and milk tanks fresh
From southwestern farms into markets where we buy it,
Pray over it and take it, as if it were holy, into our flesh.

**Allison Adelle Hedge Coke** (Santa Paula, CA) is the Paul W. Reynolds and Clarice Kingston Reynolds Endowed Chair at the University of Nebraska Kearney, an American Book Award poet, memoirist, fiction writer, scriptwriter, anthologist, and performer in major poetry festivals in Colombia, Venezuela, Argentina, Canada, and Jordan. She was visiting poet at Shandong University in China and Hawthornden Castle Artist-In-Residence. She came of age working in fields and factories.

### Street Confetti

*—for Stephanie*

Right across Turk Street, south side intersection Hyde,
in the tenement where 911 won't summon up a blue,
a man beats his woman,
the twentieth time or more, their kids bawling.
Over here, in this flat up on the third,
above blazing red neon signs highlighting
the *Triple Deuce Club* low below, I listen while
wired white hippies move furniture across checkered tiles
other side my sister's arched plaster ceiling till way past 3 a.m.
Shuffling with a sofa as if rearranging the heavens in my mind.

Me, I sleep. Or try to. Nothing else I can do.
Each day I slip off and out looking for work, gliding into the
streets of San Francisco
winding, curving, like turbulence.
Daybreak brings sweet Cambodian street children out
into a Feinstein-era playground,
still filled with hypes, winos, yellow-green from the night before,
still smelling like piss and lizard.

These kids though, they climb atop steel swing-set bars,
fifteen, twenty feet high,
as if they're walking joint lines in concrete.
Easy balance, Mohawk grace.
Their sisters provoke a paper war in the street,
      closed-off      block party.
  Paper flying by, I
catch a piece, fold it origamically, create
a mock financial pyramid, toss it back,
watch little girls with black shiny ponytails make confetti
for this ongoing ticker-tape parade,
right across Turk Street, intersection Hyde.

## First Light Edging Cirrus

$10^{25}$ molecules
are enough
to call woodthrush or apple.

A hummingbird, fewer.
A wristwatch: $10^{24}$.

An alphabet's molecules,
tasting of honey, iron, and salt,
cannot be counted or weighed—

as some strings, untouched,
sound when a near one is speaking.

So it was when love slipped inside us.
It looked out face to face in every direction.

Then it was inside the tree, the rock, the cloud.


## French Horn

For a few days only,
the plum tree outside the window
shoulders perfection.
No matter the plums will be small,
eaten only by squirrels and jays.
I feast on the one thing, they on another,
the shoaling bees on a third.
What in this unpleated world isn't someone's seduction?
The boy playing his intricate horn in Mahler's Fifth,
in the gaps between playing,
turns it and turns it, dismantles a section,
shakes from it the condensation
of human passage. He is perhaps twenty.
Later he takes his four bows, his face deepening red,
while a girl holds a viola's spruce wood and maple
in one half-opened hand and looks at him hard.
Let others clap.
These two, their ears still ringing, hear nothing.
Not the shouts of *bravo, bravo,*
not the timpanic clamor inside their bodies.
As the plum's blossoms do not hear the bee
nor taste themselves turned into storable honey
by that sumptuous disturbance.

**Jane Hirshfield** (Mill Valley, CA) is author of six books of poetry, including *After* (HarperCollins, 2006), named a best book of 2006 by *The Washington Post, The San Francisco Chronicle,* and England's *Financial Times.* She has also written a book of essays, *Nine Gates: Entering the Mind of Poetry* (Harper Perennial, 1998). Hirshfield's honors include fellowships from the Guggenheim and Rockefeller foundations, the National Endowment for the Arts, and The Academy of American Poets, as well as the California Book Award, the Northern California Book Award, and the Poetry Center Book Award. She reads frequently at universities and literary festivals in the United States and abroad.

## The Dark Hour

The dark hour came
in the night and purred by my ear.
Outside, in rain,
the plush of the mosses stood higher.
Hour without end, without measure.
It opens the window and calls its own name in.

## Sonoma Fire

Large moon the deep orange of embers.
Also the scent.
The griefs of others—beautiful, at a distance.

## Green-Striped Melons

They lie
under stars in a field.
They lie under rain in a field.
Under sun.

Some people
are like this as well—
like a painting
hidden beneath another painting.

An unexpected weight
the sign of their ripeness.

## Sign of the Times

Very few people have heard of Peg Entwistle. There's no entry for her in Ephraim Katz's *Film Encyclopedia,* yet she left her mark on Hollywood the hard way. Born in Wales in 1908. When her mother dies, she moves to New York with her father who's run over by a truck, leaving young Entwistle penniless. Marries Robert Keith but divorces him when she learns that he has another wife & child. All the same, Peg pays his alimony to keep him out of jail. Tries her luck in L.A. where she rooms with Uncle Harold, who is "good to her." Stars in *Thirteen Women* with Irene Dunne and Jill Esmond, Lawrence Olivier's wife. But the mystery thriller is so depressing for 1932, RKO cans the film and fires Entwistle. *No money, no man, no nothing.* Despondent, she puts on her favorite fragrance, Gardenia, the "happiness" flower, climbs the fifty-foot sign behind Uncle Harold's bungalow and jumps from the 13th letter in HOLLYWOODLAND. Years later, LAND rots away and is never restored. Soon after her death, she receives a generous offer from the Beverly Hills Playhouse to star as a destitute young woman who is driven to suicide. According to Griffith Park Ranger John Arbogast, Peg still haunts the scene of her demise, the 13th letter, the sign, especially on foggy nights when there's a strong scent of gardenia in the air.

**Maggie Jaffe** (San Diego, CA) is author of six books of poetry, including *7th Circle* (Cedar Hill Books, 1998) and *The Prisons* (Cedar Hill Books, 2001), which won the San Diego Book Award for Poetry. She is also the recipient of fellowships from the National Endowment for the Arts and the California Arts Council. *Flic(k)s: Poetic Interrogations of American Cinema* was published in 2009 by Red Dragonfly Press. She teaches at San Diego State University in the English and Comparative Literature Department.

**Ilya Kaminsky** (San Diego, CA) was born in Odessa, Ukraine, former USSR. He is author of *Dancing In Odessa* (Tupelo Press, 2004), which won a Lannan Fellowship, Whiting Writers Award, and American Academy of Arts and Letters' Metcalf Award. He teaches in the Department of English and Comparative Literature at San Diego State University.

## We Lived Happily During the War

And when they bombed other people's houses, we

protested
but not enough, we opposed them but not

enough. I was
in my bed, around my bed America

was falling: invisible house by invisible house by invisible house.

I took a chair outside and watched the sun.

            In the sixth month
of a disastrous reign in the house of money

in the street of  money in the city of money in the country of money
our great country of money, we (forgive us)

lived happily during the war.


## To Live

To live, as the great book commands,
is to love. Such love is not enough!—

the heart needs a little foolishness!
So I fold the newspaper, make a hat.

I pretend to Sonya that I am the greatest poet
and she pretends to believe it—

my Sonya, her stories and her beautiful legs
her stories and legs that open other stories!

And I say: a human being
understands the universe: its music

makes us foolish. I see myself: a yellow raincoat,
a sandwich, a piece of tomato between my teeth.

I raise my infant daughter to the sky—
I am singing as she pisses

(Old fool, my wife laughs)
on my forehead and my shoulders!

**George Keithley** (Chico, CA) was educated at Duke, Stanford, and the University of Iowa. He has been a visiting writer in Russia, traced the Emigrant Trail from Illinois to California, and with marine biologists followed the migration of the Pacific grey whale along the coast of the Baja Peninsula. His award-winning epic, *The Donner Party* (Braziller, 1972), a Book-of-the-Month Club selection, has been adapted as a stage play and an opera. *Song in a Strange Land* (Braziller, 1974) earned the Di Castagnola Award from the Poetry Society of America.

## The Red Bluff Rodeo

1
They travel the ranch roads that connect
with paved roads feeding into the freeway
to enter town by car or truck
or on horseback,
the main street blocked by traffic—
Not one empty seat in a bar and grill
for a mile around the fairgrounds.

"Let me have coffee and three eggs."
"How do you *like* your eggs?"
"I like 'em fine!"

2
Clowns in costume (cow-
boys, ranch hands)
fall off
a plow horse
too old to mind the jeers
of spectators. One clown
climbs a cow, flings
his feet in the air,
slaps her rear and lifts
his eyes to the sky,
asking why she won't buck—
Little laughter now
people slide close,
settling onto the wooden slats.

3
They roar for the first rider—
What's caught the eye of the crowd
is the swift stride of his horse
and the queer stiff legs of the calf.
His lasso loops her neck
to stop her short.
He drops beside her in the dust,
ties her legs tight with one length
of rope, and one twisted sweep of his arm.
Throws his hands in the air to show he's done,
like a man surrounded, forced to surrender.

Applause rattles the grandstand from its full height;
man and horse trot toward the gate.

The clowns come for the calf; hurry off.

The p.a. announces another number. The chute opens.
Out flies a fresh horse, a hat, hands
too quick for the calf
rolling helpless
in the grip of the rope.

4

Girls squirm in the sun.
Small boys turn their eyes
to women unwrapping
sandwiches. Wives
worried if a man might earn his entry fee
lean heads together
ignoring the noise, the nervous heat.

>       "Did he come home sober last night?"
>       "In the dark he tripped over a chair."
>       "What did you do?"
>       "I laughed so hard I fell out of bed."

5

The last man on a saddle bronc
provokes a rough ride
to impress the judges.
Jabbing flesh,
his spurs urge
the bronc to kick
three ways at once—

He flies from his mount
in mid-air, tossed
free. Falls
like a sack of meal in the dust.
The throng disapproves and boos.
On hands and knees he crawls away from the hooves.

>       "Some sort of fun."
>       "I'm glad it's done. All day
>       I been dizzy as a squirrel."

The crowd staggers out of the stands,
pressing into the parking lot.

Evening dresses the country in cool stars.

Far in the night a fitful line of light
searches the length of the valley
where families follow one another home
beyond the lost barns and deserted fields.

**Steve Kowit** (Potrero, CA) lives quietly with his wife, six cats, and two dogs in a tiny house in the hills in the back country of San Diego County, a few miles from the Mexican border. He is a war resister and political activist. He teaches at Southwestern College.

## Kiss

> "I could never take lightly that people were
> making love without me."
> — Jean Genet, *The Thief's Journal*

On the patio of that little cafe in the Del Mar Plaza,
across from the Esmeralda Bookstore, where you can
sit sipping latté & look out past the Pacific
Coast Highway onto the ocean, a couple is tangled
in one of those steamy, smoldering kisses.
His right arm coils her waist, arching her back
& drawing her toward him. He could be Sicilian,
or Lebanese, with that gorgeous complexion,
those chiseled forearms, that clutch of dark curls.
The young woman's skirt, lilac & sheer, lifts
as she stretches, levitated out of her sandals, out
of her body, her head flung back, fingers
wrapped in his curls. Her long chestnut hair
spills toward her thighs as she clings to his mouth,
to his loins, to his chest. How wickedly
beautiful both of them are! To their left,
off the North County coast, on an infinite sea,
two sailboats triangulate heaven. In the sheen
of the morning you munch an apricot scone
& sip your caffe latte, that blue cup of light at your lips,
with its genie of steam. In its vase, on your table,
a white tea rose shimmers. Your fork
shines on its plate. Everything trembles & glows.

**Karen An-hwei Lee** (Santa Ana, CA) is author of *Ardor* (Tupelo Press, 2008) and *In Medias Res* (Sarabande Books, 2004). She is the recipient of the Kathryn A. Morton Prize and the Norma Farber First Book Award. Her chapbook, *God's One Hundred Promises*, received the Swan Scythe Press Prize. Recipient of a National Endowment for the Arts Fellowship, she chairs the English department at a faith-based college in southern California, where she is a novice harpist.

## White Gardenias and a Letter

Noon columns of sheer eucalyptus light,
all the windows in the day room flung open;
on my shoulder, a corsage of white gardenias . . .
large white camellia or peony to the left.

Our women press blouses and sheets with irons:
Skirts, sleeves, and napkins are clipped to the line.
Silk routes open today? I ask ourselves, singing
*Sunday is missing a fish bone, a lavender moon,*

*bold-leafed kale, beautiful and ragged.*
I broke my arm falling out of the fig tree:
Shin of light, the thinnest bone in a girl
imagines a red scarf as I move my wrist.

*Am I bleeding? What do you see in the glass?*
Night, the blind woman, and I write a letter.
More contrast, less contrast, brightness or less.
Crop the image, rotate it, grayscale or white.

World inverted by a retina . . .
Won't be long, she says, sealing the fold.
I sit down to a broiled trout supper.
Fish are slain by prayers at four o'clock.

Our letter is mute as a fish sings:
*May our women's souls float*
*May our women's bodies be whole*
*May our songs be warrior-swords*

Our bodies are silver lines
ghost words
phantom gardens

alive . . .

We are writing
white gardenias;
we are writing
this letter

starting
with sheer
eucalyptus
light.

## In the White City

After the earthquake the seven hills
remained as before, staring
heavenward without the least
comment. Centuries passed.
My father arrived on the *Tasman,*
out of Alexandria with a load
of fine cotton and one deserter.
February, 1919. He took a room
above a cafe in the Alfama
where he could unload. Sleep
was impossible, so after dark
he descended on foot to where
the ships groaned and sighed
patiently and he could think
at his ease. The seventh night
low rain clouds blew in from
the sea and broke across the hills
so that when he climbed back
it was against a black river
rushing toward the Tagus. Later,
forty-seven years later, when
I arrived alone at the airport
at dawn, fevered and searching,
I hired a driver, Manuel de Alvaros,
a thief and a smuggler, who drove
only Buicks stolen before the war.
Together we found the room
just as it was, my father's suitcase
under the bed, his journal left open
to a blank page on which I wrote
his three names in the one language
we shared. Suddenly I could feel
the land slowly sliding from under me
as though released from Europe
and the past. My father and I,
together once again, heading
somewhere, across the seas or back
to childhood. It was our summer
for one last time, the window
opening on bright flags
of laundry, the cries of vendors,
of kids at play, a trolley gasping
up the staggered hills, all
of Lisbon spread out below
and clarified in exact detail
for those no longer here to see.

**Philip Levine** (Fresno, CA) is author of sixteen books of poetry, including *Breath* (Knopf, 2004); *The Simple Truth* (Knopf, 1994), which won the Pulitzer Prize; *What Work Is* (Knopf, 1991), which won the National Book Award; *Ashes: Poems New and Old* (Atheneum, 1979), which received the National Book Critics Circle Award and the first American Book Award for Poetry; *7 Years From Somewhere* (Atheneum, 1979), which won the National Book Critics Circle Award; and *The Names of the Lost* (Atheneum, 1976), which won the Lenore Marshall Poetry Prize. He taught creative writing for many years at California State University, Fresno.

### 1934

You might hear that after dark in towns
like Detroit packs of wild dogs took over
the streets. I was there. It never happened.
In the old country before the Great War,
my people were merchants and butchers,
and then the killings drove the family
first to England, then Canada, then here.
My father's brother had a shoe repair shop
for a time on Brush Street; he'd learned
the trade from his father back in Kiev.
My mother's family was in junk. The men
were huge, thick chested, with long arms
and great scarred hands. My uncle Leo
could embrace a barrel of scrap metal,
laugh out his huge laugh, and lift it up
just for the joy. His wife, Rebecca,
let her hair grow out in great wiry tangles
and carried her little fists like hammers.
Late summer Sundays we'd drive out
to the country and pick armloads
of sweet corn, boil them in sugar,
and eat and eat until we couldn't.
Can you believe those people would let
dogs take what was theirs, would cross
an ocean and a continent to let
anyone or anything dictate?
After dark these same men would drink
out on the front steps. The neighbors claimed
they howled at the moon.  Another lie.
Sometimes they told stories of life
back in Russia, stories I half-believed
of magic escapes and revenge killings,
of the gorgeous Ukrainian girls they had.
One night they tore up the lawn wrestling until
Leo triumphed, Leo in his vested suit,
gray and sweat stained. My uncle Josef
was different; tall and slender, he'd
come into the family through marriage
here in Michigan. A pensive, gentle man,
when stray dogs came to the back door
of the shoe shop he'd let them in, even

feed them. Their owners, he told me,
barely had enough to feed themselves.
Uncle Josef would take a battered pair
of work shoes and cut the soles off
with a hooked cobbler's knife and then
drawing one nail at a time from his mouth,
pound on a new sole. He'd pry off
the heel and do the same. I was just a kid,
seven at most, and never tired of watching
how at the polishing wheel the leather
took on its color and began to glow.
Once he made a knife for me, complete
with a little scabbard that looped
around my belt. The black handle too
was leather, taken from a boot no one
reclaimed. He pounded and shaped it
until it felt like stone. Whenever you're
scared, he told me, just rub the handle
three times and nothing bad can happen.

**Samuel Maio** (San José, CA) is the author of *The Burning of Los Angeles* (Thomas Jefferson University Press, 1997), *Creating Another Self: Voice in Modern American Personal Poetry* (Truman State University Press, 2005), and *Dramatic Monologues: A Contemporary Anthology* (University of Evansville Press, 2009). His poems have been featured in the *Los Angeles Times Book Review* and appear in several anthologies, including *California Poetry: From the Gold Rush to the Present* (Heyday Books, 2004). He is Professor of English and Comparative Literature at the California State University, San José.

## South Central L. A.

Leaving the University Park,
The daughters of movie stars,
Heirs of Disney, Goldwyn, and Getty,
The assured sons of money titans—
Each a loyal fraternity brother
And future privileged "alum"—
The insular boundaries of European
Brick columns and wrought iron,
The quiet Romanesque courtyard
Of the old philosophy library—
Its clock tower and gargoyles
Used in the original "Hunchback,"
Now hoarding in basement storage
A rare 16th Century collection—
Where today I nibbled cashews
And mingled at a special reception
Welcoming the selected summer
Honor students, gifted and aloof,
We're hoping to enroll next year
To gain on the private northeast.
Our lures are stately architecture,
The rose gardens and fountains,
Grand museums of natural history
And *beaux arts*, presently displaying
"Star Wars" tech-creatures aside
The Folger Shakespeare exhibit.
And frequent gatherings like these:
Good wines and dilettantes' talk,
A Dean's address, a pretty blonde
In a loose, off-white, silken gown
Delicately pulsing a golden harp. . . .

Returning to the excluded nearby,
To the only duplex I can afford
In what we call "The Neighborhood,"
The Rolling 40s' owned territory,
I assume aristocratic detachment
And lower my gaze to their patrol
Of the long avenues lined by palm.
Poor men gather in the parking lot
Of the liquor store on the corner.
Its mad security cop once smashed
A drunk's crotch with a sawed bat,
Breaking the bottle of Colt Malt
Tucked inside his reeking pants

While I watched from the counter.
And when caught staring was asked,
In a speech that might have been
The Bard's accentuated another way,
"What mixture *you* be, dear cuz?"
Alone in my Mediterranean color,
I am home, back to the mailman's
Delivering goods, Mr. Owl's Pharmacy
Dispensing crack, bennies, and ludes,
To the ice cream truck handling fix—
My neighbors get richer by the day.
And during the vast, sordid night
The circling police helicopters
Obscure the gunshots and screams.
The gang rapists and car thieves
Outrun them and sleep disquietly
As any of us behind barred windows
And steel doors hoping we're safe.


## Pleasanton Villanelle


The long-awaited raise has come and gone.
My vow of poverty is poetry.
The need to make ends meet goes on and on.
My neighbors' stocks (bought low, of course) hold strong—
I'm the lone pauper in Silicon Valley.
The long-awaited raise has come and gone.

The only home without designer lawn,
My peeling two bedroom's the scourge of the city.
The need to make ends meet goes on and on.
The house to my right is worth two million,
The house to my left worth two million three.
The long-awaited raise has come and gone.

How can I live poetry in Pleasanton,
Where money rules the emperor of ice cream?
The need to make ends meet goes on and on.
The teachers' strike settled, all placards gone,
Town leaders returned to the market's rally.
The long-awaited raise has come and gone,
Yet the need to make ends meet goes on and on . . .

**Clarence Major** (Davis, CA) is a painter as well as a poet. His first book of poetry, *Swallow the Lake* (Wesleyan University Press, 1970), won a National Council on the Arts Award. His book of poetry *Myself Painting* (Louisiana State University Press, 2008) was a finalist for the Paterson Poetry Prize. He is Professor of Twentieth Century American Literature at the University of California, Davis.

# Photograph of a Gathering of People Waving

*—based on an old photograph bought in a shop at Half Moon Bay, summer, 1999*

No sound, the whole thing.
Unknown folk. People waving from a hillside of ripple grass
to people below in an ongoing meadow.

Side rows of trees waving in a tide of wind,
and because what is moving is not moving,
you catch a state of stasis.

Opposite of this inactivity
you imagine distant music and buzzing and crickets
and that special hot smell of summer.

To the garden past the Bay to the meadow,
cliff sheltered with low clouds, offset by nodding thistle.
Tatter-wort and Stinking Tommy along footpath
worn down by locals. But who and why?

In the photograph itself you're now looking the other way
to unknown clusters of houses.
Where forces are balanced to near perfection.

Who could live
in such a great swollen silence and solitude?
You hear church bells
from Our Lady's Tears breaking that silence nicely
but just in the right way so silence continues
as though nothing else matters day after day.

And anyway, each face seems so familiar.

What do you do when you wave back?
You wave vigorously.
You remember your own meadow,
your cliffside and town,
photographs forgotten,
the halfhearted motion of your hand,
your grandmother's church-folk
gathering on a Sunday afternoon in saintly quietness.

You name the people
whose names are not written on the back.
You forgive them for wrapping themselves in silence.

You enter house after house and open top-floor windows
and you wave down to future generations like this.

## The Doll Believers

This lifeless construction,
Yellow hair curled and twisted,
The forever motionless face of rubber,
The dark marked eyebrows,
The flexible pug nose,
Spongy red cheeks,
Camel's-hair eyebrows
Moving up and down.
Lifting her up, her eyes fly open,
They stare into space—
An unmoving blueness.
Those never winking, moving balls,
Controlled from the inside,
And that thick rubber body,
The imprint of a navel,
The undersized hands,
The thick soft knees,
The screwed-on head,
The air hole behind her back,
All this in its lifelessness
Gives me a feeling
That children are amazing
To imagine such a thing alive.

**Michael McGriff** (San Francisco, CA) was born and raised in Coos Bay, Oregon. His work has appeared in *American Poetry Review, Slate, The Believer,* and *Field,* among other publications. He is a former Stegner Fellow and Jones Lecturer at Stanford University. He is the translator of Tomas Tranströmer's *The Sorrow Gondola* (Green Integer, 2010) and is author of the poetry collection *Dismantling the Hills* (University of Pittsburgh, 2008).

### Seasons between Night and Day

Somewhere between eternity and the filthy skin
of the millpond, the stars.
My mother sleeps. Somewhere between her and the stars,
my father and hundreds of other men
punch out of Georgia Pacific's sawmill forever,
the forklifts behind them at half-mast,
other machines chained to barges
with Japanese names
before the workers file out from the alien yard.

My mother's asleep. My father, on the edge
of the mattress, stoops down to unlace his boots,
unlace the sound his joints, ligaments
and sockets have saved.
When he curses his body for needing to be a body.
For now, my sister and I live a different sleep:
the dandelions outside our window
have petals that cartwheel into the night
on yellow fists.

In the morning my father will enter the garage.
Above him, the hours will reach
through the rafters one finger at a time.
He'll fire up the Chevy,
gutted dirtbikes and sick carburetors
glowing red in the exhaust
like broken engines of sleep.

Until then, his hands work the razor in the light
crawling the bathroom mirror. It means nothing
when he tells me he hasn't shaved
his beard since Vietnam, because I'm five.
*Laid-off* means no more forklift rides, he says.
He says, *Asia*. It sounds pretty and soft
as my sister's blond hair. So much happens
in the seasons between night and day:
this morning I enter the kingdom
of my father's hands as they scrape away
one face for another.

## Buying and Selling

This father and daughter
        sell wood by the cord
in an empty lot
        by the nickel plant.
They sell rugs
        that hang like cured skins.
Wolves, dreamcatchers,
        rebel flags. They sell
bumper stickers
        and used fishing poles.
They buy mushrooms
        and they sell mushrooms.
They sell butterfly knives.
        The daughter
can make one dance.
        They sell the Buddha
and Mexican leather.
        She has scraped knees
and heavy eyelashes,
        a shirt that says
*Speak English or Die.*
        They sell big American flags
and little American flags.
        MIA. POW.
They sell under a blue tarp.
        Chinese throwing stars,
switchblades.
        They sell bowie knives
with hollow handles,
        a place for wire and flint
and whetstone.
        They sleep in a Buick
near the edge of the mill yard
        and watch the sun
turn from orange to red
        as it rises
through the nickel dust.
        It's almost November.
Frost spreads across everything
        like the universe
blooming from its origin.
        In the oldest story he tells,

he's commissioned
      by Kublai Khan
to sail 100 bolts of silk to Jerusalem
      and return with a vial of holy water
to the Empire of a Million Horses.
      But this is the story
he doesn't tell: a girl
      on her father's shoulders,
how he trades
      a heap of copper wire
for a full bottle of penicillin,
      so the girl
eventually drifts back
      into the port of her body
on the edge of the charted world.


## Foxgloves


The dreams of those buried in winter
push through the ground in summer.
Among the orders, my dead
belong to the ditches of county roads.
Before the Walkers came over
to negotiate the easement
with their version of a city lawyer,
my father hung dozens of foxgloves
above our door. A dead crow
hung by its feet from the same hook.
Even in death, that purple luster
is a kind of singing.
Dead Man's Bells. Witches' Gloves.

**Sandra McPherson** (Davis, CA) is author of ten full-size poetry collections and many briefer ones. She taught twenty-three years as Professor of English, University of California Davis, four years at the University of Iowa Writers' Workshop, and briefly elsewhere. She is founder and publisher of Swan Scythe Press.

## Grouse

This water flows dark red
from alder tannin:
boot-stain river

between white rocks.
An ouzel, flannel-feathered,
sips the current up.

Mossgatherers
spread their patches
across a dry, flat turnaround.

They seem embarrassed,
want to shelter in the dark.
A coyote running in broad day;

stumps ruffling
with sulphur polypores
woodsy to the tongue,

woody to teeth.  Early
yellow leaves paste river to its bed;
blackberries drop, the last,

many out of taste
and strictly smudge.
Puddles loop in the road:

Bottomland—
the foolhen
waits there for

the fool gun,
gray throat-down free in a burst,
the pose, the afterslump.

Carcass beside spirit.
O come to my hand, unkillable;
whatever continues, continue to approach.

## Phlox Diffusa

*—A Poem for My Fiftieth Birthday*

Is it calm after midnight on its rocky slope,
exactly fitted to its nice little rubble?
Easy to think it's a bedtime slipper of a flower, owning no boots.
It lies flat on its back and looks at stars.

"Undaunted by stern surroundings," Mary Elizabeth Parsons says
in the *Wild Flowers of California*, 1907.
Like the game pummeled seapalm on outer rocks in breakers
the phlox spreads happy in its xeric meadow.

The flowers completely hide the leaf cushion,
the way a lot of enthusiasms obscure
the inner idiot. Actually clothe it,
but wildly as a shipping spree.

Charmed and usually older hikers want to lie right down beside it.
Starlike, delicate.

"The tiny crammed leaves live in a pocket of calm partly
of their own making, and there they trap
windblown particles
that slowly become a nourishing soil."

Taproots eight to fifteen feet.
A throw pillow bolted to granite.
Easy to think it's only three inches tall,
until you think of that, think of that root.

## Condolence Note: Los Angeles

The sky is desert blue,
Like the pool. Secluded.
No swimmers here. No smog—

Unless you count this twisting
Brushfire in the hills. Two kids
Sit, head to head, pool-side,

Rehearsing a condolence note.
Someone has died, "Not an intimate,
Perhaps a family friend," prompts

The Manners Guide they consult.
You shouldn't say *God never makes*
*Mistakes,* she quotes, snapping her

Bikini top. Right, he adds—You
Could just say, *He's better off*—or
*Heaven was always in his future.*

There's always a better way to say
"We're sorry that he's dead"—but
they're back inside their music now,

Pages of politeness fallen between them.
O do not say that the Unsaid drifts over us
Like blown smoke: a single spark erupts

In wildfire! Cup your hands, blow out
This wish for insight. Say: Forgive me
For living when you are dead. Say pardon

My need to praise, without you, this bright
Morning sky. It belongs to no one—
But I offer it to you, heaven in your future—

Along with silent tunes from the playlist,
the end-time etiquette book dropped
From the hand of the young sleeper.

It's all we have left to share. The book
Of paid respects, the morning's  hot-blue
I-pod, sunlit words on a page, black border.

**Carol Muske-Dukes** (Los Angeles, CA) is author of seven books of poems, including *Sparrow* (Random House, 2003), a National Book Award finalist; four novels, including *Channeling Mark Twain* (Random House, 2008); and two collections of essays, including *Married to the Icepick Killer: A Poet in Hollywood* (Random House, 2001). She is Professor of English/Creative Writing at the University of Southern California. In 2008, she was appointed by the governor as Poet Laureate of California. She has been the recipient of many awards and has been published and anthologized widely.

**Melinda Palacio** (Santa Barbara, CA) grew up in South-Central Los Angeles and lives in Santa Barbara. She is a 2007 PEN Center USA Emerging Voices Rosenthal Fellow and a 2009 poetry alumnus of the Squaw Valley Community of Writers. Her first novel is *Ocotillo Dreams* (Bilingual Press, 2010). *Folsom Lockdown* (Kulupi Press, 2010), winner of Kulupi's 2009 Sense of Place contest, is her first collection of poems.

### El South-Central Cucuy

My uncle said I wouldn't have a life.
Sorry, la little Minnie, he snarked,
Dah, ha, ha, he laughed.
If the Cucuy doesn't get you, the Bomb will.

South Central L.A. sounds like a battlefield with its random bullets,
helicopter searches for who knows whose father, brother, son,
enemies of the state, the police call them.

The Bomb will end everything, but el Cucuy
is scarier than any bomb or bullet
flying through my window at night.

Stray bullets like sonic popcorn punctured our television in the living room.
Crackles and pop-pop sounds force me to hit the ground.

Sneaky tires of a car turning too slowly,
force me to roll off my warm bed.
Welcome to my barrio.

Bullets spared me, but took the young lives of three on our street.
Bullets and bombs are visible, unlike el Cucuy.

You can't see the Cucuy who lurks in the hallway, under the bed and in the closet.
The boogeyman with devil's feet waits to touch your hair in the dark,
 in a crowded house on Albany Street in South Central L.A.

## Grandmother Rattler

who coils in my bones,
what were you thinking that summer night
when you found the warm road
on the edge of the canyon and stopped
just there exactly at the center
where the pickups and cars
and evening walkers would see
your spiral upon spiral,
hear the singing voice of your tail,
see your black head rising?

When I stopped my car
and walked up to you,
arms spread and hands open,
why didn't you move?
Why didn't you slide down the stones
among the white oaks
and single tall stems of soaproot?

When those white people stopped,
leaned out of their truck,
whistled and hooted,
did you not recognize Owl among them
calling to me over and over
"Kill it! Kill it!"  but still
you would not move
even to save your life
but sang all the louder,
your body quaking with rage.

Then that woman came out
of her house just there,
saw you, ran back, picked up
the heaviest shovel she could find,
pushed her way past
where I tried to shield you
and said she would kill you if I would not,
said she had horses down the hill
that might get bit, or she might die
if you were allowed
to live out the night.

**Wendy Rose** (Coarsegold, CA) is author of five volumes of poetry. She served as Coordinator of the American Indian Studies Program at Fresno City College in Fresno, California. In addition to her work as teacher, anthropologist, researcher, consultant, editor, panelist, bibliographer, and advisor, Wendy Rose is also an accomplished visual artist.

O Grandmother.
What did I become?
The German mother who closed her ears
to the sound of neighbors
as they choked and burned?
Uniformed boy in a silver room,
his finger hovering over one small button
to kill thousands he will never see,
elders and infants he will only know
by the magic devil word "enemy"?
I know only this.
I took the shovel
wanting to spare you a death
at their hands, brought it down edgewise
on your soft red neck, cleanly sliced
the head from the body,
felt a shadow pass
over my womb.

Ever since
there is a dream
where opals outline
the shape of diamonds
on my back.
My mouth opens
and your high
whistling hum
bleeds out,
my tongue
licks the air.

## Cirque

Even the clean
blue-green water
of the cirque,
with nothing
in between
the snow and it
but slant
can't speed
the work,
must wait
upon whatever
makes it white
to dissipate.
It seems
so hard to think
that even lakes
so pure
should start opaque,
that something
*always*
has to recombine
or sink.

## Dew

As neatly as peas
in their green canoe,
as discretely as beads
strung in a row,
sit drops of dew
along a blade of grass.
But unattached and
subject to their weight,
they slip if they accumulate.
Down the green tongue
out of the morning sun
into the general damp,
they're gone.

**Kay Ryan** (Fairfax, CA) served as United States Poet Laureate (2008—2010). She grew up in the small towns of the San Joaquin Valley and the Mojave Desert and taught remedial English for many years at the College of Marin. In 2009, she launched "Poetry for the Mind's Joy," an initiative to draw national attention to poetry and to community colleges. Ryan's awards include the Ruth Lilly Poetry Prize, a Guggenheim Fellowship, an Ingram Merrill Award, a National Endowment for the Arts Fellowship, the Union League Poetry Prize, the Maurice English Poetry Award, and four Pushcart Prizes.

**Dixie Salazar** (Fresno, CA) has published four books of poetry: *Hotel Fresno* (Blue Moon Press, 1988), *Reincarnation of the Common Place* (Salmon Run Press, 1999), *Blood Mysteries* (University of Arizona Press, 2003), and *Flamenco Hips and Red Mud Feet* (University of Arizona Press, 2010). She is also a novelist and visual artist, working primarily in oils. She teaches writing and literature at California State University and shows her art work at the Silva/Salazar studios in Fresno. She taught extensively in the California prisons and the Fresno County Jail and participated in a project for creating a homeless drop-in center in downtown Fresno.

### Altar for the Altar-less

"The homeless people that live here are the luckiest homeless in Fresno. They have maid service. We come out and clean up for them about every other week."  —Police Officer Rey Wallace

The things they lost in the cleanup:
false teeth
bicycle
sleeping bags
laptop computer
new shoes
blankets
insulin
family photos
Paxil
dog food
heart medication
jewelry
small TV
sleeping bags
birth certificates
hand weights
tool box
inhaler
love letters
tent with baby kittens inside
social security card
shampoo
military discharge papers
service medals
birth control pills
dog house
urn with grand-daughter's ashes

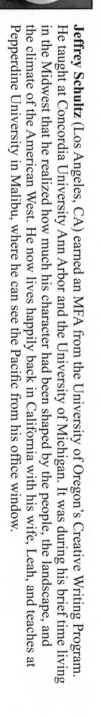

# J. Learns the Difference between Poverty and Having No Money

*—after Ernesto Trejo*

And the morning's marine layer cloud cover's just beginning to unhinge,
    to let the buttery light of another daybreak slip through
And weigh down the dead lawns and sagging roof-tops
    of this neighborhood, where cold-war era television antennas
Still cast shadows like B-52s heading offshore, where poverty, this early
    is the smell of Malt-O-Meal and the dregs of thin beer
Washed down the sink. Where the shift begins at 7 AM,
    but consciousness has a way of coming round as slowly
As this old computer monitor flickers its dull sixteen colors into being.
    On it, the names and numbers of laundromat and liquor store owners,
Fast food managers and lawn care companies; it's my job
    to cold call them, read from a script on the benefits of membership
In the Executive Dining Club, not take *No* for an answer.
    I'm no good and both the boss and I know it, and he's hovering
When the scraped-out voice of the woman on my phone answers me with
    *My husband's been killed,* and then, instead of hanging up,
Throws the receiver down next to something—dishwasher or window AC,
    I don't know—but something close, it sounds, to tearing itself apart,
Something cycling through an awful, screeching noise.
    And it's because I've paused that the boss flings a pencil
Into the wall in front of me and edges closer, and because of the fear
    of unemployment forms or the sky opening up if I were to walk out,
And because this sound—the un-oiled, flak-fouled crack of it—
    has left me standing suddenly at the end of a runway, planes
Screaming low overhead and loaded for the beginning of the end of the
        world,
    that I start back into the script, start back as if I believe each word,
Even though, in the rattle and dust of the jet-wash, no one hears a thing.

**Jeffrey Schultz** (Los Angeles, CA) earned an MFA from the University of Oregon's Creative Writing Program. He taught at Concordia University Ann Arbor and the University of Michigan. It was during his brief time living in the Midwest that he realized how much his character had been shaped by the people, the landscape, and the climate of the American West. He now lives happily back in California with his wife, Leah, and teaches at Pepperdine University in Malibu, where he can see the Pacific from his office window.

**Kim Shuck** (San Francisco, CA) earned an MFA in textiles and maintains a busy show schedule for her visual art, while also writing her poetry and prose and reading at local California venues. Her collection of poems, *Smuggling Cherokee* (Greenfield Review Press, 2006), won the Diane Decorah First Book Award from the Native Writer's Circle of the Americas. She lives in San Francisco with a collection of nearly grown offspring and various beasts that have decided to stay.

## Off Westish

Twin Peaks tucked in tight for the morning
No hint of the tower lights from this angle
Under the folds of damp and grey
It will burn off soon enough
Later there will be the drone of bees haunting
Berry vines
Bramble smells
Crushed to juice in places
So like the bloody scrapes I remember
Gathering along with the fruit and this
One of the steepest streets without stairs
Right up into the fog
Every street light still believing in the night and a
Pervasive Autumn cough season smell of
Eucalyptus
Messy things they are
Seed pods, discarded bark and leaves
Slick the concrete
City grids break down in the face of these hills but
We are almost at the crest
Nearly there
Pass the outcrop of green stone
Tossed at some point from the ocean floor
Hit the gravity shift and we are headed down
Angled towards the bakery
Between trees cracking artificial stone
Between photogenic houses
Between the quirky neighbors we will never meet
Our every Thursday unless it's raining too hard ritual
Ending with a hot cup of tea

## Waste Management

Every night a bear comes round our house to scare up
some windfall pears or to forage for fragrant garbage,
trudging on soft-padded feet & slightly open-mouthed.
He's an ursine Tony Soprano, I think, seeking refuge

from autumnal hungers as he forages the town's alleys.
Burly as a nightclub bouncer, near-sighted, he browses
through our lives' detritus, appearing as a refugee
from day's ample shadows. Our bear noisily chases

a neighborhood cat, a disemboweler of mouses,
then he eats the worst types of underworld scum—
larval worms in day-glow trousers—food storehoused
in a huge belly that sways to & fro when he travels.

Despite his slovenly slouch, our bear's a marvel
of Mafia etiquette as he curses & wantonly carouses
in the dim byways of the forest, as he sways in raveling air
to snap the bark off trees with his tough teeth & calluses.

We curse the furry rampages of our famished bear
who's surely gotten high on gruff power as he struggles
to grip trashcan rims with iron fingers—ever roused
to action by brisk whiffs of winter or our ribald catcalls.

Oh made man, living drunk or dour, don't settle
for trudging on soft-padded feet, staying tight-hearted—
know, as I do, how fear & desire drive us all. Look how
nightly a bear circumambulates our lives with such ardor.

**Maurya Simon** (Mt. Baldy, CA) has published eight volumes of poetry, including *Cartographies* (Red Hen Press, 2008) and *Ghost Orchid* (Red Hen Press, 2004), a nominee for a National Book Award in Poetry. Simon is the recipient of a National Endowment for the Arts Fellowship, an Artist's Residency at the American Academy in Rome, and an Indo-American Fulbright Fellowship. She teaches at the University of California, Riverside and lives in the Angeles National Forest in Southern California.

### Keeping Track

That's what I was doing on a Wednesday morning,
while out on Falls Road, slogging my slow way
through a foot of sodden snow, when suddenly
I felt exalted by a trail my dog and I had sighted:
deep pug marks whose petalled toes were blurred
by thick winter fur, and which raced before us
in bounding gaps, straight lines, staggered pairs.
I knew something was up when Sam's coat rose
stiffly off his back, his ears and nostrils flaring.
A mountain lion had prefaced us hours earlier,
had climbed past the same outcroppings of granite,
had paused, like us, on edges of icy precipices,
to stare far below to the ski lift parking lot,
where colorful toy cars were aligned in rows,
and where beetle-sized skiers queued up for rides.
We followed the puma's prints for more than a mile,
and so bent was I to my trail that I wholly forgot
to be mindful of other pleasures, other dangers:
for suddenly, above us, the mountainside we hugged
bellowed, buckled, loosened a thousand tons of snow
that roared down upon us a white, cataclysmic fury—
we ran, and ran and ran—then stopped to cringe
behind a boat-shaped boulder that, like a huge wall,
broke the raging avalanche into twin Amazons of death.
Like two twigs trapped in the calm, unseeing eye
of a tornado, we stood transfixed as the mountain
shuddered free its oceanic cargo, its cosmic freight,
the noise so deafening it drowned out the dog's howl.
My hand still holds that awful sound in its bones:
my hand's trembling even now; it is writing down
this poem, so that all of me flinches to remember
what I nearly surrendered one day in early March,
when I lost track of the wildness of the world.

## Romance at the River Bend Called Three Rocks

Buddha, may I rub your belly?
May I pull your earlobe and hear you laugh?
The dropped rice at your feet,
May I toss it in my mouth?

My love and I have thrown a blanket onto the rocks,
And below us, the river rushes westward.

I stand to hurl a stick in the river,
Shouting, "Oh, sky with your nonchalant meteors!"
(I had taken geology, had read maps,
And declared that I could steer earth with my little finger.)

To add to my nonsense, I strike two rocks
And proclaim to my love, "Sparks are like nature's kisses."
I skim the defective rocks across the river—
No chips of fire inside them.

I do six push ups,
Tell a fable about a tailless dog,
And admit I know nothing about geology or stars.

Buddha, may I rub your belly?
My love has undone her bikini top
And the softest boulders have rolled into view.
My hands and lips tremble when I lift them.

## Anniversary Poem

*—For Carolyn*

The moon can't decide what it wants to be—
A slice behind a cloud, a chunk of rock,
Or an old voyeur lurking in the trees.

The stars move, rotate, and pull at our fears.
A friend says they're neutral, thus godless,
These stars on a May evening

When I want to believe in something holy.
I want this to be perfect, this evening.
You said *yes* thirty-three years ago,

**Gary Soto** (Fresno, CA) is author of eleven poetry collections, most notably *New and Selected Poems* (Chronicle Books, 1995), finalist for both the Los Angeles Times Award and the National Book Award. His poems have appeared in *Ploughshares, The Iowa Review, Ontario Review,* and *Poetry.* He is recipient of the Discovery/The Nation Prize, and fellowships from the California Arts Council, the National Endowment for the Arts, and the Guggenheim Foundation. Soto has also been awarded the Human and Civil Rights Award from the American Education Association and the Literature Award from the Hispanic Heritage Foundation. He divides his time between Berkeley and his hometown of Fresno.

Yes to my black hair, my boyish body,
The craziness. A gnat is pestering me,
Same one that circled, star-like,

The lawn where our wedding was held—
The crickets, in full-suited armor,
Howled in the grass, ready to charge

And join us at the tables.
Thirty-three years, little changes.  The moon,
The stars, the insensible wars…

Perhaps a god threw a rock in the sky
And made it stay.  He did the same for us,
Both of us little stars, both of us circling

The marriage bed, both of us here to stay.


## Short Lives


I stood in front of a ruined tulip,
The rain and wind having had its way
With that Dutch flower. If it had pushed
Out of the earth a week later,
If the rainstorm had passed a week earlier,
Then it would still stand erect.
On a daily walk in the neighborhood,
Someone like me, or like you,
Might hoist their hands on their hips
And think the world lovely.

Wind passes through the leafing trees,
Rain sweeps the litter and leaves into drains.
Blossoms are thrown into the air,
And we think renewal is at our fingertips.
We can't remember today, we can't forget yesterday.
Our faces bend slowly earthward,
Flowers eventually touching mud.

## Los Angeles, 1954

It was in the old days,
When she used to hang out at a place
　　　　Called *Club Zombie*,
A black cabaret that the police liked
　　To raid now and then. As she
　　　　Stepped through the door, the light
Would hit her platinum hair,
And believe me, heads would turn. Maestro
　　　　*Loved it*; he'd have her by
The arm as he led us through the packed crowd
　　　　To a private corner
Where her secluded oak table always waited.
　　She'd say, *Jordan* . . .
　　　　　　And I'd order her usual,
A champagne cocktail with a tall shot of bourbon
　　　　On the side. She'd let her eyes
Trail the length of the sleek neck
　　　　Of the old stand-up bass, as
The bass player knocked out the bottom line,
　　His forehead glowing, glossy
　　　　　　With sweat in the blue lights;
Her own face, smooth and shining, as
　　　　The liquor slowly blanketed the pills
　　　　　　She'd slipped beneath her tongue.
Maestro'd kick the shit out of anybody
　　　　Who tried to sneak up for an autograph;
He'd say, *Jordan, just let me know if*
　　　　　　*Somebody gets too close* . . .
　　Then he'd turn to her and whisper, *Here's*
*Where you get to be Miss Nobody* . . .
　　　　　　And she'd smile as she let him
　　Kiss her hand. For a while, there was a singer
　　　　At the club, a guy named Louis—
But Maestro'd change his name to "Michael Champion";
　　　　　　Well, when this guy leaned forward,
Cradling the microphone in his huge hands,
　　　　All the legs went weak
　　　　　　　Underneath the ladies.
He'd look over at her, letting his eyelids
　　　　Droop real low, singing, *Oh Baby I* . . .
　　　　　　*Oh Baby I Love* . . . *I Love You* . . .

**David St. John** (Venice Beach, CA) is author of nine collections of poetry, including *The Face: A Novella in Verse* (HarperCollins, 2004). He is co-editor, with Cole Swensen, of *American Hybrid: A Norton Anthology of New Poetry* (W.W. Norton, 2009). The recipient of fellowships/awards from the National Endowment for the Arts, the John Simon Guggenheim Memorial Foundation, American Academy and Institute of Arts and Letters, The Folger Shakespeare Library, and the Ingram Merrill Foundation, he teaches at the University of Southern California in Los Angeles.

And she'd be gone, those little mermaid tears
        Running down her cheeks. Maestro
      Was always cool. He'd let them use his room upstairs,
Sometimes, because they couldn't go out—
      Black and white couldn't mix like that then.
              I mean, think about it—
This kid star and a cool beauty who made King Cole
       Sound raw? No, they had to keep it
           To the club; though sometimes,
Near the end, he'd come out to her place
      At the beach, always taking the iced whisky
I brought to him with a sly, sweet smile.
         Once, sweeping his arm out in a slow
      Half-circle, the way at the club he'd
        Show the audience how far his endless love
          Had grown, he marked
The circumference of the glare whitening the patio
       Where her friends all sat, sunglasses
      Masking their eyes . . .
        And he said to me, *Jordan, why do*
*White people love the sun so?—*
          *God's spotlight, my man?*
Leaning back, he looked over to where she
        Stood at one end of the patio, watching
The breakers flatten along the beach below,
        Her body reflected and mirrored
Perfectly in the bedroom's sliding black glass
       Door. He stared at her
      Reflection for a while, then looked up at me
And said, *Jordan, I think that I must be*
      *Like a pool of water in a cave that sometimes*
        *She steps into . . .*
Later, as I drove him back into the city,
       He hummed a Bessie Smith tune he'd sing
For her, but he didn't say a word until
We stopped at last back at the club. He stepped
       Slowly out of the back
       Of the Cadillac, and reaching to shake my hand
Through the open driver's window, said,
       *My man, Jordan . . . Goodbye.*

## Sheepeater Cave

Last night's cooked dinner, now breakfast trout,
As bighorns appear to scrape hoofs in marl,
And beyond clouded peaks rough thunder growls
Past flake or varnish while winds fan out.
Stowing her kayak beneath a felled log, she
Races on toward an arch yawning red,
A cave carved deep past the rock's darkened threads,
And there she huddles against the storm-spree.

Sharp tines of lightning, steep drapes of rain
So fury of water wipes river from sight.
But above her head ancient pictographs fly:
Caribou and hunters with horn-bows drawn.
In awe of the shaman whose painting still burns
She bends and begs for her own safe return.

## Undercut

We're holding hands, breathing hard. The over-
hang, a gneiss cliff, part of a canyon, should
last forever, yet as we pause here—rock
can't withstand the persistence of water—
the Salmon is claiming it. Basins are
rounded by it, polished until we shield
our eyes from the glare. Slowly, the rock-strewn
current scours a wilder path. Above us,
a fever of red-orange lichen and firs
silvered by moss. Below, the canyon's under-
cut, once stone, now burly chutes, and each day
the river-song grows deeper. While we gaze,
rock is disappearing. Nothing is static.
Not lichen, not fir, not water, not breath.

**Susan Terris** (San Francisco, CA) is author of four books of poems: *Contrariwise* (Time Being Books, 2008), *Natural Defenses* (Marsh Hawk Press, 2004), *Curved Space* (La Jolla Poets Press, 1998), and *Fire is Favorable to the Dreamer* (Arctos Press, 2003). With CB Follett, she edited *RUNES, A Review Of Poetry*. She is editor of *Spillway*, edits for *Pedestal Magazine*, and is poetry editor (with Ilya Kaminsky) of *In Posse Review*. She is published widely in magazines and journals, and she is the recipient of a Pushcart Prize. She lives with her husband, David, in San Francisco and enjoys reading, hiking, and canoeing.

**Amber Flora Thomas** (Mendocino, CA) is the recipient of the Cave Canem Poetry Prize. Her first collection of poems is *Eye of Water: Poems* (University of Pittsburgh Press, 2005). She is an assistant professor of creative writing at the University of Alaska Fairbanks.

## Swarm

A honey bee queen lays the nettle
and the weather in a black cloud that falls
on two white men lifting a rotten tree
toward their truck on the fire road. It's just luck

come up from hiding, a nether world
she sends into the August groan. The men hack
and flail pale limber arms at the air, their clothing,
and their ears. They jig around the truck
in this unexpected season.

I stand alone across the gulley and kill
the helpful girl trying to rise up
in me. If they had found me alone
on my afternoon walk in the forest?

Their baseball caps shucked, the red rising
on their arms and faces. The bees go up
and come down, a dizzy swarm. The men
throw themselves in the cab of the truck,
the haze ascending on their dust, until
nothing they could have done was done to me.

## Soar

No one ever said *housemaid* or *domestic.* Pride matters more
and here's the truth of it: she was *Tantie*, a grand-mothering

substitute chained to Miss B, a former Hollywood come-hither
and Tantie's final misery. I couldn't name a single movie Miss B

had starred in but Mother told us she was a first-class bitch.
Thirty years later, watching late night television, I recalled:

I met that bitch once. Ill-preserved on celluloid, she fluttered there
amidst her ersatz brood—but not in the same way I'd seen her

flutter decrees upon my tantie. And my tantie, once a muck-a-muck
in her own right (having flown an airplane solo in days when

most women and Negroes were grounded), half-fluttered in return—
to make sure her family had dimes and nickels. Tantie didn't tell us

she was Miss B's maid, and I never knew a thing about it until I saw
this black-and-white movie with Miss B—half a star among stars—

given third-place billing—nearly unrecognizable as the cold shrew
I remembered flaunting dipped pearls, telling me to

*look and admire* because I would never own anything
quite like them. Tantie calmly laced Miss B's tea (with what?—

we never knew) so that Miss B napped a little longer on afternoons
when Tantie fed us sugar-cubes, spoke of days when she'd soared.

**Lynne Thompson** (Los Angeles, CA) is author of *Beg No Pardon* (Perugia Press, 2007), which won the Perugia Press First Book Award and the 2008 Great Lakes Colleges New Writers Award. Her poems have appeared widely in magazines and journals. She earned her J.D. at Southwestern School of Law and serves as Director of Employee and Labor Relations at UCLA.

**Joyce E. Young** (Berkeley, CA) lives and writes in the San Francisco Bay Area. Her poems have appeared widely. She has been granted residencies at Hedgebrook, Soapstone ,and Vermont Studio Center and has served as a California Arts Council Artist-In-Residence. She is the founder of Write in Peace, and she teaches at John F. Kennedy University.

## Lizard

Lizard said, "It pays to use camouflage and observe carefully." His tongue glittered in the light as he spoke and eyed me from the other side of the boulder. He teaches me that stillness pays and moving quickly when necessary is crucial, but the best thing to do in the city or in the country, is to blend in with your surroundings.

Sometimes, men and women in dark uniforms eye me suspiciously. My height, skin color and unisex, loose fitting clothing are often identical to the description of the person they're looking for, except that I have breasts. It is dark outside, so they say it is hard for them to tell that I'm not the perpetrator they're looking for.

My tongue shoots out in flames, quickly licking the air before the blue uniform in the patrol car sees it. I fold into the brick building on the corner of Alcatraz and Telegraph. My skin turns crumbly reddish brown and I freeze.

## Dawn at Oakland Airport

Aggression keeps arriving but almost never departs.
As quiet as it's kept, greed bops along for the ride.
Do you need James Brown hollering in your ear
at 6 a.m. when you've gotten all of two hours sleep,
misread your itinerary and coldly missed the flight?
I can't stand it, either, James. The Godfather of Soul
and all the other Godfathers share a mission this morning,
and that's to put another hit on peace and quietude.
You don't need no Johnny Cash, no saxophone quartet
version of the Temptations' "My Girl," no "Goldfinger,"
no "Ring of Fire," no Earth, Wind & Fire doing "Hearts
Afire," no jaunty disco deco from the decadent Seventies.
What you need is Z's and more Z's—Zambia, Zanzibar,
Zihuatanejo, no, Canal Zone, Zone 51, UFO's, out of here,
out of ear shot surely. And when two advancing armies
in the war on silence conjoin, when the foreground music
of Gate 10 crisses across Gate 8's background music,
you know no zone can ever be demilitarized again.
Green, brown, the hills that ring this East Bay underdog
airport can't compete, and sky—O lazy, hazy sky of summer,
what brings you here in April?—the sky is battling, too.
Give us Slim Harpo: "The sky is crying;/Look at the tears
roll down the street." Give us liberty to chose your death.
The breath you hold whispers the unspeakable:
"Can things actually get any worse?" Yes, saith Phoenix,
yes, saith Las Vegas, Los Angeles saith yes, and Houston agrees.
By the time you get to Newark, maybe the Sopranos and
all the electric pianos in the world will have gone on break.

**Al Young** (Berkeley, CA) is author of twenty-two books of poetry, fiction ,and musical memoirs. From 2005 through 2008, he served as Poet Laureate of California. Other honors include National Endowment for the Arts, Fulbright, and Guggenheim Fellowships. Al Young collaborated with bassist Dan Robbins on *The Sea, The Sky, And You, And I*, a poetry and jazz CD from Bardo Digital.

## American Time

You know you've come back home again
when they start snatching plates
right out from under you in the restaurants
before you get to savor all your food;
there is no time, there just isn't time.
The country of mad hatters, this is
that; the Wonderland it took a mathematician
with a penchant for myths and nymphets to imagine
the way it truly is: Hello/Goodbye/Drop me
a line/Let's grab a bite/Give us a ring/
Damage estimated at six million dollars/
Instant replay/Times Square squared/Everything
you ever wanted in a beer and less/rushes
and rushes and rushes of early returns—
there is no time, there just isn't time.

You know you've come back home again
when you turn up at the office on Sunday
morning to find the trees that stood
in front of the building only yesterday
have been dug up and hauled away so clean
you think you've lost your mind. But what
about the stores shut down since you've been
gone and the buildings leveled and the whole
blocks excavated to leave you standing
frozen in your tracks trying to remember
in January what had been there in December?
And the neighbors who casually say, "Oh, hey,
the moving van'll be here Saturday, we forgot
to tell you we're pulling up stakes for Oregon."
Computerized dating, Disneyland waiting,
queues and cues and oolyacoos of twisty bebop
drop you constantly into to-be-continued
new waves of slaving variations on a theme.

## Process

From looking at things Navajo
& Native American, I am learning
to re-picture all that lies around
& within me as process; as step
by step I come to understand
where we go wrong when we cling
to the notion of there being
such things as fixed objects that
exist outside of ourselves in some
external world of which we are only
momentarily a part because of our
ability to perceive, that's all.

No, perception itself is process.
The thing perceived & the perceiver
are one; everything is in flux,
subatomic particles are dancing
by the trillions on the stump of your
big toe; subtle radiation bombards us
everytime we remember that universes
reside within a glistening slice of
seeded red-green-neutral-almost-white
watermelon cut from its vine & harvested
from a specific patch of earth where
the sun shines down & cool nights come.

And where do we come from? Clearly
there's something exciting & mysterious
going on here; something or, rather,
some process of enchantment so vast
& giddying that we're moved to turn
our backs on it & go to movies instead.
One glance at the sea is more than we
can handle. Snap a picture & let's go!

# *Colorado*

**Peter Anderson** (Crestone, CO) teaches writing at Adams State College in Alamosa, Colorado. He has worked as a river guide, backcountry ranger, small town newspaper reporter, and editor. He is author of *First Church of the Higher Elevations: Mountains, Prayer, and Presence* (Ghost Road Press, 2005) and lives with his wife and two daughters on the western edge of the Sangre de Cristo Range.

### Night Drive on I-80

Remember when you were headed west out of Wamsutter
measuring the after midnight miles with a half-emptied sixpack
and you had the hammer down and nothing but empty up ahead?

Remember, somewhere west of Bitter Creek, you stopped
for that roughnecked renegade leaning into the wind, who told
you he was so hungry he could eat the ass off a skunk?

Remember the eatum-up truck stop neon, blazing like Christmas
with the voltage cranked and all those big buckets of bolts
blowing diesel in the parking lot?

Remember how your roughneck pal went silent over chicken fried steak,
and you picked at a piece of pie from the Pleistocene, but the cat-eyed
waitress called you "hun" and made it all ok?

Remember dropping your new friend off at daybreak—highway 189
north to Diamondville—and how he told you to keep the shiny
side up and the greasy side down, and how you said "fer sure"

and how it was easier to believe, back then, that everyone
was a good buddy just waiting to happen?

### True News from a Small Town Beat

"Give me all the money in your cash  register," he said.
"Are you serious?" asked the clerk at Lou's Quickstop.
"Yes," said the old man.
"Who do you think you are?"
" Never done anything like this before," he admitted,
" . . . how much do you have in your register, anyway?"
"Not much," she said.
"Could you give me $20?"
"No I can't."
"How about $5?"
"No."
"Well, how bout a pack of cigarettes?"
"I'll give you a couple," she said.
The old man took the cigarettes and left.
"He was desperate," the clerk would say later on.
Police are investigating.

**Aaron Anstett** (Colorado Springs, CO) is author of three books of poems: *Sustenance* (New Rivers Press, 1997), *No Accident* (Backwaters Press, 2005), and *Each Place the Body's* (Ghost Road Press, 2007). His awards include the Balcones Poetry Prize and the Nebraska Book Award. From 2008-2010, he served as the inaugural Pikes Peak Poet Laureate. He lives in Colorado Springs with his wife, Lesley, and children, Molly, Cooper, and Rachel.

## Indeed I Was

Skinny then, little more than skeleton,
naked next to an actual skeleton,

my *memento mori* 3-D X-ray. The professor lifted
each bare limb then made me mimic the skeleton's

positions, asking the anatomy art class to see
the bones in my skin matched the skeleton's

poses. Easy to see so early and cold
on plywood stage in a studio how soon I'd be a skeleton,

what little dress of hair-on-end flesh above *tibia* and *ulna*,
*cranium*, *mandible*, fluorescents on the skeleton

and me merciless, and a square of skylight sun.
Charcoal and pencils scratched. I didn't ask, "Whose skeleton,"

or exclaim, "Alas, poor ____,"
the palm of my hand open like the skeleton's,

eyes above easels everywhere, clothed legs below.
On their sketch pads I imagined me and the skeleton

synchronized: *tai chi*, Rockettes, country line-dancing,
me on a bar floor, skeleton

kicking my undressed ribs. "Now, Mr. Anstett,"
Professor Something said, "if you could embrace the skeleton . . ."


## Prayer against Dying on Camera

Lord, not shot in liquor store stick-up,
jugular uncorked and finely misting or

splatter-patterning display case plate glass
and me so many pixels collapsing

at the feet of bikini'd cardboard
cutout models, purchase a puddle,

last words of my kind, "Oh, shit,"
lip-readable. Jesus not suddenly

in latex novelty emporium or slam-
bang stroke on jumbotron in a coliseum

screaming, not tumbling
from the burning building in a series

of photographs, speed increasing,
one frame famous because I look so calm.

**Dan Beachy-Quick** (Ft. Collins, CO) is author of four books of poetry: *North True South Bright* (Alice James Books, 2003), *Spell* (Ahsahta Press, 2003), *Mulberry* (Tupelo Press, 2006), and *This Nest, Swift Passerine* (Tupelo Press, 2009). He is the recipient of a Lannan Foundation Residency, and his poems, essays, and reviews appear variously. He teaches in the MFA Writing Program at Colorado State University and was Visiting Professor at the Iowa Writers' Workshop in spring 2010.

### Walking through the Room

When I became a traveler through another's grief,
When her face became for me a kind of architecture,
I could wander the halls, I could turn
The porcelain knobs and leave my evidence, I could
Be present, sit on the bare mattress, look at the sheets
Draped over the furniture, I could see that landscape
As the dust fell on it, I could lie down across the plains,
Stare at the crack in the sky, the crack circling the sun,
Long ago the sun went out, long ago the filament
Burned a slow orange and died, it does not stop the light
From completing its work, falling on things,
Falling on my hand that spins the globe on its axis,
It does not stop the light from pacing across the floor,
It does not stop the dust from catching slow fire in the current.
When her eyes became for me a kind of river where I could walk,
Where I could slake my thirst by cupping my hands,
Where the water runs over the stones the water wears away,
Where I can reach through the water and pick up a stone,
Where I can hold it in the light, where I can see the filament
Coursing blackly across the sphere, marking the halves,
Dividing the upper world from the lower, mapping the fault,
The line in the palm that ends where the hand ends,
Pointing to the horizon when the hand is held out, the line
Points at the dirt when the hand drops, the line the hand
Curls around when it holds onto nothing to hold itself,
Standing beside the river, hands clenched, refusing to drop
The ash into the river and let the river carry the ash away.

## Beyond the Black Iron Bars

—United States Air Force Academy,
April, 2007

On patrol, I see two cadets walk across the terrazzo.
Thin runner's shorts inch up her tanned legs.
He unlocks the gate—black iron bars swing back.

They turn the corner and hold hands,
Casually breaking the regulation
Against Public Display of Affection.

They have memorized George Patton's quote,
"If you can't get them to salute when they should
salute and wear the clothes you tell them to wear,

how are you going to get them to die for their country?"
He's carrying a blue pack with bread and water.
They can die later, if life comes to that.

I'm supposed to break them up, take names.
And I know where love can lead—late
Withdrawal, back-and-forth blame.

But I find myself cheering them on. Hoping
They'll stop to kiss, glad to see them obey,
Like Antigone, love's deeper laws.

If only for the moment, since that's
Where I find myself, I find myself
Cheering for us all.

**James Gleason Bishop** (Colorado Springs, CO) has worked as a reporter, toymaker, Air Force officer, and farmhand. He is widely published in literary journals and reviews, and he was nominated for a Pushcart Prize. He is Director of Human Resources and Assistant Professor of English at the United States Air Force Academy.

**Kathy Conde** (Superior, CO) has published poems in *Cutthroat, Orbis, The Lyric,* and others. She won the Hemingway Festival Short Story Contest in 2008. She herded cows and trained horses in *Wyoming* and studied writing at the University of Montana and at Naropa University. She is past associate editor for *Bombay Gin,* Naropa University's literary magazine. She lives in Colorado with her husband and son.

### Seekers

I was a seeker those years at the bar
staring into beer bottles,
endless trudge,
backed up three deep in front of me,
going through them one by one
with the devotion of a scholar.

Sometimes it seemed another seeker at the bar,
gazing into his own puzzling glass,
had found something there. But we spoke
delirious monologue and never knew
the difference between truth and heartburn.
Every night at closing time I oozed out the door
into blackness stuck with stars.
The night was a hammer I used on my head.

One night the truth I'd been seeking blazed up.
My life was melting away
like the snowbank under my cheek
where I briefly passed out
as I tried to get home.

### Climbing after a Fall

I hold back, feel the pull
of gravity through my boot.
Mac says it will be easy
scaling the vertical
rock face full of cracks
and quarter-inch ledges.
I climb and granite
turns to flat gray.
Handholds visible from below
vanish at a certain height.
Everything is gone—
summer grass, Mac's red car
gleaming from the road,
green silhouette of tamarack
against blue sky, screech
of a redtail hawk. All gone—
even the wind that blew
dust across the dirt
road when I took my first
look at the wall.
All that is left
is rock, my body pressed
against it like a lover,
the pull of gravity
seductive.

## Saturday Matinee

Gene Autry galloping hard on his pony,
in black and white, the ground and bushes gray,
toward gray mountains under a gray sky
where white clouds drift, hooves pounding
in the small theater as I sat forward
in my seat, my heart in my mouth with envy,
with longing for freedom, for Gene Autry,
the boy beside me sliding his hand over
for mine, the odor of popcorn in place

of sagebrush, and I saw myself inside
that movie, black hat on my head while
I rushed after him, my pony dapple-gray,
my hair long and blown back by the wind,
galloping so hard but upright western style,
a real cowgirl, and the hand in the theater
like some kind of insect I was brushing away,

my body wanting to rush after my mind—
away from that kid in his button-down shirt,
away from the white clapboard houses,
the dark deciduous forest on the edges
of town, the asphalt, the street lights,
and my father forbidding me to go
to the movie, while I sobbed, sobbed
for love of Gene Autry, for love
of the wide open west, of horses,
and galloping, for love, for love.

**Mary Crow** (Ft. Collins, CO) is Colorado Poet Laureate and has published poetry and translations. Her books of poetry include *I Have Tasted the Apple* (BOA Editions, 1996), *Borders* (BOA Editions, 1989), and three chapbooks. She received the Colorado Book Award, three Fulbright Fellowships, a National Endowment for the Arts Fellowship, and a Colorado Arts Council Fellowship. Her poetry translations include works of Jorge Teillier, Roberto Juarroz, Olga Orozco, and an anthology of contemporary Latin American women poets.

## Fault-Finding

Even now the ground is slowly shifting
beneath your feet. Even now
zones of weakness are building
behind your back, ready to crack
into fractures. Even now pressures
may exceed the power of rocks
to resist. Think of it:
thousands of faults lace this region.
You live inside a ring of fire
where walls can loom up overnight.
Forces in this landscape
are trying to rearrange your world.
You stand here feeling
you can control nothing,
at any second it is you
who may be heaved up,
and broken.

## Marfa, Texas

This landscape—new to me—is like a set
for *Giant*—vast and empty as if cast and crew
stand behind me as I gaze outward to
the distant horizon, over sand-colored hills
dotted with yucca and clumps of a dead shrub,
foothills fringing the lip of a stage speckled
with stiff antelope. Somebody, throw some
pain out there! Somebody, hurl a hallelujah!
Some red and blue! Songs and lies! Where
can we find a magenta boa? Potted palm trees?
Look how the fists of yellow grass shake in the wind!
That's more like it! And here's a gray roan mare!
What is the text? What are the stage directions?
Is there no other way but the sky's? Focus!
The suspense is bearable, waiting for clouds.
I'm here! Still here! Action, someone!

## Skinning the Elk

"There's a whole lot of life in these animals,"
George nods, almost like a prayer
as I hold the hoofed leg
steady for the knife,
mist rising from the gutted belly,
skin still warm.

Tempered steel peels back
thick hide. Fur.
The dark meat of the interior.

Secret organs slide steaming into full moonlight
on the bed of Greenbank's battered pickup.

I can't stop peering
into the glazed crystal
of those antlered eyes.
Two perfect rivets
welded to the girder of that
skeletal moment when
the bullet's magic
cut life short.

Later,
after the carcass is hung
in a cottonwood tree,
I go inside to wash my hands.
But the blood won't come off.

There's no mistake.
I am marked for life.
I wear the elk's tattoo,
as its meat becomes my meat
& its blood stains my blood.

Spirit leaping
from shape to shape.

**Art Goodtimes** (Norwood, CO) is a former poetry editor for *Earth First! Journal* and *Wild Earth*. A four-term Green county commissioner, he has served for more than twenty-five years as poet-in-residence/director for the annual Telluride Mushroom Festival and continues as founder/ director of the annual Talking Gourds poetry gatherings.

**Noah Eli Gordon** (Boulder, CO) is Assistant Professor of English at the University of Colorado, Boulder. He is author of several collections, including *Novel Pictorial Noise* (Harper Perennial 2007), which was selected by John Ashbery for the National Poetry Series and subsequently given the San Francisco State University Poetry Center Book Award.

### All Orange Blossoms Have to Do Is Act Naturally

And all the sky does is wait around for weather to consume it.
Although, one could argue that it's simply an extension of itself,
that one form describes another in the sails of outrigger canoes
before a landward breeze blows them toward the Philippine coast.

If I stand still long enough, the painting will go on without me.
Forget the mechanics of rainfall; Plutarch said it was war caused
a cloudburst. I say the only thing in the air is an evolving suspicion
that the laws of the atmosphere have accumulated out of a desire

to turn judiciousness on top of its Draconian head, reclaiming
sound judgment from the silver gavel affixed to our internalized sense
of fanciful reasoning taken for fact. All Galileo does is build a thermometer
and immediately—you believe him. Trade winds and doldrums in the tropics.

Delicate mobility in the deer. I love the tiny molecules that make up matter,
the tinier atoms inside them. If I stand still long enough, someone will walk
            around me.

## The Moment

In those days, Betty Crocker
always called for sifted flour, and so
in homes across America, women sifted.
When my mother's mother turned
the wobbly red knob, hulls and stones
jumped in the wire basket,
but by my mother's time
the flour was fine—
now women sifted to achieve
precision, purity, perfection.
It made the white flour whiter.
Then flour came in bags,
already sifted, and women stopped
making their own cakes and bread,
and didn't have time anyway
for sifting. But for a flicker
of history, my mother stood
staring down the tin cylinder,
the moment shuttered
into tiny parts, slowed
by the fanning blunt blades—
nothing to do but watch
the perfection of time, falling
into the waiting bowl.

**Jane Hilberry** (Colorado Springs, CO) is author of *Body Painting* (Red Hen Press, 2005), which received the Colorado Book Award for Poetry. Her poems have appeared in *Hudson Review*, *The Women's Review of Books*, *Virginia Quarterly Review*, and other magazines. Hilberry teaches literature and creative writing at Colorado College in Colorado Springs. She also teaches workshops in the United States and Canada on the subject of creativity and leadership.

**Joseph Hutchison** (Indian Hills, CO) was born and raised in Denver, where he teaches for University College at the University of Denver. He lives with his wife in the mountains southwest of Denver. He is author of four books of poetry: *The Rain at Midnight* (Sherman Asher Publishing, 2000), *Bed of Coals* (University of Colorado Press, 1995), *House of Mirrors* (James Andrews & Co., 1992), and *The Undersides of Leaves* (Wayland Press, 1985).

### Black River

You believe you must be beginning again.
The river opens to accept your first step,
and you're into it up to your knees—
the water's wrestle brotherly, bracing.
You start across, shouldering goods
you believe you'll need on the far side.
Waist-deep now. Feeling for rooted stones
through sopping boots. Surely this is where
you crossed before; there are no unknown
channels, no abysses, though the current
does seem swifter than you remember,
and darker (of course, it's only dusk
coming on, staining the air and water;
and the river—you believe—only seems
to be growing wider). Chest-deep now.
Icy water races past your racing heart,
under raised arms that ache to balance
whatever you carry, what you must (you
suddenly understand) be willing to let go.
Chin-deep. Perched on a slippery stone
that shifts with each shivering breath.
No choice but to take the next step—
deeper into the black river, farther
toward the shore of ink-black pines
over which the feverish stars have risen
and the cold comfort of a bone-white moon.

## Sleepwalkers

Twelve elk sleepwalk out of the forest, ghost
through torn March mist and hissing snow.
Rawboned, tall, ungainly—their grace

carried wholly in their upcurved necks—
they balance their heads like huge dried figs
while loose-jointed legs sway them onward

into the meadow. Around them the woods
draw back. Now one, now another halts.
Now they all bow down to work the blunt

boxing gloves of their muzzles, tugging
new shoots from last year's tangle. And as if
that were a signal, the swarming flakes let

go of winter, turning into a rain that beats
down on the gaunt haunches now, on drooped
ears twitching with the lavish clamor of Spring.


## From a Swaying Hammock

With a raw squawk the raven breaks
his glide and alights on a pine's

spring-like branch. What peaks gleam
in his onyx eye? What fat anoints his beak?

When I doze, it seems I hear my name
picked apart by his artful caws,

feel the combs of his claws
prowling among my graying hairs.

How can I sleep with him perched there?

**Mark Irwin** (Englewood, CO) is author of six collections of poetry, including *White City* (BOA, 2000), *Bright Hunger* (BOA, 2004), and *Tall If* (New Issues Press, 2008). Recognition for his work includes four Pushcart Prizes, two Colorado Book Awards, fellowships from the National Endowment for the Arts, and the Fulbright, Lilly, and Wurlitzer Foundations. He teaches in the Graduate Creative Writing Program at the University of Southern California.

## Rider

As I carried my mother from the hospital bed
across the room toward the chair by the window,
she played with my gold watch as if it were a toy,
flipping the strap up and down, then singing *Giddyup,*
*Giddyup,* but as I looked at her she did not smile
so I nodded my head, snorted, then put a pencil
in my mouth, as bit, and cantered about the room
till I was out of breath, puffing, and she patted me, saying,
*Good boy, Good boy*, so I pawed the carpet, slobbering a little
like her, as she waved and I nodded my mane
until this was how we said goodbye one spring
while the sun shrank to a white-hot BB among a thousand
others receding in the jeweled, black sky as the rivers
galloped away with her breath through the dark green land.

## Shoes

*—Matthew Shepard, in memoriam*

They cover the human foot. From the Old
English *sceoh*, akin to the German
*schuh*, from the Indo European base *s(keu)*:
to cover. The arch, heel, and sole.
The upper, tongue, and lacing. Some wore wingtips,
Oxfords, and loafers, while others sported
walkers or sandals as they left
their offices and homes in that quaint
mountain town. He was tied, naked to a fence,
then beaten. They stood on a ridge. Some, barefoot, lined
their shoes along the edge. Others wore them
on their hands watching the sky.

## About Eight Minutes of Light in the Meadow

I'm lying in tall grass, half dazed, watching
a fly on the bright opposite side of a leaf,
its dark hairy silhouette emblazoned
by a sun 93 million miles away.
By the time I remember this, the fly's gone.

I sit up. At the meadow's edge, a dead pine
has stayed caught in its fall by a living one,
branches entangled, the last three years
at least. Anything looked at long enough
becomes perfect. Three years is long enough.

Two dark soft fir stand across the meadow
from each other and this afternoon, this
moment, a small bird crosses from one
and lands in the other, sparks of singing
glittering in the middle of the air.

A butterfly passes, waggles away,
folds its wings thinly up and
disappears, a small door closing.
I wonder how many thousand others
are just now invisible in this meadow.

In the middle of such mild illuminations,
I'm dumb and simple here. At the speed
of light, its shine is about eight minutes
old, although everything is always
in this new time. And in this one.

## Now

I shuffle on snowshoes through the pines
in last night's snow—so where I am

was not here yesterday—and arrive
at a rocky creek, ice tightened
over the chatter of secret water.

Earlier I knew every question,
my name was "He-Who-Answers-Himself."

Now I am only whatever listens,
whatever sees what's hidden below
and everything hidden above.

Now I am breaking, coming together.
I am so alive I have forgotten my life.

**Robert King** (Greeley, CO) earned a Ph.D. from the Iowa Writers' Workshop in the early 60s and is now retired from teaching English and creative writing. He lives in Greeley, Colorado, near his childhood mountains and directs the website www.ColoradoPoetsCenter.org.

**Marilyn Krysl** (Boulder, CO) has served as Director of the Creative Writing Program at the University of Colorado and published poems in *The Atlantic, The Nation, The New Republic* and *Pushcart Prize Anthology.* She is author of four collections of stories and several books of poems, including *Swear the Burning Vow: Selected and New Poems* (Ghost Road Press, 2009). She served as Artist in Residence at the Center for Human Caring, volunteered with Mother Teresa's Sisters of Charity in Calcutta, and worked as an unarmed bodyguard for Peace Brigade International in Sri Lanka.

## Love, That Hugeness

Love snuggles us, and then Tagore warns:
go on your knees, the All-Destroying

has come—and will hang around a while,
then mosey on. A girl's sob

and a cup of cream. A cup of cream
and a gun. Things seem peachy keen,

then the peaches turn, and Marion Fisher,
new breasts and a crush on a boy, stands

against the wall in the Amish school room
watching Charlie Rogers tie her wrists,

her ankles. Charlie, who rose in the dark,
kissed his sleeping daughter's cheek

and went off to sing the familiar hymn
of delivering the morning's cream. *Stones*

*and bread,* Simone Weil said, *both come
from Christ.* Here come the shining moments,

yes, no, each moment we choose, and Marion
too, at one time or another, hurt the blooming

world. I didn't mean to, I told my mother.
Yes, she said, but you did it. Each moment

we do or we don't, and here comes the next
moment—don't hurry, there's time—

Charlie may say *wait, I don't know
what got into me, I want to be bread.*

Instead it was Marion who rose like cream
spilling over, stood in that high place

and put on shining garments. *Shoot me,*
she said, *and let the others go.* I see her

in that moment, and Charlie: they are
like me. Like us. Love them, love

yourself. Both are stones. Both are bread.

## Sacrament: Central Bus Station

It's about the coming and going of hearts, souls and tongues—
two home boys pass, jostling their saunter and slouch,
and that girl in the skirt slit up the side of her thigh,
nervous about her body but showing it off anyway,

the Prof with three dozen red roses for his wife's soprano birthday,
and the Mex day-laborer slouched beside the Sluggers' star pitcher,
both long limbed, both sweaty, both beat and kicking back,
both longing to be received so they can lay their aching down,

and now a mailman and mailwoman come in for a drink of water,
and Yogi, the station master, shooting the breeze with a driver,
throws a fake punch which lands just a hair from the jaw,
and both go on talking as though nothing almost happened—

we come, we strut, we warble, we offer ourselves and go,
coffee brewing, birds chirping, baby mouthing a banana,
and a driver sees me and says, I know where you live now,
yesterday I saw you shake your blanket over the balcony,

so come into the cathedral, line up, open your mouth,
receive from the day's fingers Christ's body, the wafer,
each of us is another and another and another,
some kid's mom dozing, leaning into her lover,

look at us, see how widely we display our variousness,
that transvestite wearing a sari and Sumi wrestler swagger,
and that old man, age spots and a cane, is like no other.
He eyeballs the rolling stroll of smoldering Chicanos

whose voices loose into my ears Neruda's erotic cadences,
*que me canto crecia con el agua,* song grows with the water,
and if I could take those words in my mouth like they do
I'd sing in that tongue our green being, our swaying sea.

## Song of Some Ruins

It's no use walking the beasts of my longing without you, *compañero,*
you whose name means stone the sun

moves across. Remember our house, and the statuary of clouds
drifting through the rooms? And the sheets and blankets of our habits,

and ourselves two hounds lying down. We loved
like we fought, slugging our way toward each other,
sending up flares to announce our advance. And when our city

burned, we stood in the ashes, and admired each other's
bodies. Now I ask you: how will we manage

without the steadiness of our long unhappiness? Can you say
you don't miss our furious

putting up with each other? The silver waves
go on polishing themselves. The sun goes down
alone. Tell me: is this as it should be? My body

goes on without you burnishing its crevices. Without your faults,
there is no salt. I will not again be fat.
Even my hair will abandon me, like a woman walking away

until you can't see her. So what
if I'm given other dawns? I ache
for the grandeur of uproar. Light

brings on its armadas of taxis and butterflies, and I'm forced
to go into the street

and talk to agreeable strangers.

## Las Alas

*(The Wings: A mission in a downtown barrio)*

The priest raises his palms to God,
a girl walks the mass with a dove
cooing between her light palms.

Women with dyed black hair clap
and sing, robust voices rise.
Children sit sleepily and Spanish

settles in the air. A guitarist sings;
the mass moves: stands, sits, kneels,
chants, "santos, santos." Necks bent

as shadowed faces gaze the tile floor.
The lady in the row of plastic chairs
in front of my row has fat ankles,

varicose veins. Displaced like a lilac
on the dry sand, I remember polyester
days, when K-mart sandals covered

the dry heels of women and church
laughter. Can one return to a desolate
past, before one *knew* one was poor,

before the luxurious perfume?
Jesus' eyes real and piercing, a doughy
host, God in my sour mouth.

What of all this faith among the oppressed?
Poor men hold themselves straight
when their backs cramp. The priest at Las Alas

Mission wears a white robe
unlike priests in large stained-glass parishes.
Other priests wear silky robes with gilded

ribbons. His robe is sheet-like, sparse,
and his Spanish twangs of Arkansas.
Men in polyester slacks and dirty jeans

stand shameless; calloused hands with imagined
doves, sea of dark bodies, steady lapping
of palms giving up and letting go.

**Sheryl Luna** (Arvada, CO) received the Andres Montoya Poetry Prize for emerging Latino poets. *Pity the Drowned Horses* (University of Notre Dame Press, 2005) is her first collection of poems. Her second collection, titled 7, was runner-up for the Ernest Sandeen Poetry Prize. She received the Alfredo Cïsneros del Moral Foundation Award funded by Sandra Cisneros in 2008. She teaches at Front Range Community College in Westminster, Colorado.

**David Mason** (Colorado Springs, CO) is author of *The Country I Remember* (Story Line Press, 1996), *Arrivals* (Story Line Press, 2004), and the verse novel, *Ludlow* (Red Hen Press, 2007). He is also author of two books of essays, *The Poetry of Life and the Life of Poetry* (Story Line Press, 2000), and *Two Minds of a Western Poet*, forthcoming from the University of Michigan Press. Mason lives in Colorado Springs and teaches at The Colorado College.

### Fog Horns

The loneliest days,
damp and indistinct,
sea and land a haze.

And purple fog horns
blossomed over tides—
bruises being born

in silence, so slow,
so out there, around,
above and below.

In such hurts of sound
the known world became
neither flat nor round.

The steaming tea pot
was all we fathomed
of *is* and *is not*.

The hours were hallways
with doors at the ends
opened into days

fading into night
and the scattering
particles of light.

Nothing was done then.
Nothing was ever
done. Then it was done.

## Home Care

My father says his feet will soon be trees
and he is right, though not in any way
I want to know. A regal woman sees
me in the hallway and has much to say,
as if we were lovers once and I've come back
to offer her a rose. But I am here
to find the old man's shoes, his little sack
of laundered shirts, stretch pants and underwear.

Rattling a metal walker for emphasis,
his pal called Joe has one coherent line—
*How the hell they get this power over us?*—
then logic shatters and a silent whine
crosses his face. My father's spotted hands
flutter like dying moths. I take them up
and lead him in a paranoiac dance
toward the parking lot and our escape.

He is my boy, regressed at eighty-two
to mooncalf prominence, drugged and adrift.
And I can only play, remembering who
he was not long ago, a son bereft.
Strapped in the car, he sleeps away the hour
we're caught in currents of the interstate.
He will be ashes in a summer shower
and sink to roots beneath the winter's weight.

**Maria Melendez** (Pueblo, CO) serves as editor/publisher for *Pilgrimage* magazine. She is author of two poetry collections, *How Long She'll Last in This World* (University of Arizona Press, 2006) and *Flexible Bones* (University of Arizona Press, 2010). She says, "I like thinking about the ways that poetry might prepare us to be more just and compassionate neighbors to both the human and non-human beings with which we share this planet."

### Recipe for When You're Tired of Feeding Your Family Life Cereal from a Box

            bed of coals
            fist-sized stones
            strong fan
            manzanita berries
            understanding for the lives of yellow jackets
            dry kindling
            basket tray
            boiling basket

Before light has tickled yellow jackets awake, build a fire close to their nest hole in the ground. Push smoke down the hole with the wide fan you wove last winter. After the yellow jackets are paralyzed by the smoke, dig out the nest. Carry it to a prepared bed of coals. Roast the nest. Shake out the dead larvae onto a basket tray. Mash them, then boil in a basket with hot stones. Drain and serve with manzanita berries.

### Backcountry, Emigrant Gap

I thought we fell asleep
austere and isolated—

two frogs calling across Rock Lake.

By morning, deer prints
new-pressed
            in the black ground between our tents—

            more lives move beside us
            than we know.

**Randy Phillis** (Grand Junction, CO) teaches at Mesa State College. He edits *Pinyon* and The Frank Cat Press. His work has appeared in a wide variety of journals, and he is author of two books, *A Man Explains His Posture* (Best Minds Press, 1994) and *Kismet, Colorado* (Mellon Poetry Press, 2000).

## What's a Boy to Do?

As a kid I had a choice:
stay in the car or follow him in
to Ben's, red lights and
thick smoke, sit at the bar
that came to my chin or in
a booth if I had crayons and paper.

Behind the bar, the big mirror
floated the backs of bottles
over my forehead as Dad
leaned forward,
elbow propped so his cigarette
hung above his head, studying
the barmaid's face not two inches
from his. Then he'd sit far back
and laugh, stretching carefully to ash,
and ask what went best
with pickled eggs. All that was good
with beer he already knew.

Sometimes I'd stay in the car,
play the radio and dance
my fingers across the dash, clench
the hard cool wheel and jerk
until I understood he wouldn't *be right back*.
Then I wandered the muddy lot,
floated bottle caps across puddles
and built rock solid homes for frogs.
Bored, I'd flatten my face
against the glass door for effect,
and finally drag myself in,
knuckles almost scraping across the stained
carpet and pull myself up beside him.

Other days, sent on an errand by Mom,
I'd stop in by myself, blinded
by the sudden dark and drink short
cold Cokes on Dad's tab.

But mostly, like now, I didn't like
going in alone, reading all the signs
to keep my eyes busy, never knowing
what to say to the woman next to me.

**Pattiann Rogers** (Castle Rock, CO) has authored twelve books, including *Wayfare* (Penguin, 2008), *Firekeeper* (Milkweed Editions, 2005), and *Generations* (Penguin, 2004). Her book *Song of the World Becoming, New and Collected Poems, 1981—2001* (Milkweed Editions, 2001), was a finalist for the Los Angeles Times Book Award. She is the recipient of two National Endowment for the Arts Fellowships, a Guggenheim Fellowship, a Lannan Literary Award in Poetry, and a Lannan Poetry Fellowship.

### In the Silence Following

After a freight train lumbers by,
hissing steam and grumbling curses,
metal screeching against metal, it passes
into the night (which is the empty
shadow of the earth), becoming soft
clinking spurs, a breathy whistle, low
bells clanking like tangled chains,
disappearing as if on lambskin wheels.

Something lingers then in the silence,
a reality I can't name. It remains as near
to a ghost as the thought of a ghost
can be, hovering like a dry leaf spirit
motionless in a hardwood forest absent
of wind, inexplicably heraldic. It is closest
to the cry of a word I should know
by never having heard it.

What hesitates in that silence possesses
the same shape as the moment coming
just after the lamp is extinquished
but before the patterned moonlight
on the rug and the window-squares
of moonlight on the wall opposite
become evident. That shift of light
and apprehension is a form I should know
by having so readily recognized it.

After the yelping dog is chastened
and a door slams shut on the winter evening
filled with snow and its illuminations,
someone standing outside in the silence
following might sense not an echo
or a reflection but the single defining
feature of that disappearance
permeating the frigid air.

When all the strings of the chord
are stilled and soundless, the hands
just beginning to lift from the keys,
when the last declaration of the last
crow swinging down into the broken
stalks of the corn field ceases, when
the river, roaring and bucking
and battering in its charge across
the land, calms its frothy madness
back to bed at last, then suspended
in the space of silence afterward
may be a promise, may be a ruse.


## For the Moral of the Story


For crags, for any bold, black, sharp-edged
chaos of broken rock, for pilings and high
cracking boulders and scrabbles, supreme
rising ridges, violet and buff-brown cliffs
and buttes and bluffs and deep-to-the-river-
bottom old canyons, silent, unmoving miles
and miles of granite alps and sandstone spikes,
useless peaks and impassable, deaf, mute,
without blood or breath or tongues, needing
neither sun nor night, needing no food, no
shelter, no offering, taking nothing—for all
of these that will not survive but will maintain
their fate perfectly until the last-left gust
and spiral of windblown sand has departed.

**William Pitt Root** (Bayfield, CO) taught at Hunter College, Amherst, Interlochen Arts Academy, New York University, and University of Montana. He was Tuscon's first Poet Laureate (1997—2002). He travels with his wife, poet Pamela Uschuk, when not working in a century-old stable near the Weminuche Wilderness, assembling reams of work into new collections of poetry and prose. He is also poetry editor of *Cutthroat*, and he enjoys giving readings and workshops as well as hiking, swimming, and kayaking with his cadre of creaturely companions.

### Crossing The Rez

*—for Joy*

I was hitching a ride toward twilight
southeast of Billings, middle of November,
when a pickup let me toss my gear in back.
I climbed up into the cab boozy with two old boys,
Country Western AM blaring sad songs of love.
The driver's sidekick cackled "Cold enough out there
to chrome a bobcat's balls." He hoisted a pint
of high noon moonshine, shoved it into my chapped hands.
It purely thawed my tongue as they both jawboned
down the road, pointing out into the uniform blue dark
toward Custer's Last Stand. "Never trust no Injun,
bud, no matter *how* cold it gits," they soberly
advised, shaking their heads and slowing down,
dropping me off there smack on the Rez at sunset.

And there I stood the best part of a bad hour
until along came the first car that stopped,
a rumpled one-eyed station wagon, front bumper
dangling, muffler skidding ice-glazed blacktop
just like a kid's sparkler in the dark.
                              "Hop in, par'ner,"
and in I hopped, stiff with cold, duffle on my lap,
all the wide dark faces, in front and back,
flat and friendly as old Hank Williams
carried on about good love gone bad again
from a scratchy speaker loose on the dash.
One popped the top on a Bud for me as gradually
we picked up speed, tranny wailing like a wolf,
everybody howling themselves into Hank's fix,
off-key and flat, while we hurtled through
the dark in a one-eyed comet.
                              "Where you headed?"
I answered "Sheridan." He nodded, smiled.
"Thing is, par'ner, we can't take you there.
Off-rez cops, they catch us in this heap,
hey, it's bail-time in the Rockies. When
we drop you at Wyola, just
remember this: Cold as your ass gits
        don't park it in no cowboy pickup,
you'll do just fine. And do say howdy
for us In'dins to all the pretty girls
you meet on down the line."

## Craft

Back at the rectangular harbor
sheltered by its groins of stone,
mist, I knew, still would be rising
from spaces left by fishing boats
well before dawn, since this was
the annual one-day Halibut season
when men made or lost a fortune.
But just a hundred yards inland
among the looming Sitka Spruce
older than their namesake by
many centuries, there was sunlight
on the wood-carver's shoulder
and starlight in his voice.
He chanted one of the songs
of his people, over and over
under his breath. A song
for carving totems—for Wolf
and Raven, Eagle, Salmon—
a song for the carver carving.
The place was a native museum
where the carver wore jeans and
a flannel shirt, even a watch
"so I'll know when to break."
He answered several questions
during the casual half hour
before I asked if he ever tired
of carving the same traditional
totems over and over, if ever
he thought of starting one new.
The smell of cedar rose from
his blade, he smiled, the adze
raised a few more curls. "One day
a new dreamer will come among
the People—there will be fish
again, and game, and new stories
to show us once more a path
of light through the darkness.
Then, yes, there will be new totems.
Meanwhile," he said, resuming
his task, "we tread water,
we keep our tools sharp."

**Reg Saner** (Boulder, CO) is author of four books of poems, three of which have won national prizes. His work has appeared in 150 literary magazines and more than 50 anthologies. He is also author of a nonfiction book, *Living Large in Nature: A Writer's Idea of Creationism* (Center for American Places, 2010). A longtime Coloradan, he lives in Boulder.

### Alpine Forget-Me-Nots

And if alpine terrain withheld every blessing
but the tiny forget-me-not's passion, its deep
high-country blue, what then? A world
of cold stone? Only so . . . except for grace
humble as theirs, of nearly no stature at all,
scarcely wide as the pupil of an eye.

Winter's last avalanche here is now a shambles.
Spruce trees uprooted, fir trunks snapped off, blown
or thrown downhill every whichway, like world history,
which always seems hopeless—though never to me
when held by the blue intensity of those petals,

their stamens, their pollen finer than sight.
Like keys of the kingdom, their minuscule florets.
Low as moss, perennial as sky,
tall as summer twelve thousand feet high.

### North of Wupatki

Later, where junipers gnarl and contort
like a lapsed forest living on sun-hammered
hardpan, you hear wind settle down, hear

high desert subsiding to one great quietude
this whole plateau seems to float on. It's then
at the hour when grand stone-ripened times

grow familiar as bat-flitter, Arizona's
pastels turn around, go walking steadily off
into a nightfall that kindles the evening star

for your campfire. As if desert mesas prefer
being listened to that way, constellations
rising behind them do seem to draw nearer

and burn more sincerely for never saying how far
they might take you. Yet you know yourself
native there, along with the one, the many,

the forever. And, in a hush uttered by nothing
but everything named "creation," a canyon wren
singing to the silence it came from.

## Flying with Father

He'd brake rudder, handling
the throttle and mixture, our ears
thrumming, tail lifting
like a wasp's, wheat blowing flush—

the shadow of the fuselage
raced green like a big fish
running shallows; then he pulled it up
into the sun, a magician;
my fear, his power:

The little town disappeared
with mice-teeth headstones,
playground bully, work, Jesus,
its streets running into fields
to the horizon.

He'd shout over the droning
for me to take control: I kept
the needle on the mark
that showed the wings balanced—
it wasn't his fault; he knew
there were no instruments—
"Look. You're flying."

Once, we got trapped
in clouds above highwires,
lucky enough to follow a road,
working hard together
to find an opening
that wouldn't close.

**Rawdon Tomlinson** (Denver, CO) is a retired teacher. He has written five books of poems, including *Geronimo after Kas-ki-yeh* (Louisiana State University Press, 2007). He is working on *The New Country*, poems about growing up on the plains. He says, "I'm most taken with flat lines, the sky and horizon where I grew up, landscape as metaphor."

## Deep Red

Christmas afternoon. The gifts opened
and the wrappers burned; glitter gone
from all but children's eyes, I ride out
into the country with my brother.

Winter wheat glistens keen as fur
across the fields; the cattle are dreams;
the world a postcard mailed from far-
away—so we get out to read.

Armadillos everywhere—
opossum, crow, woodpecker, rabbit.
Hungover from last night, my brother
holds up a turtle shell as though

he'd just won his first merit badge.
After war and divorce, we've come home
to look for bones and feathers in the sand
of a dry river. Cottonwoods stand guard.

I wonder at the blood between us;
how the open world contains
brothers and stars and armadillos—
the strange magnetics of love and hate.

Somewhere ahead, the crows are jabbering.
It's the owl telling them an old story
as light fails deep red
through the black tangle of trees.

## Where the Ashes Go

Gold light enters through a line of cottonwoods
winking as leaves shiver in rising breezes.

The snow that frosted Long's Peak this morning
has disappeared from mid-October's sun

just as now a sunset darkening shadow
turns the canal waters the color of wild plum.

A boy on a bicycle pumps along the dirt road,
his red dog wags its tail, and soon they pass

out of sight heading east toward coming night
moonrise, the heron's slow wings lifting it

west where along the trail to Arthur's Rock
a meadow full of bee balm waits for me.


## Raptors at Terry Lake

Eagles circle pine islands.
Midmorning. Late summer's
wheatgrass seeds ripen tawny
as a puma's flank. Sky from white
mist horizon to bluest overhead.
Raptors light on bone branches.
Far off, silica-pink tailings.
The final north peak spills gradual
to lower intervals of runoff
gurgling down pavement where
perched on a road sign meadowlarks
pause, pulse, a flow, silver fork
tines struck above a thin man
tapping his talons on his steering wheel
chewing his cigarette filter as he
stares waiting for the light to change.

**Bill Tremblay** (Ft. Collins, CO) is an award-winning poet, novelist, teacher, editor, and reviewer, whose work has appeared in seven full-length volumes of poetry. His book of poems *Shooting Script: Door of Fire* (Eastern Washington University Press, 2003) was awarded the Colorado Book Award. He has received fellowships from the National Endowment for the Arts, National Endowment for the Humanities, the Fulbright Commission, and the Corporation at Yaddo.

**Pamela Uschuk** (Bayfield, CO) is author of five books of poems, including *Crazy Love* (Wings Press, 2009). Her work has appeared widely in journals and anthologies and is translated into nearly a dozen languages. When she isn't writing, she hikes or kayaks or explores with her husband, the poet William Root. Pamela teaches creative writing at Fort Lewis College in Durango, Colorado.

## Finding Peaches in the Desert

*They taste like a woman*, you say
and bite deep into the sweet heat
squeezing through tender skin,
while I laugh, taking the fruit you offer.
We close our eyes and transport
this delicious host to our loves
flown distant as time in dreams.
*You can never eat too many,* I say and pull
another ripe peach from the desert tree.
It fills my palm, my mouth as I suck
the unhusbanded nectar.
It is as delicious as stealing light,
such innocent grace, a holiday
from history and eternity.
We bare our breasts to sun
as women have done for centuries
beside the blue water pool at ease with rabbits, shrill
wasps, the shy steps of occasional deer,
while vultures funnel midheaven.
Struck dumb by sun cauterizing
the Sonoran sky that flings its blue skirt
all the way across the ripe hip of Mexico,
we feast on peach after peach, while
peach-colored tanagers, wet
green hummingbirds and the topaz eyes of lizards
attend our anointment.
When I wipe one quarter across my breasts
and down my stomach to my thighs, I
am amazed at the baked odor of love
rising from everything I touch.
This is our ceremony to alter the news
of troops that mass for attack
in the Middle East, to alchemize all hatred
and greed, whatever name
it is given by multi-national interests.
There is no aggression in sharing rare fruit
priceless as the wide imaginings of sky
or the brilliant coinage of dragonfly wings.
Even squadrons of wasps and fire ants
with nuclear stingers turn
from attack to the pungency of this
ritual feast that celebrates love
in the desert stunned green by unusual rain.

## Loving the Outlaw

Outside, a silent arc of wings, an Osprey
so quiet doves nesting in cottonwoods might think
his passing breast a cloud.
His masked face lifts my heart
above its small dark center.
Like a trout, I imagine being stolen
by his embrace, caught inside
curling talons bright
as precise and tearing moons.
He flies, and I hold my breath
so the neighbor who'd shoot him
won't hear my arrested gasp,
the awesome clattering up in my chest.
I've always loved outlaws best,
the inky hats and habits,
their savvy laughter screened in movie houses.
This one soars
from the neighbor's trout pond
where's he's taken another Rainbow
back to the lawless sky.

*Idaho*

**Margaret Aho** (Pocatello, ID) is the winner of the Chad Walsh Poetry Prize from *Beloit Poetry Journal*, and her chapbooks have been published by Limberlost Press and Blue Scarab Press. She has taught poetry at the Teen-Parent Center and at the women's prison, both in Pocatello.

## to be flanking the petiole

to be stipules

that stipulate nothing but

basal appendants:  two small leaves fused

vas-like  beak-like    a mouthpiece for stems    to be

sessile [yes]    be sap-attached   be selah's rest-stop:      a

breather     abeyance      and canted      inclined [free]

to carry a torch      be green adductors to

bring toward to further      be

bar none     be wee

be blind-faith astride still-life        en-

jambing  [o folio]  leaflines still scrolled     still unread-

able        to be long-lipped for buds        o

to be kissing the world

## Cleaning a Rainbow

I open it with my long blade under the bright flow
of well water and there lie the finny wings
a moth is beginning to fold,
and then I see the river again, and where I stood
in sun- and rain-slant, that arc of color, the trout
coming down, pulling everything with it, the cold mountain
stream, the boulders blue and yellow and red, pines wind-pushed
among them and scrubbed to a silvery finish, current-salved, their limbs
lashed by tendrils of pale canary grass, all inside it and coming down,
the veined pebbles inside it and coming down, rolling, even the pearly
stone a raw-throated raven kicked loose, the lovesick bray
a wandering mule gave out causing a moose at first-
light browse to look up, the moony call
an owl still can't stop giving softly inside it, the slow-waking
kayaker's deep satisfying sleep washed from her eyes vividly inside it,
all inside it and coming down, finding their places, the feathered layers
of flesh making room, the pursy fir and lean young alders
in league with the willows, all bending, their refusals to snap
quietly folded inside it, their needles and leaves and aspirations, too
subtle to separate, completely inside it, tracks large and showy
and barely there become petite, hair-thin bones, become murmuring
rib-chimes, choirs, echoes from the lightest touch inside it and coming
down the river, embraced by the scent of cherry and musk, by the shy
fairy slipper, by bear's breath and the must oozing
from a single wild grape, by incense cedar, myrtle
and skittish skunk, all rank and sweet together, all
brushings and sighs coming down, through slick spidery worm-scrawl
falling, flicker-knock, locked horn and cocky treble-cry falling, famous
stalking and leaps lost in the furling eddies, the heart sucked
under, fibril and seed and viscid yolk sucked under, necks
nuzzled, licked, whirling around astonished, dogtooth violet and thorny
rosebush torn from their root mesh, garnishing all, and everyone rushing
down, down to this small washing, this curl of final composure
I hold in the bowl of my hands kneeling to receive it.

**Gary Gildner** (Grangeville, ID) received the Iowa Poetry Prize for *The Bunker in the Parsley Fields* (University of Iowa Press, 1997). His other awards include the William Carlos Williams, the Theodore Roethke, and Pushcart prizes. He has held fellowships from the National Endowment for the Arts, Breadloaf, MacDowell, and Yaddo, and Senior Fulbright lectureships to Poland and Czechoslovakia. He lives in Idaho's Clearwater Mountains.

## Ella

Hiking through the timber sometimes I still
see Ella, a flash of black and tan flank I know
can't be her, yet I pause, always, and listen,
my gaze in that fleeting direction. I stop,
at least I think I do, out of brief confusion:
it wasn't Henry—Henry remained at my side —
but what other creature looked like her? Ran hard
like her, low and lean? A coyote? wolf? mountain lion?
The truth is no animal, nothing flashed by or quick
Henry would have said so. And on we go, if in fact
we ever stop. Yes, I tell myself, I'm getting older.
I spend a lot of time alone.  That I once kept a dog
like Ella, whose spirit I loved, who drove me crazy too
because she refused to mind, means what, exactly,
as we make our way? She was the last
of the litter, a runt whom nobody, the owner said,
looked at twice. After selecting Henry, I took her
and she took me. If she learned anything she learned it
only for the treat and promptly forgot—or didn't care.
Those beautiful pearly black eyes—from the Rottweiler father—
she knew how to use on me, after dragging home
another bloody rag of fur. She ran deer, for a while
even enticed Henry along (though he really wanted to mind—
you could see it later in his smoky remorseful eyes).
I tried everything—the leash, more affection, the rolled-up
newspaper, books; nothing took; nothing won her
attention for long except Henry, who got
the Australian shepherd mother's softest parts,
which Ella loved to touch: crawling into a spoon-curl
with the accommodating brother on his
bale of straw in the sun, rarely using her own. At will
she jumped the kennel and came home smelling foul
about the face, poor Henry pacing, pacing
until they lay wrapped in their common house,
peaceful as lovers. The times she got sick
I nursed her back, at first saying I was sorry
to see her like this, later on calling her a bitch.
"*Now* will you learn?" She never did.  Hanging around
the yard, as Henry did, was not her idea of being
a dog, and the rope now holding her there made us all mournful.
But that was the story, I told her. "You've got something
nothing seems to fix." I found no joy, felt
no victory in the long hours she lay looking old
in the grass, how she'd nibble a little, notice
a nuthatch work its fussy way down a larch
and then lose interest. She refused
to get in my truck to go see the vet, and bit
my hand when I tried to pick her up.

"She's into self-pity," he laughed on the phone,
"just needs a little time to go by is all."
Weeks went by. Looking at each other we were not
betrayed or estranged or even fellow prisoners,
it was worse, I thought, this thing for which no word
seemed good or bad enough. One evening I was chopping wood.
Perhaps behind those bright, despairing eyes she understood
the way before I did—no doubt I'm rationalizing now—
but she came and stood as far as the rope would reach,
stood very still and so close to me, gazing down
at nothing much—chips of bark, dying dandelions—all
I had to do was turn the ax to its blunt edge,
and without hate or love or anything
nearly so clear, blacken my mind a moment.


## Spring Evenings


Growing up in Flint I turned the dirt
with a spade in our family's garden
while my sister Gloria watched the baby
and the baby, on bowed, rubbery legs,
watched our dad roll his eyes and wink

leaning on his rake. Mother was the one
who got this going, at the back door
wiping her hands on her apron and warning
we didn't have much time left—"Everything's
almost ready." I love this homely scene

I can't hold still. Fifty years later—
that first garden long gone, Dad too, and last
fall my sister, who looked up from her usual morning
toast and coffee to say something funny
was going on—I turn the dirt in the raised beds

on my Idaho mountain: there's Mother again
wiping her hands, and there's Dad, almost
falling over, making the baby dance and laugh,
though what I'm smiling at are Gloria's
last words working to keep something

alive. Which is why we can't just quit
and go in right away, right? Why we can't
help helping ourselves to a little more,
never mind that it's so small
we can only get lost in it.

**Larry N. Gwartney** (Salmon, ID) is a retired English teacher and an avid whitewater rafter. Gwartney's works of fiction and poetry have been published in *Idaho Magazine, Serpentine Magazine,* and Boise State University's *Cold Drill.* He is author of a novel, *The Ballad of China Lee.*

### Whistle Pigs

Rifles heavy in half-man hands,
We clambered up Black Rock Ridge.
Hunkering behind lichen-covered boulders,
We settled in like snipers,
Pushed the tips of our forefingers
Against the wet, red toads of our tongues and
Puffed out the mimicking calls.
Our sharp chirps floated over
The stone-slung hills like a death wind
And ricocheted against cross-canyon walls.
Rock chucks scrambled from their burrows
And popped up into our crosshairs.
Trembling like young lovers, we touched our triggers
And yellow-bellied critters crumpled like old lunch bags.
We waited until the echoes skittered away.
Then our whistles lied again and
Two more bucktoothed fur-balls turned to targets.
We zeroed in and they died, too.
Later, we trophy-ed the senseless bodies high
Then tossed them in the weeds as a thing that's done,
Shoulder-slung our rifles and sauntered home.

## New Year's Eve

I was driving, the kids in back asleep
as you nodded beside me.
Fat flakes of snow floated down
out of the night and were swished away
by the wipers. I couldn't see the river,
only feel it out there, urgent and black
beyond the road, its near edge
sealed by a lid of ice. Something
bolted through our lights and was gone,
the figment of a living
thing, felt, yet barely visible, that lingered
in the back of my mind and
lunged on fierce through the drifts,
beast or its ghost receding, circling.
There is no end to our separateness—
what makes us love one another
is knowing how frail and lost we are.
At the cabin, each with a child bundled
in our arms, we climbed to the loft
and those rickety web-strewn cots.
Far in the night I woke to the sound
of snow falling, a soft tampering,
lovely, indescribable. Above each cot
a dim halo of breath rose in the cold,
hovered for a moment and was woven
with the others, then nothing if not gone.

**William Johnson** (Lewiston, ID) is Professor Emeritus at Lewis-Clark State College. He is author of *At the Wilderness Boundary* (Confluence Press, 1996) and *Out of the Ruins* (Confluence Press, 2000), which won the Idaho Book Award. He has received fellowships from Fishtrap, the Environmental Writing Institute, the Idaho Humanities Council, the Idaho Commission on the Arts, and the National Endowment for the Arts. He served as Idaho Writer-in-Residence from 1998—2001.

**Ron McFarland** (Moscow, ID) has been teaching literature and creative writing at the University of Idaho for nearly forty years, and he's still not tired of it. He has served as Director of the Creative Writing Program and faculty advisor to the literary magazine, *Fugue*, and to the University of Idaho Soccer Club. In 1984 he was named Idaho's first State Writer-in-Residence. He has edited four poetry and critical anthologies and authored five scholarly books, three books of poetry, and two collections of prose.

## Fishing in Last Light

Fishing in the dying light I notice
something is killing the white pines,
bark beetles probably,
and off to the west
Plum Creek Timber Company has drained
another mountainside.
Someday this stream will yield to silt,
and its trout will spill away or die
trying to stay against the odds.

A sudden splash from the far bank
draws me back to the moment.
As the air darkens
I search for something light,
dun, mothy, drained of color,
something I can see on the current,
a Light Cahill
riding high on the ripples.
The rainbow reads in ultra-violet,
finds color and light,
and strikes.

I used to fish with a neighbor
who lies now in a coma
hoping to die.
His eyes went fast,
and then his body began to lose itself.
His blood
ran in strange currents
against its own flow, surged wildly.
I watched his daughter take him out
on long walks late in the evening
when all the colors had run together.

We never got to know each other well.
When we attacked a stream
he would go one way and I another,
and at the end of the day we'd meet,
happy to have fished so well
alone together.

Two rainbows now lie in my creel,
clean and cool.
In the last light
an old fisherman comes around the bend.
He wears a bright red pork-pie hat
bristling with trout flies:
Caddis, Grasshopper, Stonefly, Adams,
Coachman, Humpy, Renegade, Gnat.

Of course in the growing dark
I can only imagine the names
of those old feathery acquaintances.
The fisherman smiles and nods
like someone I've met before.

## The Bird Hunter's Art

My two old shotguns propped in the corner
mock my wife, who believes our home
a work of art.
           I tell her they're temporary,
just until I get around to cleaning them,
reminding her with a glance at the ceiling
of her long deferred dust mop.
                 Enter our front
door to a spare and decorous assemblage of
furniture in muted colors: aqua sofa, ecru
easy-chair, tawny carpet, a Turkish prayer rug
featuring pairs of leopards, panthers:
                   Two cranes
soar overhead looking left and right over their
outspread wings. Gift of a former lover.
At eye level, left and right of the blinded window
onto the deck in back, two well-framed
pencil drawings, gifts of an old friend.
Over the gas fireplace we never use,
                 that bright
bush orchid painted by an Australian artist
whose oils never seem to dry. Balanced plants
whose nomenclature escapes me; the carved gourd
candleholder featuring four perfect dragonflies,
gift from her sister;
            the serving plate commemorating
our first anniversary hung from the wall: Two herons
in blue on blue-green-off-white background,
their long necks entwined in love;
two champagne flutes hand-blown in Virginia,
wedding gift from her cousin.
               In the next room
a Steinway grand Van Cliburn played on fifty years ago:
Brahms' Second Piano Concerto.
               I point out
the Remington twelve-gauge automatic dates from
nineteen-ought-eight, my great grandfather's last gun,
and that beloved double-barrel Lefever
belonged to the grandfather of an old friend
now deceased.
           Antiques, then: They don't make them
like that anymore, the solid walnut stocks, the men
who raised them to their shoulders before the wars,
artists and lovers of another sort.

**Tiffany Midge** (Moscow, ID) is a member of the Standing Rock Sioux and recipient of the Diane Decorah Poetry Prize Award from the Native Writers Circle of the Americas for her collection of poems, *Outlaws, Renegades and Saints: Diary of a Mixed-Up Halfbreed* (Greenfield Review Press, 1994). She earned an MFA from the University of Idaho.

## After Viewing the Holocaust Museum's Room of Shoes and a Gallery of Plains Indian Moccasins: Washington, D.C.

The portrait is clear:
one is art, the other evidence.
One is artifact
the other atrocity.
Each is interned
behind glass,
with diagrams
and panels,
a testament to miles
walked. Both
are worn,
each a pair,
one is cobbled
one is beaded.

At my tour's end
can I buy a key-chain shoe?
Will I be assigned
the ID card
of one of the perished
at Wounded Knee?

The moccasins
are beautiful.  Seed pearls
woven intricate as lace.
We don't mourn
the elegant doe skins,
we admire the handicraft.
We don't ask from whose soles
do these relics come from?
We don't look for signs of resistance,
or evidence of blood.

Nor do we wonder
if he was old
and passed in his sleep,
or if this child
traded for a stick of candy
or a pinch of dried meat.
We do not make assumptions
of original ownership at all.

Their deaths were not curated,
not part of an installation. We
don't absorb their violent
and harrowing ends under soft
lights or dramatic shadows.

We look right
through them,
more invisible
than the sighs
of ghosts.
And then we move
on to the next
viewing,

and the next,

and the next,

to another
collector's trophy
lying beneath
a veil of glass.

**Diane Raptosh** (Boise, ID) serves as the Eyck-Berringer Endowed Chair in English at the College of Idaho, where she teaches literature and creative writing. She has published widely in journals such as *The Los Angeles Review*, *Michigan Quarterly Review*, and *Women's Studies Quarterly*. Her poetry, fiction, and nonfiction have appeared in anthologies in the United States and Canada. She has won three Literature Fellowship competitions sponsored by the Idaho Commision on the Arts. She lives with her family in Boise.

## Husband

She didn't have one, and never had, if *have* was the right verb for knowing someone in this way and referring to someone with this word. She had had children. Two of them. She had had friends. She had had, or, as she had heard it said, had *taken* lovers. Still, through all these years she had felt more or less tended to, almost thoroughly husbanded, though by what or whom exactly it was hard to say— certainly by some of the men she had been with, and some of the women, sometimes by her own mother even, but equally often by a single idea, such as Schoenberg's, who believed all progress in social thinking and feeling had come about through force of longing. With equal frequency, though with less predictability, she had felt cared for by certain objects, such as a spotted yellow pear, the dark fetal curl of the dog's tail, or an ancient hay derrick, tall and rangy, pointing out the far end of the world. Sometimes when she went to a movie by herself—something she often did—she would tell the ticket-taker that her husband would arrive at any minute. She simply liked the sound of the word, and she took it entirely, and many times a day, as hers.

## At the Truckstop Cafe

After open house at school, my children and I
find the only place open this time of night. A steamy cafe,
filled with men. The room is intimate with them,
their smell, their hair, their tired clothes.

Most of these men work in the mountains,
where wind and snow and solitude crumble
even the craggy rock face. These men have lived
their whole lives here, not like us.

Covered in grease and pine pitch after a day's work,
our neighbor Earl joins our table. He sighs
as he sits, the way a tree groans in the wind,
lonely on the shadowed slopes.

*How's Ruth?* I ask, knowing their five children
are grown and gone. His wife is living
three hours away in a college town.
She wants Earl to come too.

But he won't. He's going to stay here
and work the skidder. *These are the best years of your life*
he tells me. Turning to my sons, he says,
*Don't let your wife get an education. She will ask*
*you questions you cannot answer.*

**Wendy Simpson** (Coeur d'Alene, ID) has published poems, essays, articles, and movie review columns. She and her husband have two grown sons, and she enjoys reading, writing, and foreign films. She is working on a novel about the Dirty War and the Mothers of the Disappeared, whose children were victims of Argentina's dictatorship.

**Georgia Tiffany** (Moscow, ID) has received a Washington Commission for the Humanities Grant and a National Endowment for the Arts Fellowship and was an Institute Fellow for the Washington State Arts Education Project. Her poems have appeared in various anthologies and literary journals including *Agenda, Weber Studies, Tar River Poetry, Flint Hills Review, Willow Springs, Mid-America Poetry Review,* and *Rhino.* Her chapbook, *Cut From the Score,* was published by Night Owl Press.

## Trouble with Kindness

The baby raccoon holds out his paws.
I stand disarmed.
Already he has devoured a cookie
and the half-eaten sandwich
my daughter brought home from school.

Now he wants more, and I think how lovely
to be trusted by another world.
To this masked carnivore
I offer up bread,
a glob of peanut butter,

a sentiment or two
about creatures great and small.
He is all cocked head and gratefulness,
licking his fingers,
and I am sentiment reassured.

But when he learns
to turn the doorknob, raid the cupboard,
unscrew the peanut butter jar,
and leaves a bird's head on the stoop,
a trail of robin breast and entrails in the yard,

when he stands guard on the back porch,
waits for my return from shopping,
insists on being first
to check the Camry trunk for apples, pears,
free-range chicken thighs,

I think, Everyone knows how this will end;
everyone knows
the little mirror behind the eye reflects light.
His ancestry goes back 30 million years.
Do I pretend not to know

he is the one who can see in the dark?

## The Other World

So here is the old buck
      who all winter long
had traveled with the does
      and yearlings, with the fawns
just past their spots,
      and who had hung back,
walking where the others had walked,
      eating what they had left,
and who had struck now and then
      a pose against the wind,
against a limb-snap or the way
      the light came slinking
among the trees.

Here is the mangled ear
      and the twisted, hindering leg.
Here, already bearing him away
      among the last drifts of snow
and the nightly hard freezes,
      is a line of tiny ants,
making its way from the cave
      of the right eye, over the steep
occipital ridge, across the moonscape shed-horn
      medallion and through the valley
of the ear's cloven shadow
      to the ground,
where among the staves
      of shed needles and the red earthy wine
they carry him
      bit by gnawn bit
into another world.

**Robert Wrigley** (Moscow, ID) is author of seven collections of poems. He is a former Guggenheim and two-time National Endowment for the Arts Fellow and teaches at the University of Idaho, where he also served as Director of the MFA Program in Creative Writing. His books include *Earthly Meditations: New and Selected Poems* (Penguin, 2006); *Lives of the Animals* (Penguin, 2003); *Reign of Snakes* (Penguin, 1999), winner of the Kingsley Tufts Award; and *In the Bank of Beautiful Sins* (Penguin, 1995), winner of the San Francisco Poetry Center Book Award.

**Progress**

You begin to fear all the nowheres are somewheres now.
Everywhere's been discovered. Is there anywhere you can go
and find a hair-netted octogenarian wrangling a walker
and four massive, camp-sized cast iron skillets full

of Sunday dinner fried chicken at 9:00 am
and ask if she's serving breakfast, then have her say
"Sure thing, hon, but you'll have to wait on yourselves"?
Remember how pretty you were? Well, your sweetheart was

beautiful and all you wanted was some
sunnyside up eggs and bacon with hashbrowns
a white boat of peppery pan gravy,
and a mason jar of homemade apple butter

you'd have to pry the disk of wax out of
and dollop on your toast with a long-shanked teaspoon.
These days Main Street features two antiques emporia,
a coffee shop, and a wine store offering Friday night

tastings of the latest regional Cab Franc cuvee.
The café's become an office dealing in view lots,
weekend lakeside rentals, and time share condominiums.
That was a twenty-five years ago, you tell yourself.

The old chicken-frying woman probably never saw
what's become of the place, though what with the baskets
of brightly colored artificial geraniums hanging
from the vintage lamp posts and the new pocket park

with a memorial to the loggers of yesteryear,
she'd probably approve. There's a new high school too,
and according to its electronic marquee sign,
not only is there a girls' basketball team but they've won

the state three-B championship for the second time this year.
And probably the granola and yogurt breakfast parfait
with seasonal fruit from California's central valley
you had this morning was better for your arteries anyway.

Your sweetheart's still beautiful and you're willing
to settle for distinguished or fairly well preserved,
but the jam this morning comes in those tiny single-serving jars
sealed with a stirrup of foily paper, and you remember

how that morning's apple butter was explosive with cinnamon
and cloves, how the tang came from the cooked
to submission red and golden mottled peelings,
and how the old lady wheeled and toddled

over to the kitchen doorway and called you back to
"Try this for a finish up," and it was a plank of sweet cream
strudel still warm from the oven, a perfect square of butter
liquefying itself on top, and you and your sweetheart split it

and because of it all fell more deeply in love than before,
and after paying the ridiculously tiny bill and thanking
the kindly cook, drove up the lake road and found
a perfect spot in what is now an eighteen hole, pro-designed

golf course, and made love on a grandmotherly quilt,
within a body's length of the cold clear water,
and lay there for an hour in the sun, as naked and at ease
as no one in that place will ever be again.


## Misunderstanding

They've made love in the woods again
and now she's asleep, her head on his belly,
and he only wants to study her as she naps.

But the black carpenter ant, the one he's watched
climb the curve of her right breast,
now wanders from the pinkish aureole borderlands

in spirals round and round and round again,
which is why he reaches as carefully as he can
and plucks the ant up and flicks it back to the forest,

apologizing at just the moment she opens her eyes
and smiles, then closes them, and allows herself
to sleep again, although he was talking to the ant.

**Nadine York** (Boise, ID) is grateful to be enjoying retirement from a lifetime of multiple careers as teacher, landscaper, and mental health therapist. She says she has "plenty of time now to write and enjoy the pursuit of life, liberty, and adventure." Her poetry has appeared in *Albatross, Cabin Fever, The Talisman, Standing: Poetry by Idaho Women,* and *The Boise Visual Arts Chronicle.*

## Practical Math

I remember thirty
how I slunk around the corner of twenty-nine
and entered the back door
quietly
No horns or whistles

Oakland's MacArthur Park
was the party
and an apple
shared with children
aged four and three
was my cake

Pocket knife through
red delicious flesh
sliced in half and in half again
gave us four quarters
for three of us

Who gets the fourth piece
they asked
We do of course
So half and half again
the quarter into four
for just us three

They laughed as each fourth piece
smaller and smaller
got divided
right down into invisible
which was indivisible
by anything

# *Montana*

**Sandra Alcosser** (Florence, MT) works with Poets House and the Language of Conservation in collaboration with scientists and libraries to support sustainability of tribes and species. Her book, *Except by Nature* (Greywolf Press, 1988) was selected for the National Poetry Series and received four national awards, including the Academy of American Poets' James Laughlin Award. James Tate selected *A Fish to Feed All Hunger* (University of Virginia Press, 1886) for the Associated Writing Programs Poetry Series Award. Montana's first poet laureate, Alcosser teaches in the graduate programs of San Diego State and Pacific University.

### Spittle Bug

I watched an insect dive
upside down in a crystal bowl.
Magnified, it resembled
a friend's identity crisis—
red eyes, amorphous body
arched like a scorpion.
Probing the water with an iris stem,
I rescued the swimmer,
helped it crawl to the vase lip,
then complimented myself, as if
the bug were my own invention.
It rested on the flower's parchment,
hyperventilating, while I went off
to a day's work. When I returned
it had climbed higher, slathering
purple flesh with froth. Stalled
in one spot like an indulgent head
lost in shampoo, it had taken
the sweet petals with it,
rolling them in babble,
till they were stunted and scabbed.
It looked so harmless at first
roiling in its own spit,
I think I shall call it
gossip bug.

## Glory Monster

Tipped goblets, the blue heron
flap across the glassy pond.
Two then four they chase each other,
stop at the penciled shoreline
to wrap their necks together.

How like you, Iris, twisting
your green stems in the grasses.
Heron flowers, humid and patient as fists
that spring to flying buttresses,
stained cathedral naves—

if I were to make a monster, Iris,
to chase me, to suffocate in its bloom,
it would be you. Here comes Iris
marching across the pasture, waving
her rapier skirt, twirling

her caterpillar furs. Oh sing
of the brevity of life
and the ephemeral nature of pleasure,
erotic and funereal anguish,
dark-rivered nectar.

Once I lay by a bed of iris
and once by my dying father.
Each time I pressed my face
against the damp
and shriveling flesh.

**Minerva Allen** (Dodson, MT) grew up on the Fort Belknap Reservation with her grandparents. She entered school at age five speaking Assiniboine and Gros Ventre and learned English so quickly she served as tutor for other students in her elementary school. She is a life-long educator. She has worked as Head Start Director, Bilingual Director and Federal Programs Director at the Hays-Lodge Pole School District, and served as President of the Montana Bilingual Education Association. She is the mother of eight children (and raised six more) and numerous grandchildren.

## My Indian Relatives

Where are you now?

How far away do you live?

Where are you going?

Did you leave to the Sky?

Your thoughts are small.

Walk the Earth.

Medicine is strong.

Look at the Earth.

Look at it all.

The Sky and Earth are big and round.

Stand back, look hard at the Sky.

It is hard to return from the Sky.

Tipi is round like the Sky and Earth.

The door is open for you to see.

The Sky and Earth are for you to live.

If you go you will never return.

Talk, they say, the wind will listen and bring it back.

Everyone will listen

When the song drums pound, they will listen.

In the Spring the wind will say,

Where are you, and how are you?

## Nakoda Meda Goo Yeah Be

Dough ka he be?

Dough ta hon ya nee?

Dough ka E na nah?

Max be ya eNa Na ching ga?

Da goo you Ching ga Jusina.

Ma Ko cha yeah Mani.

Pe Zuta me hane.

Ma Ko cha a key da.

Max be ya, mako cha nee na tonga.

Me ma nee.

Na she max be ya nee na a kee da.

Yea knech da ching yeah kneck da suedax da.

Tipi me ma nee Max be ya, Makcha zhe cha.

Ti oba ushpha zhe cha a kee da.

Max be ya, makocha Zhe cha yea nee.

Eyeah yeah chanyeah kneesh.

Ga new za geche woe knaga Na xoo be.

A cha goo beck, oyate nax oo be day.

Ga moo be no wa be nax oo beckla.

Wedu Ga news ya a yeahka day,

Dokey ya oo, dokey ya hone?

## Zu Yea E Nanah

Zu yea E nanah.
Woe yea be wache gra a.
Ooshe ma ghee yea.
Chay yea wa oo
Tay hon was che mnog knik.

Ah bay do wajee
Cheek su yea.
Zu yea E nanah.
Woe yea be was che gra a.
Ooshe ma ghe yea.
Chay yea wa oo .
Chanda ma seejaw.

HayXada wake su yea.
HayXada we cho nee yea.
Wake su yea
O to weigh da a che yea,
Wache mnage wache hay.

Zu yea E nanah.
Woe yea be wa gra a
Chay yea waoo
Wana tay hon wakinikt day no.
EyaXa makocha
Zhe che yoda wa kinknt da.
O yea ghee he unkash me yake su yeash.

## You Went to War

You went to war.
Have pity.
I go crying.
I will not see you for a long time.

One of these days, I might forget you.
You went to war.
I will write to you.
Have pity on me.
I'm going crying.
My heart is sad.

I will not forget yesterday.
I will not forget yesterday.
When you come home to this place,
I want to see you again.

You went to war.
I'm going crying the long way home
To the mountain country.
That's the way I'm going home.
Do not forget me.

## Circle of Time

Summer grew old.
Wind of the South slept.
North Wind awoke, singing his song.
Howling. Pushing his way
in to the lodges.
Mother Earth slept under her blanket.
Old Man North was angry at this moon;
he made the fires burn brightly.
The Storm People didn't stay.
The Thunderbird came
and frightened Old Man North away.
The People sang welcome songs to him.
"Age gee ya ho."
Summer came back, young and wrapped
in her robes of beautiful colors.

## Beautiful Existence

Death my friend is not long.
Wrapped in a tanned buffalo robe,
painfully I sank to the floor,
forcing my aching knee joints to bend.
I sat cross-legged.
Fumbling for my ceremonial pipe,
filling it with tobacco from a
small pouch, I lit it.
Smoke wreathed around my head.
I felt for my drum and began a faint
tapping on the taut rawhide.
The voice that once rang from mountain
tops, echoed along beaver streams.
Softly I sang a chant of death.
All is quiet.

**Judy Blunt** (Missoula, MT) spent more than 30 years on wheat and cattle ranches in northeastern Montana, before leaving that life to attend the University of Montana. She recounts her ranching years in her award-winning book of essays, *Breaking Clean* (Knopf, 2002). Recognition of her work includes the National Endowment for the Arts and Guggenheim Fellowships. She teaches in the creative writing program at the University of Montana, Missoula.

## When Cowboys Cry

In a nearly shadowed corner
beyond his mother's open
coffin, just a dozen running
steps from the calm ranks

of flower carts and mostly
empty folding chairs, the whole
of my father's face simply turned
and came apart, like an old wall

falls one hard brick at a time.
And the whispering all stopped
and the little girls crossed
their new Mary Janes and watched

the new empty place this all
left behind, and the mourners
stared hard at the mother's
sealed eyes, and the men read

their hats for signs—like nothing
solid can grow on soft ground
or things usually heal best
when they're left alone—so no one

meddled until it all came together
and the mother was wheeled away
with her flowers and the gunmetal
chairs were paired neatly and put

aside and my father took his place
in the first pew and gave his mother
away with good solid grace and shook
hands with everybody after. Later

at the big supper they all said
they thought the better of him
for a few tears, and if not here
for chrissake, among friends, then where?

## Showdown

Grounded to her room, my daughter shook out
wings on her way up the stairs, spread them
at the window, then bailed out of childhood
in freefall, an evolution of will I caught
by chance as she sailed off the eaves
to the back lawn, a flash of color
filling ten empty feet of air, and gone.
Captured two blocks from home, she weighs
my invitation and shrugs, folds herself, clipped
and calm into the car, surrendering
nothing on the short ride back, discovery
defined in lofts and curves pulled sharp
as sealing wax, solid as new muscle,
as final as that.
                    There will be no humble
retreat from this one, no return
of the martyred princess who drifted
through past trials with great show
and moderated sighs. At sixteen she's grown
a first way to leave, and I find it
impossible to choose between fear and pride
at her poise, this defiant crossing
of lines that separate a mother
and a daughter, stepping into power
she's pieced together from scraps
of mine.
                    Right now I can imagine
no ritual of distraction, no moving on
to other things with this near-woman
caged in my house, cocked and sure
on her feet, bangs spoiled stiff
over eyes that measure me
by inches, this
girl, pacing by the window, turning
to stare outside, leaning to touch
the pane with no reflection, no
backward glance and nothing
but time, spinning, loaded
on the tips of her fingers.

**Heather Cahoon** (St. Ignatius, MT) is a tribal member from the Flathead Indian Reservation in western Montana. She earned an MFA in Poetry from the University of Montana, where she was the recipient of the Richard Hugo Fellowship. She also holds an interdisciplinary Ph.D. in History, Anthropology, and Native American Studies. Her book, *Elk Thirst* (University of Montana, 2005) won the Merriam Frontier Award. She lives in Missoula, Montana, with her husband and son.

### Rescue at L8000 Road

A broken axle promises nothing
eleven miles above Niarada.
Logging roads lead to Dad,
Carol, and the broken boom truck.
Everything is white. Pines shrug
under the weight. Tracks place deer
in openings among trees.

Kneeling at the back dually
we take apart the axle.
Two hours later, hands and faces
blushed pink, we crowd a fire
that burns clean, almost no sound at all.
Our boots and pant legs steam dry.
We leave before dark, wanting
to look for deer on the way out.
We're invisible.
Snow silences our moving.

A buck moves outside Dad's window.
He shoots. It falls, tries to run once
then falls and is quiet. Daniel and I run
down the ravine to drag it to the truck.
We reach him as his lungs heave out.
Nothing. His leg moves and I think
he's alive. I don't touch him.

Dad comes. He and Daniel drag
the deer to the road, leaving blood
for me to follow, a trail across snow.
The leg moves again. I ask
if he's still alive. Daniel says it's just
his nerves. He tells me to touch its eye.
If he blinks he's alive, if not he's gone.
I move to touch the eye, deep brown
and shining my reflection—my face
almost entirely hidden behind
my outstretched, cautious hand.
He doesn't blink.

## "Every Bit Helps"

*(Under the Orange Street Bridge,
Missoula, Montana)*

On the under-bridge shelf, cocooned
in sleeping bags, overcoats, Salvation Army-
issue blankets: Willie "Railman," Injun
Tom, Anthony. Willie's first

to rise—he drank the least
of the day's proceeds from
grocery sales. Bought a 30-
pack—Anthony had most. Willie

troubles at the wide-mouthed
gasps, pulls a cover up to
shield Anthony's neck. "Okay?"
Tom wakes, "He okay?" Willie

shrugs, "No man drinks like that
and be okay." Tom shakes out
of his huge overcoat, huge man, moves
down bank to the Clark Fork

River, removes a yellow stone, white
stone, black stone, red stone from
his jeans' pocket, lifts each, bows
East—South—West—North, raises

open palms to the blue sky, lowers to
the green earth, rejoins Willie: "Prayed
the directions for him—Indian-style—
Lord's Prayer too. Every bit helps."

**Ed Chaberek** (Superior, MT) has worked for the Missoula Salvation Army and in local schools. Ed's chapbook, *The Berkshire Polish Bar*, was published in 1999 by Ibbetson Street Press. He is author of a collection of poems about Missoula street people, *The Market Under the Orange Street Bridge.*

**Victor A. Charlo** (Dixon, MT) writes: "I was a stutterer, 'Wheeeeere is my coat?' I would say. They sent me home from first grade because of it. I had my new clothes on and all. And they teased me, too. My father said, 'Boy, you're really smart. You finished school in one day.'" Vic is the great-great grandson of Chief Victor Charlo of the Bitterroot Salish. Through lineage, he is recognized as a spiritual leader. His daughter, April, translates her father's poems into the Salish language. He is author of *Good Enough* (Many Voices Press, 2008).

## Agnes

*—for Agnes Vanderburg 1979*

We hide-tan here at Agency Creek
and at Valley Creek. Hard work
that lets your mind go as you wait
for the rest of your life. Soft hide,
so soft wind blows like cloth.
Hair white with hide.

She, Agnes, watches and lets us know in old
Salish tongue the word for scraper that I
remember now. So hard. So to the point.

Why did I learn how to write? Why did I want to?
Is it worth the loss of your world going away?

## Bad Wine

You can love a dying Indian,
But when he drinks bad wine
And breaks your best glass
You give him to the wind.

## Remember This Time

This girl with stops in her throat
makes me remember Evaro school house
    the first day of school.

I stutter like this girl yet I want
to stay in this one room warmth.

Fear shakes my feet to teacher desk.
When she asks my name,
I know if I try to tell her
I, I, I will stutter
and she will send me home.
I cry instead. She sends me home anyway.

This girl lives in Boulder, she says,
and the smell of Evaro school house brings me home.

## Buffalo

Buffalo on the edge of life

On the edge of my life

We see the buffalo

Sky lined

Against the moon

.We sing ancient songs that bring us

Fun racing against the prickly pear

We dream of a new life

Full of wonder

We will know forever

Buffalo on the edge of life.

Buffalo on the edge of life.

## Q̓ᵂeyq̓ᵂay

Q̓ᵂeyq̓ᵂay i čłčmcin i nxᵂlxᵂiltn

čłčmcin i isnxᵂlxᵂiltn

Qe wičm t q̓ᵂeyq̓ᵂay

Es kᵂłłip i sččmasq̓t

Č̓ł̓e? i spq̓ni?

Iše qe nkᵂnem t sqsps q̓ᵂelm

X̣s q̓ᵂiq̓ᵂo ci i i ċiq ččmċmus

Iše qe nspsu ?u i t sic
nxᵂlxᵂiltn

Q̓ᵂect t sckᵂłpax̣

Nem q es mi stem̓

Q̓ᵂeyq̓ᵂay i čłčmcin i nxᵂlxᵂiltn

Q̓ᵂeyq̓ᵂay i čłčmcin i nxᵂlxᵂiltn

## You, You Missed Me

Remember old house on hill with family
laughing? Remember mother being happy
and older brothers, sisters and Mom
playing stickgame with me, the youngest, not quite
old enough to play?

Remember playing rock fight with my older
brother, Gene? We would
begin in fun, but if I hit him too hard
or with too big a rock he would get mad,
and I'd be in trouble.

Remember being chased around the house,
being hit on the back with a hail of rocks,
stuttering, "You, you, you mmmm-missed me!"

195

## Put Šeẏ

Stem̓ a spuʔus?
Stem̓ łu smim̓iʔ?

Sqlqelixʷ
Sqlqelixʷ

Spqni̓ʔ
Spqni̓ʔ
Kʷk̓ʷusm̓

Q es čłac̓xenełs
Qe uł scnk̓ʷen̓

Qe uł scnk̓ʷen̓

Ci q̓ʷelm
Iše qe qe sewneʔ
Tqe sqspsq̓ʷelm

Šeẏ łu qe sxʷlšitusm
Iše qe nkʷn̓kʷn̓em
Ẏe t q̓ʷelm še qe npiyels

X̣est

Put šeẏ

## Good Enough

What's in your heart?
What's the news?

Indian People
Indian People

Sun
Moon
Stars

Watch over us
We are the chosen
people

We are the chosen
people

We hear
our
Ancient Songs

That is our guide
We sing these songs
And we are happy

Good

Good Enough

(Translation by Sophie Mays and April Charlo)

## You're Just Dirt

*—for Willie Brown*

When I put that old connection,
Latin, on the blackboard—
*human-humus-humble*
you mutter something in the Crow language:

>When somebody is bragging themselves up
we have a saying,
*"You're just dirt."*
Only it doesn't mean the same
as when white people say it—dirty.
It's like to be humble,
like that human, humus on the board.

And you want to know
if it's all right
to write about the river:

>When we kill a deer
we cut it up into little pieces,
the parts that can't be eaten,
and feed it to the river,
entrails, legs, horn.
An old man talks to the river
with the children:

>*I give to you today, deer,*
*who gave to me,*
*so he may complete his journey.*

>We sing to the river, give thanks.
We want it to be strong.

The morning Elaine dies
you hear my voice break,
yours next to mine
softer than fawn skin.
You tell me:

**Roger Dunsmore** (Dillon, MT) taught Humanities, Wilderness Studies, and American Indian Literature at the University of Montana. He was Humanities Scholar in Residence at Tuba City High School on the Navajo Reservation and Exchange Fellow at Shanghai International Studies University. Author of a collection of essays, *Earth's Mind* (University of New Mexico Press, 1997), and several books of poetry, including *You're Just Dirt* (FootHills Press, 2010), he teaches literature and writing at University of Montana Western.

The beads on this belt buckle
mean creation's fire
in all things.

And these black beads
spaced around the edge,
they're for the bad things.
That's part of it too.

Your voice, the morning Elaine dies,
telling me:

The earth is my body.
You're in sorry shape
if you can't feel it.
I never gave up
the earth.

## A True War Story

My friend's uncle
was a Marine in Korea.
His sqaud came to a cluster of huts,
smoke drifting up from one.
The squad leader ordered him
to go into that hut,
to kill eveyrone inside.
He stepped cautiously through the doorway
and waited for his eyes to adjust.
In the dim light he saw a terrified Korean woman,
children huddled up against her.
He squeezed the trigger on his M1,
emptied it into the thatched roof,
and stepped back out
through that doorway.
No one spoke.

Back home,
when he told the old people
what he had done,
they gave him a new name:
He-Who-Takes-Pity-On-His-Enemy,
and made him
the giver of names
for new-born children.

## Back into Rock

The full moon rolls over Washington
wheat fields. An eye watches & an ear
listens to the humming of the Cummins diesel,
the revolution of 18-wheels I rein
down Route 174, a no-shoulder two lane,
that pours into the Columbia basin.
Rim rock sings an epic I try to imagine.

Lost in the glare of the setting sun
on my bug splashed windshield,
the white-tailed buck in velvet
springs from the cut slope shade, hesitates,
then leaps to catch his death, the killing
I came to do. He flies, legs akimbo,
up & away, back into rock,
like some cartoon Bambi on ice—
a deer-ball swatted over the left field fence.

The fiberglass hood popped & flopping,
no way & nowhere to stop. I watch
the gauges, hope the radiator's fine.
In my mind the deer is still flying,
climbing like the red-tailed hawk
unfurled this morning over my passenger side
fender like a blanket on a clothesline
gusted by wind. It lifted from the barbed wire
fence to warn me: "Think fast—
it's coming—something is following you
(like your father's silence & thinning bones)."

I stop at the bottom of the hill,
step down from the cab to inspect the grill.
One head light & blinker are broken;
the driver-side fender is cracked.
Fracture lines whiskered with dun colored hair
trace a scar on the tractor's thigh.
As I refasten the hood, the absence of blood
makes me wonder if the little hart died.
30 tons of steel at 60 miles per hour . . .

I shiver, pissing between the duals,
& breathe the cool smells of evening on the river:
evergreens, water, sage. As I circle
the truck, it feels good to walk.
The sky is clear. Daylight's fading.
Soon the moon will rise. I climb
back in the tractor & drive one-eyed
into night. The deer tells me to trust
the moonlight. My old man nods his approval:
"Pay attention to the shadows, what's on the ground,
& keep your eyes on the goddamn road."

*—for my father, Vincent*

**Mark Gibbons** (Missoula, MT) loves his wife and two cats in Missoula, where he teaches kids poetry. He is author of four books of poems, including *blue horizon* (Two Dogs Press, 2007). One of those small-town boys who never left home, Mark drives truck and moves furniture to pay rent. He studied poetry at the University of Montana and every place the weather and his consciousness allowed.

**Jennifer Greene** (Arlee, MT) was born and raised on the Flathead Reservation in Montana. She started writing poetry when she was 20 years old, but she (secretly) has always wanted to be a writer. She is married, has three children, teaches, works on history projects, and stays up until the wee hours of the morning to write and read. Her book, *What I Keep* (Greenfield Review Press, 1999), won the First Book Award for Poetry from the Native Writers Circle of the Americas. She is Salish and Chippewa-Cree.

### Rocky Boy Visit

I saw the faded red log house where my mom once lived
when she was younger than I am now when she wore
plaid skirts & listened to Diana Ross, before she
had babies growing inside her body.

I only know this place in the stories my family told. I grew up
surrounded by fields with piles of rocks, huckleberries, buttercups,
and glimpses of moose and lanes of traffic that never stop
humming and swarming on the Flathead Reservation.

In the fields of cut yellow wheat around Rocky Boy, I see my
Grandpa Bill's hair, a crew cut—precise rows with a flat top.

In the open prairies, I see houses with hollyhocks waiting
beside front doors. I see wind blowing the full skirt of a
young woman who's waiting for something she can't see.

Two horses run toward me until a barbed wire
fence stops them; we stare at each other, and I don't
know what to say, and my hands have nothing to offer.

My grandmother spoke Cree and thought Rocky Boy was
a lonesome place. She was a pretty woman who ironed all of her
clothes, had pin curls, and bottles of perfume. She was proud
of her soft hair, soft towels, clean walls, and her thin body.

She moved to Great Falls and didn't return to Rocky Boy
until her kids buried her there.

I went to a man's house who taught in a one room school in Rocky
Boy in 1949. He married a woman from there and said he thought
she was a beauty the first time he saw her at a movie.

My hands have no memory of this soil. I try to remember the smell
of coffee in my grandmother's stories that she told about collecting
water under pine trees after the rain to rinse her hair.

It rained when I was in Rocky Boy; I walked a small dog near a road
where people drove by and recognized me as a stranger. My glasses
were wet, and I wasn't wearing a coat. I think about that morning; I told
my daughter that fog is when clouds touch the earth. Sometimes, she
asks questions, and I don't know what to say & I can only offer what I have.

## Arlee (*my hometown*)

The deadliest highway in Montana unzips itself through
the center of town. The fanciest building is the Post Office.
At night, kids ride bikes around empty gas pumps illuminated
under artificial lights.

A maze of dirt and gravel roads make a nest around the town.

In a house with the porch light turned off, a man falls in love
with a woman. His world, his children will grow roots and
sprout inside of her. Her hands will bathe the feet of his babies.

The Stockman's bar is filled with light from the inside out on
dark nights where reputations are broken like beer bottles. Many
people go to church on Sunday where they hold hands, put dollars
in a basket, and pray for sick people in each other's families.

During the 4th of July, powwow music dances its way through town
and into the hands of people smiling bright and quiet as stars. People
love each other leaned up against cars. At the powwow grounds,
teenagers walk in circles looking for each other. At powwow time,
grownups play blackjack in tin buildings and play stickgame until
the sun comes up smelling like coffee with no sugar. Some drummers
hold their throats while they sing, and fancy dancers, jingle dress
dancers, and tiny tots wait for the next intertribal.

At the high school, some teachers have taught at least two
generations of some families. Yes, there are some white
people who hate Indians and probably anybody brown but who
choose to live on a reservation. There are others who marry
Indian women and men. Yes, there are some people who never
leave because everything they love is here.

**Tami Haaland's** (Billings, MT) work has been featured on the *Writer's Almanac,* in *High Desert Journal,* and *5 AM* and in the anthologies, *Letters to the World* (Red Hen Press, 2008), *Montana Women Writers* (Farcountry Press, 2006), and *Poems Across the Big Sky* (Many Voices Press, 2006). Her collection of poetry, *Breath in Every Room* (Story Line Press, 2001), won the Nicholas Roerich First Book Award. She is Associate Professor of English and Director of the Honors Program at Montana State University Billings. She edits *Stone's Throw Magazine.*

## Liar

He yells it before she slams the car door.
"I'll walk home" she says to the closed window.

We finish her story in our own car.
In my version, she'll go to the corner,
he'll speed around the block, feel guilty,
return, and insist she get in.

In Irena's version he'll go where he's going.
She'll have to get there another way,
hitch hiking maybe or a long walk.

The story is the same and we both know it,
the way we know there are only so many stories,
perfectly formed, and they enter us
each time in shadowy variation.

Or maybe there are as many stories
as stars and we don't see them until years
after they begin to shine, our recognition that dim.

It's summer. Our windows are down. This is
earlier in our lives and the wind whips our long hair.
We are the kind of women they joke about,
another kind of story, the blonds so dumb.

But we are smart enough to know how the story
will end for that girl, smart enough to know
that if we keep on driving maybe

there's a better version up ahead just waiting
to pull its comb through our tangled hair.

## Not Scientifically Verifiable

What if I walk around the corner and
fish swim into my mind, and when a man
I don't know walks past me the thought
leaps into his mind and later he mentions
to his wife that he would like to have fish
and so she goes out to get some, since
he asked, and the word escapes from her
thoughts into the mind of the woman
in aisle three who passes it to the checker
and so on.

        Only, what if I am really
thinking of your breath on my neck, my
fingers on your shoulders, your palm on
the curve of my waist. We could explain
how these thoughts leap from one mind
to another with words like pheromone or
hormone. It's harder to say why fish might
take this course except they have been
known to swim upstream five hundred miles
as you or I might if only for a slim chance.

**Ann White Haggett** (Dillon, MT) grew up dividing her time between the Bozeman Municipal Pool, the city library, and the Southside Skating Rink. She went to Stanford and Tufts and then jumped back to her roots in Montana, where she taught first grade for 26 years in Whitefish and Starr School on the Blackfeet Reservation. Her chapbook, *Skating Backwards* was published by Pudding House in 2007.

### She Teeters

on medium heeled
mustard yellow roper boots,
shouts, *Oh yea,*
above the jukebox
*I know what makes
a rodeo queen!* Claims
she's judged Omak Stampede,
Cody Round-up,
State Fair at Great Falls.

I'm skeptical. Her coiffed curls
match the role. But what about
those long blue nails
tapping the bar
in a fingered two-step?
Then she adds, *But
I'm no Buckle Bunny.*

She's been there all right—
heart swinging on chute gates
watching cowboys pick up
their tight little Wrangler asses
from sawdust and dirt
to do the Aw Shucks Swagger
all shoulders and hips
away from the bronc.

All this for the nervous pulse
of Queen contestants sitting tall
in satin snap button shirts,
long shiny hair under
virgin white Stetsons.
Ready to tight rein silver saddled
quarter horses, show their stuff
to judges at Montana's Biggest Weekend.

## My Neighbor

painted his house
the colors of his favorite team.
Watched the playoffs
on his big-screen TV.

In his recliner
with a beer at hand
he'd coach his players out loud.
An intimate whisper
in the batter's ear.
A rant from the dugout
over a fumbled grounder.

First I met him, he swallowed
my handshake
in his bricklayer's paw,
calloused as a catcher's mitt.

Once I watched him, Sunday after church,
watering his lawn, shirtless.
A thicket of hairs down his back,
shoulders of an old bull, beer-barrel gut.

Three neighbor boys pedaled
up the walk, into a puddle
at his feet, splashing his good shoes.
*You little sons-of-bitches*, he hollered.
Turned his hose on them
as they scattered, screaming gleefully.

We didn't have much to say.
I'm no sports fan.
Nodded hellos, mostly.

When he ruptured a disk,
I drove his girls to school
on my way to work.
And brought them back.

When tragedy befell my household
—all the cards and letters,
the sickly pious condolences and prayers—
none of these lifted me much

as the day I came home
to find a battered postcard
jammed in the backdoor seal.
His team's logo, full color.
His sincere scribble,
*I'm cheering for you, pal.*

**Lowell Jaeger** (Yellow Bay, MT) teaches creative writing at Flathead Valley Community College in Kalispell, Montana, where he is also founding editor of Many Voices Press. He is the recipient of fellowships from the National Endowment for the Arts and the Montana Arts Council and author of four books of poems: *War On War* (Utah State University Press, 1988); *Hope Against Hope* (Utah State University Press, 1990); *Suddenly Out of a Long Sleep* (Arctos Press, 2009), a finalist for the Paterson Prize; and *WE* (Main Street Rag Publishing, 2010). He lives on Flathead Lake with his wife, Amy, and their three children.

## The Missionary

She stands at the door, meek as a cornered mouse.
She's been here before; the people of this house
make small-talk, smile, accept her tracts
when her eyes glaze and she musters nerve to ask,
*Do you know the Lord?* Pre-empting my reply,
she dishes leaflets, recites a speech on why
I'll never enter into the Kingdom of Hope, unless . . . .

I notice the plain folds of her plain dress,
shoes framed like little caskets for feet.
Can't be easy, stumping block-to-block
for love. Or is it fear? Her face smiles
but her eyes leak tears. My good neighbors lock
her out. She swallows hard, endures her trials,
turns, and marches onward down the street.

## Mom Said

"Till the cows come home."
Because we had no cows,
and no hope plates of pickled beets
would disappear unless we ate them.
No prayer she'd cave. No matter
how pathetic our plea.

Or "blue in the face,"
which was worse. We'd cry
ourselves blue over whose
turn it was to clear dinner dishes
or polish his shoes,
and Mom stayed cool.

All this talk in school
about a man's right to rule
his own day. Mom said, "No way.
I'm the boss, and you're the kid."
Till hell freezes over.
Which it never did.

## Chokecherries

The Crow call this time of year the Black Cherry Moon
when the rose hips are blood-bright,
spattered on their overwrought stems, and the creek
calls so clearly in words almost our own
as we come sliding down the bank.
Last night, we covered the gardens in plastic.
The chickadees were back after their wide diet of summer.
We ate the last trout, its spine curved from disease.
So much can go wrong, I want to know
what you will promise me as our hands reach in and in
through the copper, the carmine leaves.
I know you are lonely, alone with your grief
for your parents who are not my parents, for your life,
which, despite all, is not my life. The cherries
are thick here, hanging in clusters, purple-black from frost.
It has started to rain and I am chilled by it.
Each day, we promise, we will talk of our fears
of intimacy, how we still expect to be hurt when we love.
You bring me a coat from the back of the truck,
but I want to stop our task now, to sit in the cab
of the truck while the gray spills, slick with thunder.
What if I kissed you there in depth.
After so many years, I can misunderstand the difference
between instinct and obligation, how my hand
continues to grasp the stems. Keats said
poems should come easy as leaves off the trees,
but see how they cling and wrestle with their ties.
And now, the sun shines. It is not this grace
I had imagined. When Keats said poems, I meant
love. The chokecherries roll easily
into my palm, then fall into the plastic bag that binds
my wrist. Over and over, until we have enough,
until our fingers are bruised with their dark juices.

**Melissa Kwasny** (Jefferson City, MT) is author of four books of poetry: *The Nine Senses* (Milkweed Editions, 2011), *Reading Novalis in Montana* (Milkweed Editions, 2008), *Thistle* (Lost Horse Press, 2006), and *The Archival Birds* (Bear Star Press, 2000), as well as editor of *Toward the Open Field: Poets on the Art of Poetry* (Wesleyan University Press, 2004) and co-editor of *I Go To The Ruined Place* (Lost Horse Press, 2009). Her book, *Thistle*, won the Idaho Prize in 2006. She is also a novelist.

**Iris**

> *whatever*
> *returns from oblivion returns*
> *to find a voice*
> —*Louise Gluck*

The iris bulbs huddle,

their brown rags sopped,

yet above,

the light green flumes

have barely parted.

This is when I love them best

before they speak

and risk it all—

their petals washed out

under the barreling

hooves of the spring.

All night,

the creek moving stones.

I love the birds precisely

because I don't

know what they're singing.

How the iris stay

unblossomed in silt.

What if they recede

like this rain

that rests before it seeps?

How truly imperative is form?

My neighbor believes

that men must learn to be

on earth, and that

women must learn to be gods.

The tiger-striped eye

peeks out from its lids.

Why, it seems to ask,

or why not? I mean,

what does it care

for the future of its tribe?

It lives.

Its life is almost done.

Once a mind was on fire,

then it was quenched with rain,

slowed to ashes and mud.

Better the grace

of one smooth blade repeated,

sealed as a god is sealed,

than to be wrong.

**Ed Lahey** (Butte, MT) has been writing poetry for fifty years. Ed taught high school and worked on mining and pipeline operations and in the trucking business. He also taught at the University of Montana and at Carroll College. He is author of several books of poetry, including *The Blind Horses and Other Poems*, (Montana Arts Council, 1979), and *Birds of a Feather: The Complete Poems of Ed Lahey* (Clark City Press, 2005).

## The Blind Horses

The old man in the hospital bed
with his horny yellow foot
stuck through the stainless rails,
claimed that July night—the one he picked to die on—
he smelled sulfur on his gown.

When he was my age he worked the lower levels of the
Lex in a great underground corral, yoked iron tongue to
wagons filled with ruby silver and peacock copper rock,
flaked sweet hay to horses, shot the worn out.

Dozens of tramway horses hauled hard
against whippletrees—rubbed the timbered tunnels
clean—pulling down the cribbed-up drifts,
brass lanterns swinging, work bits in their teeth,
slick with mine damp and cold to the touch.

Dry stulls in the crosscut cave of that stone corral caught
fire in '98. The horses, tunnel-blind from the lack of light,
burned up in the green flame that licked the lagging
black in the Lexington Mine.

I met his eyes cracked white
like a drunk's who hasn't had a drink in months.
He said he could hear hoofbeats ring
and click against the granite footwalls.
He complained of being cold. His nostrils flared:
"I hear them breathing, Ed."

## Gimp O'Leary's Iron Works

*—for Big Ed*

You hear a lot of lies about O'Leary
but he could seal a crack in steel
no matter what the size.
His arc welder would strike
white fire and a bead
of blue-black rod would slide
along between cherry streaks,
and acrid smoke would curl away
to leave clean married steel,
not too frail, or buttered up
but straight and strong,
hard as mill forged rail.

Of course you might say,
"Don't use that example
as a metaphor for poetry.
Welding is a matter of utility."
And you'd be right. Still,
I remember the look on his face
when he'd lift his great helmet
and sneak up on the finished
job with unprotected eyes.
It was always between him
and the piece of steel—
a struggle of molecules and will.

Often others would say to him,
"Damn good job" or some such thing.
If it was, he'd grin, and look again,
as if he thought the natural light
would show a flaw, or bridge
that didn't fuse—convinced, I guess,
that in his struggle with the steel
he could seldom really win.
He knew perfection could
conceal the wound
beneath the arc of his art.
I liked him for that.

## Inside Her

"I'm in deep trouble,"
she said to him,
the first time in history
anyone had spoken of me.

The year 1936, Butte, Montana,
not far from here.
She was 18. He had
just come down the hill,
a shift in the Neversweat,
$2 a day on a widowmaker.

She bawled, then soft tears.
"What should we do?"
"This is a fine time to ask," he said
looking at his muddy brogans,
his face coal dark.

They fought and screamed
at one another, then a long
silence and she asked again, "Well?"
All the while I lay curled up,
my heart beating in the darkness
inside her.

## Moving

Moving is a burdensome task.
There are so many boxes
to be filled and opened, stuff
to be put away, carried to the
garbage chute.

Tina is a whiz, without her I
would be lost. Moving is like dying.
I am almost seventy. My time is nearing.
Thanatos means death in Greek.
There is clarity in death, stuff for the
garbage chute.

A wedding just went by outside
my window, horns honking, tin cans
tied to the wedding car. Life is moving.
We think we are going somewhere.
Some believe in eternal life.
I believe in the garbage chute.

What to throw out, what to save?
It costs money to move. It takes energy
and effort. Once has to identify things.
Suicide is not the answer.
I have lost a pair of trousers
which I need if I am to continue.

I must go on, life demands it of me.
The cemetery can wait. Every man is
a lighthouse waiting for the ship to come in.
Tina will find my trousers
and I will pull them on one leg at a time.
Life is moving.

**Eve Malo** (Dillon, MT) writes: "A tragedy in our family strangely gifted me as a young child with a sense of adventure. My mother's grieving led us to England and Europe. As she grieved by study and travel, she found excellent boarding schools for me, where I was exposed to many languages and enjoyed a rainbow of cultures. I tasted a smorgasbord of schools, twelve in twelve years. People ask, 'Where are you from?' I answer, 'I am citizen of this magnificent planet.'" In 2007, Eve Malo received the Montana Governor's Humanities Award.

## El Pozo de mis abuelos

regreso a mi tierra
a probar otra vez
los recuerdos de niñez
el primer trago del agua
que sorpresa
   refrío
      refrescante
         puro
la sal de mis lágrimas
ya no puede purificar
sueños perdidos

## My Grandparents' Well

I return home
to taste again
memories of childhood
the first swallow of water
what a surprise
  so cold
     refreshing
       pure
the salt of my tears
can't cleanse
lost dreams

## Blindness

As she approached the age of ninety-nine,

my mother lost her sight—dependency,

the last humiliation that her body

laid on her, threatened her sense

of who she was and how she wished to die.

And yet her other senses were intensified;

although she'd always loved to eat,

now she would chew more slowly,

lick her lips, and savor sweet or sour,

or salty, peppery, tongue-curling tart.

Her facial muscles would relax

and smile lines form beside her sightless eyes.

She'd sit on her apartment balcony

in humid Florida where she had lived

with my despondent stepfather

for forty years, and listen to the waves

pulse on the shore as if in harmony

with her strong, thrumming, stubborn heart

that still resisted letting go.

She needed a maternal caretaker

to supervise her all around the clock,

bathe her, set out her medications,

tuck her snugly into bed at night

and reassure her in the afterlife

she'd be united with her family—

each one of them exactly as they were.

I'd fly down with my sister when we could

arrange the time to visit her;

leaning on her walker for support,

**Robert Pack** (Condon, MT) is author of nineteen books of poetry, including *Still Here, Still Now* (University of Chicago Press, 2008). He served as the Director of the Bread Loaf Writers' Conference from 1973 to 1994 and taught at Middlebury College's graduate school of English, The Bread Loaf School, for over three decades. He teaches in the Honors College of the University of Montana, where he received the Dennison Presidential Award "for distinguished accomplishment that lends lustre to the University of Montana." He and his wife, Patty, live in a log home with a panoramic view of the Rocky Mountains in Condon, Montana.

she'd meet us at the door and tell me

that I'd put on weight. "How can you tell

that I've gained weight" I'd ask,

"if you can't see?" "A mother doesn't

need to see to know when her own son

neglects his health," she'd sternly claim.

The three of us would sit beside each other

on her woven couch, and she'd enquire about

my sister's kids and mine, and I would ask how she

was managing. She'd place her fingers

on my sister's eye-lids, then on mine, pressing down

until our sight went out. Her voice

rehearsed and wavering, she'd say,

"Just think the word, 'alone,' and let the sound,

that rolling "O," toll slowly in your mind

inside the dark with only you to hear

and only you to know that sound is there—unless,

unless you're able to imagine that

you're with each other, just as I'm with you,

inside that separating dark—a dark

extending further than you've ever gone.


## November


November, with the humming "m"

Mellifluous inside its name,

Meanders with the now diminished stream;

The once-green tamaracks, transformed,

Have lost their golden needles, and I see

The sweeping mountain vistas

In the morning light have now regained

Their shimmering chilled clarity.

    Now I imagine that a mellow

And mild drowsiness begins to take hold

In the laden rotund bodies

Of the rumbling bears

Who soon will all lie muffled deep

In humid dens, dreaming

Of what bears dream about, perhaps

The welcoming of sleep.

    The meadow wind has dwindled

To a murmuring, a little less

Than any hushed and human sounds

That mingled with the golden trees

I well remember, and a little more

Than what I know will soon remain

Of memory—brown buried leaves beneath

Mute snow heaped on the forest floor.

    The year has whitened to a frost

Upon each stiff unmoving branch,

Reminding me again that I must pause

While struggling to remember

To remind myself of what is gone:

The golden needles of the tamaracks,

My dream about the dreaming bears. November,

And I'm almost ready to move on.

**Greg Pape** (Stevensville, MT) is recipient of a Discovery/The Nation Award, a Pushcart Prize, The Richard Hugo Memorial Poetry Award, and two National Endowment for the Arts Fellowships. His poems have appeared in *The Atlantic Monthly, Iowa Review, The New Yorker, Ploughshares, Poetry,* and many others. From 2007 to 2009, he served as Montana Poet Laureate. He is author of many books of poetry, including *Black Branches* (Carnegie Mellon University Press, 2005) and *American Flamingo* (Southern Illinois University Press, 2005). He teaches at the University of Montana and in the brief-residency writing program at Spalding University.

### Storm Pattern

On my living room wall hangs a Navajo rug
handwoven by Virginia Yazzie. A Storm Pattern
with a black and white border, through which
the spirit line passes, a design like silhouettes

of mesas on the Colorado Plateau. Within the border
it's red, Ganado red, with black and white
figures, the sacred water bugs, the mountains
and the clouds, and the intersecting lightning bolts

that shoot out from the center to the four corners.
I love to look at it hanging on my wall.
I love to run my fingers over the wool.
Virginia Yazzie raised and tended the sheep

and sheared the wool and spun it by hand,
mixing in a little hair from her goats.
She dyed the wool and she built the loom
on which to weave it. She made up

this variation on an old pattern, and
she took pleasure in the work of her hands.
But there's coal and uranium and maybe oil
on her land, and the government says she

and her family have to move, relocate
is the word they use, to Flagstaff or Winslow
or Tuba City. Think of Virginia Yazzie
with the relocation blues. Imagine her

telling the government she'll never move.
Then remember the water bugs, the mountains,
the clouds, the lightning, the border through which
the spirit line passes, the storm pattern in her eyes.

## Lower Yellowstone Falls

Standing on asphalt laid down on rock
just at the place where the Yellowstone River
has come around a bend, riffling,
picking up speed, hugging a big rock
cutting the current, island-like,
just before the river forms
a last slick run to a ledge of rock,

a brief horizon,

and falls down the cliff face
into the chasm of the lower canyon
in a continuous roar
a white-water storm hosannaing hard
down through layers of air
watery columns collapsing
waves breaking into shafts
shafts breaking into tumbling ovoid
shapes pulling apart
colliding in a rush the eye
can't stop or hold
so the body feels its falling
as uprush through legs hips
into the solar plexus the heart
the blasting synapses
sheathed in water—step back.
Hold on.
             A golden stonefly
lifts off the lip of the falls,
hovers like a spark in the mist.

### View of the Bitterroot

Way out on gold slopes
of the wheat field,
once shoals of an ancient
glacial lake, three deer
wade shoulder-deep in wheat
and seem to float
like leaf boats on a gold stream.

A dark stand of Ponderosa pine
backs the scene, still spires
brushed and dabbed with morning sun.
And past the pines
the mountains build in steel-blue waves
to saw-tooth ridges in the sky.

The new owners of the wheat field
plan to develop the land, cut
the acres, where the sandhill cranes
return each year, down into small lots,
five hundred houses packed in tight
like gold bars in rows
over the shallow aquifer
at the edge of the marsh.

## Six Women Laughing

Backdrop: spirit mountains,
rustling trees, sounds and scents
of late spring. Evening sun
squanders deepest crimson.
To this we drink and to our lives
come together fleetingly and full.
Birds flash at the feeder, call
of a Eurasian dove, an enormous
bee bumps into the glass.

She launches into story
and we with her.
It's like catching the perfect
wave but in unison:
the swell, the timing,
the exquisite crescendo,
the ride down.
A riot of laughter,
crash of water and foam,
all six of us swimming,
floating, playing
in a gorgeous, heaving ocean.

**Carolyn Pettit Pinet** (Bozeman, MT) was born in South Wales in Dylan Thomas country and has lived with her family in Bozeman for 28 years. Her work has appeared in many publications across the country, including *The New Republic, Northern Lights,* and *The Big Sky Journal.* Her collection, *Poésie,* is housed in the Montana Poetry Archive. She teaches Spanish at Montana State University-Bozeman.

**Lois Red Elk** (Wolf Point, MT) has been a television talk show host, an FM radio broadcaster, an actor, a freelance writer, and teacher of high school English, poetry, and Native American language. Currently she is an adjunct professor at Ft. Peck Community College on the Ft. Peck Reservation. Besides writing poetry, she values her forty-year marriage, her children and grandchildren.

| Wakanyeja | Sacred Gift |
|---|---|
| | *(a child)* |
| Apetu ki | This day |
| wicin cana wan ici mani | a female traveler |
| | has arrived |
| kimiminawa | a butterfly |
| omaki yaka | said to me |
| Apetu ki | This day |
| wana hi | she has arrived |
| Mitakana | My little sister |
| wanayaka | behold |
| Apetu ki | This day |
| wicin cana wan ici mani | a female traveler |
| | has arrived |
| Wakanyeja | A sacred gift |
| wana hi | has arrived |
| Mitakuyapi | My relatives |
| wanayaka | behold |
| Wakanyeja | A sacred gift |
| wana hi | has arrived |

(A female traveler has arrived means a baby girl has been born. This poem was written on the arrival of my youngest granddaughter.)

## Porcupine on the Highway

Amos:  They said sister is stranded on the highway.
         Her car is about 10 miles east of town.
Sister:    I might as well pick up this porcupine or
         it'll be smashed by tonight.
Porcupine:  I give my body to a quill worker,
         and laugh at magpie on the fence.

Amos:  Mom, I'm taking Myrna to help sister.
         Her car quit and I might have to tow her in.
Sister:    Oh, it's a big one and the quills
         aren't damaged. It's got long hair, too.
Porcupine:  Clouds are fading. Earth is cooling.
         Grass is calling me home.

Amos:  There she is. She put something in her trunk.
         It looks like a big old porcupine.
Sister:    This sure is a mess. I should skin it here.
         All the cats will be coming into the yard.
Porcupine:  They used to read my bones, study my
         entrails for health and weather.

Amos:  What happened? Did you break down?
         Don't tell me, you're scavenging road kill?
Sister:    Yeh, both! All of a sudden this thing
         stalled, then I saw this huge porcupine.
Porcupine:  They say our voice sounds like a
         whimpering child. People gather.

Amos:  Pull your hood latch. You're cable was loose.
         Take it home and skin it. We'll follow you.
Sister:    I'll make Myrna a quilled bracelet and
         brother some armbands. Surprise them.
Porcupine:  She'll remember later that last week she
         dreamed about a big porcupine on the highway.

**Henry "Hank" Real Bird** (Gary Owen, MT) is a rancher and educator who raises bucking horses on Yellow Leggins Creek in the Wolf Teeth mountains of Montana. He was born and raised on the Crow Indian Reservation in the tradition of the Crow by his grandparents and has punched cows and worked in rodeos. Hank speaks Crow as his primary language and feels this has helped in writing his poetry. In 1996, Hank won the Western Heritage Award for the National Cowboy Hall of Fame. He served as Montana Poet Laureate 2009-2011.

## Tail That's Light

Goin' on fresh snow
Snows been fallin'
Several days
The ground, all is white
Sagebrush tops
Stickin' out of snow
Ridin' through snow, it's quiet
River where it goes
Just the trees are black
The ground, all is white
Where there are pine trees
It's sorta blue, almost black
Still farther beyond
Wolf Teeth Mountains, pine trees are blue
There's nothing, but the cold wind
Looks sort of like smoke
Ash trees, where they're thick
It is black
Gray I'm ridin'
His breath is white
Gray . . . he is like this day
My song, I'm singin'
Lookin' around
Where the sun appears Pink, peeps out of blue sky
Goin' to get many horses
Ridin' Gray, they won't see me
In white gray, blue black winter day
My son, I'm singin'.

## The Vet Said She May Have Been Thirty

One minute from our barnyard
the universe waits
for slumbering horses
like you Nikki.
Joining the circle of sleep
you lay down on the ice
and spread your hulking frame
from north to south.
There was sunlight on your
shoes when you made
the choice to quit
all the oat buckets
to sacrifice mornings
at the manger.
We almost would have had it otherwise
with tears and halter
to pull you back
for the spring that this year brings.
Four of us tugged with a rope
only to slide on ground
that gave yearning no traction.
It took time for you to teach us
when to give up.

**June Billings Safford** (Bozeman, MT) once ran a horse boarding operation with her husband and their four children. She writes: "'The Vet Said She May Have Been Thirty' wrote itself. It began 'with a lump in the throat,' as Robert Frost has described the genesis of poetry. Nikki's owners, who lived in Canada, learned about the horse's death when they received a copy of this poem." The Saffords have since moved to town. Horses now appear more in her paintings than in her poems.

**M. L. Smoker** (Frazer, MT) belongs to the Assiniboine and Sioux tribes of the Fort Peck Reservation in northeastern Montana. Her family's home is on Tabexa Wakpa (Frog Creek), a traditional camping ground for the Assiniboine people. She holds an MFA from the University of Montana, where she was the recipient of the Richard Hugo Scholarship. *Another Attempt at Rescue* (Hanging Loose Press, 2005) is her first book of poems. She works as Director of Indian Education for the Montana Office of Public Instruction.

## Variola

"Could it not be contrived to send the Small Pox among those disaffected tribes of Indians? We must on this occasion use every stratagem in our power to reduce them."
> Lord Jeffrey Amherst, 1763
> Commanding General of British Forces in North America

"Tomorrow is promised to no one" — Assiniboine saying

| | |
|---|---|
| *Iya tuwambi zheugiyabi.* | Our nation is called Village of Rock People. |
| *Saknabi togax hibi zheha zhechen chashutumbi.* | When the French people arrived, that is what they called us. |
| *Oyadebi ugitawabi ne Winchiyabina zheugiyabi.* | We are known as the Little Girl's band. |
| *Hekda zheha Winchinjanabi zhejeenax chinjatumbi Winkjemna numbabi zapda da chinjatumbi.* | A long time ago, in one year, only little girls were born— there were twenty-five of them. |
| *Zheha winchoundabi.* | At that time there were many of our people. |
| *Oyadebi kokdoba winge winkjemnabi uyuhabi Mni uhambi.* | We numbered ten thousand and because of this, we were strong. |
| *Zheha Ashashana hunga* | At that time The Light was our Chief. |
| *Azhashana zhe, hokun iya hinkna* | The Light traveled east, down the river |
| *Tugashina Andrew Jackson tibi ekta timani i.* | and visited with President Andrew Jackson. |
| *Azhazhana nambe yuza hinkna* | The President shook The Light's hand |
| *Tugashina zheya, "Konachijiya no!" Indeduwabi eyagubi.* | and said, "I am your friend." The two even took their picture together. |
| *Azhazhana ne Tugashinambi snonyesh.* | But The Light did not know this President. |
| *Doken unkumbikta zhe snonuyambish.* | We did not know how things would be. |
| *Omaka obawige wazhi sam winkjemna shakbe sam zapda* | This was 167 years ago. |
| *Sten.* | This is how it happened. |

**** **

Stage One: "Symptoms appear suddenly. High fever, chills, dorsal-lumbar
        pain, myalgias and prostration. Nausea and vomiting also common."

*** ***

| | |
|---|---|
| *Azhazhana kni zheha* | When The Light came home |
| *Mini shoshe gakna unazhimbi* | we stood on the banks of the |
| | Missouri |
| *wada pena agag kni.* | as the steamboat arrived. |
| *Azhazhana wauyagabi zheha* | When we saw the Light, we |
| *Iyoungipibi.* | were glad. |
| | |
| *Wokbambi oda akni.* | He brought many gifts home |
| | to share. |
| *Amba zhe, higox?a tanga yuha.* | He had a big give-away that day. |
| | |
| *At?gug Chat?ga name yuza.* | He shook hands with his father |
| | Left Hand |
| *Wiyohamb?amb? Chuwiknanga yupiya k?u.* | and gave him a heavy |
| | Hudson Bay Coat. |
| *Takonagu daya ogiya zhe.* | To his good friend who |
| | always helped him |
| *Waxeyaga zizibena sha washte k?u.* | he gave a beautiful red |
| | prayer cloth. |
| *Tida kikna zheha, nahax higox?a.* | And then he returned to his lodge |
| | to give other gifts away to his |
| | family. |
| | |
| *Amba numba ga, chuwint?gu* | In two days his daughter |
| | became sick |
| *wana yaza, chuwida.* | with chills all over her body. |
| *Wichoyaza sija, wichaxnixi.* | This was a bad sickness. |

** ****

Stage Two: "After 2 to 4 days the fever will relent and a rash will appear on the face and inside of the eyes. Rash will subsequently cover the entire body."

*** ***

| | |
|---|---|
| *Wana wichoyazambi.* | The disease is among us, growing stronger. |
| *Amnigiya napabi.* | The people try to scatter, flee. |
| *Azhazhana wana yaza.* | Finally, The Light grows sick too. |
| *Tawinju, chinjabi kowa t?abi.* | His wife and children are already gone. |
| *Estenax t?inkt.* | He will die soon and meet them. |
| *Wana onowa waka tawa nowa.* | He is now singing his sacred song. |

*******

Stage Three: "Skin lesions evolve into vesicles and pustules and finally into dried scabs that fall off after 3 to 4 weeks. Death or blindness most often occur."

******

| | |
|---|---|
| *Ahagam, winchinjana wazhi* | The last is a little girl. |
| *omaka doba ehanki* | She is only four years old. |
| *Paha saba hinkna hegisu.* | Her hair is black and loosely braided. |
| *Mini shoshe gakna.* | She waits by the Missouri River. |

(Translation by Dr. Kenneth Ryan)

## Counting

Two months into divorce.
My daughter this week in her house three days out of seven,
Next week five
Her ex in a trailer somewhere south of town.
A new family structure
With six grandmothers and innumerable relatives
Cousins or aunts or steps
A crowded complexity if it weren't for the sense of absence.

These days I seek
My own place at the table, an hour or two
Nourished by small children
Lost in a schedule of come and go.
Outside, out loud, I count
The steps to shoreline, know the number means nothing
In a tally of time and effort
futile as the count of angels who may dance on the head of a pin.

Even on shore
A large body of water cannot be discounted.
Foam blows from wind gullies
And her children delight in the metronome of waves.
They count the number of skips
A polished round rock leaps before it sinks.
Today I add up the positives:
This moment, their voices, red and green rocks, one osprey diving
          like a stone.

**Cas Still** (Yellow Bay, MT) is a poet and visual artist whose inspiration is her family orchard and garden on the East Shore of Flathead Lake. A former Artist and Poet in the Schools in Montana and Florida, Cas has published her poems in magazines and journals nationally. River, mountains, and oceans frequently distract her from her work at the Belton Chalet at the west entrance to Glacier National Park.

**David E. Thomas** (Chinook, MT) grew up on the "Hi-Line" in North-central Montana; graduated from the University of Montana, learned his literary licks on the streets of San Francisco, railroad gangs, construction crews and on the road in Mexico, Central and South America, Canada and across the United States before settling in Missoula, Montana, where he remains to this day.

### The Ten Thousand Things

Well let's see there's
        shebolts hebolts and stress rods
there's make-up bolts inbed bolts and
           carriage bolts
there's nuts and washers to fit all sizes
        of each.
There's rattle guns 18
       and 24 inch
       crescent wrenches—spud
          wrenches
       and porto-power
         jacks.
There's double jacks and jack hammers
     pinking eyes and inbed plates.
There's Foreman Frank for whom
       I work
     and foreman Al and foreman
       Stan and foreman Rags
       the superintendant and his vice.
There's the dry shacks the print shack
      the fire barrels
the lumber stockpile. There's 2x4's
2x6's 2x12's 4x6's 1x2's
     1x4's 1x6's
     in all different lengths.
     There's the Safety Man and
       "Access Closed"
     signs there's roped off areas
     and KEEP OUT
      DANGER ABOVE signs.
There's water jugs on the cranes
     and there's the nip truck
     and its driver bringing in the
       goods
     nobody can find there's okum
     and tie wire big rolls of tape
       red plugs
       and rock anchors
       wing nuts
       and cable clamps
    not to mention cables and their
        shackles
       and turn-buckles.

There's the sky turning ever more purple
                    as the shift
                    swings toward
                    its end black by
                    lunch and stars
                    from then on mercury
                    vapor lamps and a
                    heavier coat.
There's pull ropes to the cans up concrete
                                        columns
                    there's catwalks
                            and scaffolds.
There's times when I wander
                        about picking up
                        and sorting bolts
there's times when a chance glance
                            at a star
                            trying to outshine
                            the lamps
is all the rest I get. It happens every night
                    from 4:30 pm
                    to 12:30 am
                    at Libby Dam

Oh damn! I forgot nails! 16 common
                    16 duplex 8's the same
                    roofing nails and blue
                                    heads.
                    There's just no end to it

                    Sorting bolts on the edge
                            of artificial light
                    the tune of an engine
                            the shadow of the dam.

**Joe Wilkins** (Melstone, MT) was born and raised north of the Bull Mountains of eastern Montana. He now lives with his wife and son on the north Iowa prairie, where he teaches writing at Waldorf College. His work appears in *The Georgia Review*, *The Southern Review*, *Mid-American Review*, *Harvard Review*, *Orion*, and *Best New Poets 2009*.

## Then I Packed You up the Ridge Like a Brother on My Back

In the blue dark I followed the ridge
towards the pines.

In a bowl of sage and dry grass
soft as the throat-hairs

of something small,
I lay down.

The sun was a long time coming,
the earth bloodless at my belly.

I waited and watched the river.
I was very still. You know how it is—

the stars closing their bright mouths,
the dew a gift on your lips.

You did not see me,
or my rifle, blue

as the dark. But I saw
you step from the willows,

give your nose to the black water.
And you were beautiful. There is so much

blood in a thing—
yours welled up from the clean hole

I made in your heart and steamed
on the river stones,

and some washed down into the river,
where it swirled a moment,

and became the breath of fish.

## Highway

The deer hide gloves slip from his hands,
                                    chafe his wrists,
fill with the scratch of alfalfa leaves. Beyond the field, the highway
glistens. The boy puts his shoulder to a bale
and heaves it over. Stunned mice

                        scatter. He turns,
sights down the neat line of bales the stacker
will soon jaw up. In the sky
                        the sun hangs. The field shakes
with heat. He walks and walks and under his boots he hears
the pop and snap of cut grass stems,

                        like the slender bones
he once found in a mudnest. His mother cries at the kitchen table.
The man who is not his father drives the stacker behind him.
The boy stops and stares past the fence,
                        at the highway,
where a diesel rig sings down the far hills. The sky is unbearably
white and wide, and the boy opens
                        his mouth and, for a moment,

that highway song is his.

**Paul Zarzyski** (Great Falls, MT) grew up in blue-collar Hurley, Wisconsin and moved to Missoula in 1973 to study with Richard Hugo and Madeline DeFrees in the MFA program at the University of Montana. A dozen years as a roughstock rider on the rodeo circuit earned him entrée into the cowboy poetry arena, including 24 consecutive appearances at the annual National Gathering in Elko, Nevada. He is the recipient of the 2005 Montana Governor's Arts Award for Literature.

## What's Sacred:

To wake because waking means something,
something you're itching to begin
living at daybreak—revelry of autumn
cottonwood leaves, shod horses
clicking over talus, far-off
cacophony of meadowlark aria with crow
ruckus, goshawk skirl, strident magpie
cries breezed through a bedroom
window screen, tinkling wind chimes
echoing steeple bells
deep out of some distant
childhood dream.
           To hopscotch
or, better odds, slip-slip
succinctly into your jeans
with brisk whispers from each
instep thrust, 50-plus
years of this denim
one-two gymnastic balancing act
on the high wire between
half-asleep and wide-awake—right leg
then left—ankles, knees, hips,
lumbar, *snap-crackle-popping*
their breakfast applause.
           To splash
well water into your prayerful hands, cotton-
towel your eyelids dry, focus,
voice with a joyous *ahhhh*
your first hot swallow of joe
kick-starting your ticker
before walking your Aussie dog
who loves you for your clockwork
newspaper fetchings
from that blue speck of a box, far
as the blue eye can see,
a long jaunt off.
           To inhale
until your lungs flex like biceps
canine windfalls of fresh scents, dry leaves
redolent in the night's wake, gold
certificates flushed from the sprung
back doors of an armored car, both
sagebrushed ditches
flitting with winged brilliance
crisp for the picking at 6 a.m.
when you shall be the only two in sight
meek enough to inherit,
breath after rich fertile breath, this earth.

*—For Ray and Barbara March*

## Partner

As you hit ground off Staircase,
number 12, at the state fair
rodeo in Great Falls, it was hard
to hear vertebrae cracking
above the murmur of ten thousand
hometown hearts. You cowboyed-up
and hid your grimace deep,
walked out of the arena,
stubborn, on sheer pain
and took the ambulance, like a cab,
front seat to Emergency.

Tonight, drunk on Tanqueray,
we vow never again
to mention broken neck. Instead
we talk tough broncs, big shows
we'll hit down south, and hunting ducks
come fall. We straggle home,
moon-struck, to the squawk of geese—
a V of snows crisscrossing
and circling the city—screwed up,
you say, when streetlight glimmer
throws them off plumb.

When my bronc stomped
down the alleyway that night,
I knew down deep our bones and hearts
were made to break
a lot easier than we'd believe. I felt
your arm go numb in mine,
took the gate, weak-kneed, and spurred
with only half the try. It's bad
and good some cowboys don't know tears
from sweat. I folded both
between fringes of your chaps,
packed your riggin' sack neat
as you'd have, and wandered
punch-drunk lost, afraid
into the maze of parking lot.

What's done is done, I know,
but once I killed
at least a dozen singles
in a season, without thinking
how they partner-up for life
and death, how the odd ones
flocking south
survive that first long go alone.

*—For Kim Zupan*

# *Nevada*

**Krista Benjamin** (Minden, NV) was born in Truckee, California, and grew up at Lake Tahoe. Her stories and poems have appeared in the *Best American Poetry 2006*, *Creative Writer's Handbook*, *Margie*, *Chiron Review*, and other journals. She is the recipient of a Nevada Arts Council Fellowship and the Robert Gorrell Award for Literary Achievement from the Sierra Arts Foundation. By day, she teaches elementary school in Minden, Nevada.

## Letter from My Ancestors

We wouldn't write this,
wouldn't even think of it. We are working
people without time on our hands. In the old country,

we milk cows or deliver the mail or leave,
scattering to South Africa, Connecticut, Missouri,
and finally, California for the Gold Rush—

Aaron and Lena run the Yosemite campground, general
store, a section of the stagecoach line. Morris comes
later, after the earthquake, finds two irons

and a board in the rubble of San Francisco.
Plenty of prostitutes need their dresses pressed, enough
to earn him the cash to open a haberdashery and marry

Sadie—we all have stories, yes, but we're not thinking
stories. We have work to do, and a dozen children. They'll
go on to pound nails and write up deals, not musings.

We document transactions. Our diaries record
temperatures, landmarks, symptoms. We
do not write our dreams. We place another order,

make the next delivery, save the next
dollar, give another generation—you,
maybe—the luxury of time

to write about us.

To June—
My first college writing teacher. I can't
believe I've known you since 1987!
Well, here's to many more good
years... Krista
Sept 17, 2010

## Café para dos

Esta guerra no es tuya ni mía
ni de nuestros padres
pero somos
peones en el tablero de los reyes
Duele saber
que jamás nos conoceremos
porque una bala hirió
el centro de nuestros espíritus
y los sueños de viajar
libres como las aves
están pasando
hacia un lugar y tiempo desconocido
Es triste saber
que nunca compartiremos los cantos
que nuestros padres cantaron en el verano
que jamás nos reuniremos
en las playas de la amistad
para ver a la luna y su melancolía
o los colores del alba y emborracharnos
en la confianza de nuestros corazones

**Roy A. Chávez** (Carson City, NV) was born in Puente Piedra, Lima, Perú. He lives in Carson City and works as a mechanical designer. He is a winner of The Nevada Arts Fellowship (2001), *Reflections in Motion* (2004), and the Sierra Arts Foundation Grant (2005).

**Coffee for Two**

This war isn't yours or mine
nor our fathers'
but we are
pawns on kings' boards
It hurts to know
we never will meet
because a bullet has hit
the center of our souls
and the dreams of traveling
free as birds
are passing toward
an unknown place and time
It's sad to know
we never will share the songs
our parents sang in summertime
that we'll never gather
on the beaches of friendship
and see the moon with its melancholy
or dawn's colors and get drunk
to the sound of our hearts

## Do Not Resuscitate

Much like Tutankhamen,
we must record the wishes
of our passing
the Advanced Directive,
not the killing of slaves
with their baskets of wheat and dates,
but the absence of feeding tubes
or hands pumping our breasts.
Only the sipping of drugs
to ease the journey.
Let me go
into the great lake,
into my own time, my soul
wrapped in its swaddling
with the spices of my life.
My body like a reed
of its own papyrus
ink still wet with the blessing
of having written.

## No Place To Anchor The Ladder

It's so far from Carson City
to Arson City, Nevada, the town
where someone starts fires.
It's far, too, from Dementia City
where they claim I get all the hugs,
and the "clerks" stop to kiss me
but the demented never get kissed.
Living in the nursing home
is like climbing a ladder
with half the rungs missing.
It's a long way up
and the dementia redefines
the length of space between the rungs.
What use is a ladder
when all the worlds are falling apart?
Joanie says, *St. Peter,*
*why are you putting all the babies on the floor?*

**Bill Cowee** (Carson City, NV) earned a living as an accountant, but his passion was writing poetry. He served as poetry editor for *Bristlecone*, co-directed the Western Mountain Writers' Conference, and was a founding member of the Ash Canyon Poets. He was the recipient of two Nevada Arts Council Fellowships and was chosen for a Governor's Arts Award for Excellence in Literature. In 2007, he donated more than 1,100 volumes of poetry to Western Nevada College, where the Bill Cowee Poetry Collection is now housed.

**Joe Crowley** (Reno, NV) is a former professor and administrator for The University of Nevada, Reno. He has turned to poetry in retirement. Recent publications include an interpretation of the academic presidency, a book of essays and correspondence, the centennial history of the NCAA, and various poems.

## Power Plants

Congress spoke: Let's dam the St. John river.
No, said hikers, hunters, trouble brewing
too from anglers, lovers of canoeing.
But hydro-hearts, my, they were aquiver—
huge energy enhancement, high finance.
On the river banks, though, new foes waited,
lonely Furbish Louseworts, loved and hated,
once near extinct, today, endangered plants.
A forb, a flower wanting room for growth,
or parasite of sorts, in short, a weed,
this lousewort's worth could not be agreed.
There would be dams or blooms, no chance for both.
Save a flower, tie Big Power in knots,
or, well, just kill a weed for kilowatts?

## To the Rear, March!

With arms, some say, Hurray! The more the merrier.
Give thanks, then get a tank, an Uzi too,
a SAM, perhaps plastique. If you're not through,
why, you could buy and bear an aircraft carrier.
Isn't there, you ask, some built in barrier?
Here's one: Militias may be malicious—
vicious mobs whose foes sleep with the fishes,
gangs that aim to make one's body . . . airier.
Private armies. Killer cults. So scary,
some infringement has been necessary.
You, sir, have no need to stock an armory.
You are not in charge of a gendarmerie.
Your weapon's there to hunt—a bird, a hare—
and to protect your home and derrière.

## Calambro

*(scheduled for execution)*

One day after Easter Sunday your last few steps of life
A quiet walk across a cold tier of grey lawn polished
Like granite lined with steel trees leading from your
Holding tomb of a cell where you were fattened for the
Kill by your last choice meal before being drugged half-
Dead senseless the prelude to the juice that will ooze like
A zephyr snaking its death potion through your veins chasing
Life as she runs away from painless acid flowing filling
Killing, it corners your last breath—Calambro—I visited
Your deathbed thirteen years ago as your civilly-dead witness
Mine the dry lethal injection of time without parole.

**Robert Gonzáles** (Carson City, NV) has participated in the Razor Wire Poetry Workshop at Northern Nevada Correctional Center for twenty years, time enough to master his epigrammatic poems that surface with almost no hint of having been written. A laconic ordained chaplain and Vietnam Vet, "Bobby" reminds the group of their purpose with his example: to be of service—whether in the discussion of a poem or the days and nights on the yard.

**Shaun T. Griffin** (Virginia City, NV) is the co-founder and director of Community Chest, a nonprofit agency serving children and families in northwestern Nevada, and the former director of the state's homeless youth education office. For twenty years he has taught a poetry workshop at Northern Nevada Correctional Center and published an annual journal of their work, *Razor Wire*. He received the Rosemary McMillan Lifetime Achievement in Art Award in 2006 and the Governor's Award for Excellence in the Arts in 1995.

## The Meth Addict out My Window

lives with his arthritic father,
third in his class at Cal—
a civil engineer, whose hand
to the post I have opened
a hundred times, and who, without a son,
stood near upright until he came home
to glitter the moon to its inky death,
the bulb burning in his eyes,
the translucent one, porch-stooped,
smoking gun, always lit
for the fun in his half-naked den—

and mother ravels the reeds of her kin,
tiny volume of misanthropes,
the son she avows
in her loft at night—
to kiss *this* bulb awry
would miscarry her mind to gin—and he

scoots the morning sun
to clean the Harley frame,
a motorcycle not quite
in the imaginary turn at 80—
girl pressed to his ribs like a throttle
to the great wide open of we

who've become his neighbors
that will not disturb him,
positioned on the crank
of every move, until he juts out
like a mole—for whom light
is darkness and food,
something to fear—

when my wife calls to confide
the dogs sniffing the yard,
the pale blue assault of uniforms
carting their prize away
from this, our town of sleep and decay:

what we need in the night
to frisk the anguish of love,
this hour removed
from his ordeal in the house like fire
for the two who no longer sleep
the worry downstairs, and so begin
to scissor his picture from the paper,
press the hornet eyes in a drawer,
and scavenge the nightstand
for a face to endure.

## Heron Dance

I circled the river of blue necks,
their heads tipped like statuary, one white eye
driven to fish the stone pools until, stooped

for the hunt, the feathers lifted in flight,
crested the rocky points in midday heat
just yards from the bridge of man—

these twelve beaks parted the precipice and we
said nothing to the river riders, rolling beams of light,
pterodactyls that might be here tomorrow—

how things become they who cannot fly alone,
crucibles of hunger that wade and wade
to find reflection below the emerald blind

of the cut bank and I am not in their midst,
but in it still, water, that will by then bestow,
to those who so long from above, stare down.


## Los Vendedores

Out of the sand they come
crowing like cocks in the morning sun

chanting their strange, melodious hymns to food:
*Tortillero, Helado, Maní tostado,*

and the children, burnished and thin
scurry to meet the musical men

and the women, smoked in their shawls,
float on brooms behind them

and the beach is never still
with the halo of hunger overhead.

**Linda Hussa** (Cedarville, CA — "just a stone's throw from the Nevada border") and her husband own and operate Hussa Ranch, which is celebrating its centennial in 2011. They raise cattle, sheep, horses, and the hay to feed them. A writer/rancher in the Great Basin with four poetry collections and five books of nonfiction to her credit, Hussa's themes are drawn from the isolated nature of ranching, her commitment to rural communities, and her appreciation of the desert landscape.

## On a Clear, Cold Calving Night

Before I leave the human world
and enter the calving shed
of muttering cows
I stop and search bright stars
for Orion
standing astride two worlds.
I've pinned my father
on the center star
—the buckle of Orion's belt—
and there he is
as long as I look up and nod.

That he ever lived
seems as improbable
as the possibility of his eternal passage
in brilliant light.
Yet, I am made of his particular laugh
and his serious errors.

I have learned to reach into the sacred womb,
grasp a placid hoof
and coax life toward this certain moment.

If only I could
from the dust of all souls
lost between here
and infinity
draw forth the ones I need.

## Love Letters

Wow!
was written in the dust
on the bedside table.

The dawn and I blushed together
as your spurs
chinged
around the kitchen
as you started the fire.

I stretched full length
on the cool smoothness
of the sheets,

a kept woman
a moment longer.

Within an hour's time
we'll be ahorseback
in a long trot
to some distant blue mountain
hunting cows.

I'll carry your message
close
knowing there will come a day
I would give a year of my life
for that . . .
Wow!

# The Un-doing of Heaven's Match

She's returning books
borrowed against the echo of an empty house.
Never read them, I bet. Doesn't taste the coffee
I set before her, doesn't feel
the pick-me-up of its intention.
So deep in the blues.

Husband's gone
from a marriage that took her
from one end of her 30s to the other.

Supper's ready. She says she can't stay.
Red silk blouse says
she's on the hunt for something in town.
But no good time will get close
without a collision on the sorrow she wears.

Grew up on a ranch, married a rancher.
A team going from dark to dark building a place.
We saw it, the way neighbors do
when there's miles and miles of work between you.

At brandings they snaked calves careful but fast
—God's gift and purely loving to rope.
Head catch with an ocean wave, heel
with a backhand over the hip, a yip and a yowl!
The ground crew timed their look-ups
just to see their dancing loops.

They lived close in a casual way.
Both wore the grease, both wore the pants.
When it came apart
it was like trying to bale up feathers.

He was there for the work
but he'd found himself a town girl,
polish on her nails and time on her hands.

I walked her to her truck.
Before she turned the key she asked the night,
"Wasn't I woman enough for him
or wasn't I enough of a man?

## The Weir

Tonight I open the ditch through the calf lot.
Ice breaks into puzzle pieces
that will freeze down
—never again with this smooth skin.
Calves stand at a distance watching.
Them freshly weaned and curious.
My head down, busy.

When my shovel goes in
dark ground breaks open
with bright pink water
as the lowering sun
lays one thin finger on my work.

It's quiet.
Geese already bedded on the lake.
The sky is wide and empty and full.

Calves crowd up behind me
(Red Light, Green Light)
sniffing puffs of sweet oats
on my back, in my hair.

There's a rustle overhead
in winter branches.
A hawk draws in long wings.
Bare limbs bloom other hawks.
One is white
but rouged with the same sunset
that fills my small ditch.

**Claudia Keelan** (Las Vegas, NV) is author of six books of poetry and recipient of The Silver Pen Award from the state of Nevada. She teaches at the University of Nevada Las Vegas and has served as director of the MFA program in creative writing. She lives in Las Vegas with her husband, poet Donald Revell, and their children, Ben and Lucie.

## Leaving Las Vegas

It's only a man with a skull on his shirt

And a boy with SCARFACE

Written on his sleeve

This is my country

The virtually dead

Still giving it the old college try

& the real ghosts silenced

In the airspace formerly known

As the sky

I looked at the moon last night

It was full between my fingers

No power & all pull

Distant thing once able to control my body

She was gone

Amiable ragamuffin formerly known as me

It was still dark

The morning she left

There'd been wet years

Rain that swept the valley clean

But the desert was just the desert

There in the dryness of your lips

**Adrian C. Louis** (Lovelock, NV) was born and raised in northern Nevada and is a professor of English in the Minnesota State University system. His book of poems, *Logorrhea* (Northwestern University Press, 2006), was a finalist for the Los Angeles Times Book Award. He is editor of *Shedding Skins: Four Sioux Poets* (Michigan State University Press, 2008).

## Approximate Haiku, 1980

Like those little bubblings
circling the head of some
drunk cartoon character . . .
Except I knew they were
angels & not soaplings.
Of course I believed in
Wovoka's ghost shirts.
Shit, I was invincible.
When the checkout girl
said my two T-Bones
looked delicious, I said
I would cook one for her.
Then she saw the buzzing
angels & shuddered.
I said, "You can eat the
steak & I'll dine on you."
She called the manager
who told me to leave.
My no to him meant yes
to approximate haiku:
two cold Big Macs in
a small town slammer.

## In the Colony

Blood sun drips
red licorice strips that
lash the longing earth
& I whisper the prayers
of a contented consumer.
I like the sun's warmth,
but I drool about those red
whips that accentuate our
slow darkness even though
it's rapidly becoming a white
light to me. I am a red ant
& swear I come from a red
ant world as I scurry & scatter
to nests made by things that
were never ants to begin with.

**Stephen Shu-Ning Liu** (Las Vegas, NV) was born in Fuling, China, the son of a hermetic painter and the grandson of a Mandarin scholar who taught him Chinese classics. After military service in the Chinese Expeditionary Army, he came to San Francisco in 1952. Liu was an English professor at the Community College of Southern Nevada in Las Vegas until his retirement in 2001. He was the first Nevadan to receive a Fellowship in Creative Writing from the National Endowment for the Arts (1981), and he won a Pushcart Prize in 1982.

## A Mid-July Invitation

The energy crisis is over. Lights are back on the Strip.
Name the place: Sahara, Caesar's Palace, Casino de Paris.
This way, please. Come, my people; drink on the house.
You, Great-grandpa, dice-thrower from Sichuan, casting away
one hundred acres of our land overnight, be of good cheer,
this satchel of gold will last you a long while;
and you, Uncle Lu, widower and recluse of Fuling, accost
this Dixie belle, dare what you've never dared before:
this bottle will make you bold; and you, Da Shing, you
longed for a journey, you read by midnight lamps and drained
your blood between Confucius' pages and Newton's first law
of motion. Don't despair, little brother. I'll see you
enter a college this fall. And you, Shu-Ying, how your
windows framed those lonely mountains. How winter light cast
pallor on your skin and bones. How you withered in spring wind.
Like our lily pond, your eyes had never reflected a stranger's
face. Come to the party, my sister. I'll teach you to dance.

Let me hear your moans, let me feel your bony hand.
Come, I know you all. Come, away from the Yellow Springs.
It's mid-July: clouds cross the moon, the earth shudders,
and the mice must not catch you sleeping under the wormwood.

## A Visit to the Country

When tree roots nourished our steps, peaches
Ripened with our pleasure; brilliant far reaches
Of the heart were visible at last, in a joke
You and the hawks know; when stellar kinfolk

Spoke from sunrise with you and your child,
When, at our visit, you and the mountains came
Down to meet us, and history was beguiled
By stories strong in backyard honey, and the fame

Of just-born foals—just to see you, friend
And child, your forthright planetary family,
I would give a city for you, the city
Would give a country for you; we depend

On you and your life here. We come for tradition—
Blackberry commandos, love is your mission.

**Steven Nightingale** (Reno, NV) is a native Nevadan and author of two novels, *The Lost Coast* (St. Martin's Press, 1994) and *The Thirteenth Daughter of the Moon* (Thomas Dunne Books, 1996). He has also authored four books of sonnets. He divides his time between his home state, the Santa Cruz Mountains of California, and Granada, in southern Spain.

**nila northSun** (Fallon, NV) has been writing for over three decades. A Shoshone/Chippewa Indian, she works as a grant writer for her tribe in Nevada. She's received the Silver Pen award from the University of Nevada Reno, the Indigenous Heritage Award, and a Sierra Arts Foundation Literary Award. Nila enjoys involvement with the local arts community around Reno, particularly related to the Burning Man event.

## country

the cool thing about living
in the country
is you can see animals
and land
and changing leaves
you can sing
old mcdonald had a farm
and time it
so when you say
he had a cow
there they are
with a moo moo everywhere
and when you say
he had a goat
there they are
and you can throw in tigers
with a roar roar here
and a roar roar there
and the landscape is
so much more interesting
specially if you're on
a long road trip
and your mom says
she'll give you a quarter
for every white horse you see
with a neigh neigh here
and sometimes
you can pull over
to stretch your legs
and get up close
and pet the animals
feed the goats
and your dad says
he'll give you a dollar
for every elephant you see
it keeps you on your toes
scanning the countryside
singing old mcdonald had a farm
instead of mcdonalds has
fatty foods.

## the little shits in daycare

substitute teaching one day
they, too young to be properly diagnosed
a.d.d., a.d.h.d., FAS,
abused, neglected,
child of an alcoholic
3rd born in a line of 5
whatever
they were out of control
unmedicated
unruly
i walk in to rule
not
in one day can i undo
all that's been done to them
instead
of being the calm in the eye of the storm
i become the wicked witch upon which
the house lands
barely
escaping with my life
as i wave goodbye
have a nice day
wish you little dickens the best of luck
cause you'll need it.

**Gailmarie Pahmeier** (Reno, NV) has been a Nevadan for 25 years. She teaches creative writing and contemporary literature courses at the University of Nevada, where she has been honored with the Alan Bible Teaching Excellence Award and the University Distinguished Teacher Award. Pahmeier and her carpenter husband share their homes—a little house in Reno between the Truckee River and the railroad tracks and a mountain cabin in Northern California—with two cats and two pit bull mixes. She says it's a good life.

### Saving Face

Nearly 35 years from today
she'll be asleep on a Sunday morning,
her second husband spooned against her,
the two cats cornered at the bottom
of the bed. She'll rise to the ring
of the telephone, shuffle through the hall
to the kitchen, leave the man, a carpenter
she's loved for years, loved from the day she knew
he could build her this house, its open spaces
and secrets (her name carved into a truss,
their own handprints pushed into stucco),
she'll leave this man to sleep in. When she picks
up the telephone, it's her mother's voice,
coming to her from a little brick house
in the hometown she left decades ago,
and she'll hear that house in her mother's breath,
see its tidy lawn and tomato plants,
the rose trellis and the chain link fence,
the blind poodle, the fireflies, mosquitoes.
Her mother will say—Oh, honey. It's bad
news. Laura Thompson has shot herself
through the heart, has saved her face, she's gone,
gone, she's done such a sad and common thing.
This news will take its clear and careful time
to bring her down, but she will on that Sunday
morning go back to bed, back to the man
who loves her, his uncovered chest a mat
of black and grey, and she'll think of the wolf
come to blow a house down, and then she'll sleep
awhile, rise again, make coffee, break eggs.
But on this very day in 1969,
she and Laura Thompson ride a tandem
bike through neighborhoods they'll never live in.
Both she and Laura have boyfriends,
thirteen-year-olds with substantial Greek
names and the town's fullest promise. She and Laura
wear their heavy ID bracelets, talk of how
when they marry these boys they'll have porch lights
and horses, barns and patios, gardens
with statues, welcome mats at both screen doors.

And on this day Laura laughs from the front
seat of the bike, turns her soon to be
heartbreakingly beautiful face, says
*Look! Look at that one! The people*
*in that house could be happy forever*
as she pedals them farther and faster
through tall grass, toward deep woods, and into stone.

## Home Maintenance

Sometimes my father's hand shakes, sends fat drops
of paint to splatter my patio.
He's fond of this work, and I like the way
this man feels in the sun, healthy and honest
and responsible. I work next to him
on the shorter ladder, my hair sticky
against my neck. He says, This heat's a bitch.
I say, Wears my ass out. I'd like more talk,
but it's too hot, too hot to wrap our mouths
around vowels, urge consonants into
the air. We'll finish my house by Saturday,
my father will go home, live through another
familiar summer in his own backyard.
We both know he'll never be back, that this
job is his last large gift, that he will tell
my mother about the heat, tell her
this paint will last seven years at most,
that he worries about who will help me
next time, who will work beside me in the sun,
who will love me in ways simple as sweat.

**Ismael García Santillanes** (Carson City, NV) has been in the Razor Poetry Workshop at Northern Nevada Correctional Center for two decades. Poet, painter, and desert shrew, "Izzy" is a leader in the workshop. He received a Literary Fellowship from Sierra Arts Foundation in 2008 and held a solo art exhibition at Truckee Meadows Community College in 2004. He has chronicled the life of the workshop through stipplings of poets, painted for the thirteen annual covers of the prison literary journal, *Razor Wire.*

## Jimmy Took Too Long to Die

Old bastard, rigid from the pain,
bleached-bone dentures
strained shallow breaths
down the sides of his neck
vile-lined and nerves so taut
every muscle in his twisted
body was a dry, leather knot.

Tired of his wheelchair, he stood
but Parkinson's legs were too bent
for nothing more than to stalk
like Nosferatus in the classic B-movie
who crept tiptoed, hands
before him like a praying mantis
while the virgin slept . . . .

But unlike the black & white vampire,
whose only perversion was
puncture wounds on the neck,
Jimmy took his victim's head clean off.

He never told them where he hid the head,
believing some glorious day he would get out
to claim his prize, to look again
upon her bleached-bone screams . . . .

Had he not died in the prison hospital,
had the rest of us not seen him—
as he stammered around the yard
growling at everyone he hated to *fuck off*—
deform into an elongated cat's claw
that couldn't hold a cup
or change his clothes,
one would believe even now
Jimmy's ghost does bad things.

## Teaching Poetry to 3rd Graders

At recess a boy ran up to me
with a pink rubber ball and asked
if I would kick it to him. He handed me the ball,
then turned and ran
and ran and ran, not turning back
until he was far out in the field.
I wasn't sure I could kick the ball
that far. But I tried,
launching a perfect and lucky kick.
The ball sailed in a beautiful arc
about eight stories high,
landed within a few feet of the 3rd grader
and took a big bounce off the hard playground dirt.
Pleased, I turned to enter the school building.
And then (I don't know where they came from
so quickly) I heard a rumbling behind me
full tilt. They were carrying pink balls and yellow balls
of different sizes, black and white checkered
soccer balls. They wanted me to kick for them.
And now this is a ritual—this is how we spend recess.
They stand in line, hand me the ball and run.
The balls rise like planets
and the 3rd graders
circle dizzily beneath the falling sky,
their arms outstretched.

\*\*\*

In class the kids are making similes and I write them
on the board as they call out—
*A river swishing like a cat's tail.*
*Smooth as a window, quiet as pain.*
*The rain clattering like a spilled jar of marbles.*
Then a wave of laughter sweeps the room.
In my new shoes I must have shuffled
across the school carpet rife with static.
My hair is standing straight up
as if I'm a shocked cartoon character
or a scared and cornered cat.
When I write on the chalkboard,
blue sparks fly from my hand
to the metal strip that frames the green.
Everything I touch crackles.
When I help a student at her desk,
a yellow four-inch arc of lightning streaks
from my hand to hers, shocking the pencil from her grip.
The students watch amazed. "Pick up the pencil!" I say,
"Don't be afraid."

**Gary Short** (Virginia City, NV) taught high school and coached basketball in Wells and Virginia City, Nevada. He earned an MFA from Arizona State University and was a fellow at the Fine Arts Work Center in Provincetown and a Stegner Fellow at Stanford University. His book, *Flying over Sonny Liston* (University of Nevada Press, 1996) received the Western States Book Award. He currently teaches and directs the graduate creative writing program at the University of Mississippi.

\*\*\*

(a note found on the playground
pinned by wind against the chain-link fence)

From: Daniel A.
To: Missy

In case you guest
  I love you     it is a present
    to see you.
          When I dreem
  I dreem you       Not gold
not a cristal pond      not a bird
    singing evry song
      you ever herd      jus you
          Only.           None else.

Because I love you
      and love to say your name
  I see you
    and remem ber      this
  Thanks you for a dreem

Who?      Can take
    Your plase

## Test

> "You people who live near Nevada Test Site are
> in a very real sense active participants in the
> nation's atomic test program"
> —Atomic Energy Booklet, March, 1957

The sky brightens with a flash.

A rancher feels the earth shudder
beneath his red roan.
He shields his eyes—
flesh is transparent,
his hand a diagram of bones.
My God, he whispers.

The mare shies,
only the pressure of his boots
urges her
through Condor Valley to a ridge where
the only boundary is the sky.

In the sparse shade of a Joshua tree
the pink clouds hover
over the ranges of his retina.

He rubs his burning nostrils
and tries to spit out the bitterness,

the metallic taste.

## Magpies in the Graveyard

They are not beautiful,
although their blacker feathers glimmer
like rainbow oil in the sun.
Yin-yang birds, black/white
with a long tail. Flash
of white patch with each wing-beat.
We say a murder of crows. A covey of quail.
But I can't recall
the term for many magpies.
A cemetery of magpies. A sunrise of them.
I'm here this morning
because I want to be lonely
among the tombstones—the dates and names.
It takes one beating heart
to make a magpie, two wings,
four thousand feathers, a handful
of fluted and hollow bones.
One flies and the others follow.
Listen. The surprising flutter.
They rise like an undulating road
of magpies, black with white dashes, they lift
like prayer into the blank graveyard air.
Something into nothing.

# New Mexico

**Tacey M. Atsitty** (Kirtland, NM) is Diné (Navajo) of the Sleep Rock People and born for the Tangle People. She is a recipient of the Truman Capote Award. Atsitty holds a BA in English from Brigham Young University and a BFA in Creative Writing from the Institute of American Indian Arts. She is a candidate for an MFA in Creative Writing at Cornell University.

### Alch'a'abaa'

At the wash's edge:

a daughter of Noah stands in pools
of azure beaded stone, a half circle
on the warmth of her clay neck.

Ask her clan and she'll tell you beneath sackcloth:
*I am of the Sleep Rock People.*

Barefoot on steps of sandstone; waveless,
she trails down, sliding fingers along
river rocks like ripe melons, and their vines
the winding ripples of pure water. Her palms
catch white feathers zigzagging from
the Cedars of Lebanon,
ankles in mire.
Back to the cedar frame, covered with mud,
a floor of bark inside around a pit on the
North, she drops rocks into a blaze of wood.
She chants *The waves and winds still know*
*His voice who ruled them while He dwelt below.*
Stone after stone she carries with the help
of her stomach, struggling like a pregnant
woman up and down a hill, shuffling.

*I am born for the Water Edge People,*
She releases a dragonfly into the opal air.

The rocks glow red and she hands the pitchfork
over, grips a pail and trots to the stream where
bodies glitter in green;
His emblem hangs
above sleek brows:
a silver cast of the Male Shooting Way,
two thick level wings soldered together
by a darting torso, balanced.

Inside the blanket door is the crack of water
on red, and a bursting steam. In her lap she
stirs cedar, water, and the piñon needles
struck by lightning. With the bowl pressed
to her lips she blinks:

*I believe I am of the Mud People:*
the web of the wing, half earth, half water.

Her grandmother's sister calls her
Female Warrior Who Split in Two.

## Fourteen Days After Shimá's Vision

Around noontime on Highway 666, they were driving to Gallup. It was Pepper's fifth birthday. My dad is working in Red Valley. Cloudless. He is probably running laps with students. Our two vehicles left the Chuskas. I want a sucker. Cheii takes me. My little brother Vince and baby sister Billie are with mom, Pepper, Shelley Dee, and Aunt Vicky in her maroon car. It is too bright today. Two weeks ago my mom dreamt of night birds chanting amidst juniper berries. Today, the land formations look like owls. Mom was smiling in the passenger seat: Billie in her arms. I walk out of the Little Water Trading Post with Minnie Mouse's heart in my mouth. Cousin Shelley Dee was singing, "Jesus Wants Me For a Sunbeam" with my older sister Pepper. I sit alone, in the back of my Cheii's truck, trying on Aunt Olivia's make-up. Vince is drinking root beer and Billie is sleeping. It was May. I don't understand the dream or the land formations— Grandma clenches my hand as we stand on the side of the road in Newcomb. The sun takes them. I rest my eyes from the shattered rainbows at my feet;

Red Valley pepper-grass gathered in a pink plastic cup, here Daddy.

## Amenorrhea

> *When love gets into the heart there is nothing*
> *to be done but to clear it out . . . I shall forget*
> *it all . . . I shall tear it out of my heart.*
> —Anton Chekhov

I.
The heart is a uterus. *A wei o o hei yąą hei yąą,*
    A wei o o hei yąą hei yąą.

On the last day of school a sixth grader pulls down her panties in the restroom of a laundromat to discover her childhood in dry splotches. Kinaaldá, should follow. Earlier that year, girls would half-cover their mouths, "She's been gone for a week for her puberty ceremony, I heard." Tainted. She stuffs a wad of rolled tissue up there. Her first day, she squeezes her muscles, a stiff walk. Her father told her about this day. Miss Indian BYU taught her the songs. But her questions always to her aunt. Auntie, can it come in the shower?

It will come anywhere. Even with water tapping.

II.
*Yé hąą, yé hąą, a howo wo wo wo wo dei a hą,*
        *a howo wo wo wo wo dei a hą*


Inflate a balloon in the shape of a heart
with extra blood. The ribbon is a clogged straw,
a four flight newel.
                        Drag a fingernail
                            and press
against a thumb; juice drips down
a shimmery washboard of veins,     taut.


The first ovulation. Absence of the run, the raw nuggets:
   umbilical cord    slapping
her chest. Cob at cob. And grinding,
                            the grinding. Stoneless.
                    On her knees, leaning back
and thrusting forward. Only the songs. Combless.
Motherless. Skinless. Like an exquisite corpse tucked
in the nest of a cigar box. Hair frays at the string.
On a circle of pavement: companionless, running.

*Asdzáán Naadlehé! Jóhonaa'éí! Hashch'ee Yalti'i!*



III.
Even the moon stops pulling at her, a strange language
from her body. So Dr. Hay, she says *it's the rejection
of one's femininity.* The girl widens her legs and breathes.

She imagines herself inconspicuous, like a cantaloupe.
Gripping the padded handle of the zester tool, she scrapes
from the stem to the blossom end: her seed cavity, crusted
with dry love.
                *It's the air she's breathing.* His skin
is a maze of elongated sperm intertwining, circling
about scars. A negative month flow; the opposite of normal
punctuation. Her mind retains the womb's ache. Corn husks
line the hole.

Atop is a shriveled umbilical cord in a damp rag.

  Her aunt twists the cap, and folds medroxyprogesterone into the earth cake:

Áa dei hei ei ei ei ei o o ho, eiya' ei yą ei hąąngha ghei ąąnghei.

To induce the flow: sever from scar to scar, spoon out the fleshy fruit. Stand at the rite,
sing when shadowless. Sew the suture, the muscle spasms begin and spit tissue.

## XXVI (de *Meditaciónes sobre el Valle del Sur*)

Hoy talamos el olmo.
Viejo colmillo antiguo de tronco sin elasticidad.
John montaba ramas a horcajadas,
pisaba palos con brotes de semilla,
rompiendo ramas muertas. Su cabeza se perdió
entre las ramas—
        el moto-sierra colgaba de la cuerda amarrada a su cintura,
        él lentamente jaló hacia arriba,
        tiró del cordón,
        crepitando, gruñó aserrín hacia abajo
                por
                        el aire.

Las ramas chocaron al caer
con gemidos que estremecían y una agonía que rajaba,
aterrizaban con golpes muertos,
sacudiendo el aire a su alrededor mientras caían.

Los arrugados trozos de corteza como piel
rugían hacia abajo. John bajaba paso a paso
desde las ramas más altas,
hasta su melena densa—
        cortando en forma de cuña diez pies a la vez,
        haciendo cortes planos desde el otro extremo;
lentamente se volteó el tronco principal, se ladeó crujiendo, chupando aire,
revolviéndose hacia abajo, bramando
con un enorme golpe y caída,
respirando un último tirón de hojas, como elefante
en el suelo, el choque tembloroso se quedó en silencio.

Donde antes estuvo el árbol
una cascada plateada de cielo ahora vertía desde arriba.
Aire tranquilo.
Crepúsculo rojo. Sentí que acababa de matar
a un hombre anciano.

**Jimmy Santiago Baca** (Albuquerque, NM) ran away from an orphanage at age 13. He was later sentenced to five years in a maximum security prison, where he began to turn his life around by learning to read and write and unearthing a voracious passion for poetry. Baca devoted his post-prison life to writing and teaching, conducting hundreds of writing workshops in prisons, community centers, libraries, and universities throughout the country. He is author of many books of poetry. He has also written several novels, including *A Glass of Water* (Grove Press, 2009).

### XXVI (from *Meditations on the South Valley*)

We cut down the elm tree today.
Ungiving, old ancient tusk of trunk.
John straddled branches,
stepping through seed-bud sticks,
breaking dead limbs. His head was lost
in branches—
                chainsaw dangling from his waist rope,
                he slowly towed up,
pulled the cord,
crackling, it snarled sawdust down
           through
              the air.

Limbs crashed down
with shuddering groans and cracking throes,
hit the ground with dead thuds,
trembling air they fell through.

Wrinkled chunks of hide bark
growled down. John worked his way down
from the upper most branches,
down to its thick mane—
                wedge-cutting ten feet at a time,
                flat cutting from the opposite end;
slowly the main trunk tipped, lean-creaked, sucking air
thrashing down, bellowing
with one massive blow and fall,
breathing one last leaf-heave, like an elephant
grounded, the trembling crash became silent.

Where the tree had stood
a silver waterfall of sky now poured down.
Still air.
Red dusk. I felt I had just killed
an old man.

## VIII (de *Meditaciónes sobre el Valle del Sur*)

Una película trasnochada.
No puedo dormir.
Un bandido
en una vieja película del oeste
salta del techo de una cantina
a su caballo
y galopa al llano.
Mi corazón es un viejo poste
al que amarré los sueños que tuve hace años
y le dan tirones
para liberarse.
Apago la tele
y en la oscuridad, los suelto—

        un chavalo anda en bicicleta
        al amanecer por la carretera Barcelona,
        apretando rosas entre sus dientes,
en la cesta del manubrio
hay manzanas que tomó de los árboles al azar en la calle.


## VIII (from *Meditations on the South Valley*)

Late night movie.
I can't sleep.
A bandit
in an old western movie
jumps from a saloon roof
onto his horse
and gallops into the llano.
My heart is an old post
dreams I tied to it years ago
yank against
to get free.
I turn the tv off
And in the darkness,     let them go—

        a chavalo riding his bicycle
        at dawn down Barcelona road,
        clenching roses in his teeth,
in the handle-bar basket
are apples he took from random trees on the road.

**Jim Barnes** (Santa Fe, NM) is author of many books of poems, including *Visiting Picasso* (University of Illinois Press, 2007). He and his wife have a ranch in Atoka and a hacienda in Santa Fe. He served as Distinguished Professor of English and Creative Writing at Brigham Young University and as Oklahoma Poet Laureate (2009—2010). He edited *The Chariton Review* for over thirty-five years. Salt Publishing (UK) released *The Salt Companion to Jim Barnes*, a critical study, in 2010.

## Autobiography, Chapter 5: Ghost Town

Boards the shape of shadows, windows blued by the awful
      sun, the black hollow of gone doors, and always the
      surrounding sound of wind.

You try to take this absent town in one bound of soul,
      afraid you'll stumble on the derelict years only
      the headstones name.

You fail. The mind finds a stop: a rainbow in broken
      glass, a stream of dust in the washed-out street,
      footsteps you can't possibly hear.

The half saloon bangs its half a door the wind walks
      through. Night falls like hail, down with the
      thirsting hills.

You spread your blankets before the blank eyes of the
      town and lie in wait, a poor thief, for the permanence
      of stars. Inside your throat hangs a silence: there
      are no words, no words.

## Paiute Ponies

Silhouettes, they lean against a ringed moon,
their heads down against the threat of snow.
Below, a distant diesel moan runs
along the tracks, where dead coal cinders
gather frost, and plays out toward Winnemucca.

No Movement. They hump against the night.
Only quivering patches of skin crack the air,
memories of a summer fly.

Mane and tail hanging vertical as ice,
they sleep dead centuries,
or if ponies dream they dream.

Below on the flat where light strikes water,
a last ember sparks out. A dog complains.

The diesel warns again, begins its roar, passes.
They raise their heads like automatons, blink,
then drop once more into centuries or dreams.

## The Ranch, Wild Horse Canyon, 1943

The mountain south of the ranch leaned hard through
a heavy sky almost blocking the winter sun
at noon. The canyon ended there, dammed by the blue
haze that Winding Stair became after a winter rain
or snow. You could hear all the horses neigh at you

from the timbered slopes on clear December nights
when the wind was down. Stars were always on the move
across the narrow patch of sky. Lying just right
in your bunk by the window, you saw ridges shove
all the higher constellations across the night

and thought of all the things you'd like to do before
your light went out and your small voice was stilled. At ten
you were wise enough to want a few summers more
to ride the ranch with the hired hands, to pretend
no end of things. But things began to end. The roar

of warplanes overhead each day made the air dance
and the canyon echo with the drumming of stampede.
The rancher's elder son joined up, finding a chance
in war to leave for a wider world. You felt a need
to keep the horses free and cried to see them prance

into the boxcars, into soap and glue, to save
the world. Days were full of planes and nights of solemn
radio, commentators mournful and slow, wave after wave
of static as the battery wore down. You were dumb
with grief at the loss of horses, dumb with the ways

to call them home, yet old enough to know the dead
horses would not neigh again under the mountain moon.
You wept as a child at the stockyard gate, your knees red
with earth, and swore in time to come horses would run
free as far as the mountain's end and the canyon's head.

271

**Marianne A. Broyles** (Rio Rancho, NM) is a citizen of the Cherokee Nation of Oklahoma and earned her creative writing degrees from Emory University and the University of Memphis. In addition to reading and writing poetry, she enjoys spending her time visiting the Bosque Del Apache Wildlife Preserve in Socorro, New Mexico, watching baseball, and leading a poetry group for her patients at the VA, where she is a psychiatric nurse.

### American Island

I carry ice water for him,
this veteran in the dawn of alcohol withdrawal,
whose eyes are an outgoing tide,
and hands are two islands of a chain,
balled into fists to try to contain
tremors wanting to gallop through his body like
wild horses on Shackleford Banks.
Each bead of sweat is a banker pony leaping from a sinking ship,
swimming toward the beach.
An appaloosa, a bay, a palomino,
swimming, swimming, weightless legs
kicking through the current,
doing what they never thought they could—
survive another day.

(According to legend, "banker ponies" populated North Carolina's
barrier islands before people. When the ships sank in storms, these
horses lept from them and swam to the safety of the beach.)

**Jon Davis** (Santa Fe, NM) received his MFA in Creative Writing from the University of Montana. Since 1990, he has taught creative writing at the Institute of American Indian Arts in Santa Fe, New Mexico. Among his awards are a Lannan Literary Award and two National Endowment for the Arts Fellowships.

## Horse in Shadow

Cold, the wind that riffs through the west end door
sounding its low moan, grieving the moment's passing.
And cold the nose of the near-black gelding
where he stomps once in the glistening darkness,
the gentled night. My twelve year old daughter,
stiff in her jodhpurs and boots, removes one glove
and reaches a carrot toward the shadowed head.
"Good boy," she purrs. "Good boy." *Good boy,*
who'd bucked and lurched, galloping hellbent
at the corrugated wall, whirling until he'd launched her
from the saddle into the dust-dazzled air.
"Good boy," she says. And he *is*—furious teacher,
unendurable bliss—because she *says* he is, loyal girl,
good friend, forgiver, profferer of carrots, wielder
of whips, tiny commander in her wafer-thin saddle.

## Loving Horses

—for Grayce

Yellow aspen. Quaking leaf. Metal barn creaking.
Dust like rain against the roof. What could be better
than a horse dreaming in a sunlit stall? The heave
of chest, the nostrils flaring. The head carving light
into shadow and deeper shadow. The sheen of a horse's coat
is a form of weeping, the form weeping takes
when it hears the solitary cry of the flicker
in the fog-softened morning. The cry of the flicker
which is the word tear lengthened and brought to bear
upon the meadow's longings, the longings we bring to the meadow.
Which are the same longings we bring to the horse in the dawn.
The eye seems bottomless. Fetlock and pastern seem designed
more for flight than galloping, tendons taut as the bones
in a bat's wing. The bats which veer across the barn's mouth
in the dusk, feeding on the flies which feed on the horses
which feed on the hay scattered in their outdoor runs.
Yellow aspen. Quaking leaf. Metal barn creaking.
Dust like rain against the roof. What could be better than a horse
galloping with horses in a rain-freshened meadow?

The young women lean and listen to the soliloquy of hoofbeats.
In a gallop, as we first saw in Muybridge's photographs,
all four hooves are off the ground at once. *Walk.*
*Working trot. Extended trot. Canter. Gallop.*
*Count strides to the fence. Fold. Take the fence.*
*Sit up. Gallop on.* It is thought that the horse,
because it cannot see immediately ahead,
must remember the jump it jumps blindly, guided by the rider's
hands and seat and legs. And the rider must look past the jump,
*head up,* to keep the horse's energy moving forward
so that of the three—horse, rider, spectator—only the spectator sees
the actual jump as it is jumped. Which is a metaphor for life,
the way this moment I am in, this moment I am trying to be in,
does not exist until I am in the next one. The *nextness* of the fences—
the way a man who is leaving his wife for another woman
can no longer see the wife he is leaving. Or the way the child struggles
with the piano concerto until she begins to work
on the next, more difficult, concerto which makes the first one
easy to play and filled with something like joy
where before there was only agony. Which reminds me of an afternoon—
it was the son's birthday, and the mother invited the father
to a party at the house she lived in with her new lover. The father
brought his current lover who spent the afternoon measuring
the distance between herself and the ex-wife, between the father
and the wife's new lover. These were fences that needed jumping
at a full gallop, and she could only see them
when she turned her head to one side and then, when she
needed to jump, they would have already disappeared. *Dad,*
my daughter might say if she were watching over my shoulder.
*Why do you turn everything into a lecture? The poem*
*is about horses and horses are about themselves.*
Yellow aspen. Quaking leaf. Metal barn creaking.
Dust like rain against the roof. The horses stomp and sway, shift their weight
from leg to leg. *So handsome,* my daughter says. We are sitting in my Jeep,
leaving the barn on an afternoon on which I'd struggled,
in a counseling session, to explain how I had tried
desperately not to fall in love with the woman
I had already fallen in love with. It is late afternoon, the sun is setting
magnanimously over the Jemez Mountains, and her horse, Codeman—
half muscular Hanoverian, half elegant Thoroughbred—has come out
to dip his light-sculpting head into the water trough. *Look at him, Dad.*
Her voice is hushed, almost a whisper. *Just    look at him.*

## Songline of Dawn

We are ascending through the dawn
the sky, blushed with the fever
                                        of attraction.
I don't want to leave my daughter,
                                        or the babies.
I can see their house, a refuge in the dark near the university.
Protect them, oh gods of the scarlet light
who love us fiercely despite our acts of stupidity
our utter failings.
May this morning light be food for their bones,
for their spirits dressed
                        in manes of beautiful black hair
in skins the color of the earth as it meets the sky.
Higher we fly over the valley of monster bones
left scattered in the dirt to remind us that breathing
is rooted somewhere other than the lungs.
                                    My spirit approaches with reverence
because it harbors the story, of how these beloveds
                                        appeared to fail
then climbed into the sky to stars of indigo.
                And we keep going past the laughter and tears
of the babies who will grow up to become a light field
just beyond us.
And then the sun breaks over the yawning mountain.
And the plane shivers as we dip toward
                                an old volcanic field.
It is still smoldering
motivated by the love of one deity for another.
It's an old story and we're in it so deep we have become them.
The sun leans on one elbow after making love
                                savoring the wetlands just off the freeway.
We are closer to the gods than we ever thought possible.

**Joy Harjo** (Albuquerque, NM) is a member of the Mvskoke (Creek) Nation. Her seven books of poetry include *She Had Some Horses* (Thunder's Mouth Press, 1984), *The Woman Who Fell From the Sky* (W. W. Norton, 1989), and *How We Became Human: New and Selected Poems* (W. W. Norton, 2003). She is the recipient of a Lila Wallace-Reader's Digest Award, the New Mexico Governor's Award for Excellence in the Arts, the Lifetime Achievement Award from the Native Writers Circle of the Americas, and the William Carlos Williams Award from the Poetry Society of America. She performs internationally solo and with her band, Joy Harjo and the Arrow Dynamics Band.

### Perhaps the World Ends Here

The world begins at a kitchen table. No matter what, we must eat to live.

The gifts of earth are brought and prepared, set on the table. So it has been since creation, and it will go on.

We chase chickens or dogs away from it. Babies teethe at the corners. They scrape their knees under it.

It is here that children are given instructions on what it means to be human. We make men at it, we make women.

At this table we gossip, recall enemies and the ghosts of lovers.

Our dreams drink coffee with us as they put their arms around our children. They laugh with us at our poor falling-down selves and as we put ourselves back together once again at the table.

This table has been a house in the rain, an umbrella in the sun.

Wars have begun and ended at this table. It is a place to hide in the shadow of terror. A place to celebrate the terrible victory.

We have given birth on this table, and have prepared our parents for burial here.

At this table we sing with joy, with sorrow. We pray of suffering and remorse. We give thanks.

Perhaps the world will end at the kitchen table, while we are laughing and crying, eating of the last sweet bite.

## Rainy Dawn

I can still close my eyes and open them four floors up looking south
and west from the hospital, the approximate direction of Acoma,
and farther on to the roofs of the houses of the gods who have
learned there are no endings, only beginnings. That day so hot,
heat danced in waves off bright car tops, we both stood poised at
that door from the east, listened for a long time to the sound of our
grandmothers' voices, the brushing wind of sacred wings, the rattle
of raindrops in dry gourds. I had to participate in the dreaming of
you into memory, cupped your head in the bowl of my body as
ancestors lined up to give you a name made of their dreams cast
once more into this stew of precious spirit and flesh. And let you go,
as I am letting you go once more in the ceremony of the living. And
when you were born I held you wet and unfolding, like a butterfly
newly born from the chrysalis of my body. And breathed with you as
you breathed your first breath. Then was your promise to take it on
like the rest of us, this immense journey, for love, for rain.

## Eagle Poem

To pray you open your whole self
To sky, to earth, to sun, to moon
To one whole voice that is you.
And know there is more
That you can't see, can't hear,
Can't know except in moments
Steadily growing, and in languages
That aren't always sound but other
Circles of motion.
Like eagle that Sunday morning
Over Salt River. Circled in blue sky
In wind, swept our hearts clean
With sacred wings.
We see you, see ourselves and know
That we must take the utmost care
And kindness in all things.
Breathe in, knowing we are made of
All this, and breathe, knowing
We are truly blessed because we
Were born, and die soon within a
True circle of motion,
Like eagle rounding out the morning
Inside us.
We pray that it will be done
In beauty.
In beauty.

**Phyllis Hoge** (Albuqueque, NM) spent 20 years in humid Hawai'i, where she taught poetry at the university and invented the first Poets In The Schools Program in the United States. She then chose to live in land-bounded and arid New Mexico, where wide blue skies, mountains, and open miles of desert spaces prevent her from missing the islands or the ocean. Since she and her four children visit one another frequently, she continues to enjoy the best of both worlds.

**section iii** (from *El Paso*)

"Señor."
        "Sí."
                "Mi esposa—she is here."
"Lopez, verdad?"
           "Sí."
                  "Did you hear her name
When I read the list?"
                "No, señor. All the same,
I want to sit with her."
                "You will. Yet for fear
You may get separated, I will place
Both of you on one list. Guard, make a space
For Senor Lopez in the last file. Bueno."

A stocky man with black hair, copper skin,
And a pleasant face gets up and squeezes in.

Mid-row at the back.
              "Your country?"
                   "Mexico."
He sneezes, and from his pocket pulls a rag.
He blows his nose on a small American flag.

## Blanco Ascending

My horse who changed his name
from Whitey Martinez to Blanco
was last seen eating apples
in a deserted rancho in Chimayó.
We were drinking margaritas
at the Rancho de Chimayo before it burned,
Blanco née Whitey was cruising a small orchard
down the road when he ascended,
making him the world's first holy horse or
maybe they are all divine.

The fence was intact, the neighbors
saw nothing. But next day he was gone.
Apples still bore the imprint of his old teeth,
teeth that always lied about his age
since the day we bought him from
a family in La Villita.

Blanco bore me through sweetness
and betrayals. He suffered everyone
who came to ride, always galloped up
the side of gullies, eternal fat darling of all.

Now he is ascended, garlands of roses.
Some suspect aliens, others say heroin
dealers sold him, turned him into smack.
He didn't escape or would have turned up
at the pasture. No one would steal such
an ancient horse branded on his left flank
with a large angel holding a gun.

So since he vanished standing up in
the village of weavers who weave standing up
he became the keeper of apples, purveyor
of holy dirt, God's mule, white powder
of heroin and cocaine shrouding him forever.

Sacred beast, every day I pray for a sighting,
a miracle on a saddle blanket, a tortilla
burnt like Appaloosa, hoof prints on the clouds.

**Joan Logghe** (Española, NM) works off the academic grid in La Puebla, New Mexico, where she and her husband, Michael, raised three children and built three houses. Awards include a National Endowment for the Arts Fellowship, Witter Bynner Foundation for Poetry grants, A Mabel Dodge Luhan Internship, and a Barbara Deming/Money for Women grant. She taught poetry in Bratislava, Vienna, and Zagreb, Croatia.

**Carol Moldaw** (Santa Fe, NM) is author of five books of poetry: *So Late, So Soon: New and Selected Poems* (Etruscan Press, 2010); *The Lightning Field* (Oberlin College Press, 2003), which won the 2002 FIELD Poetry Prize; *Through the Window* (La Alameda Press, 2000); *Chalkmarks on Stone* (La Alameda Press, 1998); and *Taken from the River* (Alef Books, 1993). She has also written a novel, *The Widening* (Etruscan Press, 2008). She lives near Santa Fe, New Mexico, with her husband and daughter.

### Festina Lente

Rake marks on gravel.
Flecks of straw in adobe.

Four and a half feet down,
a blue-glass flask flaking mica,

charred wood, a layer of ash,
a humerus, if not animal,

then human. What looks
like the slatted side of a crate,

the backhoe driver says
is an old well shaft.

Mounds of displaced dirt,
dug up for new leach lines,

rise higher than the walls.
All we know of the pueblo

is that they burned trash here,
in our courtyard; spoke Tewa;

and dispersed—were driven out—
to Santa Clara, to Hopi.

Did the same ditch irrigate
their beans as our flowering plums?

And where we sleep, is that
where their turkeys flocked?

The man who built this house,
scavenging bridge ties for beams,

died in the courtyard,
his sickbed facing sunrise.

His wife's "stitcheries"
still cover some of our windows.

When we reburied the humerus
under a cottonwood, with incense

and a patchwork prayer,
we were only putting it back,

*festina lente*, into the mix
of sieved dirt, sand, and straw.

## Out of the West

Out of the west, unexpected, lyric,
a stand of yellow irises
rises from the pond muck.

Two horses graze the field,
one limping from the fire they fled.

Matter and spirit meet, love,
*argue,* wherever you rest your eyes,
on microscopic midges, horseflies.

**Sara Marie Ortiz** (Santa Fe, NM) is an Acoma Pueblo memoirist, playwright, poet, scholar, youth trainer, and Indigenous Peoples advocate. She earned a Bachelor of Fine Arts Degree in creative writing from the Institute of American Indian Arts in Santa Fe (2006) and a Master of Fine Arts Degree from Antioch University Los Angeles (2009).

## From First Emergence to Last

I bade you
come lie
by my side,
for just
a little while.

But *your wings*
were broken.
But
your wings
were broken.

And mine were too.
And mine were too.

So I wrote this song
So I wrote this song

What cord is not all severed?
*Sever the cord.* No other way to be free. From *first emergence* to
last.

Madness is vital in getting it done.

The cord begs us to cut it.
Who are we to refuse?

Remember, child.
*Remember.*

## Sparrow of Española

Here's to that bedraggled sparrow
at the Sonic Drive-In in Española, New Mexico,
famous Low Rider Capital of the World.

Sunday there is a holy day of cars;
the summer afternoon we passed through
all the discount auto parts stores were open, lots full,
and out on the drag a parade
of huge Dodges and souped-up Chevys crept along,
engines throbbing, drivers in mirrored shades just visible
above the steering wheels made from chain,
the carpeted dashboards, soft dice bouncing
as car after car reared up and dropped down,
reared and dropped like perfect black stallions
in movies at El Pasatiempo down the road.

Sunlight ricocheted off tinted windshields,
metallic-flake paint and chrome trim
as the drivers idled bumper to bumper
up and down U.S. 285, route of the Pueblos,
route of Oñate and Escalante, of Spanish priests,
American trappers, traders and tourists on their way
somewhere else, stopping for coffee, a bite to eat,
a tank of gas to get them out.

In Española the low riders drove all afternoon,
all evening, all their lives for all we knew.
For half an hour we ate in our car and watched them
go by and go by. They were home there,
with the hard-luck sparrow that accosted us at the Sonic:
small, brown, skinny, half its feathers gone,
others poking out at odd angles,
it looked ravaged and incapable of flight,
sparrow of present misery forever.

Yet it flew, popping from beam to beam
holding up the corrugated steel roof
above us, flying about or bouncing around
on the ground, peeping its one note over and over.

**Michael Pettit** (Santa Fe, NM) is a recipient of a National Endowment for the Arts Fellowship. His books include *Cardinal Points* (University of Iowa Press, 1988), which received the Iowa Poetry Prize. His nonfiction account of ranching in Texas and New Mexico, *Riding for the Brand* (University of Oklahoma Press, 2006), received the New Mexico Book Award for Southwestern History.

There, out of the hot sun that bore down, crowning
the cars out on the strip, softening the asphalt
everywhere except in the shadow of the Sonic,
was home, was the known world: cheap speakers
squawking, waitresses hustling trays, overheated aroma
of fries and tacos, crumbs all the sparrows fought over.
Ours and the others of the flock—those bigger,
less tattered, maybe not so hopelessly stuck in Española—
went begging shamelessly from car to car,
ours and the hot machines of low riders
in for a rest, a break in their ceaseless revolutions
up and down 285. Give them tenacity.

Here's to that lost sparrow, that least bird
cheeping on the hood of our car, ornament
of desire that creates and defeats failure.
Here's to the insistent call of its belly and heart
that won our hearts and tongues:
when we rolled out of the Sonic into the parade
and away from Española forever, we were singing
its song over and over and over.

## Driving Lesson

Beside him in the old Ford pickup
that smelled of rope and grease and cattle feed,
sat my sister and I, ten and eight, big
now our grandfather would teach us
that powerful secret, how to drive.
Horizon of high mountain peaks visible
above the blue hood, steering wheel huge
in our hands, pedals at our toe-tips,
we heard his sure voice urge us
*Give it gas, give it gas.* Over the roar
of the engine our hearts banged
like never before and banged on
furiously in the silence after
we bucked and stalled the truck.
How infinitely empty it then seemed—

windy flat rangeland of silver-green
gramma grass dotted with blooming cactus
and jagged outcrops of red rock, beginnings
of the Sangre de Cristos fifty miles off.
All Guadalupe County, New Mexico,
nothing to hit, and we could not
get the damn thing going. Nothing to hit
was no help. It was not the mechanics
of accelerator and clutch, muscle and bone,
but our sheer unruly spirits
that kept us small with the great desire
to move the world by us, earth and sky
and all the earth and sky contained.
And how hard it was when,
after our grandfather who was a god
said *Let it out slow, slow* time and again
until we did and were at long last rolling
over the earth, his happy little angels,
how hard it was to listen
not to our own thrilled inner voices
saying *Go, go*, but to his saying
the *Good, good* we loved but also
the *Keep it in the ruts* we hated to hear.
How hard to hold to it—
single red vein of a ranch road
running out straight across the mesa,
blood we were bound to follow—
when what we wanted with all our hearts
was to scatter everywhere, everywhere.

**Leo Romero** (Santa Fe, NM) has been a bookseller since 1988. His current bookstore is called Books of Interest, which he runs with his wife, Elizabeth. Leo has previously had two other bookstores. Before being a bookseller, Leo worked at the Los Alamos National Laboratory as a technical writer/editor. Besides writing, Leo enjoys drawing/painting and building rock walls.

### Perros Del Diablo

Elena walks everywhere
on crutches. She only
has one leg.

"My children ate it,"
she says out loud
whether there are
people around
to hear her or not.
"Esos perros del diablo!"
she says with revulsion.

Those dogs of the devil.

Everyone sees Elena
walking around town
with her crutches.
She's not from around here.
The rumor is she's
from somewhere in Nayarit
where so much
drug trafficking
has been going on.

She arrived on the bus
one day.
Her leg was already
missing.
No one knows
how she gets by.

And since that day
people have continually
heard Elena
complain about her children,
how they pushed
her husband
over a cliff
when he threatened
to turn them in
for selling drugs
if they didn't stop.

Then they came after her
like a pack of wild dogs
believing she had
turned their father
against them
which she had.

She had been
telling him for months
to get a gun
and shoot them all
saying the drugs
were making them crazy.

After they ate
one of her legs,
she just managed
to escape
before they got
to her other leg.

It horrifies people to hear
Elena talk
this way,
but no one
doubts the truth
of what she says.

We've all seen children
turn on their parents
and treat them horribly.

"Here! Take my leg!"
Elena will shout
causing shivers to go
down our spines.

"And they took it,
esos perros del diablo!
They tore into
my living flesh.
And no matter
how much I screamed,
they continued until
even the bone was gone."

**An Angel Aids Jesus**

An angel's feather
poked Emilio in the eye
when the angel raised
her wings.
One of the more delicate
angels in heaven
with wings
like those of a crane.

The angel had stopped
to come
to his assistance
thinking Emilio was Jesus
because of the blood
that was pouring
down his chest.

He didn't have a shirt on.
Just pants.
And bare feet.
Someone shot him.
Mistaken identity.

Emilio had just moved
into a new apartment
and had opened the door
to enjoy a beer outside
when he saw a man
about to knock
who he had never
seen before
and who then shot him.

The man hadn't looked
at his face
and fled
in a waiting car.

Emilio staggered outside
and that's when
the passing angel
saw his bleeding chest.

She landed next to him
and in her distress
kept flapping her wings
until a feather
poked him in the eye.

*Damn!* Emilio thought, *First
I get shot and then this
crazy bird has ruined my eye.*

## Step

Marie's got stuck on repeaters today.
*Knees up! Knees up!* Our benches groan.
She moves like a cat just ahead of the beat,
ponytail tapping either shoulder blade.
She's taken off her shirt, down to Batman bra,
lycra shorts. A blue tattoo peeps over the hem.
What is it? A dolphin? A spider? *OK!* she shouts.
*March it out!* Her buttocks flex. *Basic left!*
Turn-turn, thud-thud, turn-turn, thud. *Arms!*
Up they go, braced for imaginary weights.
The fat guy hates the butterfly arms, does them
halfway. We *glute-squeeze*, we *abductor*,
we *travel-straddle*, we *round-the-world-and-kick*,
we *up-and-lunge*, *power-lunge*, *double-lunge*.
Miss Latina with the gun-barrel eyes gets me
in her sights in the mirror. Caught me eyeing her.
Marie's spine bends desirably as she ballerina-kicks.
My sneakers turn to clay, my shirt drips
and clings. Not Marie—dry as a bone.
*Take a pulse*, *warm-down time*. That tattoo—
a butterfly, a bat? An orchid? It's stretches now,
and *back-rolls*. Marie's light and young,
strong and hard, everything I want to be.
Come on, let's back-roll together, you and me.
The boxer in the gallery quits thumping his bag,
peers down, gloves dangling over the rail.
The raquetball players glance from the door
as the class groans and gasps like a rusty machine,
grins on every face now because it's *big-inhale*
time, *grab-some-water* time. We sigh, we clap
ourselves as Marie marches it out one last time.
She tweaks her shorts, peels back the hem
like a fruit rind, smiles over her shoulder,
and there it is, branded on her rump: an open fig.

**Henry Shukman** (Santa Fe, NM) won the 2003 Jerwood Aldeburgh Prize for his first poetry collection, *In Dr. No's Garden* (Random House, 2002), which was also a Book of the Year in the (London) *Times* and *Guardian*. He was Poet-in-Residence at the Wordsworth Trust and a Royal Literary Fund Poetry Fellow at Oxford Brookes University. He lives in Santa Fe, New Mexico, where he writes for *The New York Times* and teaches at the Institute of American Indian Art.

### The Airport Shuttle

*Mightn't be this ain't the last run of the day*,
says the driver, and whichever way the negatives work
he's right. A night like this, swamped by snow,
you don't know when your last chance might come.

At the intersection the red goes deep as midnight.
AutoZone and Long John Silvers, the Chevron
and the Lamplighter—the ballad of Cerrillos Road:
this artery of tar and rubber, the local life-support.

The bus splashes its axles in the slow lane.
We crunch through frozen slush.
Close to town, the houses are hung with lights.
Just the elderly couple and me now, chortling

down the long red wall to the last hotel,
and the driver bobbing on his seat.
It's falling again, a swarm coming thicker, faster,
until it's all the wipers can do to keep things clear.

**Arthur Sze** (Santa Fe, NM) is author of nine books of poetry, including *The Ginkgo Light* (Copper Canyon Press, 2009) and *Quipu* (Copper Canyon Press, 2005). He is also editor of *Chinese Writers on Writing* (Trinity University Press, 2010). Professor Emeritus at the Institute of American Indian Arts, he lives in Santa Fe.

## Looking Back on the Muckleshoot Reservation from Galisteo Street, Santa Fe

The bow of a Muckleshoot canoe, blessed
with eagle feather and sprig of yellow cedar,
is launched into a bay. A girl watches
her mother fry venison slabs in a skillet—
drops of blood sizzle, evaporate. Because
a neighbor feeds them, they eat wordlessly;
the silence breaks when she occasionally
gags, reaches into her throat, pulls out hair.
Gone is the father, riled, arguing with his boss,
who drove to the shooting range after work;
gone the accountant who embezzled funds,
displayed a pickup, and proclaimed a winning
flush at the casino. You donate chicken soup
and clothes but never learn if they arrive
at the south end of the city. Your small
acts are sandpiper tracks in wet sand.
Newspapers, plastic containers, beer bottles
fill the bins along this sloping one-way street.

## Qualia

"Oviparous," she says, "A duck-billed platypus
is oviparous." Strapped in her car seat,
she colors an array of tulips on white paper.
Stopped at a light on Highway 285, he stares
at a gas station, convenience store. A man
steps out with a six-pack under his right arm,
while she repeats last night's queries:
Why does the Nile flow north? Who was Nefertiti?

And as cars accelerate, he knows the silver
one in the rearview mirror will pass him
on the right before he reaches the hilltop.
She sounds out "red": what was the shape
and color of a triceratops egg? Though
a chart can depict how height and weight
unfold along time, no chart can depict
how imagination unfolds, endlessly branching.

As sunlight slants over the Sangre de Cristos,
he notices Tesuque Pueblo police have pulled
a pickup off the highway. At school, lined
up for kindergarten, she waves, and he waves
back. As classmates enter, she waves, and, again,
he waves back, waves at apple blossoms
unfolding white along a studio wall, at
what is shed and slithering into pellucid air.

**Diane Thiel** (Albuquerque, NM) is author of eight books, including *Echolocations* (Story Line Press, 2000), which won the Nicholas Roerich Prize; *Resistance Fantasies* (Story Line Press, 2004); and *The White Horse: A Colombian Journey* (Etruscan Press, 2004). Thiel's translation of Alexis Stamatis's *American Fugue* (Etruscan Press, 2008) recieved the National Endowment for the Arts International Literature/Translation Award. A recipient of many awards, including the Robert Frost and Robinson Jeffers Awards, and a Fulbright Scholar, she is an Associate Professor at the University of New Mexico.

## Wild Horses, Placitas

This old village is known for its horses, wild herds
which consider these foothills their home. They are said
to have run here for centuries, since they were left
by the conquistadores. You rarely will catch
any glimpse—only traces, the dust cloud kicked up
or the high-pitched calls traveling far in the cold
morning air. Very soon after moving out West,
I encounter them, first those mysterious calls
at the break of a dawn, re-inventing my ear
and my eye and the day and the trail with a still
unexplainable peace, like a long desert rain

but then, suddenly breaking, the radio's news
like a murder.

            Why is it, again and again,
we will know of such beauty just as it is lost,
one herd harvested, auctioned—the lead stallion's neck
snapped, as he tried to resist. On a morning like this,
I can't help but want one, at least one mystery
to remain—I want something that large and that fast
and that—costly—to still be out there running free
to have even the tiniest possibility
on an average morning, on waking, or heading
off to work in the city, our sprawling Albuquerque
to hear their hoofbeats in the valley—echoing.

## At the Mailbox

The first few times we met, our hearts would rise.
You must have thought that I had no excuse
since I am over a thousand times your size.
But ever since my brother introduced
the two of us, and showed his sibling love,
by catching you to put you in my hair—
I've had the kind that lizards can't get out of.
Now I tap the box to let you know I'm there,
a ritual we both appreciate.
Between my much awaited mail, you leave
your gifts. What would I do, if every day
*my* little house would open and receive
a mountain, where my living room once stood?
I'd move. At least, I like to think I would.

## laid off

they hold their heads high
say they saw it coming
(they did) and knew
how to take it in stride
(they didn't)
all week whispered conversations
about unemployment benefits
and maybe going back to school
then the planning out loud for all to hear
about meeting at a local bar Friday after work
to get blasted and let it all hang out

if you were one of the lucky ones
you'll pass because after the 3rd round
weird looks will begin to come your way
the comic book bubbles over their
heads where you can read their thoughts
will say the same thing:
"why not him?"

then you'll blink an eye and see it
reflected back at you in their faces
the shotgun someone will clean tomorrow
and come Monday you're sitting at your
desk taking a phone call
whipping around to see what made
the loud metallic click behind you

you'll blink again
now you're back at the bar
Hank Williams is on the jukebox
they're all lifting their glasses
in your direction

you read someone's lips
as he/she says:
"watch out man,
you could be next."

**Richard Vargas** (Albuquerque, NM) graduated from California State University Long Beach, where he studied poetry and literature under Gerald Locklin and took part in the local small press scene by publishing five issues of *The Tequila Review* from 1978—1980. He is author of two books of poetry, *McLife* (Main Street Rag Publishing, 2005) and *American Jesus* (Tia Chucha Press, 2007). He has lived in Colorado and Illinois and now resides in Albuquerque, New Mexico.

## baby brother's blues

he was just a kid who loved to tease
our sisters and counted on me to keep
the neighborhood bullies at bay
but our stepfather did not like him as he was
right away he tightened the screws
shaved his head
slapped him around
played mind games with him
like waking him up at two in the morning
and making him shine his shoes
he was only seven or eight
the time he took him to downtown L.A.
made him get on the floor of the car
so he could not see where they were going
then he was told to sit up and before he
could ask about the tall buildings and all the people
scurrying about like ants the old man opened the door
kicked him out on the sidewalk
drove off without saying a word
years later my brother would say he had never been so scared
cried as he realized he had been dumped
on the street like an unwanted pet, until
our stepfather circled the block
laughed as he picked him up like
it was a big joke

his childhood became a thing to endure
losing a piece of himself with every blow
to his head, carrying what was left of his psyche
in the palm of his hand
like pieces of precious glass

last year i drove up to see him
surrounded by cold stone walls
and fences with razor sharp edges
men with loaded guns watched from above
as we hugged and talked
this is how i remember my baby brother

in Folsom blue

trying to fill the holes in his soul
with Camel cigarettes
and crude tattoos

## ancestor

word has it he crossed the river
at El Paso when the streets were still dirt
when a mexican had to step aside to let
a white man pass
he planted his seed here
started a whole branch of the family tree
and then he killed a man
(i don't know why or how
but i'm sure money and a woman were involved
also several shots of tequila
and an old pistola from the revolution)
the sheriff got word to him
he was good as dead if he got caught
so he crossed the river back
to Mexico . . . the mother of our people

and word has it he crossed back
several times to visit his family
once he had to spend all day
in the outhouse while the sheriff's men
searched the place
terrorized his wife and children
but he always got away
like the fox he truly was

some would say it is a shame
to have a killer's blood in my veins
and worse, to be proud of it
but i think back to the times
i refused to be fucked with
convinced guys bigger than me to back off
knowing if my bluff was called
i would be history
maybe they could see the old man's craziness
in my eyes . . . the button they dare not push

it's a good thing to have some bad blood
it's a good thing

**race war**

"yeah," he said, "guys at work are buying
guns and shit . . . storing 'em in the desert
for the big race war."

immediately i begin to regret
the many times i refused to go
hunting with my stepfather
never acquiring the taste for
blood and guts, the violent
scattering of feathers in mid air
or the nonsensical pumping of shells
into a ball of fur.

taking a sip from my wine cooler,
i study him . . . an aryan bull.
i imagine him and myself
locked in hand to hand combat,
a classic battle.
but i know that's not how it will be,
because a scared man is a crazy one.

it will come from behind, and i won't even know
what hit me.

**Erika T. Wurth** (Albuquerque, NM) is Apache, Chickasaw, and Cherokee. *Indian Trains* (West End Press, 2007) is her first collection of poems. Her work has appeared in *Boulevard, SAIL, AMCRJ, Cedar Hill Review, Fiction, Raven Chronicles, Pembroke, Ellipsis, 5AM, Global City Review, The Bryant Literary Review,* and *Red Ink.* She was a visiting writer at the Institute of American Indian Arts in Santa Fe, and she also teaches creative writing at Western Illinois University.

## Oh, Cousin

How we rode on your motorcycle that summer and every summer,
on those back roads behind my house,
the smell of the raspberry bushes after the rain everywhere.

I buried my mixed blood hands in your mixed blood hair, cut it, you said
and make it look like yours, but darker.
And I couldn't though I loved you more than anyone else.

How we laughed all night, tormenting
my brilliant younger sister who would grow up so angry and sad
just like Dad, just like your dad too, both of them.

Oh, Ab, we grew up and got off that bike too quick,
you with babies and fists, and me, with words and nothing else.

Oh, Ab, let's get back on the bike, and stop, and pick those raspberries
and make something beautiful out of them and let's take my sister along
this time, I miss her so much.

## In Order to Save the Woman

I've been told a million times that I've got to kill the Apache in order to
save the woman and if I would love blindly love blind I would see the
beauty of white hands, the beauty of white hands on me, I would feel
them everywhere, especially inside but I like the look of brown eyes too
much to enjoy the death and besides it's already begun, my skin yellow
and my mind empty of the words that my grandmother used to explain
exactly how she felt the first time she walked into the kitchen and the
whole room was empty of the holy words that had filled the room only
moments before.

**Venaya Yazzie** (Huerfano, NM) grew up in the eastern region of the Navajo Nation. Venaya is of the Manyhogans clan, born for the Bitterwater clan and the Hopi Nation. She has worked for several years in the Four Corners community, spreading the importance of literacy and teaching poetry to children both on and off the reservation. Venaya has participated in the Bisti Writing Project Artist-In-Residence Program since 2006 and has recorded children's stories for *Cuentos, Hané and Tales* radio program for San Juan Community College. She is an alumnus of the Institute of American Indian Arts in Santa Fe, New Mexico, and Fort Lewis College in Durango, Colorado.

### The Pine Nut Eaters

You've seen them.
Sitting still. Sitting peaceful.

Sitting with *chizhi* fingers pinched at their desert mouths.
Their granular tastebuds
waiting for that earth taste.
Pine nut taste.
Nutty taste of desert earth mingled with pine nut.

Navajos have scurried to and fro.
Navajos from Teesto, AZ traveled east
in the direction of *Sisnaajini*.

Packed into double-cab trucks, Navajos
from Tuba speed down Interstate 40 east.
After pit stops in Gallup, they exit at Bernalillo
and drive north to Cuba area.
Where they got word
that the piñon nuts are huge!

They sleep, but only with cloud visions
of salted, roasted piñons dancing
above them. Just like the night before Christmas
story, but instead of visions of sugarplums,
they see only deep brown piñon shells.

Huge, monster brown pine nuts
dancing circles around their *chxoshi* bed heads.

Just last weekend
in Hopi the women shouted,
*"Bring us piñons. We want pine nut taste on our mesa tongues.
The trees 'round here don't have piñons on them. We want to eat
piñons too!"*
You've seen them.
Sitting. Standing. Kneeling.
Sitting with empty piñon nut shells all around their feet.


Translations:

*chizhi*—rough, dry skin
*Teesto, AZ*—community in western Navajo reservation
*piñon*—nut from piñon trees
*sisnajini*—Navajo sacred mountain to the east
*chxoshi*—messy, unorganized, hair that is unkempt

## Ma'ii Ałkidááyee Yénałníí

*hayokaalgo,*
*ma'ii*
*hayokaalgoo h'a'aahgo*
*ma'ii*
*e'e'aahgo iinaasgoo yilwood.*
*hastiin naat'áani barboncito wolyé-*
*a'ahteeh hastoi naat'áani*

*ma'ii bi stéé natsi'liid na'halin.*
*ma'ii bi stéé . . .*
*ma'ii bi stéé alchini bii naa'to'*
*hweeldi łeezh.*
*łichxíí*
*odoo tátł'idg dootł'izh*
*doo łigai*
*ma'ii bi sis ałki'daago Hweldíí bahané.*


## Coyote Remembers

it was

at dawn
that *ma'ii,*
that coyote
led the way west.
*hastiin naat'áani barboncito*
*a'ahteeh hastoi naat'áani*
followed *ma'ii's* rainbow tail
full of burrows
and tears of children.

dust
at *hweeldi,*
tattered
red, green and white
sash belts
caught up old stories
of
the
time
at
fort sumner, nm, u.s.a.

299

# *Oregon*

**Ginger Andrews** (North Bend, OR) was born in North Bend, Oregon, and lives there still. She is author of two poetry collections, *Hurricane Sisters* (Story Line Press, 2004) and *An Honest Answer* (Story Line Press, 1999). She runs a small housecleaning business with her three sisters, who all live within walking distance.

## Rolls-Royce Dreams

Using salal leaves for money,
my youngest sister and I
paid an older sister
to taxi an abandoned car
in our backyard. Our sister
knew how to shift gears,
turn smoothly with a hand signal,
and make perfect screeching stop sounds.

We drove to the beach,
to the market, to Sunday School,
past our would-be boyfriends' houses,
to any town, anywhere.
We shopped for expensive clothes everywhere.
Our sister would open our doors
and say, *Meter's runnin' ladies,*
*but take your time.*

We rode all over in that ugly green Hudson
with its broken front windshield, springs poking
through its back seat, blackberry vines growing
through rusted floorboards,
with no wheels, no tires, taillights busted,
headlights missing, and gas gauge on empty.

**Prayer**

God bless the chick in Alaska
who took in my sister's ex,
an abusive alcoholic hunk.
Bless all borderline brainless ex-cheerleaders
with long blonde hair, boobs,
and waists no bigger around than a coke bottle
who've broken up somebody else's home.
Forgive my thrill
should they put on seventy-five pounds,
develop stretch marks, spider veins,
and suffer through endless days of deep depression.

Bless those who remarry on the rebound.
Bless me and all my sisters;
the ball and chain baggage
we carried into our second marriages.
Bless my broken brother and his live-in.
Grant him SSI. Consider
how the deeper the wounds in my family,
the funnier we've become.
Bless those who've learned to laugh at what's longed for.
Keep us from becoming hilarious.
Bless our children.
Bless all our ex's,
and bless the fat chick in Alaska.

## Real Men

work at the sawmill and
refuse to eat bologna sandwiches.
They like leftover meatloaf or tuna
—if it's not that damn grated crap
with damn ground bones in it.
They work lots of Saturdays,
pay for groceries with cash,
wait in their cars while their wives
shop with one baby on their hip,
one in the cart, one at their feet,
and one on the way.
They have garages they built themselves
with really big vises on the end
of a workbench, and hundreds
of Gerber baby food jars full
of nuts and bolts and screws
that are screwed into the lids
that are nailed to the ceiling
by the light bulb that hangs
in front of the calendar
with pictures of fancy cars
with shiny bumpers
and women with long legs
and low-cut summer tops
and red lipstick and high heels.
They will give you a nickel
for penny candy
if you get in their way.
They say Jesus Christ a lot.
They don't like preachers, but
they are happy to drive you
to church on Sundays,
drop you off and pick you up
at twelve o'clock sharp.

## The Spirit of Place

Handwritten in curlicues of ink on vellum,
orders made the evacuation official. Unofficial
threats followed, then a little rifle fire.
A volunteer from the garrison in Walla Walla
wanted to play with matches and Colonel
let him play. A Cayuse horse broke its hobble
and they shot it. Clouds of smoke, much obliged,
obscured the view from town on the nearby hill.
Who did those fools think they were dealing with,
setting up camp beside the river, making utterly
irresponsible and unacceptable claims on a place
not rightfully theirs? Those ratty squatters
and their wives, worn-out and good for nothing,
wanted to argue with logic of superior force. Good
for their kids, who ran like gophers, trying to find
a hole where they might hide. They found one, too,
at the sporting distance of two-hundred paces.
Sway-backed horses weren't good for dog meat,
and tents had to be burned to protect public health.
The skirmish took an hour to mop up. The ladies
auxiliary erected a marker: God, Law, Necessity,
&tc., &tc. Colonel Shaw claimed the land
as his own. His son sired a son with a limp
and withered arm, who sold the land to settle
debts and taxes. Because sheep eat grass to dust.
Loggers liquidate trees. Miners gouge for gold
they never find and gravel pits aren't much profit.
It unravels like this year after year, right down
to the present, at the riverside, the anniversary
of the battle, the channel choking with algae,
the Chinook extinct, and cows going mad
from eating each other's brains. It's crazy,
this place. Enough to make us all ill.
Who will ever figure it out—the river
poisoned, the valley cursed? That campsite
of sixty vagrant Cayuse with nowhere else left
to go on earth but into it, after the magpies
and maggots finished with their corpses.

**David Axelrod** (La Grande, OR) is author of four collections of poems, including *The Cartographer's Melancholy* (Eastern Washington University Press, 2005), which was a finalist for the 2006 Oregon Book Award, and *Departing by a Broken Gate* (WordCraft of Oregon, 2009). His poems have appeared or are forthcoming in *New Letters, Boulevard, Alaska Quarterly Review, Hotel Amerika, Quarterly West, River Styx, Verse Daily,* and many other magazines. He teaches at Eastern Oregon University and is associate editor of *Basalt: A Journal of Fine & Literary Arts.*

## It's for Our Own Good, Actually

There's no way I know, short of screaming,
to express how a razor-winged fighter jet
appears in the treetops without any warning,
banks away just above our upturned faces,
and roars east out of the valley. A machine
faster than any thought, and a split-second
of confusion, before I begin remembering
what it's all about: barbecue. National holiday.
Waiting for fireworks at dusk. And that blast
of jet engines in the trees, a "fly-over," is just
another benign gesture of our independence
from a ludicrous king, a way to divert us
from the boredom of waiting. For that split-
second, though, I got totally de-contextualized—
despite my job, car payments, mortgage, pension,
and my wealthy-educated-arrogant friends,
a hot cramp loosened up my bowels. I mean,
what are taxes for? But then I'm pissed off,
same as during the last little war, when pilots
from the nearby base practiced strafing us
campesinos in the countryside: we stood there,
agog: at our feet the row of onions we hoed.
Being caught in the open like that, humiliated,
and then a smart ass voice catcalling: "Psych!"
as when we were children, and the reversal came.
And really, it's a game, right? No harm intended.
"Motherfuck," I shout across the quiet lawn,
and all the nice people's children at the party,
who just now were gaping at the sky, turn
toward me and start howling for their mothers,
who glare at me, too, as though I were to blame.

## Train Whistles in the Wind and Rain

In some Havana of the heart I still
imagine my father, his broken English
explaining why that morning he left
he never looked back but went on
into his life. And was it a good life?
The last time I saw him was before
the war, on Christmas Day. I was two,
watching the toy train he'd brought
slow down until, minutes after he left,
my mother wound it too tight and broke it.

I gave his name up for a stepfather's but
whenever I thought of it, and I tried not to,
I hated him for leaving, for not writing.
I hadn't a photo, even, to tell what he had
looked like, only his shadow, and images
of trains. Later, in Klamath Falls,
my mother told me tales to scare me
from the tracks: horrible stories of hoboes
who tortured children, and of a kid with
both legs cut off at a crossing.
But nothing kept me away. On my tricycle
I watched the trains roar past, huge
Mallets, four-eight-eight-fours, with
pusher engines to scale the Siskiyous, until
my mother, missing me, switched me home,
pedaling and howling for my life.

In Seattle, Uncle Andrew took me to the yard
to watch the engines shuttling boxcars.
And standing by the track, clutching his hand
as the switchers passed, bathing us in steam,
how could I know I wouldn't see him again, that
somewhere in the Ardennes a German mortar
round would fall behind the lines where
he stood drinking coffee beside his tank.
Mother, not his mother—though she had nurtured
him after my grandmother's religion tore the
family apart—hung a gold star in our window.
That Seattle morning's all I remember of him.
I can almost see his face, almost hear him,
Mother's youngest brother, explaining
the complicated mechanisms of pistons
and drivers, of boilers and steam valves,
as the engines rumbled and huffed, bellowing
steam and smoke, their bells clanging.

**Henry Carlile** (Portland, OR) was born in San Francisco and educated at Grays Harbor College and the University of Washington. He taught for thirty-four years at Portland State University before retiring in 2003. He is author of three books of poetry and recipient of an Ingram Merrill Fellowship, National Endowment for the Arts Fellowships, and the Devins Award. He lives in Portland with his wife, Genevieve.

And years later, a young man just broken up
with my fiancée, I took my grief to a river,
as I always had, and stood knee-deep
in the chill winter current, casting
toward a far bank where the steelhead lay,
their icy blue backs freckled with black,
their noses aimed upstream, fins sculling
in place. But nothing hit that day.
One by one they broke ranks to let my lure
drift past, then reclaimed their places.

I was almost ready to leave when I heard
the far whistle of a freight, one of the
last steam engines,
its carboniferous breath blooming beyond
a far curve of pinkish, bare alders
where the tracks followed the river,
then curved to cross a bridge upstream
from where I stood. Like soot, a flock
of crows started from the deep boom of
its drivers, the screech of trucks on rails,
the headlight, though it was almost noon,
swiveling its lizard's eye. And suddenly,
something, not nostalgia for trains,
or the woman who had left me, or my
father, or my uncle, caused my eyes to brim
and scald as they had once in St. Paul
when I leaned off an overpass to stare down
a passing engine's funnel and got an eyeful.

So tell me why, this late at night, I love
to hear that far hoot through the rain.
Why does it comfort me, when it's not steam
but air sounds the whistle, not coal
but diesel quakes the house and windows?
Tell me why so late in life, engine, father,
uncle, lover, your loss gathers to a sweetness
in one voice to sing a past more
perfect than it was.

## The Book of the Deer, the Bear, and the Elk

You never wrote the small green book
like the poems of Edward Thomas.
It was a book I dreamed.
But watching the green report of your heart
on the monitor it came to me as I stood
like one of the doctors in my cap and gown,
home, where you've lived like a bachelor
at the far end of the house,
there is a green diary:
the book of the deer, the bear and the elk,
with snapshots of Julian and Bob and Harry,
old hunting friends
dead as the game strung up on poles
or drooped across fenders.

It took four shots to bring it down.
Your father never praised you.
Rising from dinner that night he beckoned
toward the woodshed where the skinned deer
hung draped in burlap.
Then he whipped you with a belt.
"Don't ever bring home meat
shot up like that!
One bullet is enough."
I saw you kill a running buck
at three hundred yards with one shot.
It's a brutal art that fathers pass to sons.

When the propane tank ignited
you took the flaming cylinder in your arms
like a lover
and fought it out the door.
Now you dream each night of the trailer burning.
My mother screams and beats the fire out of her hair.
She was not burned like you—
twice, and three times, for your care.

Now the deer are safe from us,
I have one photograph to add to our book:
a doe running through a field.
My best shot.
Somewhere in the grass behind her
a fawn is hiding.
You can't see it,
but it's there waiting for its mother
to draw us away.
Later, she'll return
And the two of them will be saved.
Stepfather, Father, be like the fawn.

## Nature

My wife can't stand those programs where something
is killing something else. And who can blame her?
It's nature, I tell her, as if that made a difference.
The death of the least furred thing brings her to tears,
as if she were responsible and might prevent it.

The cheetah streaks after a Thompson's gazelle,
trips it and seizes it by the throat. A mother wildebeest
tries in vain to save its calf from a pack of hyenas.
And Genevieve turns her head from this carnage,
angry because I go on watching night after night,

the Serengeti, Sarajevo, trying to sort out the difference
between the lion that kills a cheetah's cubs and leaves
them to rot, and a sniper's estimate of the distance
between himself and a mother out gathering wood.
I know I should try harder to shield my wife from what

she cannot bear, and yet some streak of yellow-eyed
watchfulness instructs me to wait and do nothing,
like the scientist who will not interfere because nature,
as he perceives it, condemns the weak to inherit nothing.
Once, a harder-minded woman scoffed when

I broke up a fight between two stupid mallards bent
on murder, or so it seemed to me, the air full of down.
It must have looked silly, a man in up to his knees,
shouting at ducks, so I didn't blame her for laughing.
But let me always right the beetle struggling on its back,

stand between the dog and cat and the cat and sparrow,
foolish and impractical as she accused me of being.
And let me remember also why I married Genevieve.
Because she is kind and will not accept what others take
for granted: that nature is otherwise and man no better.

## Some Days

It's winter in Oregon
and I'm thinking about the snow in Ann Arbor
where my brother lives in his happiness,
the masculine huskiness
of corned beef stewing inside its own juices,
filling the heavy bottomed pot,
big enough to hide a small teenager,
the grease of a thousand mornings
darkening the iron and copper,
the two brown eggs lying on the cutting table, femininity
doubled up, a stereotype in stereo,
the sun breaking over the ladles and knives like water.
Any cook would want to hold them,
their perfectly formed shells,
the yoke inside its yellow limbo, both
in one hand, my brother cracks them over the steel bowl
while the snow falls
like really expensive French sea salt,
the kind that comes in little blue bowls
with cork tops and the words
*Sel de Mer* written in French loops and flourishes,
like someone's number on a pack of matches
after you've closed a bar or maybe
not even that, not even closed it
but drank real fast so everything
was French and flourishy.
In the morning you can take your hangover to work,
when everything feels more German than French, and work
will straighten you out. Work will make you
see clearly even if, like my friend Mike,
you wake up early so you can deliver candy bars
and soda pop to the machines
scattered across the University campus
where you used to go to school before taking this job,
putting on the gray jumpsuit, starting up
the truck, the robins staring at you from the barbed wire
fence. He is working
so students can drop their parents' coins
into little slots so that THUNK!
a piece of chocolate or a can of cold
Coca-Cola will fall into a larger slot.
Slot to slot Mike worked all day and drank
on the Sabbath with a book or two in his head
and some car in his heart.
When I worked the job opening a café
at five in the morning, I knew beautiful women
were getting out of the shower, drying off, not even thinking
of coffee yet, or the croissants I was making,

**Matthew Dickman** (Portland, OR) is author of *All-American Poem* (American Poetry Review/ Copper Canyon Press, 2008), which received the 2008 APR/Honickman First Book Prize, the May Sarton Discovery Prize from the American Academy of Arts and Sciences, the Kate Tufts Award, and the 2009 Oregon Book Award. He is also the co-author, with his brother, Michael Dickman, of a fine press chapbook *August 20, 1975* (Kunst Editions, 2009). His work has appeared in *Tin House, Dossier Magazine*, and *The New Yorker*, among others.

folding and re-folding the dough
over the cold marble slab, some hopefulness
pouring out of me, waiting
for them to arrive, the bell
around the doorknob jingling
a little behind them, the bell
somehow like a dimple
above the ass
of a person you love, I can't explain it,
it's somehow silver
and supernatural. It didn't matter.
I never saw them. I worked
in the back, behind the closet
filled with detergents and toilet-paper,
until the soups were done and the chicken cleaned,
the guts tossed, the boning knife
washed and sheathed, my apron
covered in blood
darker than the darkest cigar.
Some days a kitchen can
save your life. Carl would
come in and have one piece of brown
pumpkin bread, reading the *Times* or the *Oregonian*
or that late, great, magazine, *The Sciences*,
where even a guy from Harvard, Illinois could understand
Biophysics. Every time he opened
*The New Yorker*, each time he picked up
the warm bread
and placed it to his red mouth, he was not
thinking of how much he'd lost
or who he would love desperately
with nothing but wind
moving through his hands like a rope.
When I was broke and hungry and worried about the dogwood trees
I thought of my brother
making croutons and blintzes in Michigan,
the corned beef steaming,
the sun with its yoke running over everything.
I thought of him, and almost,
as if he had pulled it from his own wallet,
a ten dollar bill lay folded
on the sidewalk, where I picked it up
and went directly out to lunch, a bowl of onion soup, a pint of dark
beer, the bread was free, and all because
of my brother, that old apron,
that great and mythic friend of mine,
that lucky charm.

## Driving One Hundred

We went, in 1956, in Sarah's boyfriend's car
out on the new highway south of Coos Bay,
toward Millington, named for a mill,
and the Shinglehouse Slough,
where years later someone's father's ashes
would be scattered, his last wish.
We went in Sarah's boyfriend's car,
a black convertible,
and she, wishing to try on speed,
drove fast, fast, faster,
pushing the speedometer to sixty,
seventy, eighty, as we screamed
and laughed and held ourselves down
in the seats without seatbelts.
Our hair in the wind lashed us
like something breaking over a waterfall,
and afraid our young meat and bones
would be scattered,
we screamed at Sarah, slow down slow down,
Sarah, and then she did ninety
laughing, "He'll kill me if he ever finds out,
you guys, don't tell," and pushed the pedal
down and held it, as we went fast, and faster,
screaming and dying and laughing at Sarah,
until the needle stood at one hundred,
and Sarah relented, and we chided her then,
and began to breathe again,
at sixty, fifty, forty, did a U at twenty,
turned around at the cutoff to Coquille.
"I almost died," we all said.
"I'll never do that again."
And our flesh settled down to go on living
as we secretly thanked her, like a goddess,
for the terrible experience.

**Barbara Drake** (Yamhill, OR) is retired from Linfield College and lives with her husband on a small farm in the foothills of the Oregon Coast Range, where they raise sheep and wine grapes. She is author of a book of essays, *Peace at Heart: An Oregon Country Life* (Oregon State University Press, 1998) and several books of poetry, including *Driving One Hundred* (Windfall Press Books, 2009). She also authored *Writing Poetry* (Wadsworth Publishing, 1994), a college textbook.

**Michele Glazer** (Portland, OR) has received fellowships from the National Endowment for the Arts, Oregon Arts Commission, Regional Arts & Culture Council, and Literary Arts. She directs and teaches in the MFA program at Portland State University.

## To the better view

With the better view out back,
we sit where the storefronts dangle
starfish on strings (for your rearview mirror, for your Christmas tree),
shirts festooned with sandbuckets, and the titular rumble of ocean
is only a backdrop to a thought we might or might
not have, the way traffic sounds back home
(back home—the freeway sounds
around us—we tell ourselves *that's the ocean*).

There isn't much to do so we have to make do
and describe the early summer
visitors walking past licking their cones, the dogs their balls.
"Rat dog," John begins, loud enough they can hear but so what
is heard came out of which mouth? And George gives
"best of show" to a woman in white capris,
pink shades, cream-colored head
band "mostly for her purse" that is also white and who
would think to carry that to the beach?

The man sitting next to us
would hear our chatter if he weren't already somewhere
else. And wasn't it for him not us we said
all this?        Now here's where
it gets rough. Where I should step off the porch and go inside
myself, move in closer, a little, to the scene
I've set myself
up to watch. Still there is an ocean inside
of the man sitting next to us.

*In the ocean is a world of things*
*eating each other* one of us
says and how is it
the show you're watching is not the show
you sit down for.
Now another passerby has stopped to admire the yellow Porsche
the man sitting next to us parked in front
of Osburns Ice Cream, then came up to sit on the porch and watch.

## Anything a Box Will Hold

Our line inches forward.
One postal clerk on duty and shift change
at the mill, the trailer plant, both prisons.
We all want to go home.
The man ahead of me carries his box
tucked under one elbow—a toddler snatched up
mid-laugh from run-and-tussle on the grass—
except, of course, it's winter. His mackinaw's
unbuttoned to the cold.
The poor buy money orders.
Someone behind me
sets her package on the counter
to push along, then reaches out
to clutch it back.
For $7.95 we can ship anything
a box this size will hold
to soldiers in Iraq, Afghanistan:
wet wipes, soap and razors,
cookies. Five boys dead
so far, one home without his legs.

The man shifts, cocks his box
on one hip. In plain view now: PAROLE CLOTHES.
Black marker letters square as his fist.
All six sides.

At last it's his turn.
*This wasn't my idea.* His voice
a daisy-cutter spiraling the room
one pitch too high.
*It's nothing fancy. Just enough
to get him home, maybe
he's learned enough
he won't go back.*

We stare at passport signs,
posters of stamps. That hanging Appaloosa quilt.
Outside, the flag's at half staff
for a boy from Warm Springs.
Then, again, the litany of questions—
Is anything inside our boxes fragile?
Liquid? Hazardous?
Perishable?

**Bette Lynch Husted** (Pendleton, OR) is author of *At This Distance: Poems* (Wordcraft of Oregon, 2010) and *Above the Clearwater: Living on Stolen Land* (Oregon State University Press, 2004). She was a finalist for the Oregon Book Award and the WILLA award in creative nonfiction. Her essays, stories, and poems have been published by *Northwest Review, Fourth Genre, Prairie Schooner,* and other journals, and she received a 2007 Oregon Arts Commission Award. She lives in Pendleton, Oregon.

**Garrett Hongo** (Eugene, OR) is Distinguished Professor of the College of Arts and Sciences and Professor of Creative Writing at the University of Oregon. He is author of two books of poetry, *Yellow Light* (Wesleyan, 1982) and *The River of Heaven* (Knopf, 1988), which won the Lamont Poetry Award from the Academy of American Poets and was a finalist for the Pulitzer Prize in 1989. His memoir, *Volcano* (Knopf, 1995), won the Oregon Book Award for nonfiction.

### On the Origin of Blind-Boy Lilikoi

I came out of Hilo, on the island of Hawai`i,
lap-steel and dobro like outriggers on either side of me,
*shamisen* strapped to my back as I went up the gangplank
to the City of Tokio running inter-island
to Honolulu and the big, pink hotel on Waikīkī
where all the work was back in those days.
I bought a white linen suit on Hotel Street
as soon as I landed, bought a white Panama too,
and put the Jack of Diamonds in my hatband for luck.
Of my own, I had only one song, "Hilo March,"
and I played it everywhere, to anyone who would listen,
walking all the way from the Aloha Tower to Waikīkī,
wearing out my old sandals along the way.
But that's okay. I got to the Banyan Tree
on Kalakaua and played for the tourists there.
The bartenders didn't kick me out or ask for much back.
*Zatoh-no-bozu, nah*! I went put on the dark glasses and pretend I blind.
I played the slack-key, some hulas, an island rag,
and made the tourists laugh singing *hapa-haole* songs,
half English, half Hawaiian. Come sundown, though,
I had to shoo—the contract entertainers would be along,
and they didn't want *manini* like me
stealing the tips, cockroach the attention.
I'd ride the trolley back to Hotel Street
and Chinatown then, change in my pocket,
find a dive on Mauna Kea and play *chang-a-lang*
with the Portagee, *paniolo* music with Hawaiians,
slack-key with anybody, singing harmonies,
waiting for my chance to bring out the *shamisen*.
But there hardly ever was. Japanee people
no come the bars and brothels like before.
After a while, I give up and just play whatever,
dueling with *ukulele* players for fun,
trading licks, make ass, practicing that
happy-go-lucky all the tourists seem to love.
But smiling no good for me. I like the stone-face,
the no-emotion-go-show on the face,
all feeling in my singing and playing instead.
That's why Japanee style suits me best.
*Shigin* and *gunka*, ballads about warriors
and soldier song in Japanese speech.
I like the key. I like the slap and *barong* of *shamisen*.
It make me feel like I galvanize
and the rain go drum on me,
make the steel go ring inside.

Ass when I feel, you know, ass when I right.
Ass why me, I like the blues. Hear 'em first time
from one *kurombo* seaman from New Orleans.
He come off his ship from Hilo Bay, walking downtown
in front the S. Hata General Store
on his way to Manono Street looking for
one crap game or play cards or something.
I sitting barber shop, doing nothing but reading book.
He singing, yeah? sounding good but sad.
And den he bring his funny guitar from case,
all steel and silver with plenty *puka* holes all over the box.
Make the tin-kine sound, good for vibrate.
Make dakine shake innah bones sound,
like one engine innah blood. Penetrate.
He teach me all kine songs. Field hollers, he say,
dakine slave g'on use for call each oddah
from field to field. Ju'like cane workers.
And rags and marches and blues all make up
from diss black buggah from Yazoo City,
up-river and a ways, the blues man say.
Spooky. No can forget. Ass how I learn for sing.

## Kubota to the Chinese Poets Detained on Angel Island

*—to the memory of Him Mark Lai*

My geography does not match yours, surrounded by the bay
And the city so close by you can see it from the hill of Island.
I am at the middle of an ancient sea, raised up out of water
To make a dusty land of red and pink rock, yellow cliffs,
                                    and snowpeaks
far from the Great Ocean you crossed from your home villages.

But we spend our days alike—gazing at bare walls,
Composing poems to carve on them, bedding down at night
To the whistling of wind through bars and barracks.
When the moon shines and insects chirp under our bunks,
Grief and bitterness wrap around us like cold, winding sheets,
And we rage against the whites and the promises
This land made to us it would be a heaven of gold mountains.

Hard living through confinement—our families not near,
Interrogators trying to catch us in stories
That do not match what your immigration papers say,
That do match lies informants have said about me.

Can you remember how many steps to the duck pond?
How many houses were south of the village well?
Which order brother died in the Year of the Ox?

They ask me about the inkstone and the radios in my house
The FBI took on December 8th, about the military school
I attended in Hiroshima, though I was born in U.S. like them.

We try to act bravely, as we were taught, chests full of blood.
But we are not heroes. The wild geese of the bay echo your cries,
The coyotes mimic mine, and only ghosts escape these places,
Rising from the cold bodies of men who hang like butchered meat
In the lavatories, pale lights shining through the thin gauze
                                                    of their clothes.
They will see their families, but only from the clouds.
I pity them, but share my dreams with you, poets of Island,
Trapped beneath the guard towers of history.

When they ask you your brother's name, say *It is Kubota.*
When they ask me what light attracts the fish at night,
I will answer *The light of angels from Island.*
When they ask what fish come to the light,
I will say *A fish that swims The River of Heaven.*

## Sawdust

> "There is no other life."
> —Gary Snyder
> (Why Log Truck Drivers Rise Earlier
> than Students of Zen)

When log trucks roamed this land
as thick as bison across the Great Plains
Dad drove himself home from the woods,

a flannel shirt tied around the tender
tissue of his knee that had been sliced to white
by the chainsaw's kick.

Mom sent us up to Gran's,
placed a grain sack in the pooling blood,
had him swap seats for the ride to the doctor's

office, six miles away. Back home with criss-cross
stitches and aspirin he ate dinner late, worried
about the chainsaw exposed to the damp night.

## Escape

In the moonlight I watched
the mare push the gate
and walk out

I knew I should stop her
what did she know
about going on

Though no animal is wholly wild
(nor wholly tame)
what did this one know
about the long night
and the dark woods

What does anyone know?

**M. E. Hope** (Klamath Falls, OR) is a native Oregonian who lives, writes, and works in Southern Oregon's high desert region. She is a veteran, a wife, a mother, and—most heavily indicted of all—a community (poetry) organizer. She lives outside of a mid-size town on a small acreage with five cats, two dogs, and one man, in their now-empty nest.

**Lawson Fusao Inada** (Ashland, OR) is an Emeritus Professor of writing at Southern Oregon University. Inada is author of five books: *Legends from Camp* (Coffee House Press, 1992), *Drawing the Line* (Coffee House Press, 1997), *In This Great Land of Freedom* (Japanese American National Museum, 1993), *Just Intonations* (Graven Image Gallery Press, 1996), and *Before the War* (Morrow, 1971). He is editor of *Only What We Could Carry: The Japanese-American Internment Experience* (California Historical Society, 2000). He is the recipient of fellowships from the National Endowment for the Arts and the Guggenheim Foundation, and he served as Oregon State Poet Laureate.

## Nobody, Nothing

Big Lencha, just because
I was small
and standing there,
smiling,
as she lost
her turn at jacks,

chased me
all the way home
and stood there,
shaking her fist
at the window.

Huff-puff, huff-puff,
phew, as I
turned on the radio.

"Who's that out there?"
"Nobody, Mom."
"What's she doing?"
"Nothing."

Well, the program
ended, night fell,
dinner came
and went—

but there was Lencha.

Now, I kid you not
when I reveal
that, as things
were wont to happen
in youth and Fresno,

she stayed there
like a fixture
day and night
through several
seasons, long enough

to be taken
for granted
by the accepting
community . . .

But, as you
might guess,

the expected
happened at dusk,
on Labor Day—

Lencha simply
lowered her fist,
like some tired
Statue of Liberty,
shrugged, shook
off the stuff
and went home.

Except
I followed, stood
outside all night,
and that morning
tracked her
like a shadow
to school—

where, since it was
the first day,
I changed
my schedule
to sit beside
her in basic
home economics,
intermediate
sewing, introductory
stenography—
because, you see,
Big Lencha
had become
a different person,

a smaller, larger
version named Lorenza,
with mysterious
scents and tresses,

and a smiling answer
for her surly father
inquiring about
the unsmiling youth
sulking on the lawn:

"Nobody, nothing."

### IV. The Legend of Lost Boy

Lost Boy was not his name.

He had another name, a given name—
at another, given time and place—
but those were taken away.

The road was taken away.
The dog was taken away.
The food was taken away.
The house was taken away.

The boy was taken away—
but he was not lost.
Oh, no—he knew exactly where he was—

and if someone had asked
or needed directions,
he could have told them:

"This is the fairgrounds.
That's Ventura Avenue over there.
See those buildings? That's town!"

This place also had buildings—
but they were all black, the same.
There were no houses, no trees,
no hedges, no streets, no homes.

But, every afternoon, a big truck
came rolling down the rows.
It was full of water, cool,
and the boy would follow it, cool.
It smelled like rain, spraying,
and even made some rainbows!

So on this hot, hot day,
the boy followed and followed,
and when the truck stopped,
then sped off in the dust,
the boy didn't know where he was.

He knew, but he didn't know
which barrack was what.
And so he cried. A lot.
He looked like the truck.

Until Old Man Ikeda
found him, bawled him out.
Until Old Man Ikeda
laughed and called him
"Lost Boy."
Until Old Man Ikeda
walked him through
the rows, and rows,
the people, the people,
the crowd.

Until his mother
cried and laughed
and called him
"Lost Boy."

Until Lost Boy
thought he was found.

## X. The Legend of the Magic Marbles

My uncle was going overseas.
He was heading to the European theater,
and we were all going to miss him.

He had been stationed by Cheyenne,
and when he came to say good-bye
he brought me a little bag of marbles.

But the best one, an agate, cracked.
It just broke, like bone, like flesh—
so my uncle comforted me with this story:

> *"When we get home to Fresno,*
> *I will take you into the basement*
> *and give you my box of magic marbles.*
>
> *These marbles are marbles—*
> *so they can break and crack and chip—*
> *but they are also magic*
>
> *so they can always be fixed:*
> *all you have to do is leave them*
> *overnight in a can of Crisco—*
>
> *next day they're good as new."*

Uncle. Uncle. Uncle. What happened to *you?*

## The Legend of Targets

It got so hot in Colorado we would start to go crazy.
This included, of course, soldiers in uniform, on patrol.
So, once a week, just for relief, they went out for target practice.
We could hear them shooting hundreds of rounds, shouting like crazy.
It sounded like a New Year's celebration! Such fun is not to be missed!
So someone cut a deal, just for the kids, and we went out past the fence.
The soldiers shot, and between rounds, we dug in the dunes for bullets.
It was great fun! They would aim at us, go *"Pow!"* and we'd shout *"Missed!"*

## Everything

When the river rose that year, we were beside it
and ourselves with fear; not that it would do anything
to us, mind you—our hopes were much too high for that—
but there was always that remote, unacknowledged possibility
that we had thrown one stone too many, by the handful,
and that by some force of nature, as they called it,
it might rain and rain for days, as it had been,
with nothing to hold it and the structure back,
and with everything to blame, including children
on into late summer and all the years ahead,
when it would be ours to bear, to do much more with
than remember and let it go at that—some mud,
some driftwood, some space of sky as a reminder
before getting on with the world again;
no, the balance was ours to share, and responsibility
for rivers had as much to do with anything
as rain on the roof and sweet fish for supper,
as forests and trembling and berries at sunrise;
thus it was, then, that we kept our watch,
that we kept our wits about us and all the respect
we could muster, sitting in silence,
sleeping in shifts, and when the fire died,
everyone was there to keep it alive;
somehow, though, in the middle of the night,
despite our vigils, our dreams, our admonitions,
our structure, our people, and all our belongings
broke free with a  shudder and went drifting away—
past the landing, the swing, the anchored cages,
down through the haunted rapids, never to be found;
when we awoke that morning, the sun was back,
the river had receded under our measuring stick,
and everything had been astonishingly replaced,
including people and pets, the structure intact,
but in the solitude of all our faces as we ate,
the knowledge was there, of what we all had done,
and that everything would never be the same.

324

## Lake Forest Memorial

A dead young female, white,
lying in a prairie stream between mansions
alarmed a stroller two days ago.
Nothing about it in the news till now—
a jogging nurse's aide from a nearby dorm.

Against the reddening morning
the crusty arms of elms outside my porthole
stretch black and flat. Their blackness
is not political like mine. Your letter
with its *i love you* brings me
the comfort of goose down.

Where in heaven or hell am I?
These mansions are not like my father's house.
Nor more proof against the stumble into oblivion.
She was twenty-two.

## Smell Theory

We hugged. Her thick black coat told
of fire, and the scent was in her hair
when she returned from the studio.
A tramp, to escape the cold snap, had no doubt
got into the lower part of the building
and built himself a little fire that prospered
too much, that alarmed the street before dawn,
smoked out the architects upstairs and
the manikin shop and the artists above them.
One of the neighborhood homeless that roamed
below the lofts, perhaps a Nez Perce
from up the river, shivering here
ten thousand years later without trees
or family or animals under steel and concrete
that curb the river. Stiff, puffy guys with
cigarettes stuck to lips, trying to keep warm.
Maybe a woman with them. They've got coats
but this freeze feels big as the nation.

**Harold Johnson** (Portland, OR) is a former teacher. His poems have appeared in *Fireweed: Poetry of Western Oregon, Hubbub, Portland Review, Northwest Magazine, Willamette Week, Reflex,* and numerous anthologies. He is a fellow of the Ragdale Foundation's Africa—USA Project and is completing his novel, *Private Birdsong Speaks*.

### And You, Gilbert Stuart

*—For Richard Rezac and Julia Fish*

Sometimes it appears to be
all buying and selling:
at the capital
in the National Gallery
I stared (again, with vague hope
of riddling the ambiguity of my citizenship)
at the salmon-colored faces
of the first few Presidents
chanting of soap and water and beef
above foaming white collars and waistcoats
locked in the legerdemain of your brush
as long as paintings last.

And now back home out West
I sit in my studio
before an empty canvas
thinking of Celilo, the dam-doomed falls
where men stood on rocks and logs
dipping nets, facing cold spray
in the red rays of their sinking day,
ellipsis to the long sentence
of their history
and the drowned future of their rights
(power must be served)
and I think of Yakima
up the river
where a black boy
whose grandfather was born
the year of the Proclamation
loved schools
called Adams, Madison,
Jefferson, Washington…
Washington,
The Good Slavemaster,
master of the minuet,
refuser of crowns,
surveyor of free ground
that he sold for many dollars.

And you, Gilbert Stuart,
painter of Presidents,
who they say had a habit
of reeling in suckers twice,
didn't the Great American Purchaser
sit for you
to begin the century on canvas?
And by 1805 weren't you still
dancing around his inquiries with the excuse
that you weren't satisfied with the painting?
And didn't you sell it
to the Fourth President?
(Whom you'd also painted, along with Dolly)
And didn't you finally, in 1821,
slip the old sage
a slick copy, purportedly the original
(His daughter remarked the wet paint),
on a mahogany panel?
(Canvas had been embargoed since 1801)
Oh yes you did.

**Dorianne Laux** (Eugene, OR) grew up in the border town of San Diego and has lived in the wilds of West L.A., Berkeley, and Petaluma, California, as well as Eugene, Oregon and Juneau, Alaska. She now teaches poetry at North Carolina State University and is a founding member of Pacific University's Low-Residency MFA Program. She is author of five books of poems: *What We Carry* (BOA Editions, 1994), *Smoke* (BOA Editions, 2000), *Facts about the Moon* (W.W. Norton, 2005), *Awake* (Eastern Washington University Press, 2007), and *The Book of Men* (W.W. Norton, 2011).

## Bakersfield, 1969

I used to visit a boy in Bakersfield, hitchhike
to the San Diego terminal and ride the bus for hours
through the sun-blasted San Fernando Valley
just to sit on his fold-down bed in a trailer
parked in the side yard of his parents' house,
drinking Southern Comfort from a plastic cup.
His brother was a sessions man for Taj Mahal,
and he played guitar, too, picked at it like a scab.
Once his mother knocked on the tin door
to ask us in for dinner. She watched me
from the sides of her eyes while I ate.
When I offered to wash the dishes she told me
she wouldn't stand her son being taken
advantage of. I said I had no intention
of taking anything and set the last dish
carefully in the rack. He was a bit slow,
like he'd been hit hard on the back of the head,
but nothing dramatic. We didn't talk much anyway,
just drank and smoked and fucked and slept
through the ferocious heat. I found a photograph
he took of me getting back on the bus or maybe
stepping off into his arms. I'm wearing jeans
with studs punched along the cuffs,
a t-shirt with stars on the sleeves, a pair
of stolen bowling shoes and a purse I made
while I was in the loony bin, wobbly X's
embroidered on burlap with gaudy orange yarn.
I don't remember how we met. When I look
at this picture I think I might not even
remember this boy if he hadn't taken it
and given it to me, written his name under mine
on the back. I stopped seeing him
after that thing with his mother. I didn't know
I didn't know anything yet. I liked him.
That's what I remember. That,
and the I-don't-know-what degree heat
that rubbed up against the trailer's metal sides,
steamed in through the cracks between the door
and porthole windows, pressed down on us
from the ceiling and seeped through the floor,
crushing us into the damp sheets. How we endured it,
sweat streaming down our naked bodies, the air
sucked from our lungs as we slept. Taj Mahal says
If you ain't scared, you ain't right. Back then
I was scared most of the time. But I acted
tough, like I knew every street.
What I liked about him was that he wasn't acting.
Even his sweat tasted sweet.

## The Rest I Imagine

There are things men and women don't talk about,
things like brutal acts of war, miscarriages and
in the woods, the graphic way a man can die.
After the accident with the helicopter, my husband is stoic.
He was the first man on the scene, the first with a stretcher,
the first to see what a helicopter's tail rotor can do
to the head of a forester from Wisconsin, a forester
just out of college, a young man who for a split second
forgot about the flying blades, saw only his bags of fertilizer.
The tail rotor suffered damage. The helicopter could not fly.
Another helicopter did the evacuation. My husband claims
it's the best thing when the kid dies in ICU six hours later.
The rest I imagine while I mix corn muffins and ladle out chili.
Our son tells us about the tree fort he and his friend are building.
The cat jumps on my husband's lap, circles and starts purring.
It doesn't take long to bake brownies. This time I frost them.

## Unfinished Rooms

Dad breaks two wooden reaches in one day.
Mother jots the cost figures in the loss column.
She worries plenty about the money, the risk
of borrowing for log truck expenses, down time
and the weather. Together, my parents budget
two weeks of down time during summer fire season
and two weeks in the winter when snow covers roads.
Anything else cuts into money to finish building the house.
The rooms are finished except for an extra bedroom
and the coat closet on the first floor. Then, two weeks
before Christmas, the unbudgeted happens.
Dad dies. He's thirty-seven. His heart attack comes at night.
Mother's uncle buys the truck and adds it to his fleet at the mill.
Mother wants the truck working. Dad would have wanted it that way.
On Sundays, after church, Mother takes us on a country drive.
We circle around the sawmill, looking at the line of trucks,
hoping to see the one Dad owned. Back home, the upstairs bedroom
remains unfinished. Money is short and there will never be more kids
in need of a room. The coat closet looks naked. Raw two by fours
show black marks from Dad's carpenter pencil. Behind our coats,
his fishing poles and rifles are propped against the hot water heater.
At the back of the closet, beside a brick chimney,
a plaid Mackinaw and red felt hat wait on a nail.

**Joy L. McDowell** (Springfield, OR) is a University of Oregon graduate who writes from her home above Oregon's Willamette Valley and from a studio at the edge of the Coos Bay estuary. She often shares stories of men and women who earn their living through physical labor. Her words and images are infused by the tidal rhythm that comes twice each day to flush and replenish the salt marsh.

## Wedding Vandals

The loader operator is the first to discover
what's left of his work station. The vandals
have pried off fuel caps, run the dozer over the bank,
torn up the landing and taken a knife to a leather seat.
A lot of damage. They used one machine to bash another.
Machines can't be used to finish the job. The logging site
waits to be wrapped before the rains come and close off
dirt roads. Then the rigging slinger finds the book,
the textbook with the name of a local athlete
and scattered essay papers. College kids.
The cops make the case. The parents
buy the boys out of trouble, except
for the kid whose dad doesn't own
his own business and isn't prominent
in the local education profession.
No one goes to jail. Money changes hands.
Just the crew loses wages for the down time
it takes to fix damaged equipment. Someone says
the kids were celebrating a friend who got married. Just kids
getting drunk and being stupid. They are all about twenty, including
the young logger with a wife and baby who loses a paycheck
and his trailer for missing yet another loan payment.

## 1962: Gods of the Afternoon

Rude messages have been fingered into
dust on the logging crummy's rear door.
Sex and women, the cartoon breasts
a woods worker artist rounded
where the emergency exit sign
will never again show through.
At the abandoned railroad yard
the battered yellow bus brakes to a stop.
Men spill sullenly from its accordion door.
Young men come first, anxious for release
from their cage of company labor.
Broad hands swing spiked boots,
a lunch box and maybe a thermos.
Veins like ropey vines snake along sculpted forearms.
Dirt masks make a canvas for watery Adonis eyes.
Finally come fathers and grandfathers, lame, stiff,
whatever is left after a life of chokers and logs.
These bodies move slow, sure of what this day
and all others can possibly hold. A big man
with a tree trunk torso smiles as a young logger
is met by an eye-shadowed girl. The girl teases
and whispers, "Don't touch, you'll get me dirty."

## So That's It

We are all reflections of original catastrophe.
So the poor in spirit are dumbstruck
As a rabbit of inconceivable size
Is pulled by an even bigger hand
From a hat of limitless darkness.
So the unemployed go on and on,
Survivors of eons of random collisions;
So the loveless, wandering in their grief,
Imagine the sweet madness of tendrils
Shooting heavenward in an ecstasy of photosynthesis.
Who lives and who dies?
The cosmos breathes and stars are born, stars go out.
It takes forever as it happens in a heartbeat.
The miracle, I guess, is that the vast soul and puny soul
Are somehow like the centered rider on the trail
Amid solar wind, rubble, and debris,
Their course through chaos the only way home.

## War

The sun comes up, an eye detects alarm.
The field erupts with thunder, running horses
While men drive us, intending to disarm

The pestilence that bears down on the farm.
The breakfast curdles in its steaming courses
As the sun comes up and eyes detect alarm.

Survivors gather round a hill-top cairn.
The children wail, their blocks all in pieces,
While far below men struggle to disarm

The terror.  The undead appear. They roam
The country backroads. The scent of apples teases.
The day warms up, a bird detects alarm.

At last, the only sound a windblown can,
Then quiet so sudden the air inside it freezes.
Some men showed up but failed to disarm

The thing that flattened them. A worldly harm
Is the only thing the ticking clock discloses.
The sun goes out, no ear detects alarm,
And none arrive intending to disarm.

**Robert McDowell** (Talent, OR) is author of *Poetry As a Spiritual Practice* (Free Press/Simon & Schuster, 2008). The author/editor/translator of nine other books, he co-founded Story Line Press and served as its director for twenty-two years, selecting, editing, and ushering into print 250 books. Robert is an acclaimed teacher/mentor/speaker/coach, having taught at Esalen, Kripalu, and conferences throughout the world. He mentors businesses, organizations, and individuals, improving writing and communication skills through poetry and journaling.

**Carlos Reyes** (Portland, OR) is a poet and translator who lives in Portland, Oregon, when not traveling to Ireland and South America. Two years ago he was honored with a Heinrich Böll Fellowship, which gave him two weeks to write on Achill Island, Ireland. In the spring of 2009, he was poet-in-residence at the Lost Horse Ranger Station in the Joshua Tree National Park.

### The Old West

Half-way through the night
outside Fallon, Nevada

the Greyhound pulls
to the shoulder, stops.

In shadowy light
two deputies have come aboard.

They handcuff a man, shuffle him
from the bus into the squad car.

They return (by now
I'm half-awake). One says

to the other, as they start
to open the suitcase

in the rack above my head,
Better not, Bob,

till we get it off the bus . . .

The suitcase slowly floats

in the arms of the deputy
down the aisle.

Through the bus' windshield
the revolving red light

disappears
into the misty night

of my dreams.

## August Wind

The sudden northeast gust
through the backyard hemlock

becomes a breeze, not enough to disturb
the thin waves of chalky clouds

overhead in the baby blue sky
but stirs lost memories of other Augusts.

What comes before, wind in trees,
what comes after.

Fire to hurricane force.
Whirlwinds that suck trees into the sky.

Fires that invent their own weather, clouds . . .
reminding me of sleeping at night

in a paper bag on the fire line.
Shivering in the cold,

in the updraft of that fire.

**Jenny Root** (Eugene, OR) has published poems in *The New Southerner; Common Ground, Windfall: A Journal Poetry of Place, Poetry International, Fireweed: Poetry of Western Oregon, Bellowing Ark,* and other literary journals. She works with independent booksellers and the Lane Literary Guild, promoting the written word in performance. Formerly with Story Line Press and Tsunami Books, she now works as an editor and graphic designer with a nonprofit organization in criminal justice.

## Money to Burn

*—Middle Fork Gorge Fire,
Oakridge, Oregon, 1998*

Federico and I stretch a lateral line
500 yards sidehill off the main.
B.L. cranks up the pump's
high whine at the creek
and the hose stiffens to life.
I train its direction, blackening
every scorched grey inch, while he
churns shovel through thick ash,
finds embers lurking in the duff
beneath rotting Douglas fir.
Boots wedged between edges
of scalding rocks, ankles cocked
on the bone, spray from the hose
dowses for heat, hisses its find.
My axe leans against a salvageable log
and I'm calculating my overtime.

We work methodically
from one smoke to the next
through a forest of black snags.
Silent ghosts coil from cedar trunks
logged a century ago, each stump
a burning furnace on a burned-out land.

Federico is at home with this work,
graceful as flame, while I'm
the clumsy rookie, trying too hard.
We speak a recipe for friendship
in English and Spanish: one part
inquire to three parts shy.
He wants to know if I believe
in God—how do I tell him
She is all around us, parched
beneath our boots, sifted into our hair?
I want to know if he will ever
return to Mexico, start a family?
*Pues si*, he says, *but not yet.
Your country has mucho dinero
fighting fires—money to burn.*

Three weeks mopping up the Oakridge fire,
two hundred acres torched by two kids'
rockets and we've heard the feds
could charge their parents a million bucks.
We know we're due to take a break
soon with the rest of the crew
but keep talking—and drowning
and butchering this stump.

Awake to the orange and ashen air,
the grace of *mi compadre*, the entire afternoon
stained with the scent of burnt, wet cedar,
a scent curling into my veins. My arms burn
with their own fire now
and Federico says *Con permiso*
as my axe misses and misses its mark.

**Vern Rutsala** (Portland, OR) is author of *The Moment's Equation* (Ashland Poetry Press, 2004), which was a finalist for the National Book Award. Other awards include a Guggenheim Fellowship, two National Endowment for the Arts Fellowships, a Masters Fellowship from the Oregon Arts Commission, two Carolyn Kizer Poetry Prizes, the Kenneth O. Hanson Award, the Mississippi Review Poetry Prize, the Juniper Prize, an Oregon Book Award, and the Akron Poetry Prize. From 1961 to 2004, he was member of the English Department of Lewis and Clark College.

### Speaking Her Lonely Greek

Daily we have the sea's commentary,
that large green voice
rising and falling, speaking her
lonely Greek hour after hour.
At sunset she takes the sun quickly
and we walk the sand
in darkness listening to that gloss
on our days, that muttered
interpretation we thought we
understood—salt and water, pressure
and release. We listen sifting
for those cries and drums, the voices
of something lost, our own
voices out there. We listen these days
away as our past sifts through
our fingers—all the times
we've walked this sand and heard
the surf knock its wind out
beating hard on the shore, and watched
lights come on in the houses,
the sea lion lift his head
like a dog and carry on
his silent dialog. But tonight
we feel a change, some shifting
of sands and birds and we can't
explain, a wind swerving
out of the east, a darkness deeper
than we remember. The sea lion
is gone, the surf continues
its gibberish, and we are alone here
in a way we never knew before—
each of us walking apart, parsed,
with fog coming in, the moon lost,
direction scattered everywhere, the sea
pounding her fists on the sand and weeping.

### Prospectus for Visitors

Here are some things
you should know: First,
if you come here
be ready to spend long

days in thought, long days
indoors, deeper indoors
than you've ever been.
In the steady sweet
rain you'll get beyond
the anterooms of thought,
you'll explore rooms
you've never seen.
You should know as well
that all this rich green
always loses to the gray.
Even the winter roses
fade, even the camellias
fail—or seem to under
that sky. It's the low
sky that's always there,
that knitted cap. If
you want to stay
learn to wear it
from October on. Wear
it as you explore
those neglected rooms
you boarded up so long
ago. Learn to delve
and consider, learn to test
each thing you think
you love. And even
on clear days you must
know that the mountains
you can almost touch
don't care—mainly they
display their vast
indifference just as,
to the west, the Pacific
remains aloof, clearly
representing a system
of values beyond your
pettiness. But come, walk
the trails, go out among
that green, follow rivers—
but be ready to think
of all those things you
shelved for years. Force
those doors and find
those caustic packages—
unwrap them here,
poke and shudder at
what you see, believe
it finally and learn
to live the life you have.

337

**Maxine Scates** (Eugene, OR) has lived all her life on the West Coast. Born and raised in Los Angeles, she has lived in Eugene, Oregon, since 1973. She has taught at Lewis and Clark and Reed Colleges and now teaches privately. Her poetry has received the Agnes Lynch Starrett Poetry Prize, the Lyre Prize, a Pushcart Prize, the Oregon Book Award for Poetry, and fellowships from Literary Arts and the Oregon Arts Commission.

### What I Wanted to Say

On the trip I did not take I'd thought waiting
in the plastic seats eating energy bars and apples
and drinking tepid tea would help me find a way
to talk about the Cage Fight taking place
one Saturday at the Roseland Theater, the tickets
available at any Safeway, or so the sign said
along the interstate. But I got sick instead
and did not take a trip, made my way home,
awakening to March snow falling through the firs.
I listened as I had listened every morning
for the last ten years for the neighbor's dog.
But he did not bark and has not barked for a week,
and I don't know whether to be happy or sad
his long days on the chain are over. I'd thought
the waiting, the canned air and the cancelled flights
might help me understand why anyone would watch
a Cage Fight, but instead read my old blue book,
growing groggier when I reached Paradise
in the long poem, its perfections so much less
interesting than the fall, thinking of our living room
on 97th, so small and even smaller when my father
and brother fought and fell into the furniture.
The Indian plum was greening now, the flowering
red currant in bud and the cherry yet to blossom
and even though I'd wanted to say *transfigure*
for the longest time, I saw instead how the owl
and the red-tailed hawk sat patiently
strapped to their perches, wings broken by bullets,
as we swarmed around them at the fair. I'd wondered
if they still saw twilight, the moment of awakening,
if they still felt the glide to fencepost behind
their hooded eyes? And then I wanted lilacs. I wanted
a voice I seem these days to know only as echo,
its lilt and fall, its little song, its dance so deep
in dream. But when the call came it was my mother
who had fallen down in the street a thousand miles
south, a stranger who took her to the hospital,
a nurse who called her a tough old bird
as she stitched her up. Then just this morning
I remembered ushering Roller Derby in college,
whole families came to watch what must be
a little like a Cage Fight, not so much
the steel wheels on the boards, the bearings whirling,
but those ponytails worn simply to be yanked, necks
wrenched, the cries, the hurt you can and cannot fake,
the bang and thud of bodies falling.

## What Do We Know
## and When Do We Know It?


Hot day, an old guy is climbing into a tractor,
bright orange, as yet ungouged by gravel
or tree stump. He's testing levers and gears
and settling into a seat built only for him
while we sit at the signal next to the tractor lot,
next to an oil drum painted blue, bright
with utility. And on the weekends outside
the ballpark a man does play the oil drums,
a dog sits wearing sunglasses with a hat at its feet,
its owner nowhere in sight in these last shabby days
of summer. The days right before the mist
starts to rise in a fusion of twilight and evening
over the neighbor's garden, when the hollow shafts
of sunflower stalks almost whistle, when we think
we can see the golden thread that will lead us
out of the labyrinth despite the stories people stop
to tell us at every turn, the glass bead rolling away
catching light, the ink on the page growing spindly,
each story feeding the one we don't know
how to say yet, the one waiting in us for the right story
to come along. And sometimes it does,
like that moment in *The Bicycle Thief* when the boy
and his father go off to work and each is proud
of the other and the boy is, I'm certain, my brother
walking to work with our father after the war,
walking down to the Water and Power yard,
and later, when the father is beaten by the crowd
for stealing the bicycle, the boy is no longer my brother
but me, the silvery entrails of failure swirling
in chiaroscuro, the man beating his oil drums
and the dog with its paw outstretched in the last days
of August grimy with dust, blemished by indifference,
when, finally, we know there is no way out. There is
a rusty dredger in the Umpqua hauling up gravel
from the riverbed, there is a river and we're in it,
an osprey nest resting in the cradle of stadium lights
and now a woman telling a story riven with such loss
she has to tell someone and she has told you,
your head barely above water as you follow
the current filled with branches and upended trees,
filled with pawn shops and homecomings
and a boy who could be you or me
or my brother watching his father fall down.

**Penelope Scambly Schott** (Portland, OR) is author of the verse biography, *A is for Anne: Mistress Hutchinson Disturbs the Commonwealth* (Turning Point Press, 2007), which won the Oregon Book Award for Poetry. Author of seven books of poetry, she lives in Portland, where she hikes, paints, grades papers, and indulges her family and dog.

### In This Time of War,

I've rummaged too long in my dresser drawers sniffing
at dead sachets. Even the rose petals are scraps

of paper with no names written down. So how
must I dress myself to walk about upon

this reddened earth? Today I will wear my snazzy
new panties of snake skin, those cool translucent scales

that slither in only one direction, up.
Never to droop or gather about my ankles.

I once knew a woman who lived through the London Blitz,
and her knickers were stitched from German parachute silk—

all the elastic had gone to the army, only
a safety pin to hold her homemade panties

up; she stood on the platform at Waterloo Station
where a long troop train chugged in with the wounded,

and just as her right hand ascended to her forehead
in quick salute, her slippery silk panties descended

and puddled over her sensible shoes, and she stepped
right out of them and kept on walking,

leaving all that tender and airworthy silk
under the crooked and shell-shocked wheels

of the gurneys, many,
so many gurneys.

## April, Again

The most brutal movie I ever saw
was time-lapse film of fruit in a dish,
all that tender ripeness caving in
on itself: the collapse of is into was.

When I glimpse my face in a mirror,
I remember a chipped colander
mounded with yellow cherries,
some rotting and some just dried.

Remarkable, all remarkable,
like this loose pebble in my palm,
its sparkle of mica, speck of lichen
thinking of nothing but *cling, cling.*

My fists are clusters of blossoms,
and inside them, the stone knuckles
with whatever of flesh will adhere,
adhering. Yes, I am old enough

to discuss April with a certain
earned authority: how pale petals
on the cherry tree guess nothing
about the hard pit.

**Peter Sears** (Corvallis, OR) came to Oregon in the mid-70s to teach at Reed College in Portland. He now lives in Corvallis and teaches in the Pacific University MFA Writing Program. His latest book is *Green Diver* (CW Books, 2009). His poems have appeared in *Field, The Atlantic,* and *Saturday Review.*

## Plane Down in Moriches Bay

I didn't know what my brother meant
when he said the sound of the explosion
reached our town, and he still didn't know
what had exploded when he and the other volunteers
gathered uptown, before dawn, and drove west,
to Center Moriches, to the bay,
where wreckage of a huge plane
sprawled across the night-gray waters.
Volunteers waded into the shallow bay,
my brother said, formed lines,
held both hands out to the man in front of them,
bending over at the waist, their elbows dipping
into the water. What was passed to each man
each man passed on: a piece of fuselage,
a piece of corpse, a broken lobster pot
long on the bottom. They stepped gently,
all the volunteers said so. Some said
there was too much debris in the water
for the people's souls to rise off the bay.
What helped, the volunteers said,
was to take deep breaths and let them out slowly
across the water. A couple of young guys
said they felt souls in the water.
They were led back to shore.
Now and then, the volunteers in the lines
looked out across the bay to the inlet
and out to the ocean where the sun
was coming up—but not for long
for fear of not being ready
when the man in front turned to them
with something in his arms.

## Dowsing for Joy

The dowser says he can discover joy
as well as water or the whereabouts
of elk in hunting season. Unfurled wire
hangers and forked sticks nestle in a leather
quiver he carries up our gravel drive
until a fold of land calls him to the west.

In the woods he seems half his eighty years
and his pale blue eyes deepen to sapphire
as he gazes where the breeze disappears.
He says there are signs everywhere,
obvious things that most of us simply miss
like the scent of blooming lilies carried on air,
or hidden fields of force that call us home
when we can no longer bear to be alone.
What is music but waves plucked from the sky
and is color not light disturbed before the eye
can find it? He reminds us no one doubts
the fact that wild animals know weather
well enough to hide before a storm arrives.
Are we not animals too? The agitation of a boy
lost in the forest pulls like the moon on tides
if a dowser is tuned in, if he can ask
the right question at the right time and cast
his spirit before him into the dark.

He stops to stake a vein of water for the site
of our well and strings ribbon over limbs
to track its turnings. Something tells him
there is more to know here. Among the oak
and fir he whispers questions to the night
ahead and smiles first at me, then at my wife
as the wires in his fists cross to find us both.

**Floyd Skloot** (Portland, OR) is author of *Selected Poems: 1970—2005* (Tupelo Press, 2008), which won a Pacific Northwest Booksellers Award. He has won three Pushcart Prizes and a PEN USA Literary Award in Creative Nonfiction. After living for thirteen years in the middle of twenty hilly acres of western Oregon woods, Skloot and his wife, Beverly Hallberg, now live in Portland.

**Primus St. John** (McMinnville, OR) lives in Oregon and teaches literature and creative writing at Portland State University. He is author of *Communion* (Copper Canyon Press, 1999) and co-editor of the Oregon anthology, *From Here We Speak* (Oregon State University Press, 1994).

## The  Sniper

That night
when the sky showed me
every star it had
and the biggest moon
I'd ever seen,
I aimed my gun
for the first time
and shot him.
Being nineteen
I rolled on my back
and chewed grass
and counted everything carefully.
Now when my students ask me
"What are their names again?"
I wonder who will forgive me.

## Water Carrier

The water carrier
has your skin
has stolen your wrinkles
your flute voice,
and so the fruit trees
in the valley are fed,
and so she walks toward me
without a sign of war in her hips
a sweet community
well fed.

## The Marathon

At the eighth mile
my daughters start to pull away from me.
I smile.
Soon in the large hand
of this ambitious sun
I will be far behind
in the irony of all this,
seeing as how where we're really heading
I'll get there first
and that's cool.

## At the Indian Cemetery on the Oregon Coast

Take that path at the bend in the road (easy to miss)
and then up through salmonberry and salal

to where they had to chop away a long
spruce root to fit a few graves. You find only

the soldiers marked with stones: marble for James,
World War I, granite for Leonard, World War II,

then Raymond and Agnes, married in '45—
plastic roses, drenched flags in moss.

From there, a dozen wooden crosses, crooked
aluminum letters still: here lies NG, here W.

Someone made a bench of cedar planks nailed
to a cedar tree so the old ones could rest

after they cleared the fallen alder branches,
stamped flat the tracks of elk and deer.

Sit there. Time turns over. Remember
when they said it would be alright,

that peace would come, and we would be
so happy we wouldn't need to speak of it.

Look how Leo's cup has filled with rain.

**Kim Stafford** (Portland, OR) is author of a dozen books of poetry and prose, including *Having Everything Right: Essays of Place* (Sasquatch Books, 2002) and *The Muses Among Us: Eloquent Listening and Other Pleasures of the Writer's Craft* (University of Georgia Press, 2003). He has taught at Lewis and Clark College since 1979, where he also serves as founding director of the Northwest Writing Institute and as Literary Executor for the William Stafford Archives. He writes, "We live in a world where a few people could destroy us all, but a few people cannot save us. The math doesn't work that way. We can only be saved when many people—and finally all people—recognize and live by our true interdependence on earth."

## Louise

*—for Louise High Eagle*
*of Lapwai, Idaho*

I went upriver to visit Louise—
stopped at the market to give her a call.
She's always home, working on her beads—
    you know Louise.

I knocked at her door, she shuffled me in—
had all her beadwork spread out on a board.
I bought some things, and asked how she was.
    She turned away.

I looked out the window to say my good-bye.
The sun was low and the day was cold.
But then Louise started to speak,
    and I listened to Louise.

She said, "We went down to Phoenix to visit the Pope,
that summer when he was there.
I was wearing my red dress that day,
    with the white shells on.

My friends, they all said they saw me on TV.
They said, 'Louise, did you touch the Man?'
Well, I reached out my hand, but then I was afraid,
    and I pulled away.

The man beside me touched the Pope's hand,
and then the crowd moved him along.
We got in our truck, and started for home,
    driving toward Idaho.

As we drove along I was working on my beads.
My fingers shook and I dropped a few.
My little grandson, he laughed and he said,
    'Why do those old things?'

I took his arm, and I looked in his eyes.
I didn't like what I felt then.
I said some things that I'd say again—
    I love that boy.

I said, 'It is hard when you sew one bead at a time.
My hands are shaking, my eyes have grown dim.
But are you too lazy, or are you too rich
    to sew one bead at a time?'"

Louise was through, and I said good-bye—
drove over the bridge at Spaulding for home,
on up the canyon, past Kendrick for Troy,
      as the dark came on.

I went up the switchbacks, out on top
came into the wheat, left the car,
looked up at the stars, and thought
      about Louise:

It is hard when you sew one bead at a time.
My hands are shaking, my eyes have grown dim.
But am I too lazy, or am I too rich,
      to sew one bead at a time?

## Beside the Road While Our Nation Is at War

In our son's young hand,
borrowed from the ground in California,
five acorns glisten and roll.
"Dad! These could be bullets!
Will you help me make a gun?"

His eyes look up into mine.

"Or Dad! They could be magic
seeds! Will you help me make
a bag with a hole—so
they drop along the path
and grow?" I take his hand in mine.

"Little friend, we must decide."

**Patricia Staton** (Astoria, OR) and her husband, watercolorist Noel Thomas, build aged miniature structures for collectors and museums and teach their techniques at workshops around the country. *The Woman Who Cries Speaks* (Lost Horse Press, 2008) is her first book of poems.

### Walking After Dinner

we head out the levee road
to where three gray donkeys
hold down one corner of a pasture,

their croaky voices anthems
tugging us across the rocky landscape.
Lulled by the half-light I think

the older one has reached the bottom of things.
It sways me the way their ears hang
out. In the field of weeds

blamelessness lies everywhere.
How their feet don't get tangled
where the barbed wire is down.

It isn't grief that curves toward us.
It is a kind of mercy.
Stepping in to the opening

we scratch their available necks,
raising slow clouds of dust.
They let us,

standing dopey-eyed in their beggar sleeves.
In the rise and fall I think even this
is a kind of survival.

It's a consolation
the way they stand in the light,
gold clinging to the air around them.

## Geography

In grade school, I never quite perfected
the task of drawing continents on the skins
of oranges. My ball point pen bumped
along dimples until countries lost their
shapes to each other. Nor was I any better
at making salt maps. I added too much water
until glistening landmasses oozed together
then dried and cracked on the cardboard.

So, my extra credit projects were dioramas—
carefully blocked scenes of Indians
and explorers taped into K-Mart shoe boxes.

Now, if I could scale down this view from
the kitchen window, I'd make a morning like this:
sky papered with scraps of cloud,
jagged mountains waxed with snow,
cardboard horses and matchstick fences,
and along the irrigation ditch,
yellow threads of grass, bending and bending.

## Hands

The winter we fed Henderson's cattle,
you taught me how to warm my hands
by curling my fingers into fists inside my gloves,
then navigated bumpy fields in low gear
while I stood on the flatbed, cutting strings
and heaving broken bales into the snow.
I learned how to ride the shifting weight
of the load, keeping my back to the wind
and how to pound on the cab for attention.

What artifacts did we leave to be swallowed
by thawing fields? Snarls of baling twine,
rotting gloves, a rusted pocket knife, its open blade
floating in the dirt like a ruined compass.

**Pamela Steele** (Echo, OR) was born in her grandfather's house on the banks of Laurel Creek in West Virginia. At age six months, her parents took her across the Divide on a train to eastern Oregon, and she has been traveling back and forth since. On one of those trips, she received an MFA in Writing from Spalding University in Louisville, Kentucky. She has been a recipient of Jentel Arts and Fishtrap fellowships, and her work has appeared in *Rattapallax*, *High Desert Journal*, and *Rosebud* magazines, among others.

**Lisa M. Steinman** (Portland, OR) teaches at Reed College. She is author of three books about poetry, including *Invitation to Poetry* (Blackwell, 2008), as well as four volumes of poetry, including *Carslaw's Sequences* (University of Tampa Press, 2003). Her work has received recognition from the National Endowment for the Arts, the National Endowment for the Humanities, and the Rockeller Foundation, among other places. She co-edits the poetry magazine *Hubbub*.

## Elegy with Policeman

One might have told the officer one was distracted by thoughts
of one's father, an old man with barely the strength of will
to die at the end. Miles away. Tubes and so on.

But that would have suggested thought, to which one probably
did not rise. And then there were the officer's lights.
And the stop sign for which one probably

did not stop, not even by rote. Rote: like family, like love, not
unfailing. The last thought was probably of how the consolation
of imaginary things is not imaginary

consolation. One might say it was embarrassing. But it was more
that it seemed it should be. It was a short—but completely full—
stop in any otherwise unremarkable day.

## Thought Under Construction

There's no first stanza and maybe we should all go home,
since thinking isn't easy under any circumstances. And if

'home' is what's under construction? The work crew first
disconnects the stove, then turns up the radio. Omelets and broken

eggs, yes, but quiet and even the chips and cracks
*were* the script. Like the script of a one-note seasonal bird

when a chill moves over a lake. But not like the radio.
The first rule of construction? Destruction. Even the bees

are irritable, launching preemptive strikes. Says the radio.
And how trite of the sky to be enamel blue for days,

the white rose bud, a small finger—thumbs up—in the green
& scorched brown garden. Voices in the background fill

dismantled space, while, hands over ears, not to listen,
every one is thinking, "So what if the background voices

murmur in, as they say, harmony, if the fist in the garden
unfurls the lineaments of rose? If the rose seems to *mean*

something?" Voices growl at the edges
 of mind, mind skittering away from thought, saying

(in a mother's voice), "This will never do."
"Safe as houses," *we* say, without any idea what that means.


## Puzzling


My father expressed himself
with talismans: a can opener, a ruler,
uncostly but material things. Thinking this
as I brush the crumbs of light off
the counter, water the garden.
There are spaces between
words here: sites of possibility, states
of mind for which we have no words.

The cosmos is in full flower; the birch,
full of early birds, all branches atwitter.

Each night, looking at the night sky,
it's all dipper, dipper,
dipper. Not *only* dippers, but *all*—
everything—in the great soupy
universe dipped or dipping: soft
ice cream cones in hard hats; ballroom

dancers out for ratings not melting
hearts; bodies fretted by heat next
to bodies of water; sine-waved charts
on office walls; all singing a cappella. *Dip.*
*Dip. Dip. Dip.*
                    It's as difficult
when dots connect in just one way
as when they do not, but that's
another can of worms.

**Ellen Waterston** (Bend, OR) has had essays, short stories, and poems published in numerous journals and anthologies. Her collection of poems, *Between Desert Seasons* (Wordcraft of Oregon, 2008), won the 2009 WILLA Award in Poetry. Her memoir *Then There Was No Mountain* (Rowman Littlefield, 2003) was selected by the *Oregonian* as one of the top ten books of 2003. She is recipient of an Oregon Arts Commission Fellowship and an honorary Ph.D. in Humane Letters from Oregon State University Cascades for her work as an author and in support of the literary arts. She is founder and director of The Nature of Words, Bend, Oregon.

### Spring Calver

The sky reels from clear to madness.
Rain, startled from the clouds,
erases the last tracings of snow,
washing down the earth so we can rework
what was done this time last spring.

I can see a coyote trailing his own
shadow along the ridge, eyeing
the carcass of the heifer we finally
gave up on. Threw too big
a calf. Pulled it dead. Her first,
poor thing, trying to calve all
those days out in the hills
before we found her.

He slit her stomach after,
so the dogs could have at . . .
Oh! The water's boiled away
on the eggs. Be hard by now. Some
have described him that way:
"Hard as a picnic egg."

In the hen house the other day
actually saw a hen lay. Always
thought they set to do it. But she
stood in that cramped little box,
her downy white breast rubbing up
and down against the splintery harshness
of the wooden sides, her tail feathers curling
with rhythmic effort. Then finally that white,
warm egg. Let me tell you, she did hop
out of there. Fled the hen house.
Squawk! Squawk! I couldn't decide
if she was boasting or cursing the trouble it was.

I'm due again in March.
He says: "You're no heifer anymore."

## Drought Dirge

One mile up bone-
dry road, bawling
calves trip along-
side mothers'gaunt half-
notes. Phone lines
droning in the heat
sag to breaking
point from the weight
of sere discords.
The ransacked
hide of a deer lies
scored, pitched, fly-less
in the draw, clef
of sun-cured skin
foretelling a waterless future.
The fretted ribs and fractured
femur intone crevasses, flats,
clefts, sand bars, sharp
mountain peaks, ancient
tremor. The hide of this land
is stretched thin beyond recall.
In the parched creek below
an antler pierces the stagnant
muck recording the receding
watermark. I part the scum
with my stick: a buck,
his head still perfectly intact.
With my baton I poke
the lip, the jowl. Loosed
fur, rotten flesh floats
gently off the face, pink,
bloodless. The jaw,
now buoyant, opens—
a sluggish yawn or wide—
mouthed silent scream.  One
blind, pickled eye stares up
at everything.

**Painted Shut**

Here life is meted out in sections. Farm
machinery parked arrow straight. Coming
or going takes right angles. All those tidy,
yellow-bright rows of weed-free annuals. Even
the unimportant knick knack—meticulous
on your mother's white sill, long painted
shut. She excises crusts from triangular
sandwiches, pays the neighbor girl a penny
for every dead housefly dropped into the bean-
bag ashtray—while you, the good son, plow under
miles of dried cornstalks and all thoughts of ever
doing anything else. As your wife, I sit and crack
snap peas on the porch swing and dream . . .

of circles. Here, only the curlicuing rivers confound
the grid. Well, once, at the county fair, the round trip
of the Ferris wheel briefly lit up your face, softened
your jaw. More time has passed. I can tell because
it begins to weigh something. I smell it like the rain.
The years fill my gauge with a lightness. Some other
gravity pulls me away. For you words are roadblocks.
But they are how I travel. Get off your plow. Talk to me.

## After a Class in Seaweed

These names like exotic diseases—*Alaria, Porphyra,*
*Fucus*—or terms transmitted from darkrooms (try
*Iridia,* try *Laminaria*). Still, it's hard to
imagine our world's future food supply
blessed with names like Bull Whip Kelp, though
that's what it looks like, and history shows

Maiden's Hair is poisonous, leaving us
(if we stick with the representational) Sea
Palm and Lettuce—high in iron, potassium,
iodine, protein, you name it—and once you see
how good they can taste, who knows, you might
impress your friends with your daring, you might

start a new trend. Believe me, these new scientist
cooks know what they're up to. Last week I stir-fried
some kind of algae with onions, green peppers, garlic
and soy sauce. Forgot it wasn't spinach. Tried
Porphyra chips with salsa, disguising an aftertaste
clinging like limpets, like shriveled up slug trails

that don't wash off. Anything's possible. Like
tonight, the casserole I took to the potluck
full of Sea Palms everyone took to be diced
black olives (smothered with hamburger, tucked
into a sauce of tomato and cheddar). Like finding
good intentions not only tricking the tongue, but blinding.

**Ingrid Wendt** (Eugene, OR) is author of four books of poems and is co-editor of the Oregon poetry anthology, *From Here We Speak* (Oregon State University Press, 1994). Ingrid Wendt's many awards include the Oregon Book Award, the Carolyn Kizer Award, and the Editions Prize. She and her husband, Ralph Salisbury, divide their time between Eugene and Seal Rock, Oregon.

## Benediction

*As it was in the beginning, is now and ever shall be*

Because I'd once been told what women always had done—though never
how, or why—after you died, the last tube taken out and gone,
and they offered to leave us alone, I asked if I could wash you.

The soapy water was warm, as you were, still, and soft. The basin was round.
The towels and wash cloths thick and white. And there was no strangeness in it,
really. And I didn't cry, and that, too, was part of the wonder.

I began with one smooth, pliant arm. As once you daily must have done with me,
as once you must have done at your own mother's death, I carefully dipped one
        cloth,
and carefully wrung it, and carefully bathed the whole freckled length of your arm,

your docile hand, each finger light in its yielding.
And though you had no choice in acquiescing to my love, I did not
revel in my power, but slowly lifted, washed and patted dry each limb, in turn,

your crooked toes and in between the toes; your shoulders, breasts,
the secret folds between your legs, thin pubic hairs, and with a different cloth,
which would have been your way, your face.

I took my time. I lingered in this unexpected absence of condition or demand.
And when at last with nothing more to do, I sat beside your bed and took
the hand I'd long since lost the need to hold, and laid my grown-up hand inside:

Oh, familiar shape my fingers knew by heart and had forgotten
that they'd ever known. How long this total rightness had been gone.
And, as leisurely as once I must have done, when simple being was enough

to please you, I let my eyes, without distraction, wander every
tiny detail of your face, its astonishing calm. I saw again your chin,
unguarded; saw your knuckles worn, arthritic; sang a tune that came

from who knows where: *This is the hand that fed me,*
*Hand that held me, Hand that punished me, Hand that led me.*
For hours, sunlight was the only thing that moved. And soon

would be gone. And your hand in mine, still warm!
I stood to kiss your forehead. It was cold. But I had been
in the presence of holiness. World without end. And was done.

## Truck

I shall now
praise my neighbor's truck
crouched on its slab black and metallic candy-apple red

emblazoned
with chevrons and swashes of gold
his only chariot why shouldn't he treasure it glistening

like unto
the color of beryl the mirrored
grillwork and foglights on the roof the little trumpets

of annunciation
the leaping trout and bull elk
the eagle airbrushed wheeling over a mountain lake

who can tell
the shape a dream might take
the appearance of animals round about within it moving

in a cloud
of exhaust the waterfall spilling
over a fender a great plain spanning the hood the desert

silhouette and deep
ocean all the world a likeness
of the firmament and its weather why shouldn't he cherish

this his ark
his rescue carrying him forth turning
neither right nor left but whither the spirit might go.

**John Witte** (Eugene, OR) has published poems in *The New Yorker; The Paris Review;* and *American Poetry Review.* He is author of *Loving the Days* (Wesleyan University Press, 1978), *The Hurtling* (Orchises Press, 2005), and *Second Nature* (University of Washington Press, 2008). The recipient of two fellowships from the National Endowment for the Arts and a residency at the Provincetown Fine Arts Work Center, he lives with his family in Eugene, where he teaches literature at the University of Oregon.

**Elizabeth Woody** (Portland, OR) writes poetry, short fiction, essays, and is also a visual artist. Her first collection of poetry, *Hand Into Stone* (Contact II Publications, 1990), received an American Book Award. Her second and third collections are *Luminaries of the Humble* (University of Arizona Press, 1994) and *Seven Hands, Seven Hearts, Prose and Poetry* (Eighth Mountain Press, 1994). Ms. Woody is the secretary of the founding board of the National Native American Arts and Cultures Foundation. She is Navajo/Warm Springs/Wasco/Yakama, born for Tódich'íinii (Bitter Water clan), and her birthplace is Ganado, Arizona.

## Flight

Eagle hovers as immobile Cross.
The blue clarity of tableau is critical detachment.
It drops from vision as simple hunter.

Afternoon hail, lightning and mist light blue-gray years between birth and mother.
Color-filled finches, mourning dove, and canyon wrens sing.

Smell sage rolling back and forth between fingers.
At the edge of Juniper berries is the matter of prayer.
The evergreen crests collect arches of pinion to mingle with ozone.

Locate a circle of copper in a sliver of rock. A burning red draws eye to the circle.
Palm open with hot lifeline, the rock fits along lined path of light's shadow,
comfortable in small mounds of muscle.

Our eagle plume stands up in the path.
Breath moves on the brown edge of filmy down as divination of the proper
        direction.

## Reveille

The rose bush lies across the path.
Heavy waves of petals and blush
a neglectful sun pushing through cedar.

The upper house is alive with a new baby.
Stirring the window gauze dishes ring
in morning and pear tree.

Nightshade twists through the laurel
to one companion rhododendron.
Waxen leaves reflect dawn's sheen.

Sentinel crow on the wire
is hoarse from wake up calls.
Warning and blessing are the same song.

# *Utah*

**Sandy Anderson** (Salt Lake City, UT) was the 1997 recipient of the Salt Lake City Mayor's Award in Literature and the 1995 Writers at Work Writing Advocate Award. She has been artist-in-residence at local schools and has given workshops to groups of disabled, veterans, and prisoners. She is currently editing her forth anthology of work by the disabled. She has been writing seriously since she was eight years old and teaches piano for a living.

### David Emmanuel's Wife

*Three days after her husband (who believed he was god) committed suicide in August, 1978, Rachel David pushed or coaxed her seven children off an 11th floor Salt Lake City hotel balcony, then jumped herself.*

I am pushing my children over.
All of them.
One by one.
There are those
who jump by themselves,
look down before jumping,
but jump.
I cry as each of them go.

The baby is easiest,
still one with my will,
welded to my sense of
what to do with the world.
But there are those others
who fight and hang on to the ledge.
They do not want to go.
Cry out at me.
Hideously.
Claw at me.

The world has gotten into them.
Warped their vision, their love,
their ability to love.
Jumping up and down on their fingers
is breaking the world's hold on them.
They will follow their father,
the crowds below are helpless to stop me,
my last child falls.
The lord gave me the power to create,
I come to him.
I follow.

**Rob Carney** (Salt Lake City, UT) has done readings at colleges and festivals across the country and on National Public Radio's "The Poet and the Poem from the Library of Congress." His work has been published in *American Poetry Journal, Mid-American Review, The National Poetry Review, Quarterly West, Redactions: Poetry & Poetics,* and dozens of other journals, as well as *Flash Fiction Forward* (W.W. Norton, 2006).

## January 26, 2009

Forty-three thousand job cuts in one day,
in just one morning. Thirty thousand more

by late-afternoon. Mine wasn't one of them.
We're not part of the millions since last May

who've lost their homes—lost porches and front doors,
the mantel 'round their fireplace, the trim

they painted 'round the windows one April:
pale green to go with her flower garden.

Or the place where he first saw her naked.
Or their kids' favorite hiding closet. All . . .

whatever the details, whatever their plans. . . .
How do you fit that in boxes, tape-gun it shut?

I don't know; the news didn't answer. Instead they ran
the weather: *Cold.* Then a story about a duck.


## Two-Story, Stone and Brick, Single-Family Dwelling

If there's added value in a ceiling fan,
then there must be value in a hawk. They come

for the doves, the ridiculous quail, and quick sparrows
squabbling daily on our neighbor's lawn,

suddenly plunging from nowhere, suddenly gone—
launched off before my eyes blink open.

And there must be value every time they miss
so *plunge* becomes *pursuit,* becomes a game

played out in fan-tailed figure-eights; it's wild:
your heartsong humming, the sky brighter blue. . . .

I know this won't go into the appraisal—
just bedrooms, baths, etc.; two-car garage.

There isn't any math that factors this.
No box to check if the front yard comes with a hawk.

**Elaine Wright Christensen** (Sandy, UT) is author of *At The Edges* (Utah State Poetry Society, 1990), which won the Utah State Poetry Society Book Award. Her second book, *I Have Learned Five Things* (Lake Shore Publishing, 1996), was selected by Michael Dennis Browne as winner of the National Federation of Poetry Societies' Stevens Contest. Her poems have appeared in numerous journals, and she has been nominated for a Pushcart Prize. She is mother of five children and grandmother of eleven. Living near the Wasatch Mountains, she draws inspiration from quail, fox, deer, sagebrush, and sego lilies.

## I Have Learned 5 Things

1.  The sulfurous flame
      sunbeams in corners
         lightning like cracked glass
            the bulb of an idea
               your dark eyes
    all
    have one source.

2.  Pain is truer than people
               truer than a full plate
               truer than God.

3.  Joy is a suitcase
    packed with everyday things
    no beaded gowns, no hats
    no umbrella
    just pajamas, a toothbrush, sneakers.
    If it rains
    stand there
    soak up every drop
    like applause.

4.  I have learned that I want less:
            the sound of lake water lapping
            tadpoles listless in sun-heated shallows
            wispy grass, knobby reeds
            greeting me, my name
            caught in their raspy throats
            one or two clouds
            and a bird, maybe,
            if it doesn't sing.

5.  Old age is where you started,
      a child
      looking up at the light
               at jumbled faces
               at mouths whispering,
    "There, now, go back to sleep."

## Inside

me
there is a dancer.
Inside this middle-aged body
of a housewife
there is a dancer.
Don't laugh.

I have danced with sunflowers
in sandy September fields

   with fruit trees each spring,
   blossoms in my hair

      at the lake's edge in winter
      where tall grass
      and thin reeds
      wobble on pointed toes
      in the wind

         and in summer
         with the sea

where anyone can find the dancer
inside.
Don't laugh.
Barefoot,
arms outstretched,
palms raised to the sky, to the birds,
to the clouds, to God,
who choreographed it all,
I danced.
I knew every step
and the waves stood up and bowed.

**Christopher Cokinos** (Logan, UT) is author of *The Fallen Sky: An Intimate History of Shooting Stars* (Tarcher/ Penguin, 2009) and *Hope Is the Thing with Feathers: A Personal Chronicle of Vanished Birds* (Tarcher/ Penguin, 2009). The winner of a Whiting Award, Cokinos has had essays, poems, and reviews in *Orion, High Country News, The American Scholar, Poetry, Western Humanities Review, Science,* and *Birder's World.* He teaches at Utah State University and lives along the Blacksmith Fork River in northern Utah's Cache Valley.

## Solstice Poem 2005

*—for my friends, especially Ken Brewer*

Today I glimpsed
a short-eared owl above
a rise just south
of Little Mountain.
Gone, when I looked again.

Of course this is metaphor
for the beauty and brevity
of life and for tragedy.
The owl will kill,
the owl will die.

At home, at dusk, in snow,
I hauled cut flood-wood
from the other side
of the river then
stacked logs by the willows

where we've talked and looked,
where we've listened to murmurs
of water and fire.
It was cold and nearly dark
when, stooping, I stopped

and heard the dipper's song go on and on.

# Natural Disasters

1.  A mother's lifelong rage. The slow burn
of a wire behind an old house wall, its paper
ornamental to the last, going

sepia before the fire
eats it out from behind.
                 No ignition:

in the end, at our old tinderbox,
no harm done. The firetruck bellied up,
sirenless, lights pulsing against the night,

and the fireman's industrial flashlight showed the source,
electricity turned to a slow smolder, smoke

we swam through.
                In winter's dark, we warmed
our hands before the voluble
flicker of television, which brought disaster

safely into the designated room.
We bought it on purpose, the neighborhood's
oldest house. Walls dried to tinder. Walls at last so thin

one good jolt of earth (the fault
a block above us and poised to go, sometime
in the next millennium) would reduce them.

And then, of course, the mountain
crumbling down. We don't think

of the inevitable: empire fallen, citizens—
schooled in the way of a city
blazing like heaven's declension—

extinguished at once, our tidy block
reduced to rubble. On the tube,

families huddle in the cold,
their homes burned to ashes, or taken

by hostile forces, by dry rot, by the bank.
If we change the channel, famine burns

another continent's children to the bone.
We opened windows, let out the smoke.
It was as cold as our house would get all year,

**Katharine Coles** (Salt Lake City, UT) has published four collections of poems and two novels. She teaches creative writing and directs the Utah Symposium in Science and Literature at the University of Utah. She also serves as the Inaugural Director of the Harriet Monroe Poetry Institute at the Poetry Foundation in Chicago. In 2006, she was named to a five-year term as Poet Laureate of Utah.

though the weather was heavy, record-breaking.
Then we went to bed.

2.                              Imagine this:
a man with a name requiring of him either
impossible dignity or the world's best sense of humor—

neither of which he's gained by fifty-six—
holds his hand to his heart, its charges

wired brilliantly awry, and falls
to his knees in a parking lot stitched with rain.

The janitor finds him. Too early—five a.m.—,
the hospital a block away sunk into winter half-light,

the ambulance drivers playing a game
of rummy. Someone had a good hand. Too late

the emergency technician's palms pumping down,
electrical paddles to shock the muscle

back to the rhythms of work, of play.
Half an hour: entropy wins the day.

How much, in America, a white man's life is worth
(the deep south; winter deeply green)—
more than anyone's on earth, and no more—

not even a life spent learning impulsiveness,
mapping tissues, the nervous skin

conducting the charge. He knew that machine.
Knew by heart his family's history.
Died, like everyone, surprised

by the fault ticking inside him. He paid it no mind;
had the words, but refused to name it.
All this, even his name, engraved

on the still electrified hearts of those left behind.
Over coffee, we shake the newspaper:

children, boulders, trucks plucked up, driven
inland by a tide we've ignored,

swelling so far out at sea, traveling,
we thought, to such desolate shores,

nobody paid attention
to the final turn toward our own beaches,
the building force.

3.                    This couldn't be more personal,
or less so. The new year, 1993.
My mother will live for years,

her anger building like ice
she won't chip away. Her own mother
passed it on, and the world

collaborated—little endearments,
gestures, the weights of civilization

sticking like burrs around a heart
that will not turn to stone. I harden myself

to feel the ways I'm charmed.
In the yard, three feet of snow and counting:
icicles form on the eaves, blades

drawn toward us by their weight.
Another storm cauterizes our city.
All over the neighborhood, men scale

their houses' ice-glazed pitches, and start to shovel.
Their wives pace the walkways.
But roofs collapse in our best neighborhoods.

Drivers abandon their cars—suburban streets
lost to white, unpastoral meadows—

and forge on foot toward porchlights.
They will be lent the phone, then turned away.
From the whited-out mountains, a herd of elk

drifts toward the valley through a canyon
buried twenty-feet deep in snow. Ghostly

in car headlights, the sensible elk
take the freeway the whole way down.
In the canyon's mouth, the wind

concentrates its rage on them.
Then they shoulder over snowbanks into our yards,
persistent as dream.

4.                              Still there when we wake

to heavy skies, another storm barrelling in.
They bare their teeth to the trunks

of cherry and dogwood. What we inherit,
too great a tenderness. I planted
those trees myself, but give them up

to watch the elk browsing,
lying in my yard's snow. On days like this

we may not feel luck churning
through us like blood. Look at that sky—

how history carries us here, a current
we're barely aware of. We don't resist

flying at the storm's eye.
This ring of peaks holds danger

back, makes the world peripheral.
But the elk are here. And a fire burns

even under this winter, the dormant garden.
The cows, gravid, sleep in our frozen lilies.
And above us, where the elk will turn

at first thaw, glaciers, traveling so slowly,
push before them mountains, reshaping the earth.


*—For T. P., 1936—1993*

**Star Coulbrooke** (Smithfield, UT) is responsible for Helicon West, a bi-monthly open readings/ featured readers series in Logan, Utah. She directs the Utah State University Writing Center and organizes an annual Beat/Slam Poetry Night. Her poems appear in *Poetry International, Ellipsis,* and others.

## How I Stopped Selling Life Insurance

I

My aesthetician does the best pedicures
this side of the Rockies,
hot soapy water, soft white towels,
three grits of emery stone,
massage that tickles your bones
toe-knuckles to knees. When she's
done your calves are weak,
balm of washed feet, a blessing.

II

Her name is Lucy. Dark eyes, deep
layers of burgundy hair and skin
like you can't get enough of, peach
under porcelain. Whatever she's using,
you want it. So I bought her wares,
then she bought mine. Life insurance.
A hundred for her, ten thousand per child.

III

After the funeral, after the company
issued the check, policy plus interest
for her boy killed in the crush of an AC/DC
concert crowd, I went to her salon
where flowers and tributes lined the counter
and we talked of his grace and beauty,
the joy he gave her all his fourteen years.
After I left her there, check in hand,
that's when, and that's how.

## Men Working

They have ulterior motives,
the worker I live with admits.
And I almost enjoy
the insinuation of sex
into my mundane middle age,
apprised of men's pleasure
in flexing their bodies.

I see them on rooftops
of the tallest buildings in town,
some in hats and flannel,
faces lined from years of sun,
the younger ones oblivious
to heights and UV danger,
bare-chested, muscles rippling,
heat-bronzed, pants tight
over hard butts and thighs.

I watch them in my front yard
on bobcats and backhoes
scraping out the worn driveway,
pouring new cement, workers
with triceps like knotted cedar,
hormones thrusting, confident
my eyes are on them, on the one
who strides across my lawn,
hoists a three-gallon cooler
to his shoulder like a whiskey jug,
bottom to his lips, and presses
the dispenser. Water streams
into his mouth and mine.

**Halina Duraj** (Salt Lake City, UT) is a Ph.D. candidate in Creative Writing at the University of Utah. Her writing has appeared in journals, including *Witness, Fiction,* and *Hayden's Ferry Review,* and one of her pieces is a recommended story in the 2009 PEN/O'Henry Prize Anthology. She lives in Salt Lake City.

## Vertiginous

Over a pot of tea,
my friend looks up from her book
and tells me she likes the word vertiginous.
Doesn't it mean green, she says, like verdant?
I say I always thought it meant being on the verge of something.

Later I look up the word in the dictionary.
We were both wrong.
But if only vertiginous did mean what it sounded like:
something on the cusp of turning green.

Instead it has more to do with what I heard on the radio
as I drove to meet my friend:

The dam proposed for China's Yanghtze River
will be a mile wide.
The reservoir will stretch 150 miles upstream
and when filled will inundate
an area the size of Switzerland—

a weight so great it will
literally tilt the earth,
the scientist said,
by a fraction.

**Michael Hicks** (Provo, UT) is author of three books: *Mormonism and Music: A History* (University of Illinois Press, 1989); *Sixties Rock: Garage, Psychedelic, and Other Satisfactions* (University of Illinois Press, 1999); and *Henry Cowell, Bohemian* (University of Illinois Press, 2002). He edits the journal *American Music*, and his poetry has been published in *Dialogue, BYU Studies, Literature and Belief, Sunstone*, and in the anthology *Cadence of Hooves: A Celebration of Horses*.

## Whaling

After ham baguettes and Martinelli's at the museum café,
my new friend Gary drove me to see the 9000 LPs
stored above his garage, all plastic-sleeved, cube-shelved
onto three walls: a mausoleum of tunes, souls of our heroes
floating in mildewy air beside the last unshelved wall
which wore a poster of the pyramids at Giza, the insert
for Pink Floyd's *Dark Side of the Moon*, a first pressing
of which Gary held up, sliding the vinyl from its sleeve,
as if to illustrate the title, and declared, "Stone mint."
I said, "I hear it's going to be repressed," to which he said,
"Aren't we all?" as if he were lifting a tonearm, as if a pun
could retract the sorrow of record hounds everywhere
for their black fetish's erosion, its extinction by neglect.
Each new pressing means preservation, I told Gary:
mummification and resurrection at once. What high priests
tried in pyramids, which, like any collection, one keeps
excavating and refilling. Gary said he wanted to reorganize
by genres with cardstock slats for dividers. "Where
would you put *Songs of the Humpback Whale*?" he asked.
"Start a 'whales' section," I said, as if I were some
new Enlightenment stumbling into the room. Crumb's
*Vox Balaenae*, Hovhaness's *And God Created Great Whales*.
Maybe some Paul Horn. "Hendrix belongs there,"
he said. "The feedback is pure whale." So we talked
for hours about the ecology of rhyme and about memory's
tilting architecture and about how whales can hear
each other's songs a thousand miles away, one ocean
to the next. Which led us to our various ex-lives,
most now capsized or collapsed like waves. And soon
it got dark, though we knew the physics of planetary
surfaces and knew that it's always day somewhere
on earth, that, even as we spoke, a sunlit Giza was tipping
its worn styluses onto heaven to play the B-side.

### Sunday's Tie

I  slip the  tie

through a Y

I choreograph

each silken end.

One is centered

within like a long

bow. Windsor knot.

I try to still my love,

clasp his shaking fists.

We grasp beneath the tie.

His proper tie can not hide

his worsening tremors which

stir us both though we hold on

knuckled tight as knots. I to give

my care loving him so as he

dies.  I am true until

death claims the

end

.

**Linda M. Jefferies** (Lehi, UT) enjoys seventeen grandchildren, yoga, skiing, biking, and travel. With numerous poems now published, she is assembling a book-length collection, *Bdellium*. She is a Mormon and serves in a Latter-day Saints Temple in American Fork, Utah.

**Kimberly Johnson** (Salt Lake City, UT) is author of two collections of poetry, *Leviathan with a Hook* (Persea Books, 2002) and *A Metaphorical God* (Persea Books, 2008), and she has translated Virgil's *Georgics* (Penguin Classics, 2009). Her poems, essays, and translations have appeared in numerous publications, including *The New Yorker, Slate, Yale Review,* and *Modern Philology.* Recipient of grants and awards from the National Endowment for the Arts, the Utah Arts Council, and Sewanee, Johnson lives in Salt Lake City, Utah.

## Voluptuary

Fifty-mile Creek in the extravagance
of June, a fullness of flowers: paintbrush
and larkspur, beeflower and attendant bees,

the cedars *sough*, the sunfired pines
forge filigree at the timberline.
My ballerina sister on the riverbank

balances, rod cocked to rearward,
released, and retracted, line tripped
terpsichorean by the weight of the fly.

Her tacklebox cockeyed reveals homemade
damsels: the Emerging Sparkle, the Orange
Sunrise, the Dark Scintillator, and a Green

Butt Skunk. A ridiculous scene, tableau past
cliché, with verdure and soughing
and blah blah blah. She hooks a splake,

flips him to shore, yanks her knife open,
swipes anus to jaw. With a finger inside
she slides guts, gore, and shit in a shining

red pile. She dunks him, lets the stream
clean the gash, chucks him to me
for the icebucket, and here the suckerpunch

of beauty: white vault of ribs in their arch
to the spine, one red vein bulging faithfully
skull to tail, red gills fragile, useless

beneath the operculum, ordered
like layers of vellum. Scales flake off
and stick to my palms like glitter.   Like silver.

## Pater Noster

This garden is a miracle.
Aphids dropped with April, gorgeous emeralds
with teeth. They preen against the petals,
distill sweet sap to honeydew.

Down bark, down fencepost, tazzled branches
dart and pull their braiding shadows, a slapstick
of diffraction. Downwind the barnstormers
perfect their spectacle—stiff cloth, wood

prop, 2-cycle engine ascending like a prayer
to flame out, hang breathless, cartwheel
over and power swooping earthward.
It's all for show, the windswept scarf

from forties matinees, the smoky trail,
the drama of the stall. The pilot streaks
to level, tilts a greeting as he buzzes
overhead, milks the throttle, rolls

headlong into a spin, whining, frictive, the form
of glory, and gloriously sunstruck. Seasonal
the ritual, pinching aphids as I kneel
upturned, squinting sunward for the sleek

daredevil flight, for the promise of the climb,
of sunlit wings, of plain things charged
and fulgent, of one perfect
performance, of *earth as it is in heaven.*

**Lance Larsen** (Provo, UT) is author of three collections of poems, including *Backyard Alchemy* (University of Tampa Press, 2009). His work has appeared in *New York Review of Books, TLS, Raritan, Paris Review, Southern Review, Poetry Daily, The Best American Poetry 2009,* and elsewhere. He has received a number of awards, including a Pushcart Prize and a National Endowment for the Arts Fellowship. He serves as Associate Chair of English at Brigham Young University.

### Americana

I found Old Lady Kuhni's yard strewn with garbage,
a confetti of junk mail and potato peels,
trash can knocked over—and her
in a purple kimono thing trying to clean up.
"*Wild dogs done this,*" she said, followed by complaints
about her Jack, *damn him, he gone up*
*the mountain to shoot him another deer, and could you,*
*please . . .* Who was I to turn her down?
I was a paper boy on foot, a thrower of bad news.

So I stooped and gathered—grapefruit rinds
like speckled snakes, charred toast,
wallets of dryer lint, bloodied wads of t.p.
When she handed me a badminton racquet,
I thought, "A gift?—why not, I've worked hard."
Then she motioned me to the fence
and pointed. Lying in a bed of scraggly mums,
a deer head. Prim as a handbag but chewed,
one eye missing, the other staring across frosted lawn.

She knew boys like me were brave in stupid ways
and wouldn't mind using a racquet
as a spatula. So I scooped up
that face and carried its soft ears and final
grimace across the yard. Carried it.
We're always auditioning for something.
Me: for paper boy of the decade, plus tips.
Old Lady Kuhni: a little respect.
That partitioned deer: a blind date with eternity.

Which is why I carried what was left of its face
in front like a torch. *Not into the trash,*
she said, *that would bring the dogs again.*
I followed her into the garage, to the freezer,
which gasped in white when she opened it,
a cauldron filled with dry ice. I settled that face
atop a bed of frozen peas, and she closed
the lid. We traded then. I handed
her the racquet, handle first, and she buried me

in thank yous, then I trudged back into that cold
masquerading as Sunday morning.
What I didn't know hung
everywhere. Tricky Dick Nixon and the price
of bananas from my shoulders, secret
lives from lit windows.
I was a carrier, worth 87 cents a day,
plus rubber bands, right arm two inches
longer than my left. I looked back then and saw

in the side yard the rest of the doe—upside down,
in an apple tree, tied in place
with a blue jump rope, rib cage stuck open
with kindling. What I breathed
out was only breath, but it felt like moths.
Moths that climbed and dissolved,
climbed and dissolved, till I too circled
that exquisite scarecrow of hanging
meat, weddings and want ads banging my thighs.

## Like a Wolf

You had to admire the shapeless genius of his outfit—
upside-down garbage bag over purple shorts.
Just a slit for his bald head, holes punched
through for his arms, and a draw string
he could tighten in case of rain.
I made him my pace car, and tried to stay
no more than five or six strides back.

My purpose: not win or place, just finish.
Like the rest of us, he knew that on race day
suffering must brave leg cramps and wind,
angst and winding climbs, and hope
must first be numbered and pinned to your shorts—
in his case, #88. I loved the symmetry
of those eights. Twin infinity signs standing

upright, one chasing the other just as I was chasing
him. At mile eleven, when the sun bled
through red rock hills and I tied my warm-ups
at my waist, and real runners flung
theirs into after-race oblivion, I learned
wisdom. Mr. Hefty tore off his garbage bag,
like the Hulk shredding another Armani suit.

And tossed it high.  An updraft caught it,
till it floated above what we were, an undulating
river of huff and wheeze pouring out
of the canyon. Floated—an effigy he ran under,
as if he had escaped himself. Old man nipples
peering out at a new world, he tipped
back his head as if drinking the sky and he howled.

## Why Do You Keep Putting Animals in Your Poems?

I open windows to catch a glimpse of *grace*
on the horizon, and in they sneak, coyotes and crows,
pikas and the scholarly vole, dragging scoured skies
I can see myself in. Much cheaper than booking
a flight to the Galápagos. And they teach me.

Badgers rarely invent stories to make them sad
about their bodies. And the wrinkliest of Shar Peis
never dreams of ironing its face. My happiness
is like a flock of sparrows that scatters when a bus
drives by, then re-strings itself two blocks away,

a necklace of chirps festooning a caved-in barn.
Capuchin monkeys will bite a millipede to release
a narcotic toxin, then hand it to a neighbor
as if passing a joint at a concert. In a Rhode Island
nursing home, Oscar the miracle cat curls up

with residents hours before they expire, converting
death into purrs for the next world. A poem is grave
and nursery: the more creatures you bury in one place,
the more hunger bursts forth somewhere else,
like bats at Carlsbad when the brightest day shades dark.

The night I stood on my sister's feet and learned
to waltz, a porcupine braved four lanes of asphalt
and hurtling machines to chomp our windfall apples—
two miracles of syncopation held together by a harvest
moon. As Marianne Moore taught us, an hour

at the Bronx Zoo in a tricorn hat leaves one happier
than nine months with a shrink. Comes a time
you just have to wiggle your pin feathers,
wag your ghost tail, feel your teeth grow long
for the ragged salmon throwing their bodies upstream.

**David Lee** (Cedar City, UT) splits his time between his new home base in Bandera, Texas, and Seaside, Oregon, where he and Jan summer. Retired, he spends his time scribbling, wandering available trails and greenbelts, dawdling, and concentrating on his goal of becoming a world class piddler. His new book, *A House Made of Time* (Logan House Press, 2009), is written with William Kloefkorn.

## Racehogs

John calls and sez Dave
when I say hello and I say hello John
and he sez come down Dave
you gotta see what I got
I say fine I'll be right there and he sez
bring Jan I'll show her too
and I said I will
so Jan and I got in the car to see
what John bought.

John bought four hogs
starved half to death, bones out
everywhere, snouts sharp enough
to root pine trees and the longest damn legs
I've seen. What do you think? he sez
and I don't say anything so he sez
I sez what do you think? and I say
them's pretty good-looking racehogs John
and he sez what? and I tell him
I heard about a place in Japan or California
(because he's never been there) where they
have a track and race hogs
on Tuesday nights and he sez do they
pay much? And I say yes or so I heard
maybe a hundred to win and he sez
goddam and I say those hogs
ought to be good with them long legs
and skinny bodies and he sez goddam.

Jan's walked off so I go find her
but she's mad and says I ought not to do that
and I say oh I was just bullshitting
but when we come back John's standing
by the fence throwing little pieces of feed
all around the pen making the hogs
hurry from one place to the next
and when I get up close he's smiling
and I can hear him whisper
while he throws the feed
run you skinny fuckers, run.

## The Tale of the Graveblaster

On the way to the auction in Salina to sell our pigs John told a story about a graveblaster he knew in Pioche.  Not a digger, the ground was too hard so he had to blast his graves out with dynamite. John couldn't remember the man's name but he had a son named Manuel who the story was about anyway. There was a day when the father was ill and had to be taken to the hospital in Ely. Afternoon, the mortician called and asked for the father; only Manuel was left to blast the grave.  He loaded his father's truck with the sticks from the case, fused the charge, walked behind a small knoll and detonated the explosives.  The blast carved a huge gap in the earth which spread much farther than Manuel had anticipated. Nearby graves were upthrust and several coffins disinterred and scattered profusely about the area.  John's story struck me as being somewhat sardonically humorous and I laughed.  Incredulous, John slowed his truck, cut me off with a glance.  "It ain't funny you sonofabitch," he said. "That was his daddy's grave he was blasting."

## Attachment

It's carved into a rockface
in a canyon somewhere in the Swell,
buried in a cemetery, or just scattered
about the graves
of ancestors who settled this valley.
It's in Dugout Canyon
where we take the dogs,
where Sweetie and Holly chase water striders
in the pools of the stream
and we walk for miles
through this high desert of juniper,
thinking, when we talk about leaving Utah,
how it all turns about
and comes back at us until we're old enough
to move away from the places we love,
where our son, who can't wait
to leave this small desert town,
has waded the canyon streams,
watched me bury Winchester, Groucho
then Sweetie beneath the crabapple tree,
keeping them close, where he said
he was sure they wanted to be.

**Jan Minich** (Wellington, UT) has published poems in many journals and is author of *The Letters of Silver Dollar* (City Art, 2002) and two chapbooks: *History of a Drowning* and *Wild Roses*. He is Professor Emeritus at the College of Eastern Utah, where he taught literature and writing for twenty-five years and was the Director of the Wilderness Studies Program for several of those years.

**Rod Miller** (Sandy, UT) is author of a Western novel, *Gallows for a Gunman* (Pinnacle Books, 2005), and two nonfiction books, *John Muir: Magnificent Tramp* (Forge Books, 2009) and *Massacre at Bear River: First, Worst, Forgotten* (Caxton Press, 2008). He earned a degree in journalism from Utah State University and worked as a copywriter and creative director in advertising agencies in Idaho, Nevada, and Utah. He also rode bucking horses for the Intercollegiate Rodeo Team.

## A Bolt of Broomtails

Across alkali flat and sandhill,
Over the sage-covered plain
The mesteñada flows like fabric,
Dancing ahead of its dusty train.

> *chestnut, claybank,*
> *coyote dun,*
> *buckskin, black,*
> *blue roan, bay,*
> *piebald, palomino,*
> *pinto, paint,*
> *grulla, ghost white,*
> *dapple gray*

Rippling in the morning light
The hues shimmer and shift;
Mustangs run as colored threads
Through the warp and weft.

## Go Home Again

Pull the snap from the hasp and squeak
neglected hinges. Stare into the dim past.
Taste dust dancing in light beams that leak
where shingles gap like teeth that didn't last.

Smell leather seasoned with horse sweat,
blankets lined with variegated hair crust.
Straighten a reluctant latigo strap. Let
your thumbnail scratch cinch ring rust.

Hear tarnished bit chains on a stiff headstall
rattle, lifted from a used-horseshoe hook
nailed to the warped, weathered wood wall.
Read the brittle pages of an old book.

## A Small, Soul-Colored Thing

The dog walked out of the forest with the deer in its mouth.
No. The deer came out of the forest. The dog
ran beside it, over, under: the dog slipped itself
into the animal lurching to my side of the road,
one of its throats bent back to the sky,
one of its dark spines dissolved to pear-white belly.
The throat was red. And the long legs looked broken.
But I made a mistake. The legs were not broken.
And the deer did not appear dead, though it must have been,
animated by the dog's hunger so that the deer moved
when the dog did, shivered like the soul inside the body,
the dog's face all red, which is the color of the soul.
The back of the dog was sleek and brown
and expensive-looking. When I stared at him,
I could see the lawns he must have escaped from,
the gravel drive winding down from the hills in the gold tags
jangling at his chest: the clean, pink flaps of his ears
flushed with cold. Now they were froth-covered.
And his eyes were glazed with a furious longing.
The dog tore at the deer's throat as if he could dig
himself inside of it. The dog became a dog
again, and I watched him do it, and the deer became
something else: it left the soft ash shape of the doe
grazing by the bus stop, it abandoned
the buck's bright energy leaping over the stone wall
that separates my house from the cemetery,
its low border taut as a muscle that herds of deer trace
in moonlight, cast out of the canyons choked with snow.
The deer became some shadow torn between us:
beneath it, the beautiful legs, the elegant ribs
twisted into the road. I stopped and watched
this wrestling, the dog half deer, the deer
half dog, myself poised behind them
so as to remain invisible, though a low,
slow growl loosed itself at my approach.

**Paisley Rekdal** (Salt Lake City, UT) is author of a book of essays, *The Night My Mother Met Bruce Lee* (Vintage, 2002), and three books of poetry: *A Crash of Rhinos* (University of Georgia Press, 2000), *Six Girls Without Pants* (Eastern Washington University Press, 2002), and *The Invention of the Kaleidoscope* (University of Pittsburgh Press, 2007). Her work has received a Village Voice Writers on the Verge Award, a National Endowment for the Arts Fellowship, and the University of Georgia Press' Contemporary Poetry Series Award. She serves as Director of the Creative Writing Program at the University of Utah.

It entered the deer and reverberated there
until its fur grew long and thickened,
and its face took on the shape of a lion,
a wolf, a bear. It became the shape of a mouth
tearing and tearing as I watched it, wanting
to pull the velvet antlers down from my head,
to take my share of it, kneeling at the walk
and putting my mouth to the flesh, letting
blood and fur both coat my tongue, while my hands
reached into the stomach to rip and empty it.
I wanted to loose my gray hair out
upon my shoulders, letting my own heart be pierced
and the soft pulse shiver in the skin. No.
The dog tore at the deer's throat. And I watched it.
I was the human that could watch it. I was the small,
soul-colored thing that wouldn't change.
The deer trembled and lay still.
It grew slack in the deepening snow.
The road disappeared and the sky turned white.
The snow piled up. It kept falling.

## Reading Henry Fowler's *Modern English Usage* in Salt Lake City in November

You note the one "r" in iridescent,
from the Greek, *iris*, rainbow, not the Latin,
*irrideo*, to laugh, and I smile

to think of your idiosyncrasy,
scrupulous care in life as well as work.
Today light streams in, the bright surprise

of it risible, as amazing to me
as sagebrush and pinons. First Western fall,
felicitous, pumpkin custard sending

clove into the air as the cats quibble
over the patch of hottest sun. Gone:
Old house, old roads, old friends. Gone as well

that blue hour when solitary
lovers in cafés console themselves.
That city's farther than it's ever been,

differs *toto caelo*, by the whole sky,
from these nights of shooting stars
and sunny days that beam across the floor

like lace. If you were here, Henry,
you'd advise exactitude, tell me to love
the narrow difference between "broad"

and "wide": a distance that separates
the limits, an amplitude of what
connects them. Some words refuse wide,

admit broad: blade, spearhead, daylight.
And some allow them both: A wide door
open to miles of snowy peaks. The view

from where I am is wide *and* broad, and if
I lose myself in its expanse, will mountains
rein me in, or clouds as volatile as grace?

**Natasha Sajé** (Salt Lake City, UT) is author of two books of poems, *Red Under the Skin* (University of Pittsburgh Press, 1994) and *Bend* (Tupelo Press, 2004), and many essays. Her work has been honored with the Robert Winner and Alice Fay di Castagnola Awards, a Fulbright Fellowship, the Campbell Corner Poetry Prize, and the Utah Book Award. Sajé is Professor of English at Westminster College in Salt Lake City and has been teaching in the Vermont College MFA writing program since 1996.

**Michael Sowder** (Logan, UT) is author of *The Empty Boat* (Truman State University Press, 2004), which won the T. S. Eliot Award, and his *Calendar of Crows* (New Michigan Press, 2001) won the New Michigan Press Award. He also authored a study of Walt Whitman, *Whitman's Ecstatic Union* (Routledge, 2005). Featured in Ted Kooser's "American Life in Poetry," his poems appear widely, as do his essays about poetry, Buddhism, and the natural world. He teaches at Utah State University, where he is poetry editor of *Isotope: A Journal of Literary Nature and Science Writing*.

## The Lost Verse

In your birthday-present aquarium
*Hypostomus plecostomus*
rests in the lap of the Buddha—
his body divided bow and stern,
half black, half a pale tangerine,
like a yin-yang cigar,
or a half-lit submarine.

An algae eater, all morning
he's been sucking the scum
from the Buddha's body—
cleaning that great roundness,
hands and face, chest and thighs,
while Gautama sits quietly,
two feet under, without
breathing.

All about them shimmer
the spangled host: neon tetras,
silver angels, prayer-flag gouramis,
rainbows, fire mouths, pearlfish,
a water filter their only choir.

While there at the center
Mister Plecostomus lies
content—knowing the lost verse said:

Blessed is the scum of the earth,
for it shall adorn the body of God.

## The New Year at Albertsons

Price, Utah

Sometimes the store is better than the Internet.
Getting out in the icy parking lot
to have your young neighbor, a basket pusher,
insist he lift heavy cans into your trunk,
ask if you can use some hired help
to shovel your snowy drive.
Running into Carol in Produce,
who tells you the sad story of another friend's
death when you were away last summer.
Or laughing with Rick you missed
at the solstice party, as he charades
how he fell off his dog sled,
the team yipping and gliding
and getting smaller
near Starvation Lake.

A woman I just met in Tai Bo
says she's hurrying to a Caribbean cruise
just to hear Les Claypool—*You know, the old
guitarist from Primus?* But when she starts
with the dates and times of her flights and boat,
I begin rolling away with a nod to Giselle
at the deli, slip my own words in about tilapia
I came in for, and what's all fished out
as the woman ends her story with her landing
in Florida by morning, and we all look out
at the falling snow.

There are the surprises of those
you want to avoid, or who want to avoid you.
As I wait at the pharmacy in One,
Misty, my husband's non-trad student,
always calling to get help with her sentences,
veers to a stack of pies near Three.
I cut down the cereal aisle as my
former dentist opens the door to the milk.

I know I could meet the student
I caught plagiarizing, or my Mormon neighbors,
when I'm loading beer for a party.

**Nancy Takacs** (Wellington, UT) is Professor Emeritus at the College of Eastern Utah in Price. She has lived and taught in Utah for thirty years and worked also as a wilderness studies instructor. Takacs served as an artist-in-education for the Utah Arts Council, and she taught poetry in prisons and schools. She received an MFA from the University of Iowa and is author of three books of poems, including *Juniper* (Limberlost Press, 2010).

Mostly it's all good, the free coffee,
the ongoing life-swapping stories with Jane,
the young checker, no longer engaged
to healthy wealthy Bob,
but now dating Tom,
a hamburger cook at the Balance Rock Café.

Today I'm checked by Betty
who survived breast cancer years ago.
She has rusty car brakes in her voice
that could still run forever, asking
if the deer herd has wandered my way lately,
if they've eaten any of my trees,
says how they're climbing
on her porch for cat food
along with the raccoons,
since she and I live
just a few miles apart
along the same river,
and we know they're there
under the moon at midnight
hoofing through snow
for the fallen apples.

## The Bowling Alley's Giant Neon Pin

is visible from space,
or so says local wisdom
and I'm frankly tired anyway of all
the "just take our word for it"
satellite shots of the Great Wall,
Great Barrier Reef, Grand Canyon.
I haven't met those places yet.

I love the subterranean clamor
that greets me at the door,
the warm smell of spilled beer
and smoke that lingers
blue in the air. I love indicating
with a dumbshow of fingers
my size 8 foot
and the oriental moment
of slipping out of my shoes.

The astronauts who agreed
they'd identified the giant bowling pin
were weary from space travel,
loopy for lack of oxygen, sick for home.
They would further report
that the earth appeared to them
as a blue and white and green-swirled world,
a hand-span in size,
and the most beautiful thing they'd ever seen.

I love, yes, best of all
standing in the shiny hardwood lane,
my fingers curled
up inside the ball, cradling it to my chest,
feeling lucky this time.

**Mike White** (Salt Lake City, UT) is a graduate of the doctoral program in Literature and Creative Writing at the University of Utah and a former editor of *Quarterly West*. His poems have appeared in numerous journals, including *Poetry, The New Republic, The Iowa Review, The Threepenny Review, The Antioch Review, Western Humanities Review,* and *Denver Quarterly*.

## Go Around

Happiness may not be communicable.
Yet there are cables under the ground.
Have you seen the men digging?
This one shoulders a section of pipe.
That one is directing traffic.
Go around his arm says.
It is late afternoon and wavy hot.
He has forgotten his arm
is connected to his body.
Here was once a seashore.
Here was once a dinosaur.
There is a tiny horse in the concrete.
There is a brain we share.

## Basho, Glimpsed

miles from
anywhere, NV

head down
walking

              nothing
on his back

but the moon

## Aftershocks

Long ago in California, my Dad
went out to sea. I stood,
hand inside my mother's. The ship
receded; the horizon
swallowed it up. The earth beneath
us did not move

                    but waited. Then dishes
rattled in the cupboard; a vase fell
to the floor; my mother's hands
trembled. We huddled

under a table, my full five years
upturned. If the earth moves,
       I knew at once, a first certainty,
anything could happen. I dreamt

paws, claws to sink in shifting
ground, roots, long arms to pull the world
close, within me, to soothe the planet. By
rocking. Rocking

it back to
how it was. Or sinking
down, into deep stillness. As a breath

drawn in the wake of a vacuum, you
never take earth for granted after the first quake.

Years pass, lie jumbled among flowers
on my parents' graves. By the iris
is my 18th birthday; under the rose,
my 48th. And then, on the horizon, a ship

which only I see.
              It is fading.

The earth moves; a father leaves; anything can happen;
everything does.

**Laurelyn Whitt** (Spanish Fork, UT) is author of *Interstices* (Logan House Press, 2006), which won the Holland Prize. Her work appears in numerous journals in the United States and Canada, including *The Malahat Review, Hawai'i Review, PRISM International, Puerto del Sol,* and *The Fiddlehead.*

## Deertime: Spanish Fork Canyon

They stand, more sensed than
seen, diffuse
twilit beings
shapes merging & emerging,
evasive dreams.

Intermediaries of dusk & dawn,
we hold them in our breath;

cars pouring down the murky canyon.

When we spill from its mouth,
exhaling softly,
they are still with us

spread casually
on the bunkers of a
dynamite factory;

go-betweens of worlds,
their dark bodies
move
behind razor-wire fences.

We gaze from our windows,
hearts caught in dry throats,
stacking what we see
and what we know
in a precarious column:

the deer, the dynamite
the fault below.

# *Washington*

**Sherman Alexie** (Seattle, WA), a Spokane/Coeur d'Alene Indian, grew up on the Spokane Indian Reservation in Wellpinit, Washington. His honors include a 2010 Lifetime Achievement Award from the Native Writers' Circle of the Americas, a 2007 Western Literature Association's Distinguished Achievement Award, and many others. His most recent books include *Face*, a collection of poetry from Hanging Loose Press, and *War Dances*, a collection of stories from Grove Press. He lives with his family in Seattle.

## Wreck League

1.

Whenever I leave
The house to play
Hoops, my wife says,
"Please don't get hurt."

It's not exactly
What a man wants
To hear from the woman
Who shares his bed.

Things he would prefer
To hear include, but
Are not limited to:
"I would rather fuck

You than Michael Jordan
Or LeBron James."
"Bring back a dead
Animal, any animal."

"While you are gone,
I will think of you
Spinning through the key
Like the love child

Of Earl Monroe
And Emily Dickinson."
"Darling, you are my
Asphalt playground."

2.

Eighteen years ago,
Eighteen of us,
Fresh from college,
Began this weekly game.

There are four
Of us left.
Year by year,
We've added other

Players, some of them
So good and young
They don't yet know
How it feels

To wake the next
Morning so sore
That you have to roll
Out of bed and crawl

Into a hot shower
In order to stand.
I suppose I could
Only play against

Other men my age,
But I still need
To stare into the eyes
Of a stronger

And better man
And try to kill him,
If only on the court
And only metaphorically.

3.

Twenty-one years ago,
At an All-Indian
Basketball Tournament,
I scored fifty-five points

Against a team
Of college players,
Then went dancing
At the rez tavern,

And slept two hours
Before I scored forty-eight
In the early game
Against a high school team.

Forgive my immodesty,
But in my youth,
I was sometimes
(Say it!) beautiful.

Last night, I missed
More jumpers than I made,
And cramped so badly
As I drove home

That I had to pull
Into a 7-11 parking lot
And fall out of the car
Onto the pavement

Where a homeless old man
Helped me to my feet
And into the store
Where I purchased

Two bags of ice
(And a 40 for the old man)
And sat on them
Until my hamstrings froze

In place and allowed me
Just enough grace
To make it back
To my five-bedroom shack.

4.

"Daddy," my son asks,
"How come you keep
Playing basketball
If it hurts so much?"

"Son," I say,
"I keep playing
*Because*
It hurts so much."

## Daughter, Athlete

Lifting the pages, glancing sideways
at the gathering of families and friends sitting
on the folding metal chairs
crowding the neighborhood library,
she wavers for a moment, pausing
to get her balance,
like a wind surfer
pressing herself to an invisible mast
while the Colorado-blue-and-crocus-striped
sail flaunts its silk,
snapping and swelling in the wind,
leaning, taking a chance
despite the open water and the rock beveled shore,
or perhaps because of them,
I want to call "come back, come
back," but she pushes against
the wind, stands up straight, catching herself
in the silence, holding on, she's got to, we've all got to
go with it or go over,
spinning, see her turn, unexpected
hop and twirl into the current of her words
and we listen as she speaks. We listen.

**Christianne Balk** (Seattle, WA) is author of *Bindweed* (Macmillan, 1986), which received the Walt Whitman Award, and *Desiring Flight* (Purdue University Press, 1995). Her poems have appeared in *Ploughshares*, *The Atlantic Monthly*, *The New Yorker*, and other publications. She lives in Seattle with her husband and daughter, who was born with cerebral palsy. She works as a writer, teacher, and caregiver. Christianne also serves on the board of directors for Bread for the Journey of Seattle, a nonprofit that provides microgrants for innovative community-building projects in social justice, health, education, and the arts.

**Boyd W. Benson** (Clarkston, WA) lives next to the Snake River and the Idaho border, where he cooks in a small restaurant. He has also taught writing at Washington State University for the past decade.

## April Wedding

Did I mention the forty of us squeezed
into the family photo—half of us not
knowing the other half, the small
Mexican girls in pink dresses and
white tights, lined-up and smiling
like little candles, or for a ride in a
swanboat,  crammed so close I could
feel their heartbeats in my belly?
Someone put Brahms on the stereo.
Meanwhile, the lady with the hawk
face and redneck husband whispered
in his ear.  It was some sort of waltz—
a profusion of strings, maybe a piano,
we pressed tighter, the meat steaming
on the barbeque behind us, and it
began to snow.   We tried to keep
those smiles for a good (virtuous)
five minutes, some of us just noses
and eyes over shoulders, awkward
and to some extent holy, and we did.

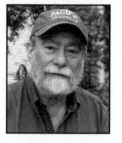

**Marvin Bell** (Port Townsend, WA) has been living portions of each year in the Northwest since 1982, mostly in Port Townsend, Washington, and also in Seattle and Portland. His nineteenth book was the wartime collection, *Mars Being Red* (Copper Canyon Press, 2007). His twentieth was a collaboration of seven poets from five countries. He teaches for the brief-residency MFA program based in Oregon at Pacific University.

# The Book of the Dead Man (The Northwest)

*Live as if you were already dead.*
—Zen admonition

*And the fish swim in the lake / and do not even own clothing.*
—Ezra Pound, "Salutation"

## 1. About the Dead Man and the Northwest

Picture the dead man in two rooms in the northwest corner of his being.
In the one, it is day, and in the other, night, and he lives in both.
His street dead-ends at a cliff above a rattling of ropes clanging on masts
   and the whimper of lazy tides.
There are lumps on the sea bottom.
There is also, as elsewhere, a worldly stomping that threatens the scale
   pan of justice.
The dead man fingers a lucky stone like Casanova his address book.
For the northwest, which may feel ashen to the displaced easterner under
   the white of a winter sky, pleases him greatly.
It is the density of forest that overwhelms his language, as the dexterity of
   the tides smooths his hours and the mountain passes frame
   the light at midday.
The dead man smells the faint fizz of froth at shore's edge.
It is the smell of the soap the adolescent rinses away before a date.
It is the loamy feel in his throat when a young man is asked to speak.
The dead man has opened the map, and run his finger along the
   interstates, and driven west to land's edge.
The dead man's distant friends look toward England, it is old.
The dead man is himself old but is forever newly at home.
He who grew up near the sunrise feels more at home near the sunset.
That's the dead man's duality, drawn east-to-west and south-to-north.

*2. More About the Dead Man and the Northwest*

Though we make a junkyard of the sea, still the fish wink.
The dead man's turf is piled with lug nuts and vinyl, tubing and wire, razor
   blades, batteries, bubble wrap and book bags—name anything.
Still the dead man toasts both the present and the absence to come.
Salmon that went against the current.
Madronas that peeled without a whimper, you seers take notice.
The dead man has a favorite heron because they see one another daily.
And the one sits in the other's tree and squawks when it flies off or returns.
What makes one go here or there, and stay, may be the rhythm of the
   heart, or the firing of brain cells or the feel of the air.
The dead man has heavy bones, he does not float.
He has small pores.
He cannot be smelled as quickly by the wolf, a trait that brought them
   face to face.
He walks by the elk and the deer who do not care.
Like them, he knows time by the look of the light and the smell.
The dead man, standing between the Pacific and Cascades, at the tip of
   the Quimper Peninsula, is almost out of time.
The dead man is not as much about *doing.*
The dead man was, and will be, and, for now, just is.

## Sun Worship

Looking like Muslims at prayer, they gather
in rows over the silk
and twig-ridges
of their tents. When the sun
commands, they do a synchronized dance—
weaving side-to-side with a snap
that quickens.

Wearing saffron yellow and
millennial black, they are
the tent caterpillars, and in their millions
an unsavory prey.

Today, we see one march the length
of a bleached log, searching
for the single sacred place where cocooning
feels right. When it pauses, and curls like something soft
you'd want to touch, my companion explains
if you see a chalky spot that glows
against the dark of the forehead, it means
this supplicant has been chosen
by a wasp who's laid an egg.

Later, inside the cocoon, that humid
rebirthing chamber, it will hatch
and feed greedily on the sacrificial host.
Swollen then with such rich nourishment, such
spiritual fat, the young wasp will poke
a portal through and,

like a moth driven ecstatic
by light, ascend.

**James Bertolino** (Bellingham, WA) is author of ten collections of poems, including *Finding Water; Holding Stone* (Cherry Grove Collections, 2009). His awards include the Discovery Award, a National Endowment for the Arts Fellowship, two *Quarterly Review of Literature* book awards, and, in 2007, the Jeanne Lohmann Poetry Prize for Washington State Poets. He taught creative writing fourteen years at Western Washington University and, in 2006, retired from a position as Writer-in-Residence at Willamette University.

**Allen Braden** (Lakewood, WA) was the last generation to grow alfalfa, wheat, barley, and beef cattle on his family's farm outside White Swan, Washington, on the Yakama Indian Reservation. Farm life informs the poems in his collection, *A Wreath of Down and Drops of Blood* (University of Georgia Press, 2010).

### Grinding Grain

The belt, tight as a razor strop,
whips from tractor to hammer mill
and scares out of our grain bin an owl.
Welded pipe coughs flour into bags

stenciled *H & H* or *Logan's Feed & Seed.*
I take another off my father's hands,
another cinched with his square knot
better than any I used to tie.

Easily I buck those bags onto the stack
that shoulders the granary wall.
The air thickens this early light
sifting around the blurred belt.

When I turn back he's gone,
inside a cloudbank of flour
the way burlap can swallow
so many pounds of ground durum.

All our lives we work this way.
He sacks and ties.
I lift and stack.
Our bodies slowly growing white.

## The Hemlock Tree

Did I mention that last night an owl swept down
from her perch in the hemlock nearby
to devour a wild dove tamed by Safeway birdseed?
Of course I can reconstruct the scene for you
from knowing how this testimony
beyond the limits of your city implies the inevitable
circuit of hunger, from knowing how all life must
enter into a kind of covenant with nature
*for the living shall consume*
                    *the flesh of the living*
and from the delicate evidence at hand:
a wreath of down and drops of blood.
And right now you might be wondering
about the wisteria spiraling up that hemlock,
inching a bit higher with each passing year,
offering loveliness in powder-blue clusters
for a few weeks of May, and all the while killing
the tree with its gradual, constrictive, necessary beauty.

**Elizabeth Bradfield** (Tacoma, WA) is author of *Interpretive Work* (Red Hen Press, 2008), which won the 2009 Audre Lorde Award, and *Approaching Ice* (Persea Books, 2010). The recipient of a Stegner Fellowship from Stanford University, her poems have appeared in *The Atlantic Monthly, Orion, The Believer, Poetry,* and elsewhere. Founder and editor of Broadsided Press, Bradfield works as a naturalist.

## Multi-Use Area

Would the day on the hay flats—
sun slight through clouds, grasses
just starting again from last year's
grasses, geese and cranes bugling
over the marsh—have been better
without the old tires, the gutted couch
in a pullout, a moose slumped alongside,
meat taken but the head still attached?

I can close my eyes to the pop bottles,
booze bottles, and orange skeet shells
in the parking lot, along the river.  Walk
past them. I can pretend my own steps
through the marsh convey a different
presence. But I can't close my ears.
There, a white-fronted goose, there
a pintail, willow branches cracking

underfoot, F-14s from the base. And there, again,
the shotgun blast and whoop which I can't
edit out, which I probably shouldn't.
It stops when I walk into view. I stop
and stare across the flats through my
binoculars, thinking *asshole.* And of course
someone's staring back at me
over a truck bed, thinking *asshole.*

## Cul-de-sac Linguistics

Today, the boys call each other penis.
*Hey penis, commere, penis, pass me the ball,*
*penis.* Last week it was *whore*, discovered

halfway through a game of h o r s e
on the mini-hoop that backs my fence.
And earlier this afternoon, the teenage girls

whose bedroom window stares
above my thumbnail yard improvised
outgoing messages in theatrical rapture:

first the easy scatological, then
a nursery rhyme that morphs
into an anti-homo riff so suddenly

I actually look up

to see if they're directing this at me
(they must be), down in the yard, reading poetry
as my girlfriend weeds the flower bed.

O, the high profanity of kickball games,
the rough posturing demanded
by even this tame street. Listen, they're learning

how well bastard fits with fucking, how ass
can't be mis-used. No one could hope to ease
their jagged entries into this profane world

which is fucking beautiful, ass-bastard gorgeous,
the evening light wild and soaring
like kickballs on a true arc into flowerbeds

of penis tulips and pussy daffodils
that nod their heads in wild agreement
with the whorish, shit-loving lot of it.

**Alice Derry** (Port Angeles, WA) is author of seven collections of poems, including *Strangers to Their Courage* (Louisiana State University Press, 2001), which was a finalist for the Washington Book Award; *Tremolo* (Red Hen Press, 2011); *Stages of Twilight* (Breitenbush, 1986), chosen by Raymond Carver; and *Clearwater* (Blue Begonia Press, 1997). Derry taught at Peninsula College for twenty-nine years, where she co-directed the Foothills Writers' Series.

## Deposition

*It's not a story-telling process,*
*my attorney reminds me.*

Today I'm in a dress and stockings,
careful make-up, even lipstick.
I am asked if it's too stuffy.
Would I like something to drink?
No one is allowed to smoke.

If this were Poland
midway last century,
I would be starving,
freezing,
sleepless,
naked.

If this were Bosnia last year,
I would be brought in, raped
under blinding light,
and the questioning
would go on even
during the rape.

Nevertheless, he begins.
*Did you say?*
*Would you assert to be true?*
*Did you believe?*
*Would you think?*
*Can you tell when?*
*tell who?*
*tell how?*

In the tiny electric shocks
of his relentless questions
which I may not, under law,
refuse to answer, I've lost
where he might be going,
I don't know how many times
I've contradicted myself,
or where my story disappeared
in the myriad tiny fragments
of *yes*
*no*
*I can't remember*
*That's not what I meant.*

And the glowing cigarette
drawn by sucked-in breath
to its hottest point
seems to glide from his mouth
to my bare arm.

Paper after paper
the court has subpoenaed from me,
opened like my dress, my calendar
revealing the secret comfort
of my body to everyone.

There is lunch.
The blur of questioning
after lunch.
His legal partner
begins *her* questions.
There is my doubt.
There is the knowledge I have lost
my side of what happened forever.
And the lies I've stumbled into—
which the written record's
cunning sequence
will later reveal.

Persistent April sun
clambers to get past
the windows.
There is the break
my attorney arranges for me,
the date for my next deposition.
Then, the final click of their heels
as we exit the room.

**Dana Dickerson** (Olympia, WA) grew up on the mean streets of Phinney Ridge and spent his summers on the Colville Reservation. He attended the Institute of American Indian Arts in Santa Fe, New Mexico, for creative writing, and the Evergreen State College in Olympia, Washington. His poetry appears in *Volt*, a literary journal in San Francisco.

### The Last Bastion for the Wrong Kind of Liberal

Squinty Seymour lives in a camper, with his *sooyapi* girlfriend Red, while they build an Earthship on his land. She hates spiders, he hates to kill them, but she finds them everywhere. He starts to collect the biggest ones in a five gallon bucket.

"What are you going to do with all those spiders, Squinty?" Red asks, disgustedly. Squinty just shrugs, but in his head he keeps a list of ex's, enemies, politicians and media hate mongers, who will be receiving a package.

It's thirty miles of bad road to the Post Office, Squinty never misses a day. "He sent a lot of odd shaped packages," a clerk at the Inchelium Post Office says, into the camera of the FOX affiliate from Spokane. "He looked like a skin, but he wouldn't take his hood and sunglasses off. I heard he was Pinky Seymour's boy . . . no, not Timmy, the other one . . . looked like the Unabomber."

## Whole-Body Counter, Marcus Whitman Elementary

*"The mobility of this new laboratory provides versatile
capabilities for measuring internally deposited gamma-
ray emitting radionuclides in human beings."*
—Health Physics, November 1965

We were warned to shut our eyes.
Everyone was school-age now, our
kindergarten teacher reminded us,

old enough to follow directions
and do a little for our country.
My turn came and the scientists

strapped me in and a steady voice
prompted *The counter won't hurt,
lie perfectly still,* and mostly I did

and imagined what children
pretend America is, parks
bordered by feathery evergreens,

lawns so green and lush
they soothe the eyes and pupils
open like love—

a whole country of lawns
like that. Just once I peeked
and the machine had taken me in

like a spaceship and I moved
slow as the sun through the chamber's
smooth steel sky.

I shut my eyes again and pledged
to be still; so proud to be
a girl America could count on.

**Kathleen Flenniken** (Seattle, WA) grew up in Richland, Washington, near the Hanford Nuclear Site. Her first book, *Famous* (University of Nebraska Press, 2006), won the Prairie Schooner Book Prize in Poetry and was named a Notable Book by the American Library Association and was a finalist for the Washington State Book Award. Her poems have appeared in *Poetry Daily, Poetry,* and *The Iowa Review,* and she is a recipient of fellowships from the National Endowment for the Arts and Artist Trust.

### Herb Parker Feels Like Dancing

*Herbert M. Parker (1910—1984), a founding father of
Health Physics, established and oversaw the measuring
and monitoring of radiation in Hanford workers and in the
surrounding environment.*

Mr. Parker's Sunbeam is shiny as an atom.
He pulls up, disembarks with grace
and makes his dance hall entrance.
Perhaps you sense his English accent
and pocket square. Women shy
like ponies to one corner. He corrals one
and trots her around the dance floor.

Herb Parker rides a shapely 4/4.
"That Old Black Magic,"
"Baby, It's Cold Outside."
Maybe it is, or maybe it's blazing,
unsafe to breathe tonight.

Her earrings are zircon daisies.
A silver belt rings her slim waist.
Herb Parker steers her toward
his dark place. "Mr. Parker?"
he hears somebody ask, like a tremble
on a seismograph, but you can't blame
Herbert Parker for his appetites.

He palms the tender center of
her back.  "Mr. Parker?" again.
Perhaps it's her voice, or her husband's,
or one of the voices in his head. He's
a Dutch boy with his finger in the dike,
a valvular, crepuscular figure.

*"Look out the window at that storm . . . "*
He takes the government's calls
and negotiates those devils' bargains,
how much of their order can he fill?
You understand they say "product"
and mean plutonium, they mean
*how many bombs can you afford to fuel?*
*"Darling, down and down I go,*

410

*round and round I go in a spin"* . . .
the river, and its sediments,
the air, capricious with winds,
the soil column, the ground water,
the vase of wildflowers on Deputy Chief
Gamertsfelder's desk! Sagebrush

and Russian thistle growing in Richland
yards. The mosquitoes, for pity's sake,
the farm animals, the farmers living
off the land, the water birds and the
duck hunters, the bottom fish and
the fishermen on Richland dock.
Everything he thinks to test . . . good god,

the entire food chain contaminated.
He's basically a shy man with
immeasurable power. A sultan
coaxing his courtesan's smile.
She only shakes a little now.
Don't you understand? *Someone*
must step forward and play God.
How much better that the man
can lead? hold you tight
in his very good hands, and spin.

## Going Down

This is the guy in the white fastback Mustang
commuting to work on a Wednesday morning.

This is the woman with wooly brown hair
in the passenger seat of the white fastback car
who goes down on the man who is driving like hell,
passing a van, passing four cars, passing a bus on his way to the job
on a Tuesday or Wednesday morning.

These are the thousands who rise before dawn,
clip on their badges and climb on the bus,
or jump in their cars if they've got enough gas,
heading up north to their nut-numbing jobs,
when a Mustang swings past and a woman goes down
on a man growing famous for driving full blown
into Monday, or Tuesday, morning.

This is a pattern of acting out
on the only road through the Hanford Works,
a.k.a. the ends of the earth,
entertaining the masses en route to the site
where they'll suit up in white, alert for alarms,
locked in a gate, protected by guards,
in a plant that makes high grade plutonium stock
for government bombs to protect us from harm
on a typical Tuesday morning.

This is the landscape bleak and brown
that can hold its secrets for only so long
till they spill and spill, but for now and instead
the woman goes down on the man driving fast,
we cop our looks while they rocket past
and the rest of us feel . . . not closer to death, but further
from life as we slow at the gate for security check
on another Wednesday morning.

## Advice to Female Deckhands

You will be the cook.
In addition to wheel watches, working
on deck, unloading fish, fueling up,
filling fresh water, mending nets,
grocery shopping whenever you come to town,
you also will prepare three meals a day
and two hearty snacks to go with coffee.
You must keep the kettle on the stove full
and the juice jug and two gallons of milk in the fridge.

You will learn to slice vegetables, prepare a marinade,
cook pasta and fillet a salmon
in twenty minute intervals
while the net is out. You will learn
to ignore the other crew members sitting
at the galley table reading. You must know
how to create a corral in rough weather,
so pots of soup don't end up dripping
down the firewall behind the stove. You will need
bungee cords to keep the cast iron skillet from sliding.
These cords melt if they touch the stovetop.
Keep a squeeze container of Aloe Vera gel
under the galley sink for the burns
on your hands and forearms.

The stove will blow out on windy days
when you're exhausted,
your skin stinging with jelly fish.
The crew will say they're not hungry on these days
but when you slide behind the Cape, it will be flat
calm and all of you will be starving. Before relighting the stove
determine how much diesel has built up.
If it's more than an inch deep,
turn off the fuel source
by flipping a breaker in the engine room.
You don't have time for ear protection. Get down there
and back before someone hollers for you on deck.
Passing the engine, watch the straps on your raingear,
your ponytail, where you put your hands.

**Erin Fristad** (Port Townsend, WA) is of the Northwest: she is the spawn of loggers, miners, and commercial fishermen. She worked as a deckhand on commercial fishing and research vessels for fifteen years and now resides in Port Townsend, where she writes, teaches, and works as Campus Director for Goddard College. Erin's work appears in numerous journals and anthologies.

When cooking, remember all odors from the galley
drift directly into the wheelhouse. Fish sauce
smells like dirty tennis shoes. Once she smells this,
your skipper's daughter will refuse to eat anything
she suspects has fish sauce. As a woman and cook
you will be expected to have a special bond with the skipper's daughter
and you will. Have art supplies in a shoe box in the galley,
a drawing tablet under a cushion, collect starfish,
Decorator crab, and Spiny Lump Suckers in a deck bucket.
Teach her what you know can kill her. When she cries
put your arm around her, kiss her
on the top of the head and let her cry.
Allow her to use your cell phone to call friends
in exchange for making salads, pots of coffee,
washing lunch dishes, carrying groceries to the boat.
Develop sign language for communicating
when she stands in the galley door
peering out at you on deck.

This isn't what I intended.
I set out to give you advice for taking care
of yourself, now it's about taking care of a girl
you're related to by circumstance.
This is exactly what will happen.
You'll notice a hum
more penetrating than the engine.


### What's Left

The voice on the phone says flatly,
"We've been forced to lay off some boats."
A long pause implies he's one of them.
His response equally flat. He fantasizes
calling them bastards, ranting about pathetic
marketing, price fixing, how unfair it feels
being forced out by huge steel boats that fish three
or four fisheries, with three or four hired
skippers. But the voice on the phone
is familiar, a man he met when
he was eighteen walking the docks
looking for his first fishing job.
This same man called to congratulate

him when he bought his own boat.
This is the man who arranged his cannery loan. Truth is
they're both sorry, and that's what they say,
and silence and they hang up.
What's left of a fisherman laughs
at the words "laying off boats."
"You're laying off people, you bastards"
finally escapes between a shout
and a whisper. A noise brings him back,
his four-year-old daughter pushes the door
open, she's giggles, bounces, points.
She wants him to see their golden
retriever wearing a sweatshirt, struggling,
wagging his tail, trying to please her. Now he's a father,
petting his dog, tickling his daughter, directing
them back out into the yard. What if I tell you
it's not that bad for this man. What if his boat is paid for,
his wife is a teacher, they have health insurance,
they own their cars. A young couple from Seattle
has phoned twice, desperate to buy
a classic wood boat, turn the fish hold
into state rooms. What if I tell you
he has a teaching certificate
he'll find work, maybe get his captain's license
run a small tour boat in the summer. But I can't let go
of the phone call, the one where he found out
the sale was final. I can't forget that same afternoon
when he drove to the harbor, sat in his truck staring
at his new boat in the slip. He walked down the dock
alone, climbed on board. I can smell it, wet wood
diesel. There he is lighting the stove
warming his hands over the flame.

**Carmen Germain** (Port Angeles, WA) teaches at Peninsula College, where she is a co-director of the Foothills Writers Series. While on sabbatical in 2008, she lived in Italy, researching the work of Elsa Morante; during part of that time, she was also a Visiting Artist/Scholar at the American Academy in Rome.

### April, Seattle to Missoula

When the doe stepped out—
eyes tight on the head beams—
you said your one word
*god* before I jolted awake,
and then she was gone.
I remembered that Wisconsin night
when I was a child trying to sleep
in the back seat of the blue Rambler,
Father and Mother talking up front.
How white pine and deer glinted
in and out of light, but more
than this—the way
a moment can change you.

How we came first on the wreck
and I saw the man, then the woman.
As though they had pulled off the road
for talk, his arm slung out the window.
His head thrown back as though
the woman had said something hilarious
as she stared out the shattered windshield.
And the velvet buck broken in the ditch?
He listened carefully, too, his great
brown eyes, like hers, slowly emptying.

## Grandmother, Cleaning Rabbits

I shot this one by the upper pond of the farm
after watching the rings trout made rising
to flies, watching small birds pace the backs
of cows, hoping all the time she would run.

My grandmother told me they damaged her garden.

I think it was a way to make the killing
lighter. She never let me clean them, only asked
I bring them headless to her. I bring this one
to the fir block near the house, use the single-
bitted axe with the nick in the lower crescent
of the blade, smell the slow fire
in the smoke-house, salmon changing
to something sweet & dark. A fly turns
in a bead of blood on my boot. I tuck
the head in a hole beside the dusty globes
of ripened currants, talk quiet to the barn cat.

In her kitchen my grandmother whets the thin blade
of her Barlow, makes a series of quick, clever cuts, then tugs
off the skin like a child's sweater. This one was
pregnant. She pulls out a row of unborn rabbits
like the sleeve of a shirt with a series of knots.
The offal is dropped in a bucket. Each joint gives way
beneath her knife as though it wants
to come undone, as though she knows some secret
about how things fit together. I have killed
a hundred rabbits since I was eight.

This will be the last.

I am twenty, & about to go back
to the war that killed my cousin in Kien Hoa,
which is one more name she can't pronounce.
I haven't told her about the dead,
& she won't ask. She rolls the meat
in flour & pepper & salt, & lays it
in a skillet of oil that spits like a cat.
She cannot save a single boy who carries a gun.
All she can do is feed this one.

**Samuel Green** (Waldron Island, WA) was raised in the fishing and mill town of Anacortes. A thirty-year veteran of the Poetry-in-the-Schools program, he has taught in hundreds of classrooms. Among his ten collections of poems are *Vertebrae: Poems 1972—1994* (Eastern Washington University Press, 1994) and *The Grace of Necessity* (Carnegie-Mellon University Press, 2008), which won the 2008 Washington State Book Award for Poetry. He has lived for twenty-six years off the grid on remote Waldron Island in a log house he built himself after living in a tent for three years. He and his wife, Sally, co-edit Brooding Heron Press. He served as Washington State's first Poet Laureate.

**Stroke**

Where is the axe, says the ice in the trough, left in the field for the cows.

      Here, says the file on the bench in the shed, stuck in a hole by the vise.

Where is the cup with a chip in its rim, says the sink with its saucer & spoon.

      Here, says the kitchen linoleum square, in fragments the color of bone.

Where is the milk, says the pail on the porch, scalded, & shining & worn.

      Here, say the bells of the shuffling heifers, stalled at the door of the barn.

Where is the cream for the cinnamon cat, says the tuna can under the stairs.

      Here, says a shelf in the cold box, with the butter & leftover pears.

Where is the heat for the dinner, says the skillet and pans on the range.

      Here, say the split chunks of alder and fir, carefully dried & arranged.

Where is the ball made of leftover twine, says the unfinished rug on the stool.

      Here, says the awkward crochet hook made from an old-fashioned nail.

Where is the woman who lives in this house, says the work coat still hung on a chair.

      Here, says the wind through the grass of the field,

      here say the waves on the bay past the bluff,

      here says the breath in the air.

*Not here*, say the cows, *not here*, says the cat, *not here*, say the boots by the door.

*Not here*, says the stove, *not here*, says the coat, *not here*, says the shape on the floor.

## Lady Slipper

This one is ten feet off the trail,
an inch from where I set down my saw,
the color of a girl's most earnest
blush, open, as she might open her lips
in mute surprise. Some call it
"Calypso," after the nymph who kept a man
seven years from his wife with the magic
of her body in bed, Greek for *hidden*.

Pick it, & the plant will not bloom
again. Dig it up, & it will die
away from where it was rooted.

Forgive me, if all I bring you
is its name, & the brief story
of how it stands in a patch of moss
swept clean in a small wash
of light no larger than a sole
into which we push with care
the small, perfectly fitting foot of love.

**Sam Hamill** (Port Townsend, WA) is Founding Editor of Copper Canyon Press, where he served for thirty-two years. He is a celebrated translator of two-dozen volumes from Classical Chinese and Japanese poetry, the author of fifteen volumes of award-winning poetry, and four volumes of literary essays. In 2003, he founded Poets Against War. He divides his time between the Pacific Northwest and Buenos Aires, Argentina.

### Children of the Marketplace

They come out of nowhere, the sad-eyed
pleading children of the streets, they come
bearing shoplifted socks, small notebooks,
pens, anything, even just a card that pleads
for change, a peso so they can eat.

From our lunch spot under the grand
acacia trees, we say, "No, gracias," wondering
if a coin encourages thievery or whether
any of them will ever learn to read.
Or we make a gift of some small change
when one rushes to open the door
of a cab we've flagged. "No, gracias,"
to the old woman selling wilting roses
on the street, wondering what life
has she whose children learned to pick
a pocket, to moan for some relief
in a world without regrets, a world of need.

We watch a pregnant girl drag her heavy cart
through busy traffic on the street,
sorting through the trash—salvaging
old cardboard, plastic bottles, a board,
a brick, old newsprint, almost anything
that ordinary trash provides. Her work
is hard, her face a mask of grief
the marketplace can't hide.

In Seattle's Pioneer Square, it's a wrinkled face
asking for a dollar for the newspaper
of the homeless, news of that other marketplace
where human life, degraded or self-abused,
comes cheap, and dignity and hope
are long forgotten dreams.

It's the same in Caracas, Mumbai,
New York City or Saigon. The world is one.
Who knows what's wrong or right,
whose coin will go for suicidal wine
and whose for mercy in a shelter for the night?
The young, the old, for them there is
no sense of time, no past remembered,
no thought of what tomorrow brings.
The marketplace is full of things.

## Because You Showed Me a Piece of Barbed Wire

that had lain in the dirt road
beside a lone sign
marking all that remained of barracks,
rowed and eclipsed by the shadow
of Heart Mountain, I thought
of my mother beginning her tour of Japan. What
would she say if she saw me with a piece of her past
cupped in my hand? Would she tell me if the guard tower
rose to her left, perhaps to her right
as she stepped down from the bus,
sleepy and holding her mother's hand?
Or would some things simply remain
unspoken? On the plane, she would be napping,
the pages of a Sunset Magazine
fanned by her breath. The small shutters closed,
the movie would flash by, unremembered.
But outside, clouds would buoy up the wings,
buffet the metal. A suitcase in each hand, she'll wait
patiently while my father scowls, passing
through customs under neon signs
she won't understand. Into Tokyo, they'll continue.
I turn the knotted path of wire smelling of ghost dust,
touching the barbs that held everything in.

**Sharon Hashimoto** (Tukwila, WA) is a writing instructor at Highline Community College in Des Moines, Washington. Her poems have appeared in *The American Scholar, Bamboo Ridge, Crab Orchard Review, The North American Review, Poetry, Poetry Northwest, The Seattle Review, Shenandoah,* and others. In 1989, she received a fellowship from the National Endowment for the Arts. Her book, *The Crane Wife* (Story Line Press, 2003), was co-winner of the Nicholas Roerich Prize. She has also published short stories.

## Wonder Bread

A thin rain is blowing all around us.
The mud flaps of your bicycle wheels catch
the broken puddles and send out a spray.
It splatters my penny loafers
and there's a dark border around my skirt
where the hooded jacket doesn't reach. Gruffly,
you huff at me: Keep those feet away
from the spokes. I sit side-saddle, balanced
on the crossbar, hanging onto a sack of Wonder Bread.

Tank-like Buicks, Fords, and Chevrolets
crowd the main road; their silhouettes overlap
and deepen the dusk. Dutiful brother, you've come to collect me
from my Brownie meeting. In the window of an IGA store,
I glimpse our reflection. You, me, and a dangling
brown bag on a Schwinn streak by.

The pencil of your headlight grows stronger
as we turn down Holly, past the overgrown hedge
of a darkened house. You lean forward into the night.
Standing up, legs pumping the pedals,
your fingers curve around the hand brakes.

We are close but not touching. Wind plays
through the gaps. As I listen to your ragged breathing,
I shrink myself out of your way. The red letter "W"
widens the tear in the sack. Ahead lies the curb
where the bread will slip from my grasp.

## Fasting on Yom Kippur

Today the pear trees wrapped in shawls of air,
the wind that bends them booming with frogs—

but I am not wearing a new blue suit. My hair
is not perfumed spikes of black that poke out

under a white skull-cap. This day each year
the Law added our sins to our father's.

All the Jewish boys were absolved
like trees that drop their foliage

all at once. We'd play at prayer and fasting,
at emptying and the chest-thumping of grown men

till sundown. A few remaining leaves scratch
and their dry cough recalls the drone

of men in prayershawls, the tinkle of glasses
later, a table heaped with herring and sardines.

My heart catches. Netted, it bangs
louder. We stiffen, our yearly rings

unbreathable armor without forgetfulness.
Without memory we repeat our fathers, slip

and vanish around the trunks of pear trees.
I fast today. I walk out past

the unpruned orchard,
nostalgia's branches clacking.

**Mark Halperin** (Ellensburg, WA) has published five volumes of poetry, including *Falling Through the Music* (Notre Dame, 2007). He is co-author of *Accent on Meter* (National Council of Teachers of English, 2004) and co-translator of *A Million Premonitions* (Zephyr Press, 2004), poems from the Russian of Viktor Sosnora. He lives with his wife, the painter Bobbie Halperin, and his dog, Dasha, near Washington's Yakima River.

### Accident

*Are you okay*? When I answered *yes*, adding
I'd already called it in and was waiting for
the tow-truck, she blessed me from the cab,
then Jesus for preserving me, then got down.
*You've no idea when the tow truck will show up;*
*you might stand in the cold for hours*, she said,
moving beside the truck, which, like her,
had been around, rummaging in her sacks
of groceries and pulled a bagel out. *No*
*thanks*, I said. She insisted. It was easier
to accept than fight with her, and besides,
there was something so natural, so direct,
for all the bless Jesus-es, the bagel, so
soft, topped with burnt onions, garlic chips,
so bereft of any *yiddishkeit* . . . I took it,
like her benediction, with a nod, a Jew,
ankle-deep in snow on a rural road in
eastern Washington, car down the steep
embankment, cradled by cattails. How
had I come to be there, hand around a roll
as much a bagel as I was a Jew, I wondered?
Only a deity who delighted in far-fetched
scenarios could have concocted a delivery
like that. Before I took a bite, rather than
a *motsi*, I peered at my precariously balanced
car, then into the shimmering distance
from whence the wrecker would come.
Hat on, I blessed her and my good fortune.

## Desperados

The floorboards were dark brown and creaked
and Mrs. Ellis who used to be Miss Jensen
brought forth a tiny, crazed marimba music
every time she moved her graceful legs between
the blackboard and the secret
border marking her turf from the province
of those eager front row faces so firmly hated
by the rest of us, especially back row laggards
like myself, who threw spit wads and giggled
snortingly and carved the word "tits" into our desks.

*Creeeek, snap, screeent,* "What is the capital
of North Dakota?"

"Tits!" we didn't say out loud.

*Hareeenk geeohhNEEP,* "How does one spell
'circumscribe?'"

'Tee' 'Eye' 'Tee' 'Es' we wrote in our all but
empty notebooks, leering and goosy with
the lusciousness of crime.

One day Mrs. Ellis, who was nearly too
beautiful to live, lifted her gaze
into our nether world of guaranteed failure
and probable arrest
and gave us all the tired pity she possessed.

The look went on and on.
The floorboards made no sound.
"Tits?" one of us wrote, experimentally
just as our faces flared with the shameful
knowledge that we would love Mrs. Ellis
all our ruined lives.

**Christopher Howell** (Spokane, WA) is a widely published author of poems, essays, and interviews and recipient of a number of awards, including two National Endowment for the Arts Fellowships, the Washington State Book Award, the Washington Governor's Prize, and three Pushcart Awards. He teaches at Eastern Washington University's Inland Northwest Center for Writers and is director and editor for Lynx House Press.

### Greenhouse Sparks and Snow

It is night and my grandfather potters around, grafting
various geraniums to other geraniums, goading to life
brilliant hybrids to amaze the window boxes
of his cadre of aging customers, and for the fun of it.

He has fired up that potbellied stove
my parents would later turn into a planter
and through the stovepipe chimney sparks dizzy up
toward the stars like a kind of interstellar spawn
going home.

The old man looks up, though he cannot have heard
my footfall on the path that passes through the orchard
from his house to ours, or the light tapping I can't resist
bringing to the glass.

Pipe in his mouth, he makes another cut, mating stranger
to stranger with the unhurried precision that comes
with a lifetime of presiding over floricultural weddings
of this kind.

The stars turn. He does not look up again, though
I think hard to bring his peaceful face
into my room, four hundred miles
and forty years away.

What have I made of myself? He would want to see
the garden
and to try out the chair I sometimes, on nights like this,
edge up to the fire. The news in general
would not interest him and he would puzzle

at my sadness as I try to say how much he is
my own life
of sparks and snow and stars but also work and, here and there,
love's mortal blossom.

## Burning Bush

I think of my father on his knees, hammering
at the floor of what would become
the new bedroom
as we, on our knees, prayed to the campfire
we were trying to kindle
in the field that bordered the dirt road.

With our lips like little valentines we leaned close
and huffed softly, just as Roy Rogers had shown us
a hundred times, and sat back, pouring
our imaginary coffee, when
*boom:* there it was! the burning bush!
Scotch broom exploding like the breath
of God Almighty and so hot! our cowboy hats
flew off. The whole field: just *whoosh!*
No time to save the horses, Tex, better run for it!
as my father ran
then, dragging three hundred feet of strung-together hose,
yelling, "Get out of there! Get out!"
just minutes ahead of the fire truck and screaming
neighbors.

I remember Cecil Morris tripping in the tail
ends of his armload of garden hoses
and sprawling full out as though worshipping the Fire Department
just then connecting to the new hydrant
on the corner, first one planted out so far from town.
They blasted the blaze to smoldering char
then assaulted the whole field with shovels and axes,
taking no prisoners.

My father,
covered in soot, half soaked and breathing hard,
stood before me and said, "Give me the matches."
I handed them over.
The crowd looked on with approving sternness.

This is it, I thought, they'll hang us for sure
this time.
I looked at the sky and the huge firemen.
What would Heaven be like?
My father put his hand on my shoulder
as though he already knew.

**Kim-An Lieberman** (Seattle, WA) holds a Ph.D. in Vietnamese American literature from the University of California, Berkeley. Her poems and essays have appeared in *Poetry Northwest, Prairie Schooner, Quarterly West, CALYX, ZYZZYVA, Threepenny Review,* and the anthology *AsianAmerica.net: Ethnicity, Nationalism, and Cyberspace.* She teaches English and creative writing in Seattle.

## Swallows Nesting

That spring, as I hauled boxes into the new house,
a pair of swallows started building their nest
at the entryway tucked just beneath the eaves.
A fascination at first, watching their erratic swoop
toward the trees and then the quick veering
back with beaks full of scraggy twig. They played, too,
around and around the clear pond next door,
shimming their stomachs along the surface.

Coming home at night, I would glance up
and see them perched smugly in the overhang,
flanking the near-finished nest and plainly ignoring
my regular traffic. Good neighbors enough.
But then droppings began to splatter the windows,
the welcome mat. My first houseguest assaulted
by a volley of indignant screeching. Half a cookie
pecked to crumbs, as the grocery bags rested
just a few short minutes on the doorstep.

Finally, splotches of white on my favorite shoes.
I knocked down the nest with a garden rake,
muttering under my breath. The birds darted out
squalling alarms, flapping an elliptical patrol
but gradually realizing they had no fort to defend.
For a time, they hovered, with intermittent prattling.
Then wingbeats, then silence, and I was alone.

In the morning, grown remorseful for my victory,
I hammered wooden boxes into nearby trees
as peace offering. But the swallows did not return
that spring, or the next. My living continued,
a parade of empty houses and uncharted cities,
each time the landscape rebuilding itself around me.
In the calmer years I wonder after them,
my fork-tails, my rudders in the turning wind.

## Translation

I take my grandmother to the doctor each weekend.
My Vietnamese is fair enough, the basics at least;
I have to get creative with "hematocrit" and "uterus."
The doctor, pale blue scrubs and a half-smile,
always addresses my grandmother by her first name
though he is 30 years her junior. He briskly nods his head
as I explain, the best I can, each phrase he assigns.
Sometimes he stops me short: *Just translate my words.*
*Don't add personal interpretations. Just say what I say.*

Appointment over, I take the keys and drive us
home through the usual stretch of street signs.
*What's that one,* my grandmother asks mile after mile
and, like some proud traffic-law expert, I say:
"Stop," "Yield," "Caution speed bump," "Exit ahead."
But the truth is I have no idea whether my words
connect, if my translations are knowledge or nonsense.
This language engulfs us in separate oceans,
longer and louder than anything I know how to name.

**Marjorie Manwaring** (Seattle, WA) is a freelance writer and an editor for the online poetry and art journal *DMQ Review*. Her work has been published in *Crab Creek Review*, *Floating Bridge Review*, *Sentence*, *5 AM*, and other journals. Pudding House published her chapbook *Magic Word* in 2007. Marjorie has taught poetry writing to children and adults and has been awarded writing residencies through the Whiteley Center at Friday Harbor and Artsmith on Orcas Island.

## Treasure

Somewhere there's a key, lost
in the rubble of a cobwebbed garage

or wedged in the corner of a moss-covered shed.
Who will find it, hold it in her hand,

rub away the rust and muck?
What you hope for—not treasure in a padlocked box

but another unlocking:
rush of strawberry air, hint of hay

that years ago kept you awake;
climbing down the fire ladder, over the gate

meeting your best friend in moonlit pasture
to ride your father's horses bareback—remember

how you'd turn toward home when you heard the horn
of the morning's first ferry crossing the bay?

## Moving On

Make a path through furnishings.
Haul out trash and rubble.
Tattered issues of *Cooking Light*.
Scuffed pairs of worn-out boots.
Rusty hubcap, leaky raft.
Single earring, solo socks.

Sift through clutter, odds and ends,
things held on to beyond their time.
Three-legged chair you couldn't fix,
blow-dryer that never worked right.
Yellowed spatulas, wooden spoons.
Empty old rooms. Let them be spacious again.

From the garden, decide
what can and won't be divided.
You can transplant squash blossoms
and roses to your next place
where they may open their white hearts
and a new world might bloom.

## September Ripens and So Do We

Me, in the kitchen,
buttering slices of whole-grain toast,
cracking fresh farm eggs
into a sizzling pan, admiring
their deep-orange suns.

You, in the orchard,
bruised peach cradled in your hand
cupping its heaviness.
Standing there, caring,
holding all that sweetness.

**Terry Martin** (Yakima, WA) is an English professor at Central Washington University. Over two hundred of her poems, essays, and articles have appeared in numerous publications, and she has edited both journals and anthologies. Her first book of poems, *Wishboats* (Blue Begonia Press, 2000), won the Judges' Choice Award at Seattle's Bumbershoot Book Fair in 2000. Her second book is *The Secret Language of Women* (Blue Begonia Press, 2006).

**Robert McNamara** (Seattle, WA) has published two collections of poetry, *Second Messengers* (Wesleyan University Press, 1990) and *The Body & the Day* (David Robert Books, 2007). He teaches in the Interdisciplinary Writing Program at the University of Washington.

## Winter, Tulalip Shores

Fog. A crescent bay between headlands.
A dozen houses climb the valley's sides.
The concrete seawall's stacked with dories,

working, wet. Three men in a wherry
feed net from the stern, their blue
and yellow coats tolling, tolling.

On the beach, four men are stiff angled posts
driven deep at the water line, hauling
net hand over hand, picking out crap—

then the glint of scales, a pocket of seaspoil,
roiling. They fling the salmon high and backward
with a shovel motion, a quick pass

onto the rocks. The fish skitter furiously
waterward. Now and again one slips and lands
at a fisherman's feet, thrashing. Two boys

tend fire in a tangle of driftwood dividing
forest and tide. Weekend tourists
in cold weather, a little fistful, watch

the work of the tribe. A fishing boat slips
net into the water, moving as though blown,
circling, circling. The large spool

at the stern turns with the pace of the tide
turning. One man thumps the water
with a hollow cone on a stick.

Bruised kings lie on the rocks, their lower jaws
jutting.

## A Tribute to Chief Joseph (1840?—1904)

*"God made me an Indian, but not a reservation Indian."*
—Sitting Bull

Hin-Mah-Too-Yah-Lat-Ket: Thunder-rolling in-the-mountains,
never reached with his people,
the Wal-lam-wat-kins, Canada's promised land.
Instead, the fugitive chief sits in a corner of the prison car
clicking its way to Oklahoma.
Chained to his warriors, he is like a featherless eagle
forced to look at a sky colorless as a square.

Out the window geese rise from the storm's center
and he remembers more men, women
and children died by snow blizzard and starvation
than by cavalry shot or canon blast.

Chief Tu-eka-kas, his father, is a dream shield
of Wallowa Valley that wraps around him
like its winding waters.
So deer and elk from the forest and mountains
of his ancestors flashed in his eyes
and Spi-li-yai, Coyote wanders alongside,
running in his famous drooling circle,
but only a cricket swallows the dark.

The war chief sang to himself morning and evening
to break the cycle of cold weather and disease
his people had coughed and breathed on the run
for more than a thousand miles
through land that drifted with ice
and shredded one's clothes like a knife.

Unable to move and sleepless as the door-guard,
the train rattles and smokes
dirt in his teeth, straw in his eyes.
Holding rage secretly in the palm of his fist,
his people's dream of home and a future
spirals to red dust, leaves his bones
on the track, his soul in the whistle.

**Duane Niatum** (Seattle, WA) has published six poetry books, including *The Crooked Beak of Love* (West End Press, 2000). He was three times nominated for a Pushcart Prize and is finishing his *Collected Poems*. He is an enrolled member of the Klallam Tribe (Jamestown Band). Duane's writing is grounded in the Pacific Northwest landscape and its creatures, birds, animals and plants, along with Klallam stories and characters. He earned a Ph.D. in American Studies from the University of Michigan.

## Tide Blossoms

She and I alone step down the shore.
I hold her close because she's a daughter of the sea.
We watch boats cross the jetty's corridor.

The autumn storm strikes our bodies with its lore
as the voices of the wind we hear and seek.
She and I alone step down the shore.

The clouds that spark return the blue to force;
the rain drowns out the breakers ebbing reefs.
We watch boats cross the jetty's corridor.

Sun-buoyed, kelp and cod drift along the shoal;
the terns dip green, turn shadow and are free.
She and I alone step down the shore.

Like a forest flower this beach leaves us transformed;
salt and sun and moon compose our dream.
We watch boats cross the jetty's corridor.

When amber waves carve oysters to the core
a sandpiper darts over its slanting ground of peace.
She and I alone step down the shore.
We watch boats cross the jetty's corridor.

## Fish

It is suspended mid-tank,
fins wilted at edges like leaf curl
on a failing plant. Blood red dots the tail.
None of us knows whether it is sick
or old, the relative span of goldfish.
The children hold vigil, mid-night
wakes detoured from the bathroom
toward aquamarine light,
the magnified fish-eye
unmoved. Its gold
turns the color of flesh, then fades.
They discuss helping it die,
and how to, but no one wants to lift it
from faint liquid life
into the closing air.
They wait until the fourth day
when it stays, a pale float
curved at the surface.
Scooping it out with a silver bowl,
the three of them carry it
to the garden, each holding the rim.
Between corn and blackberries
they shape a hollow with their trowel,
pour in the fish and watch fluid
seep slowly downward
until the blanched form clings to soil,
a fetal arc still drawn to water.
After, they sketch
on the dry shoal with their stick
the shallows of a name.

**Dixie Partridge** (Richland, WA) grew up on a Wyoming farm homesteaded by her great-grandfather and lives near the Columbia River in Washington. She is currently working on a fourth collection of poems and edits poetry for *Sunstone Magazine*. Her essays and poetry have appeared in *The Georgia Review, Poetry, Ploughshares, Commonweal, Midwest Quarterly, Nightsun, Southern Poetry Review,* and *Northern Lights.* Her books are *Deer in the Haystacks* (Ahsahta Press, 1984) and *Watermark* (Saturday Press, 1991).

## About Stones

*How good it was to practice on stones . . .*
*things we could love without weeping over.*
                    —Stephen Dunn


When rocks grew like a crop
in my father's plowed fields,
we lugged them to wagons and rock piles
spring after spring, their claptrap clatter
a brash echo of the shape and range
that sang creekwater down from the hill.
From that spring bed, my sister and I held
wet polished pebbles in our mouths like candy—
flavors from childhood wadings.
Our collections dried drab but soothed us
through early winters, when larger creek stones
showed through the ice trace
like choir mouths
to be silenced by snows.
Rock mounds edge the farm,
overgrown with sod, oxeye daisies,
nettles. Wedged into the hillside,
the soberness and power of two great boulders
have stayed the same
as fences and buildings sagged into themselves,
my father weeping at the gate
as my brothers hauled away the gray
and lichened wood.

## Angel to Love, Man to World: My Father's Great Books

He swore he'd read them all — follow the Ten-Year Plan, begin
with *Hamlet,* for instance, or St. Augustine's *Confessions,*
before diving into *The Decline and Fall* — finally attain

that liberal education he never had. Sunday afternoons
he'd pick one color-coded volume: pale yellow for Literature,
dark green for Science, red for History or blue Philosophy,

and promptly fall asleep in his recliner, the half-finished first page
folded on his chest. Weekdays after school, my brothers
and I would pile *Descartes, Spinoza, Cervantes, Darwin,*

to bank the tracks of our electric racecars. My sisters
would practice balancing *Herodotus, Thucydides,* or *Galen*
upon head-banded heads, solemnly pace and posture

like fashion models down the kitchen hall runway. We'd return
all the books to their case before father's car darkened the driveway.
Soon he was collecting stacks of glossy paperbacks

to learn himself *Contracts & Finance, Home Remodeling,
Do-It-Yourself Haircuts*. His Great Books eventually took a spot
in the basement, decorated by a vase of mother's plastic geraniums.

The pair of indexes with their intriguing titles: *Angel to Love*
and *Man to World* were abandoned to gather dust with the only
update my father ever bought: 1961. As if time

and history had stopped with Kennedy's Election,
Seventeen New Nations in Africa,
Mass Culture, and The Youth Explosion.

**Peter Pereira** (Seattle, WA) is author of *Saving the World* (Copper Canyon, 2003) and *What's Written on the Body* (Copper Canyon, 2007). He is a family physician in Seattle. His poems have appeared in *Poetry, Prairie Schooner, New England Review,* and the *Virginia Quarterly Review* and have been anthologized in *180 More: Extraordinary Poems for Every Day;* and in *Best American Poetry 2007.*

**Lucia Perillo** (Olympia, WA) has published five books of poetry, including *Luck is Luck* (Random House, 2005), which was a finalist for the Los Angeles Times Book Prize and won the Kingsley Tufts prize from Claremont University. She is also author of a book of essays, *I've Heard the Vultures Singing* (Trinity University Press, 2009). Her latest book of poems is *Inseminating the Elephant* (Copper Canyon Press, 2009). She is a MacArthur Fellow and lives in Olympia, Washington.

## The Revelation

I hit Tonopah at sunset,
just when the billboards advertising the legal brothels
turn dun-colored as the sun lies
down behind the strip mine.

And the whores were in the Safeway,
buying frozen foods and Cokes
for the sitters before their evening shifts.
Yes they gave excuses to cut
ahead of me in line, probably wrote bad checks,
but still they were lovely at that hour,
their hair newly washed
and raveling.  If you follow
any of the fallen far enough
—the idolaters, the thieves and liars—
you will find that beauty, a cataclysmic
beauty rising off the face of the burning landscape
just before the appearance of the beast, the beauty
that is the flower of our dying into another life.
Like a Möbius strip: you go round once
and you come out on the other side.
This is no alpha, no omega,
no beginning and no end.
Only the ceaseless swell
and fall of sunlight on those rusted hills.
Watch the way brilliance turns
on darkness. How can any of us be damned.

## First Job / Seventeen

Gambelli's waitresses sometimes got down on their knees,
searching for coins dropped into the carpet—
hair coiled stiff, lips coated in that hennaed shade of red,
the banner-color for lives spent in the wake of husbands
dying without pensions, their bodies used in ceaseless
marching toward the kitchen's dim mouth, firm legs
migrating slowly ankleward. From that kitchen doorway,
Frankie Gambelli would sic a booze-eye on them,
his arms flapping in an earthbound pantomime of that
other Frank: The Swooned-Over. "You old cunts,"
he'd mutter. "Why do I put up with you old cunts?"—
never managing to purge his voice's tenor note
of longing. At me—the summer girl—he'd only stare
from between his collapsing red lids, eyes that were empty.

Once I got stiffed on a check when a man jerked crazy-faced
out of his seat, craned around, then bolted
from those subterrranean women, sweaty and crippled
in the knees. Though I chased him up the stairs to the street,
the light outside was blinding and I lost the bastard
to that whiteness, and I betrayed myself with tears.
But coming back downstairs my eyes dried on another vision:
I saw that the dusk trapped by the restaurant's plastic greenery
was really some residual light of that brilliance happening
above us on the street. Then for a moment the waitresses
hung frozen in midstride—cork trays outstretched—
like wide-armed, reeling dancers, the whole
some humming and benevolent machine that knew no past, no future—
only balanced glasses, and the good coin in the pocket.
Sinatra was singing "Jealous Lover." All of us were young.

**Charles Potts** (Walla Walla, WA) was born in Idaho Falls, Idaho, and received a BA in English from Idaho State University in 1965. ISU gave him a Distinguished Professional Achievement Award in 1994. In 2008, he received a Lifetime Achievement Award from the Washington Poets Association. He raises foundation Appaloosa horses in the foothills of the Blue Mountains near Walla Walla.

## Starlight on the Trail

Packing in the primitive
Idaho Chamberlain Basin area south
Of the main Salmon River 20 years ago
I found myself in Moose Meadows at dark
Twelve miles from the cabin
On a trail I'd been on exactly once,

Stumbling through the moonless dark
With eight pack horses, two mules,
Four extra saddle horses and one
Plumb green kid from Michigan.

I shut my eyes and sighed once,
Amazed to open my eyes and see
The trail a trifle more clearly.

I rode three steps with my eyes closed
And three with them open,
Picked up enough
Starlight on the trail
To find our dark way home.

**Joseph Powell** (Ellensburg, WA) teaches English at Central Washington University. His most recent books include a collection of short stories, *Fish Grooming & Other Stories* (March Street Press, 2007), and a collection of poems, *Hard Earth* (March Street Press, 2010). He lives on a small farm with his wife and son.

## Pecking Order

The turkey hen was calm and gentle from
the egg. She didn't scratch and scrabble
for food or peck the combs and rumps
of younger chicks or the tom she came with.

But soon the others saw in her compliance
a weakness their boredom eyed with a kind of zest—
just passing by they'd take a peck this once,
then again, again, until her tail

was bloody, her wing-bone joints were sores.
And through it all, though bigger, she humped
and bore it like a saint, a Roman leper,
an odd child. Sometimes, she'd trot away

and settle in a corner, her tail to the walls
but then they'd peck the knob above her nose
until it was as red as a cherry. She'd let
one chicken roost on top of her. I suppose

it was because her wings and back were given
some respite. I finally put her in
a Pet-Porter inside the chicken house
until she healed, yet she grimly paced

the wired door as if the cruel confinement
kept her from herself. Three times she was caged
and healed, and within a week or two
the chickens' faces were splashed with red.

Reversing my logic, I let her out
and locked up the bloody beaks.
Lonely, she flapped her wings, squawked,
and ran across the head-high field of grass

like a frenzied child running away from home.
For two months, the dog held her hunger in
as the chickens passed inches from her nose—
she rolled her eyes to see if I were watching

then lay her hunger down like a carving knife
before a prayer. But the flapping flurry
through the field was a vision granted life;
it seized her smell-bound brain like a sneeze.

I punished and penned her, plucked and dressed
the turkey who then sat accusingly in the pan.
She was hard to eat, to look at, but I ate—
small bites, small bites, like all the rest.

## The Apple-Heifer

> "Could it be sweetness is the prototype of all desire?"
> —Michael Pollan, *The Botany of Desire*

From the top of the hill, the Angus heifers come running to my call,
stumbling through the creek, loping across the moguled pasture. One
comes racing to the fence in a steamy burst of breath. Weeks ago she tore
through that veil of distance between sweetness and the butcher's hands and
now eats greedily, nose close, waiting and then taking the apple whole,
rolling it expertly with her tongue, way back to the molars which crunch it
with a squeak like a wet finger down a window, and then the mashing and
slathering, her head up so the juice slides back, pleasure draining downward,
her eyelids half-closed as apple after apple disappears into the lather of joy.
Because the "sweetest fruit makes the strongest drink," this apple-addict has
stepped out of the dress of herself to stand naked and shameless. I touch
her forehead, scratch her poll, feel the fine mucousy ridge-pattern of her
nose. The other heifer stands back peering into the sweet shop's window,
will not cross that invisible barrier, but her mouth drools sympathetically,
her knees locked, two yards from sweetness, her body almost shuddering
against itself, watching the apple heifer shame herself, wanton, trollop, tart,
Jezebel that she so inexcusably is. Finally, the other heifer butts her in the belly,
pushes into her, chastising, but the apple-heifer wobbles with it softly, apple-
froth streaming from the corners of her mouth, her nose poised
toward the next unbelievable burst of Jonagold.

## Shooting the Thief

Fifteen, I stumble home after midnight from the cannery, too
double-shifted to smell the sweet-grass at the river
or the bread rising in my aunt's bakery next door.

I don't need light to find my bed on the back porch,
I need out of these berry-soaked clothes and into bed.
My pants hit the floor. I hear a ratchet *zip zip zip.*

I peel curtains aside like a bandage. A shadow of a thief
hunches over my mother's tires, her battery and generator
that she bought with her sweat and cracked, bleeding hands.

I load the old single-shot 12-gauge and *snick* shut the breech,
hold my breath and ease open our thin back door. He's smaller
than his shadow. I tap him on the shoulder with the muzzle.

"Hey, fucker," I say, and he runs. Without a grunt or a look,
he jumps up and runs. This isn't the way of things in the movies.
He's supposed to put up his hands, say he's sorry, wait for the police.

The dark blob of him nearly makes the tracks when I split the night with fire
that brings Mom, my sisters, the neighbors, the cops. My thief shows up
at the hospital to get the lead out, winds up doing seven years.

The cop, my ex-dad's ex-partner, says I have to go downtown.
"Stripping cars ain't a capital offense," he says. "Here's the rule:
If we can't hang 'em, you can't shoot 'em."  He lets me go at dawn.

**Bill Ransom** (Grayland, WA) worked as a farm laborer (berries and chickens), trapper, cannery worker, jet engine expeditor, roofer, framer, poet-in-the-schools, firefighter, advanced life-support medic, and—late in life—Professor and Academic Dean of Curriculum at the Evergreen State College in Olympia, Washington. He says, "This list of jobs seems typical to me for a person my age living in the West and probably has defined me more than any other influence."

**Susan Rich** (Seattle, WA) is author of *The Alchemist's Kitchen* (White Pine Press, 2010), *Cures Include Travel* (White Pine Press, 2004), and *The Cartographer's Tongue* (White Pine Press, 2000), which won the PEN USA Award for Poetry. She has received an Artist Trust Fellowship as well as a Fulbright Fellowship to South Africa. As a human rights worker and long-time traveler, her poems frequently reflect her experiences in Bosnia, Gaza and the West Bank, and South Africa. More recently, landscapes of the Northwest have found their way into her poems.

### Mohamud at the Mosque

—to my student upon his graduation

And some time later in the lingering
blaze of summer, in the first days
after September 11th you phoned—

*If I don't tell anyone my name I'll*
*pass for an African American.*
And suddenly, this seemed a sensible solution—

the best protection: to be a black man
born in America, more invisible than
Somali, Muslim, asylum seeker—

Others stayed away that first Friday
but your uncle insisted that you pray.
*How fortunes change so swiftly*

I hear you say. And as you parallel
park across from the Tukwila
mosque, a young woman cries out—

her fears unfurling beside your battered car
Go back where you came from!
You stand, both of you, dazzling there

in the mid-day light, her pavement
facing off along your parking strip.
You tell me she is only trying

to protect her lawn, her trees,
her untended heart—already
alarmed by its directive.

And when the neighborhood
policeman appears, asks
you, asks her, asks the others—

So what seems to be the problem?
He actually expects an answer,
as if any of us could name it—

as if perhaps your prayers
chanted as this cop stands guard
watching over your windshield

during the entire service
might hold back the world
we did not want to know.

## Naming It

Shilshole: the shape in
which the estuary threads

her way inland to Puget Sound;

or—to pull a thread
through the eye of a bead.

That same sense of direction—

staving off loss
by narrowing what we need.

*\* Shilshole is a Duwamish word meaning "threading
a needle," perhaps referring to the narrow opening in
which Salmon Bay narrows into Shilshole Bay.*

**Derek Sheffield** (Leavenworth, WA) is author of *A Revised Account of the West* (Iowa State University Press, 2008), which won the Hazel Lipa Environmental Chapbook Award. He also won the James Hearst Poetry Award, judged by Li-Young Lee. His poems have appeared in *Poetry*, *Orion*, *The Georgia Review*, *The North American Review*, *Ecotone*, and *Hayden's Ferry Review*. He teaches at Wenatchee Valley College in Washington.

### A Good Fish

*Jerk that bitch*, urges my guide,
and I give my shuddering pole
a jerk, hooking the throat
of the first steelhead of my life.
My father, uncle, and cousin
are reeling, shouting, *First fish!*
and I'm horsing my pole
and reeling, shouting, *What a fighter!*
The boat's mascot whines
deep in her body, claws
clicking as she dances.
*Let it take some line.*
A silver spine touches the air.
*There*, he points, *a hen. And guess what?*
*She's gonna join the club,*
somehow spotting in that glimpse
the smooth place along her back
where a fin had been snipped.
He leans over the gunwale, dips a net,
and scoops her into the boat.
She is thick with a wide band
of fiery scales, slap-
slapping the aluminum bottom.
*Welcome to the club,* he says,
and clobbers her once, and again,
and once more before she goes still.
*A bleeder*, he says, shaking his head
and handing her to me. I curl
a finger through a gill the way
you're supposed to, determined
not to let her slip and flop
back to the river, a blunder
I'd never live down. A good fist.
Fish, I mean. A good fish.

## Used

Little by little.
It happens.
The mare's put out to pasture,
after she's foaled
and foaled again.
The field's gone gray.

Trees cut not quite down to the stump
mark the property line,
and, white sheets or not,
the ghosts line up
waiting to be served.
Neon pumpkins in the windows.

Where did the candle go,
after it became a carrot?
Roots stitched to rot
and the wax still flowing,
crayon-colored, from its wick.
Where did the children go

in their costumes decades old?
The fridge groans and starts
up, windows darken
until they bear no resemblance
to the ruffle of daylight,
the frilless nights.

**Judith Skillman** (Kennydale, WA) is author of twelve books of poetry. Her work has appeared in *Field*, *The Iowa Review*, *Northwest Review*, *Poetry*, *Southern Review*, and *Prairie Schooner*. Her latest books are *Prisoner of the Swifts* (Ahadada Books, 2009), *The Never* (Dream Horse Press, 2010), and *Heat Lightning: New and Selected Poems 1986—2006* (Silverfish Review Press, 2006). A writer, educator, and editor, she holds an MA in English Literature from the University of Maryland.

**Laura L. Snyder** (Seattle, WA) is a naturalist, botanical illustrator, basketweaver, and spinner of natural fibers. Laura says she "mixes cattail pollen with bog mud, coaxes Raven for quills, scratches in journals, and tosses her words to the four winds." Her poems have appeared in *Front Range, Four and Twenty, Switched-on Gutenberg, Earth's Daughters, Wazee, Flutter Poetry Journal, Pontoon 9, Chrysanthemum,* and the anthology *Grrrrr: A Collection of Poems about Bears, Least Loved Beasts of the Really Wild West.* You'll find her with an open journal in art museums and wherever trees and bears hang out.

## Evidence

*Where Tracks Spell War or Meat*
—Charles M. Russell

The light is rosy and low in the scene; it could be
dawn or sunset. There is no way to know for sure.
Snow is on the far mountains and snowy plains stretch
to meet a mounted party with nine horses. The riders

wear blankets, have dark braided hair, carry lances
and repeating rifles. The horses are guided by a twist
of rope against the tongue. The cold is made flesh

by the horse's breath, clouds jet from blowing nostrils.
There is no wind, this we know—the eagle feather
lays flat against the man's braid. The scout stops

where the snow was marred by many hooves. His horse
smells the disturbed snow. Though the man squints
in the direction of the mountains, he hesitates

and does not urge his horse forward. The past comes up in bits
from dirt, from stone, from paint. There is no whole history.
It was winter; the man's head was raised; they came to a place
of many tracks; they rode across open plains; light glinted off their eyes.

## The Bus Driver's Threnody

To be
      a fireman:
             his childhood wish
Lies drowned.
         He suffers
             from *almost-growns*
                 who fish
For change
      they never carry;
          *near-deaths* who take
               so long
To find a seat
      (each one they pass
          is wrong
For their august
      buttocks);
         *you're-lates*
           who complain
About the gridlock,
      stupid drivers,
         the rain;
The *shouts*, dressed
      in prison chic,
         who strutwalk
To the back
      and sit down far
         apart
          to talk.
And *wanh-hanhs:*
      little
        liabilities
Whose  parental
      pacifiers
        whine, "Please
Sit down—
      the bus might
        hit a bump!"
He moans.
      At least
        the garbage
         in a dump
Truck is still
      and quiet.
        Reaching the end
         of the route,
He imagines
      a huge hose
        blasting them out.

**Michael Spence** (Tukwila, WA) has driven public-transit buses in the Seattle area for twenty-five years. His work has appeared in *The American Scholar, The Chariton Review, The New Criterion, The New Republic, The North American Review, Poetry Northwest, The Sewanee Review, The Southern Review, The Yale Review,* and others. In 1990, he received a Creative Writing Fellowship from the National Endowment for the Arts. His third book is *Crush Depth* (Truman State University Press, 2009).

## And Don't Forget the Fruit

Miss Fargnoli climbs the slick steps—the rain
Is light though steady. *Old Seattle plain,*
She tells me with a sigh: *little drops*
*But lots of them.* The first rider I stop
For and the last to leave, she always takes
The spot across from me. After she shakes
The water off her orange umbrella, she sits
Carefully in the Lonely Hearts' Seat—
The place where people park when they're full
Of need for a priest in this confessional
On wheels. Although small and seventy,
She doesn't lament an awful life. Like a key
Whose twist removes a set of ankle chains
From the slog of the hours, her comments train
My thoughts on the world beyond the windshield.
*Worn as a Labrador, but well heeled,*
She says, umbrella poking my gym bag
On the floor beside the fare box. The fabric sags
As though collapsed in sleep. *It's never bit*
*Anyone,* I joke. Our conversation flits
To exercise—I tell her a life behind
The wheel can lead to a life that's *all* behind.
She waves a hand: *Some drivers, oh my Lord!*
*I don't see how they can get aboard*
*Without the wheelchair lift. Now, me, I swim*
*A dozen laps a day—that keeps me trim.*
The image of this tiny woman kicking
The water out of the Y pool brings
A smile to my lips. *Back when I had my car,*
She allows, *I learned how stupid people are.*
*My bumper sticker declared, "I oppose*
*Adipose."* When I laugh, she grins: *No one knows*
*What that means these days. A man asked me*
*If I was against slouching. Dictionaries*
*Must now be foreign as the Rosetta Stone.*
I tell her I watch what I eat, though I'm prone
To chocolate binges. *It always seems that sweets*
*Are what lead one's diet to defeat.*
*Eat vegetables—and don't forget the fruit!*
*I still have all my teeth.* She shows me, then hoots
At her display. I say I usually take
An apple, grapes, something to chew on my break
At the end of the line. *Along with the candy bars?*
She teases. The bell rings; I edge some cars
And stop at the curb. A man with a keg of a beer
Gut comes up and climbs off as soon as the door

Opens. I call out that he still owes his fare.
Turning around slowly, he gives me a stare,
Then slides a hand deep into his coat.
I feel a dryness tightening my throat
When he says, *Know what happened to the last bastard*
*Who told me to pay? I cut `im.* Somehow I'm stirred
To lean and reach into my bag. *You know*
*What happened to the last guy to show*
*Me a knife? I shot him.* He licks his lips,
Taking a step away, and nearly trips
As he hurries off. When I lean back, I hold
A banana in my hand. A wave of cold
Goes through me, a grin frozen to my face.
Miss Fargnoli laughs as her umbrella traces
An arabesque in the air. *If he'd gone haywire*
*And come back on, I'd have punctured his spare tire.*

**Ann Spiers** (Vashon Island, WA) leads creative writing seminars and ecological field trips. She's been boots-on-the-ground through great Western landscapes: Mount St. Helens post-eruption round-the-mountain trek, beach hike from Columbia River to Cape Flattery, and whale chasing from Scammon's Lagoon off Baja to her grandfather's former whaling ground along the Washington coast. She earned an MA in Literature and Creative Writing from the University of Washington and is published widely.

## 4th of July: Bunker Trail

Fire over the water is Rule #1.
My boys and their friends
sit on the bulkhead, ready to shoot
off illegal bottle rockets
mail-ordered from South America,
not hundreds but a deal—thousands.

I carry out Rule #2 by running
next door to notify Spanky,
Viet Nam vet, of the impending racket
so he can hunker down for the duration.
The impatient boys, fingers already
stinking of gunpowder,
stand in yesterday's field of thin paper,
the confetti of independence.
They light the punks and stick
four dozen rockets into beer bottles.
The boys say, bending to light the fuses,
"She must have told him by now."
Watching the rockets arc and explode,
the littlest says, "He told me
it's the rocket you don't hear that kills you."
"Cool," the other guys say. "Cool."

## Hidden Memory

> (It has been a slow process to heal from the emotional shock
> of looking at the photograph of a man falling
> from one of the World Trade Center's towers.)


August in the heart of the Big Apple, on our way from Seattle to Europe,
I bought a souvenir. It was a tiny golden spoon with the World
Trade Center towers. It said: New York. I carried it with me during
the entire trip in my purse, country after country, without knowing
the gesture could have meant something. A torch in the dark.

On the second week of September, already back home, the two
towers were piles of cement and rubble. My brain spinning, I felt the vertigo,
slipping through the interstices of darkness, death, and I was one flying
and falling into the abyss, again and again.

Many years have passed and the memories of those days
still return as magnets attracting the rumble of the jets before impact.
How do I know how much mind should be memory?
What portion no longer eludes me when I look at the tiny souvenir
    in my hands?


(Translated by Carolyne Wright)

**Eugenia Toledo** (Seattle, WA) was born in Temuco, Chile. She came to the United States in 1975 to pursue degrees in Latin American and Spanish Literature. She teaches writing workshops, writes literary articles, and creates "book-objects," combining words and graphic materials. "Hidden Memory" is included in *Tazas de mapa/Map Traces*, a collection of poems in process of translation by Carolyne Wright, winner of an award from 4Culture (King County Arts Council). Eugenia is author of three books, a chapbook, and numerous poems in international literary magazines.

## Memoria escondida

(Ha sido un proceso lento curarme del choque emocional de
mirar la fotografía de un hombre cayendo
de una de las Torres del World Trade Center.)

Agosto en el corazón de la Gran Manzana, en camino de Seattle a Europa,
Compré un recuerdo. Era una pequeña cucharita dorada con las Torres
del World Trade Center. Decía: Nueva York. Lo llevé conmigo en mi
cartera todo el viaje, país tras país, sin saber que el gesto pudo haber
tenido un significado. Una antorcha en la oscuridad.

En la segunda semana de Septiembre, ya de vuelta a casa, las dos torres
eran pilas de cemento y escombros. Mi cerebro dando vueltas, el vértigo,
escabulléndose por los intersticios de la oscuridad, la muerte, y yo volaba
o caía en el abismo, una y otra vez.

Tantos años han pasado y los recuerdos de esos días aún vuelven como
 imanes,atrayendo el estruendo antes del impacto.
¿Cómo saber qué parte de mi mente debe ser memoria?
¿Qué porción me elude cuando miro el pequeño recuerdo en mis manos?

## Kissing Cousins

In Grandma's kitchen garden while whippoorwills
whooped softly between the lettuce and red beets,
my lips as dry as hers, my left hand trembling
in hers like hers, my right arm reaching almost
halfway around her through that breathless evening,
not knowing how to, I kissed Ada Rose.

She was as wide as Grandma, but for miles
there was no one else I could kiss, and the girls back home
played spin-the-bottle with older boys, not me,
and I'd been dreaming of girls with their clothes off,
and here stood Cousin Ada Rose in a garden.

We didn't breathe because I didn't dare
so close to her glasses and because she couldn't
with her mouth shut tight against the deepest longings
of asthma. With a gasp and a glancing blow
of the hips we parted, and I sneaked upstairs
to hide my life under a comforter.

If only I'd kissed her hard with a hard grin
like Humphrey Bogart, cracking some kind of joke,
or given her a sister's birthday peck
or a Jimmy Cagney smack smack on the cheek.
but I'd done it scared and solemn, a dumb cowboy
forgetting when to head into the sunset.

All night, sleeping and waking, I tried to do it
differently while the curtains billowed toward me
like nightgowns, like the vapor from the machine
that breathed in her bedroom. In the glare of morning,
I sat cold on a bus, my vacation over,
while Ada Rose, tight-lipped, didn't wave goodbye.

**David Wagoner** (Lynnwood, WA) has published eighteen books of poems, including *A Map of the Night* (University of Illinois Press, 2008), and ten novels, one of which, *The Escape Artist* (Ballantine, 1982), was made into a movie by Francis Ford Coppola. He won the Lilly Prize in 1991 and has won six yearly prizes from *Poetry* (Chicago). He was a chancellor of the Academy of American Poets for twenty-three years. He has been nominated for the Pulitzer Prize and twice for the National Book Award. He edited *Poetry Northwest* from 1966 to its end in 2002. He is Professor Emeritus of English at the University of Washington.

**Panic**

Something
is watching you. Something
is ready to savage you. You can't see
any difference in choosing one direction
instead of another, but it's in your nature to climb
out of reach or confuse the enemy by taking cover,
by trying to blend in, by taking on the colors and shapes
of what seems to get along with the here and now or to turn
bright and beautiful, to be deserving of protection and preservation
or suddenly to seem unwholesome, inedible, dangerous, poisonous,
and you don't have time to stand still. The impulse is to run fast enough
and far enough to get out of the woods where you haven't been on speaking terms
with the inaudible and the nameless, and so you follow yourself and find yourself
following an urge toward a sunset, toward the ominous reddening of the leaves
overhead, meaning an inevitable darkness in league with the same darkness
now overtaking you and bringing you to a halt where you crouch
and settle for anything less than your own dimensions,
for the smallest unit of available space
where you plant your feet,
then plant your knees,
where you can bury
your poor head
in your hands.

## Pleasant Dreams

She's seven. She's afraid
        to go to sleep tonight
                because when she lies down
the bad thoughts come rushing into her head,
        come rushing over her quilt, the bears
                and horses and elephants and bad rabbits,
and jump into her dreams. I tell her
        it's all right, everything's going to be
                all right, nothing can harm you, sleep
is your best friend, we love you, there's nothing
        ever to be afraid of, and now, now there,
                there, think of the night light
all the way till breakfast, and look
        what I'm going to do. I'm tiptoeing
                into another room and lying down
while the mattress and the floor melt under me
        and the walls fly up and I hear the call of the green
                dental assistant as the laughing gas
wears off and the whole idea of morning
        is torn out by the roots and goes *clink*
                in a basin and the drowned man
in his translucent body bag
        worms his way out of the morgue
                and slips on his formfitting cassock
trimmed with gauze and chases the interns
        out of the swinging doors into the garden
                where visitors have left baskets and baskets
of vegetables to rot into compost
        among the artificial flowers in memory
                of the dear, dear nearly departed.

**Finn Wilcox** (Port Townsend, WA) worked in the woods of the Olympic and Cascade mountains with the forest workers co-op, Olympic Reforestation, for over twenty years. From the mid-seventies through the early nineties, he was an editor for Empty Bowl Press. He lives with his wife in Port Townsend, Washington.

## Women

I'm doing dishes.
It's summer.
My wife and my mother
are outside
sitting by the fire
laughing so hard
I have to set the pans
aside
and watch.

It's important to
pay attention to joy.
To love that is serious.

Now they are showing
each other earrings,
mom's silver bracelet,
Pat's jade teardrops
looped around her neck.
The night sky
bringing its own
slow jewelry to bear.

It hasn't always been like this.
I wasn't an easy son.

To those who say
redemption
dwells only in the house
of the Lord:
I say
you haven't met these women.

## The Rocking Chair

*—for Carolyn Norred*

You say it's one of your best memories
when your first boy couldn't sleep for days, when

it took medicine 48 hours
to ease the pain in a child's ear. His

crying would stop only against a warm
body. You had been holding Chris for two

days, rocking him, the worn velvet under
you, his hot ear against your heart beating,

the sun rising dimly as tears wetted
your face. You hadn't slept for a long time

when the door opened, and your neighbor, your
mother-in-law, walked into the room. She

had seen the light in the house and thought you
might need to sleep. She took the boy

into her arms so gently that he hardly felt
the change of comfort. You go, she motioned

until tears flowed from cheek to pillow as
you fell asleep in the dark room feeling

no human being could love you more than this.

**Deborah Brink Wöhrmann** (Longview, WA) lives in southwest Washington, where she's taught at a community college for the past ten years. She loves to travel, roam forests, and wander beaches. Much of her inspiration for writing comes from the people she meets—both in the classroom and while trying to understand people who speak a language other than her own.

**Carolyne Wright** (Seattle, WA) has published eight books and chapbooks of poetry, four volumes of translations from Spanish and Bengali, and a collection of essays. Her latest collection, *A Change of Maps* (Lost Horse Press, 2006), won the 2007 Independent Book Publishers Bronze Award for Poetry. Her previous book, *Seasons of Mangoes and Brainfire* (Eastern Washington University Press, 2005), won the Blue Lynx Prize and the American Book Award from the Before Columbus Foundation. In 2005, Wright moved back to her native Seattle. She serves on the faculty of the Whidbey Writers Workshop MFA Program.

### After the Explosion of Mount St. Helens, the Retiring Grade-School Teacher Goes for a Long Walk Through the Wheatlands

*Odessa, Washington*

These were the fields of the moon:
a dream of crops
and the distant cataclysm's
new snow ghosting on the roadway,
white as elevation markers
she could no longer point to on the wall maps.

All afternoon across the wheat steppes.
Hills mauve with slant-light, spring wheat
green-graying to the horizon.
She followed the straight track between the fields
on faith: no barns anywhere
to show her what arrival looked like.

No trees either . . . No, one—
over a rise, a poplar. Its gray leaves
drooped, dejected as a scolded child.
The geography she taught
told her *Hidden Springs*. Or *History*—
a farmhouse, torn down now, and a farmer

who planted a sapling once
thinking "avenue,"
and collapsed at the end
of a drought-cracked summer
before he ever could remember shade.

She kicked ash drift at the road's edge.
It rose heavily, reluctant
as eraser dust on the hands of blackboard
monitors she kept late after school.
The road went on, endless as an open set
as if whole numbers could extend
as far as sky does over the horizon.

Her last few weeks.
The ruler-straight road
reminded her who the teacher was.
She trudged between forty-acre sections,
chalk dust from the hundred sentences
deepened the lines of a neglected
history lesson in her face.

## Tire Hut: Seaview, Washington

The shop is divided like the brain:
on one side, dull metals lie crooked
like limbs after wind. Men shout things
to each other and no one. Buckets
of bolts line a wall where red and blue
rags hang from nails, already black
with grease. A generator
or tire balancer makes the floor shake
as if the ocean were under it pushing
up, and the air tastes like batteries.
This is where the work gets done.
But the customer comes in to wait
on the other side, sees tires splayed out
in pretty black rows. This one for fifty-nine.
This one for seventy. This set on sale:
buy three get the fourth free.
Tables with shiny magazines to lift
and touch, and everywhere
the smell of new coffee, sweet gasoline.
Outside is a rusted half-barrel.
It catches the rain. My father and brother
keep it there to drown tires in,
to see where the leak is.
The water is the cleanest water
you've ever seen. No kidding.
You can look into that water
and see the mountain from which it came.

**Maya Jewell Zeller** (Spokane, WA) grew up in the Northwest, living most of her life in small coastal towns of Oregon and Washington. Her poems have appeared in various literary journals, including *Bellingham Review, Mississippi Review, New Ohio Review, High Desert Journal,* and *Camas.* Maya lives in Spokane with her husband and baby and teaches English at Gonzaga University.

## Facing

At seventeen I worked after school
and most weekends for a local grocery,
and when it was slow I would straighten
the shelves—we called it facing—
which helped me memorize where everything was,
right down to the canned loganberry topping
Eleanor loved for her cheesecakes
or the clam juice or the coriander
or the yellow food coloring I knew could give people
impotence, and really what would be so bad
about that, I was familiar with most of the customers
who came in and frankly it wouldn't hurt them
to have fewer babies, the way they laughed
at the Mexicans who brought vans on Saturdays
to fill three grocery carts with tortillas, bagged
chilies and metal-clipped tubes of ground beef,
the way they would ask me what I was doing
when I got off, did I want to come out
to their campground where they were fishing
and no, I didn't, but I'd smile, ring up
their hot dog buns and Coors Lights,
while they grinned at what little skin I had showing
beneath a black apron that said Okie's and a button shirt
and I wished instead of their eyes it was wind
at my collarbone, thistle-sweet air while I ran
the road toward Altoona, birds
following my legs with their call,
those honest phlox faces lilting in the wet ditch.

# *Wyoming*

**Constance Brewer** (Gillette, WY) is a multi-tasking poet, writer, and artist. A long time ago, in a galaxy far away, she joined the Army, saw bits and pieces of the world, and finally settled in Wyoming, amid the extraterrestrial-enticing wide-open spaces, where she now lives with a small but vocal herd of Welsh Corgis and an alien-abandoned cat.

### Downwind

Spring breezed
in on a whiff of
Angus, packed
four steers deep
in the bowels
of a cattle truck.
Earth-ripe, heavy-
handed reminder
of life outside
this active city.
Manure-scent
colors the wind
long after the
silver Peterbuilt
lumbers away
to a packing plant
downwind.

**Patricia Frolander** (Sundance, WY) and her husband own his fifth-generation ranch in the Black Hills of Wyoming. Ties to family, land, and livestock have provided a wonderful variety of subjects to journal and pen. She writes, "We are blessed with three children, seven grandchildren and two great-grandchildren, all of whom live close to the ranch. Managing family, ranching, or writing is like trying to rope the wind."

## Wringer Washer

Rural Wyoming, twelve degrees.

I bucket hot water outside to the washing machine,
more to the rinse tubs, and complain.
Weeks before, in Colorado suburbia, my clothes
washed and dried in automatic appliances.

The bunkhouse, I now call home, has four rooms
for a husband, three children, a dog, and an old wood stove.
Diapers freeze as I pin them to the clothesline.
My mother-in-law's prediction:
"You won't last a year."

I grit my teeth and fill another bucket.

## New York to Deadwood

In the hold of Grandma's trunk,
bone china rimmed in fourteen carat,
spider cracked, never used.
Embroidered towels nestle
a yellowed wedding dress,
a bit of lace at collar and cuff.
Beneath all, a diary;
fourteen years in a Dakota sod house
living on dust
and the promise of gold.
Her last entry in tight, spare script,
"I left the sorry bastard."

**H. L. Hix** (Laramie, WY) teaches in the MFA program at the University of Wyoming and lives in Laramie, where every year he marvels at how late in the summer it is before hummingbirds arrive at 7,200 feet and at how hardy pocket gophers are. (And every day he rejoices that he can survive at an altitude at which cockroaches cannot.) He is author of seven collections of poems, one of which, *Chromatic* (Etruscan Press, 2006), was a finalist for the National Book Award.

## Summer

Suspended by a strand of spiderweb, seedburst
hovers and swings, counting out time, scribbling its sign
that this world is cursed with repletion, blessed with waste.
One wind shift, and light gray fence rails darken with rain.
God gets to *assign* meaning to the three gray cats
crouched at an open door looking out through the screen,
to round rocks clattering, to the fly that insists
on returning to my arm again and again.
Even dry months host a luxury of moonlight,
a sybaresis of dry leaves, of sprinkler spray
blown onto a neighbor's yard, of last plums picked at
by thirsty birds, paving stones tree roots lift and splay,
holes eaten into leaves at even intervals and straight,
sons following fathers, swinging their arms the same way.

## Fall

Rusting bulldozer, rusting wellhead and backhoe,
rusting LTD. One last hummingbird, rust-necked,
seeks red among rusting cannas. Through the window,
a voice calling *Come on back, that's it, come on back*,
a swingset's rusty voice severed by a chainsaw,
then, thinned by the mile from the road to here, a truck
gearing down. For one moment, a dozen sparrows
pause on the screen, each clinging with its feet and beak,
caught between the mute inward spiral and the one
that speaks, between those dead leaves that as they fall
tap the dying to follow and the yellow-brown
dying that argue among themselves how to call
the dead back, between the pepper blushing top-down
and the buddleia's brown base erasing purple.

### Winter

Stubble rows, four matte, four shiny in morning sun,
show the combine's direction. What can be preserved
must be preserved as some self other than its own.
Bent cattails mimic stubble in the frozen pond.
Suet nearly gone, chickadees cling upside down
to the feeder. Above it, a hedgeapple wedged
between branches since fall. Past that, changing direction
at once like a shoal of krill, a thousand blackbirds.
Skaters on a pond, we fall into what we know,
drown in disorienting light before we freeze.
In angled afternoon sun, the fence's shadow
caresses the snow's contours like tight-fitting clothes.
Even when grass greens to re-enact spring, the snow
will linger, longest in the shadows of houses.

### Spring

Five first crocuses burst into bird-brilliant bloom
and suddenly everything flies: behind a car
scraps of paper rise, two from a flock, startled dumb.
Some lives begin in abstraction; others end there.
If I find the child's fist this universe bloomed from
I will close it again as my own five fingers,
say worlds as one sentence, fit them into a name
for gold overwhelming finches, feather by feather.
With leaves returned, we still hear birds but see them now
only when they fly. It's hard to *see* anything,
even when we hear it sing, even though we know
it's there, even if we feel it filling our lungs.
Forsythia insists all that is is yellow.
None of this had to happen, but it had to be sung.

**Bo Moore** (Green River, WY) writes poetry and literary nonfiction about the contemporary West. She has lived in Colorado, Arizona, and New Mexico and has been a resident of Wyoming for fifteen years. A degree in geology informs her view of the Western landscape and how humans relate to marginal living conditions. Her poems are as sparse as the Wyoming badlands. She is the recipient of a Wyoming Arts Council Fellowship and the 2007 Doubleday Award.

### Dry Land

Wheel tracks cut the flanks of yellow hills,
as if the lowly sagebrush and bitter creosote end somewhere,
and a person could drive that far.

### Pretty

Small tasks become precious ways to gather time;
a thread, when pulled, makes emptiness into a pretty ruffle.

On sunny days, when isolated clouds throw shadows
across the uniform land it may be said to be pretty,
as a plain woman may be pretty if she takes pride in her plainness.

### Forecast

I open the screen door to the full moon,
to clouds that push across its white face, promising snow,
and a rip saw wind that breaks our few trees, the force
behind an empty can that rattles down the street.

If it does snow tonight, the dust will yield
little water, and trash from uphill will stick to the fence,
as will weeds that tumble from the edge of town,
just two blocks away, and I will leave them there all winter.

## Night Drive

Shoulderless mostly, old
This is the road
You should not be driving

Not at night, at zero
Or well below,
Bone-stark, so cold

Each turn appears
As a figure in a dream
Sure, demanding

*Look*, fields are rising—
And they are, the bright
Snow-stripped fields,

Like a shroud
Or a female voice
*You never loved me*

And that's true
Even the farthest homes
Close enough

To your home
Where often in the dark
Downstairs in the kitchen

The beams of headlights
Moving through the room
Moved through you

**Kate Northrop** (Laramie, WY) is author of *Back Through Interruption* (Kent State University Press, 2002), which won the Stan and Tom Wick First Book Award. Her second collection, *Things Are Disappearing Here* (Persea Books, 2007), was a finalist for the James Laughlin Award and a New York Times Book Review Editor's Choice. Her poems have appeared in *AGNI, The American Poetry Review, The Massachusetts Review, Raritan*, and other journals. Northrop is associate professor of English at the University of Wyoming.

## Winter Prairie

Around which the houses darken
And the windows surface silver-pale,

Around which the ditchwater
Freezes stunned in a ditch,

The water like the windows: clear,
Secretive. One knows

A window: it gives everything away,
Nothing back. One knows

The TV light scattered through,
Blue, cold, though not as blue, not as cold

As the prairie, the winter prairie, spare
And so clean, it becomes like this

A struck note, a shape
Cut from the world yet held in the world

—like staring hard into a grave.
I speak to you; clearly someone else speaks.

## The Black and the Dazzle

Some winter mornings
dawn a wild, dazzling bright
finding and blessing everything—
fence post, phone pole
brown grasses poking through snow,
brown cattail medley at the frozen marsh—
with its particular self.
The cold air holds nothing
but transparent possibility.
My daughter
beside me on the seat
chatters along of what she remembers
of summer, the races we had
in the yard on her birthday.
We pass a snowplow, coming at us
and find ourselves for a panicked second
with nothing but each other.
My father writes:
*I am deteriorating steadily and painlessly.*
Again, the road appears, pollarded trees around a farmhouse
and a black line of cattle
strung feeding along a line of hay.

**Tom Rea** (Casper, WY) is a Western journalist and historian. He earned an MFA from the University of Montana in 1979, and he and his wife, Barbara, founded Dooryard Press in Story, Wyoming, publishing titles by Richard Hugo, Ed Harkness, Alberto Rios, Lee Bassett, and Ripley Schemm. Tom worked for the *Casper Star-Tribune* as a reporter and editor. In 1998, he left newspapering for bigger projects, and he has been freelancing since.

**David Romtvedt** (Buffalo, WY) served in the Peace Corps in Zaire and Rwanda and on a sister city project in Jalapa, Nicaragua. He earned an MFA from the Iowa Writers' Workshop. He teaches at the University of Wyoming and has served as Wyoming Poet Laureate. Romtvedt is a recipient of the Wyoming Governor's Arts Award, Wyoming Arts Council Fellowship, two National Endowment for the Arts Fellowships, and the National Poetry Series Award.

## Twenty-Five Vultures

There are twenty-five vultures
roosting in my neighbor's cottonwood tree.
They rise in high lazy circles,
patient for what might be dead below.
The flap of their wings
makes a noise I hear from far away.

This is the third year they've come
to live here with my neighbor
and he never complained before.
But now, his wife dead,
and him shot full of chemo and radiation
for his own cancer, he's got a different attitude,
been calling the mayor's office and demanding
they do something. "Like I'm living in a goddam
chicken coop," he says, and asks me to help him.
"Mayor says it's the County—we'll go to the commissioners."
"But I haven't got any complaint about the birds," I say.
"Anyway, don't you have a shotgun?"
"I do. I do," he nods, "but them damned dirty birds
is protected. You shoot 'em and the federal boys'll be all over you."
I say, "There's nobody out here but us. No federal boys at all."

My neighbor calls up Game and Fish and complains.
A few days later a warden appears in a dark green pickup.
He aims a fat pistol up in the tree and fires.
There's a whir and a trail of smoke
then an explosion and whistle
loud enough to bust the walls of the house,
knock out the windows and scare the shit
out of every living creature in two miles.
The birds flapped off in a black cloud
and didn't come back for fifteen minutes.
The warden waited for them to settle down
then fired again. Each time the vultures
scattered, returning in fifteen minutes.
The warden shot four times then the sun went down.
You could see the silhouettes in the branches.
Next afternoon the warden came back
and did it all over. Bang. Scream. The dogs howled
and the cats took off for the lambing sheds,
the vultures flapped away and the sun went down.
I hoped my neighbor felt better for the attention he was getting.

After the second visit from the warden, the vultures were gone
for two days. When they came back, the neighbor called
again and the warden came again and bang, scream,
the pistol and by then I was rooting for the vultures.

Then it was Saturday and Sunday and Game and Fish
doesn't work weekends. I saw the warden in town
and said, "Those vultures are still there. They're tenacious."
The warden shook his head and smiled, "Once vultures pick
a roosting tree, they stay. Noise won't scare them away."
"Doesn't seem very useful then."
"No, not very useful." He touched the brim of his hat,
nodded, and left. I left too, thinking about my neighbor
and how would I feel if it was me who had maybe six months,
maybe two months, maybe only a few weeks left to live?
Would I go after the vultures?
I like to think I'd be too busy getting ready
to give myself back to the earth
so that if you were going to find me,
you'd have to look down like the vultures
and fly patiently in an ever-widening circle.
But I don't know. I might act like my neighbor,
call Game and Fish, fire the gun to make the explosion,
raise my face, shake my fist, and shout
*I ain't dead yet, goddam it, so get outta my trees.*

### Artificial Breeze

I walked up and down the field
while she stood on the flatbed trailer.
The mountains in the distance,
the plains were dry and hot.
We were loading hay. Without a hook,
I lifted each bale by hand—forty pounds—
the plastic cord cutting into my gloves.
Her feet spread and her knees bent,
she grabbed the bales and shoved them
like bricks crisscrossing so that though
they rose above the cab of the truck,
they didn't fall. We went on wordlessly
under the rumble of the engine,
the thump of the bales on the flatbed
boards then on each other. Sweat
dripped from my eyelids. Sweat
ran down my chest and back. "What
a load of shit," she said. I didn't ask.
She has done this work for thirty years
and once it was mine, too, but now—
good luck and who knows what—
I earn my daily bread teaching poetry
and appear here as a guest, a former rancher,
a part-time loader of hay. "What a load
of shit," she said again and this time,
I asked, "What?" while imagining
the poetry that might be made
from drudgery and dead-end jobs.
She shook her head in disgust
and waved her arms angrily.
In the artificial breeze, the air
seemed hotter and the dried grass
rattled like a snake about to strike.

## Bending Elbows

We were two old American ranchers
at a cattlemen's conference in Kuala Lumpur,
out bending elbows.  Limousin breeders,
we'd been around the world to these things—
Western Australia, Central France, Argentina,
South Africa, and now Malaysia, mostly
talking about cows. We stepped out of the bar
and hailed a rickshaw, began to haggle with the driver
over the price. There were people everywhere,
the crowd surging left and right as if breathing
in and out. Who could tell who bumped into us
but whoever it was was slick, cleaning all the change
out of our pockets. Those guys knew their business.
Next night we went back to the bar, and stood around
outside to let the thieves try again. When they made
their move, we grabbed them and invited them into the bar,
bought them beers, explained the term "bending elbows,"
and asked them about life in Kuala Lumpur.

**Robert Roripaugh** (Laramie, WY) ranched with his parents along the Wind River Mountains and completed degrees at The University of Wyoming, where he later taught Creative Writing and Western Literature. He was Wyoming's Poet Laureate from 1995—2002. Roripaugh's poetry is collected in *Learn to Love the Haze* (High Plains Press, 1996) and *The Ranch* (University of Wyoming, 2001). One of his novels, *Honor Thy Father*, won a Western Heritage Award from the National Cowboy Hall of Fame.

### The Old Horseshoer

In late spring the horseshoer navigates
Our soggy road, his Studebaker truck
Clanging an anvil, tools of the trade,
Iron shoes in a barrel. Stooped, Day's Work
Mixed with mustache, he sets up under
Cottonwoods, keeping one eye on the corral
Where Sugar, PeeWee, wary Shorty are waiting.
Their coats are patchy, winter hair
Shedding unevenly, "bellies a little gant."

He hasn't come for small talk. Remembering
The last time, he picks out Shorty first,
Ties him high by a heavy halter-rope.
Wearing leather apron with pouches for nails,
The old man lifts a foot, swears, wields
His curved hoof-knife—spits—neatly clips
The edge with rusty pinchers, rasps it level.
He bends the calked shoe by a squint,
Pounds, fits, refits, gauging the ellipses
Against soft blue and Shorty's cautious eye.

His mouth bristling with nails, he works
Under the raised front leg, a circus
Act, gray cap on backwards, hammer near
The quick, twisting and clinching nails down,
Mutters to himself, the light
Green morning opening to sun. Shod in muddy
Boots, he limps around Shorty, picks up
One hind foot easily as a tired lover,
Asks if we've heard the first meadowlark.

## Clues

The gopher in my palm reeks.
I'm sitting on the cabin doorstep
suppressing panic—rabies?
Tularemia? Plague? Her splayed toes
balance her furry ounces on my wrist.

She flicks her tail, snatches a seed
I hold cupped, nibbles off an edge
of shell so the two halves fall apart.
She slips the kernel whole
into her mouth, selects another seed.

I lift her to my wrinkled nose
and sniff. Phew! Yet, I seem to know
this stench mixed with gopher sweat
and baked sand, shriveled sagebrush leaves
and dried prickly pear fruit.

Her fists pound the last seed
into her bulging cheeks. She jumps
down and belly-flops in a cedar's shade
to massage her shrunken teats
in the soft, cooling duff.

Getting up, I brush hulls from my lap,
dust my hands, and trot up the steep
hillside along trails dimpled with tracks—
lark and chipmunk and deer,
coyote and badger and skunk—and gopher.

August sun flames in my hair
and burning lungs, but she could
scamper the whole way in the shade
of the sagebrush that scratch my jeans.
From my pounding footfalls locusts flee—
to her they'd be armor-plated jackrabbits!

At last I reach the bunchgrass
meadow and read the evidence—the sand
everywhere riddled with holes and ransacked,
stalks hacked off and strewn helter-skelter.  Ah-ha!
Just as I suspected—she's raided this place
and stolen all the wild onions!

**Dawn Senior-Trask** (Encampment, WY) grew up in the log cabin her family built in the rugged Snowy Range foothills of Wyoming. She came to know many wild animals, including "gophers" (ground squirrels), hawks, pine squirrels, porcupines, weasels, larks, deer, eagles, and coyotes. Dawn has published poems and essays in many anthologies. She is also a professional artist.

### Silly-Day

"You Silly-nilly-daffy-down-dilly-
dumbbell-dodo-kafluey, you!" we call
each other as fast as we can,
laughing ourselves red and round
as bubblegum popping all
over our faces. At the picnic
we're laughing so hard
that Jenny snorts a spaghetti
noodle out of one nostril. We roll
in the grass sneezing and itching,
plastered with green stains
and frantic ants, spitting twigs
and clippings. We guffaw at the dog
who leaps, barking and snapping,
at the birthday balloons we bat
around. He grabs one and—*bang!*—
shakes his baffled head
wondering where that fat bird went.

Chortling, tickling, chasing, we dodge
among our tethered steeds. Rastus
the raggedy donkey sniffs
Patty's garlic breath—his rubbery lips
curl—*"Eee-haw! Eee-haw!"*
We grab manes, swing on bareback,
race at a gallop into the forest.
Alone, we whoop and hoot,
shuck our duds, dive into the pond
wearing our panties. We kick and splash,
burble and shout until—freeze!
Listen! Panic! Like bug-eyed frogs
we leap to hide in willows.
A pickup stops beside our flung-off
shirts and jeans. A family tumbles out
and patiently rigs their fishing rods.

# Books of Poetry by Poets in This Anthology:

## ARIZONA

Bakken, Dick. *Here I Am*. St. Andrews Press, 1979.

_____ *Feet with the Jesus*. Lynx House Press, 1989.

Chorlton, David. *Forget the Country You Came From*. Singular Street Press, 1992.

_____ *Outposts,* Taxus Press (UK), 1994.

_____ *A Normal Day Amazes Us*. Kings Estate Press, 2003.

_____ *Return to Waking Life*. Main Street Rag Publishing Company, 2004.

_____ *Waiting for the Quetzal*. March Street Press, 2006.

_____ *The Porous Desert*. Future Cycle Press, 2007.

Harrison, Jim. *Plain Song*. W.W. Norton, 1965.

_____ *Locations*. W.W. Norton, 1968.

_____ *Outlyer and Ghazals*. Simon and Schuster, 1971.

_____ *Selected and New Poems, 1961—1981*. Delta/Seymour Lawrence, 1982.

_____ *The Theory & Practice of Rivers*. Winn Books, 1985.

_____ *The Theory & Practice of Rivers and New Poems*. Clark City Press, 1985 (rpt. 1989).

_____ *After Ikkyu and Other Poems*. Shambhala, 1996.

_____ *The Shape of the Journey: New and Collected Poems*. Copper Canyon Press, 1998.

_____ *Braided Creek: A Conversation in Poetry* (with Ted Kooser). Copper Canyon Press, 2003.

_____ *Livingston Suite*. Limberlost Press, 2005.

_____ *Saving Daylight*. Copper Canyon Press, 2006.

_____ *Letters to Yesinin*. Copper Canyon Press, 2007.

Hogue, Cynthia. *Where the Parallels Cross*. Whiteknights Press (UK), 1983.

_____ *The Woman in Red*. Ahsahta Press, 1989 (rpt. 1999).

_____ *The Never Wife*. Mammoth Press, 1999.

_____ *Flux*. New Issues Press, 2002.

_____ *The Incognito Body*. Red Hen Press, 2006.

_____ *When the Water Came: Evacuees of Hurricane Katrina*. University of New Orleans Press, 2010.

_____ *Or Consequence*. Red Hen Press, 2010.

Inman, Will. *Surfings: Selected Poems of Will Inman*. Howling Dog Press, 2005.

_____ *I Read You Green, Mother*. Howling Dog Press, 2008.

Jay, James. *The Undercards*. Gorsky Press, 2003.

_____ *The Journeymen*. Gorsky Press, 2010.

John, Hershman. *I Swallow Turquoise for Courage*. University of Arizona Press, 2007.

Miller, Jane. *Many Junipers, Heartbeats*. Copper Beech Press, 1980.

_____ *The Greater Leisures*. Doubleday, 1983.

_____ *Black Holes, Black Stockings* (with Olga Broumas). Wesleyan University Press, 1985.

_____ *American Odalisque*. Copper Canyon Press, 1987.

_____ *Working Time: Essays on Poetry, Culture, and Travel*. University of Michigan Press, 1992.

_____ *August Zero*. Copper Canyon Press, 1993.

_____ *Memory at These Speeds: New and Selected Poems*. Copper Canyon Press, l996.

_____ *Wherever You Lay Your Head*. Copper Canyon Press, l999.

_____ *A Palace of Pearls*. Copper Canyon Press, 2005 (rpt. 2006).

_____ *Midnights* (with Beverly Pepper) Saturnalia Books, 2008.

Natal, Jim. *In the Bee Trees*. Archer Books, 2000.

_____ *Talking Back to the Rocks*. Archer Books, 2003.

_____ *Memory and Rain*. Red Hen Press, 2009.

Nevin, Sean. *Oblivio Gate*. Southern Illinois University Press, 2008.

Ortiz, Simon. *Naked in the Wind*. Quetzal-Vihio Press, 1971.

_____ *Going for Rain*. Harper & Row, 1976.

_____ *Fight Back: For the Sake of the People, For the Sake of the Land*. University of New Mexico Press, 1980.

_____ *A Poem Is a Journey*. Lieb and Schott, 1981.

_____ *From Sand Creek: Rising in This Heart Which Is Our America*. Thunder's Mouth Press, 1981.

_____ *A Good Journey*. University of Arizona Press, 1984.

_____ *Woven Stone*. University of Arizona Press, 1992.

_____ *After and Before the Lightning*. University of Arizona Press, 1994.

Rattee, Michael. *Mentioning Dreams*. Adastra Press, 1985.

_____ *Calling Yourself Home*. Cleveland State University Press, 1986.

_____ *Enough Said: A Poetry Dialogue Between Father & Son*. Adastra Press, 2002.

_____ *Everything Green Everything White*. Apropos Press, 2008.

_____ *Falling Off the Bicycle Forever*. Adastra Press, 2010.

Ray, David. *X-Rays, A Book of Poems*. Cornell University Press, 1965.

_____ *Dragging the Main and Other Poems*. Cornell University Press, 1968.

_____ *Gathering Firewood: New Poems and Selected*. Wesleyan University Press, 1974.

_____ *The Tramp's Cup*. Chariton Review Press, 1978.

_____ *The Touched Life*. Scarecrow Press, 1982.

_____ *On Wednesday I Cleaned Out My Wallet*. Pancake Press, 1985.

_____ *Elysium in the Halls of Hell*. Nirala Publications (India), 1986.

_____ *Sam's Book*. Wesleyan University Press, 1987.

_____ *The Maharani's New Wall*. Wesleyan University Press, 1989.

_____ *Not Far from the River: Love Poems from India*. Copper Canyon Press, 1990.

_____ *Wool Highways*. Helicon Nine Editions, 1993.

_____ *Kangaroo Paws: Poems Written in Australia*. Thomas Jefferson University Press, 1995.

_____ *HeartStones: New and Selected Poems*. Micawber Fine Editions, 1998.

_____ *Demons in the Diner*. Ashland University Press, 1999.

_____ *One Thousand Years: Poems About the Holocaust*. Timberline Press, 2004.

_____ *The Death of Sardanapalus and Other Poems of the Iraq Wars.* Howling Dog Press, 2004.

_____ *Music of Time: Selected and New Poems*. Backwaters Press, 2006.

_____ *When*. Howling Dog Press, 2007.

_____ *After Tagore: Poems Inspired by Rabindranath Tagore.* Nirala Publications (India), 2008.

Ray, Judy. *Pebble Rings*. Greenfield Review Press, 1980.

_____ *Pigeons in the Chandeliers*. Timberline Press, 1993.

_____ *To Fly Without Wings*. Helicon Nine Editions, 2009.

Rios, Alberto. *Elk Heads on the Wall*. Mango Publications, 1979.

_____ *Sleeping on Fists*. Dooryard Press, 1981.

_____ *Whispering to Fool the Wind*. The Sheep Meadow Press. 1982.

_____ *Five Indiscretions*. The Sheep Meadow Press, 1985.

_____ *The Lime Orchard Woman*. The Sheep Meadow Press, 1988.

_____ *The Warrington Poems*. Pyracanthus/ Arizona State University School of Art, 1989.

_____ *Teodoro Luna's Two Kisses*. W.W. Norton and Company, 1992.

_____ *The Smallest Muscle in the Human Body*. Copper Canyon Press, 2002.

_____ *The Theater of Night*. Copper Canyon Press, 2006.

_____ *The Dangerous Shirt*. Copper Canyon Press, 2009.

Seiferle, Rebecca. *The Ripped-Out Seam*. The Sheep Meadow Press, 1993.

_____ *The Music We Dance To*. The Sheep Meadow Press, 1998.

_____ *Bitters*. Copper Canyon Press, 2001.

_____ *Wild Tongue*. Copper Canyon Press, 2007.

Silko, Leslie Marmon. *Storyteller*. Seaver Books, 1981.

_____ *Laguna Woman: Poems*. Greenfield Review Press, 1974.

Speer, Laurel. *A Bit of Wit*. Gusto Press, 1979.

_____ *T. Roosevelt Tracks the Last Buffalo*. Rhiannon Press, 1982.

_____ *I'm Hiding from the Cat*. Geryon Press, 1983.

_____ *Weird Sister One*. Geryon Press, 1984.

Tapahonso, Luci. *More Shiprock Night*. Tejas Art Press, 1982.

_____ *Seasonal Woman*. Tooth of Time Press, 1983.

_____ *A Breeze Swept Through*. West End Press, 1987.

_____ *Sáanii Dahaataał: The Women Are Singing*. University of Arizona Press, 1993.

_____ *This is How They Were Placed for Us*. Helicon Nine, 1994.

_____ *Blue Horses Rush In: Poems and Stories*. University of Arizona Press, 1997.

_____ *Songs of Shiprock Fair*. (Anthony Emerson, illus.) Kiva Press, 1999.

_____ *A Radiant Curve: Poems and Stories*. University of Arizona Press, 2008.

Waggener, Miles. *Phoenix Suites*, The Word Works, 2002.
Walker, Nicole. *This Noisy Egg.* Barrow Street Press, 2010.

## CALIFORNIA

Addonizio, Kim. *The Philosopher's Club.* BOA Editions, 1994.
_____ *Jimmy & Rita.* BOA Editions, 1997.
_____ *Tell Me.* BOA Editions, 2000.
_____ *What Is This Thing Called Love.* W.W. Norton, 2005.
_____ *Lucifer at the Starlite.* W.W. Norton, 2009.
Archila, William. *The Art of Exile.* Bilingual Press/Arizona State University, 2009.
Bass, Ellen. *No More Masks! An Anthology of Poems by Women* (with Florence Howe). Doubleday, 1973.
_____ *Mules of Love.* BOA Editions, 2002.
_____ *The Human Line.* Copper Canyon Press, 2007.
Buckley, Christopher. *Last Rites.* Ithaca House, 1980.
_____ *Blue Hooks in Weather.* Moving Parts Press, 1983.
_____ *Other Lives.* Ithaca House, 1985.
_____ *Dust Light, Leaves.* Vanderbilt University Press, 1986.
_____ *Blue Autumn.* Copper Beech Press, 1990.
_____ *Dark Matter.* Copper Beech Press, 1993.
_____ *A Short History of Light.* Painted Hills Press, 1994.
_____ *Camino Cielo.* Orchises Press, 1997.
_____ *Fall From Grace.* Bk Mk Press, 1998.
_____ *Star Apocrypha.* TriQuarterly Books, 2001.
_____ *Closer to Home: Poems of Santa Barbara 1975—1995.* Fountain Mountain Press, 2003.
_____ *Sky.* The Sheep Meadow Press, 2004.
_____ *And the Sea.* The Sheep Meadow Press, 2006.
_____ *Flying Backbone: The Georgia O'Keeffe Poems.* Blue Light Press, 2007.
_____ *Modern History: Prose Poems 1987—2007.* Tupelo Press, 2008.
_____ *Rolling the Bones.* Tampa University Press, 2010.
Chernoff, Maxine. *A Vegetable Emergency.* Beyond Baroque Foundation, 1976.
_____ *Utopia TV Store.* The Yellow Press, 1979.
_____ *New Faces of 1952.* Ithaca House, 1985.
_____ *Japan.* Avenue B Press, 1988.
_____ *Leap Year Day: New and Selected Poems.* ACP, 1990.
_____ *World: Poems 1991—2001.* Salt Editions (UK), 2001.
_____ *Evolution of the Bridge: Selected Prose Poems.* Salt Editions (UK), 2004.
_____ *Among the Names.* Apogee Press, 2005.
_____ *The Turning.* Apogee Press, 2008.
Chin, Marilyn. *Dwarf Bamboo.* Greenfield Review Press, 1987.
_____ *The Phoenix Gone, the Terrace Empty.* Milkweed Editions, 1994.
_____ *Rhapsody in Plain Yellow.* W.W. Norton , 2002.
Cotter, Craig. *The Aroma of Toast.* Black Tie Press, 1989.
_____ *There's Something Seriously Wrong with Me.* Black Tie Press, 1990.
_____ *Chopstix Numbers.* Ahsahta Press, 2002.
Davis, Carol. *Into the Arms of Pushkin: Poems of St. Petersburg.* Truman State University Press, 2007.
Day, Lucille Lang. *Self-Portrait with Hand Microscope.* Berkeley Poets' Workshop and Press, 1982.
_____ *Fire in the Garden.* Mother's Hen, 1997.
_____ *Wild One.* Scarlet Tanager Books, 2000.
_____ *Infinities.* Cedar Hill Publications, 2002.
_____ *The Curvature of Blue.* Cervena Barva Press, 2009.
DenBoer, James. *Learning the Way.* University of Pittsburgh Press, 1969.
_____ *Trying to Come Apart.* University of Pittsburgh Press, 1971.
_____ *Lost in Blue Canyon.* Christopher's Books, 1981.
_____ *Stonework: Selected Poems.* Swan Scythe Press, 2007.
_____ *Small Gifts, Great Grace: The Personal Poems of Venantius Fortunatus (540—610 CE),* Bald Trickster Press, 2009.
Dofflemyer, John. *Poems from Dry Creek.* Starhaven (UK), 2008.

Espinoza, John Olivares. *The Date Fruit Elegies*. Bilingual Press, 2008.

Follet, CB. *The Latitudes of Their Going*. Hot Pepper Press, 1993.

_____ *Gathering the Mountains*. Hot Pepper Press, 1995.

_____ *Visible Bones*. Plain View Press, 1998.

_____ *At the Turning of the Light*. Salmon Run Press, 2001.

_____ *Hold and Release*. Time Being Books, 2007.

_____ *And Freddie Was My Darling*. Many Voices Press, 2009.

Gioia, Dana. *Daily Horoscope*. Graywolf Press, 1986.

_____ *The Gods of Winter*. Graywolf Press, 1991.

_____ *Interrogations at Noon*. Graywolf Press, 2001.

González, Rafael Jesús. *El Hacedor de Juegos/The Maker of Games*. Casa Editorial, 1977 (rpt.1988).

Hales, Corinne Clegg. S*eparate Escapes*. Ashland Poetry Press, 2002.

_____ *Underground*. Ahsahta Press, 1986.

Hedge Coke, A. A. *It's Not Quiet Anymore*. (Anthology) Institute for the American Indian Arts, 1992.

_____ *Voices of Thunder*. (Anthology) Institute for the American Indian Arts, 1993.

_____ *Dog Road Woman*. Coffee House Press, 1997.

_____ *Off-Season City Pipe*. Coffee House Press, 2005.

_____ *Blood Run*. Salt Publishing (UK). 2006.

_____ *Sing: Indigenous Poetry of the Americas*. (Anthology) University of Arizona Press, 2010.

Hirshfield, Jane. *Alaya*. Quarterly Review of Literature, 1982.

_____ *Of Gravity & Angels*. Wesleyan University Press, 1988.

_____ *The October Palace*. HarperPerennial, 1994.

_____ *The Lives of the Heart*. HarperPerennial, 1997.

_____ *Given Sugar, Given Salt*. HarperCollins Publishers, 2001.

_____ *After*. HarperCollins Publishers, 2006.

Jaffe, Maggie. *1492: What Is It Like to Be Discovered?* Monthly Review Press, 1991.

_____ *Continuous Performance*. Burning Cities Press, 1992.

_____ *How the West Was One*. Burning Cities Press, 1997.

_____ *7th Circle*. Cedar Hill Books, 1998.

_____ *The Prisons*. Cedar Hill Books, 2001.

_____ *Flic(k)s: Poetic Interrogations of American Cinema*. Red Dragonfly Press, 2009.

Kaminsky, Ilya. *Dancing in Odessa*. Tupelo Press, 2004.

Keithley, George. *The Donner Party*. George Braziller, 1972 (rpt. 1989).

_____ *Song in a Strange Land*. George Braziller, 1974.

_____ *The Best Blood of the Country*. Mellen Poetry Press, 1993.

_____ *Earth's Eye*. Story Line Press, 1994.

_____ *The Starry Messenger*. University of Pittsburgh Press, 2003.

Kowit, Steve. *Incitement to Nixonicide and Praise for the Chilean Revolution*. Quixote Press, 1979.

_____ *Cutting Our Losses*. Contact II Publications, 1982.

_____ *Lurid Confessions*. Carpenter Press, 1983.

_____ *Passionate Journey*. City Miner Press, 1984.

_____ *In the Palm of Your Hand: The Poet's Portable Workshop*. Tilbury House, 1995.

_____ *The Dumbbell Nebula*. Heyday Press, 2000.

_____ *The Gods of Rapture*. CityWorks Press, 2006.

_____ *The First Noble Truth*. University of Tampa Press, 2007.

_____ *Crossing Borders. (a collaboration with the Lenny Silverberg)* Spuyten Duyvil Press, 2010.

Lee, Karen An-hwei. *In Medias Res*. Sarabande Books, 2004.

_____ *Ardor*. Tupelo Press, 2008.

Levine, Philip. *On the Edge*. Stone Wall Press, 1963.

_____ *Not This Pig*. Wesleyan University Press, 1968.

_____ *Pili's Wall*. Unicorn Press, 1971.

_____ *Red Dust*. Kayak Books, 1971.

_____ *They Feed They Lion*. Atheneum, 1972.

_____ *1933*. Atheneum, 1974.

_____ *On the Edge & Over: Poems, Old, Lost & New*. Cloud Marauder Press, 1976.

_____ *The Names of the Lost.* Atheneum, 1976.

_____ *Ashes: Poems New and Old.* Atheneum, 1979.

_____ *7 Years From Somewhere.* Atheneum, 1979.

_____ *One for the Rose.* Atheneum, 1981.

_____ *Selected Poems.* Atheneum, 1984.

_____ *Sweet Will.* Atheneum, 1985.

_____ *A Walk with Tom Jefferson.* Knopf, 1988.

_____ *New Selected Poems.* Knopf, 1991.

_____ *What Work Is.* Knopf, 1991.

_____ *The Simple Truth.* Knopf, 1994.

_____ *The Mercy.* Knopf, 1999.

_____ *Breath.* Knopf, 2004.

_____ *News of the World.* Knopf, 2009.

Maio, Samuel. *The Burning of Los Angeles.* Thomas Jefferson University Press, 1997.

Major, Clarence. *Swallow the Lake.* Wesleyan University Press, 1970.

_____ *Symptoms and Madness.* Corinth Books, 1971.

_____ *Private Line.* Paul Breman (UK), 1971.

_____ *The Cotton Club.* Broadside Press, 1972.

_____ *The Syncopated Cake Walk.* Barlenmir House, 1974.

_____ *Inside Diameter: The France Poems.* Permanent Press, 1985.

_____ *Surfaces and Masks.* Coffee House Press, 1988.

_____ *Some Observations of a Stranger at Zuni.* Sun and Moon Press, 1989.

_____ *Parking Lots.* Perishable Press, 1992.

_____ *Configurations: New and Selected Poems, 1958—1998.* Copper Canyon Press, 1999.

_____ *Waiting for Sweet Betty.* Copper Canyon Press, 2002.

_____ *Myself Painting.* Louisiana State University Press, 2008.

McGriff, Michael. *Dismantling the Hills.* University of Pittsburgh Press, 2008.

_____ Tomas Tranströmer's *The Sorrow Gondola* (translator). Green Integer, 2009.

McPherson, Sandra. *Elegies for the Hot Season.* Indiana University Press, 1970 (rpt. Ecco, 1982).

_____ *Radiation.* Ecco Press, 1973.

_____ *The Year of Our Birth.* Ecco Press, 1978.

_____ *Patron Happiness.* Ecco Press, 1983.

_____ *Streamers.* Ecco Press, 1988.

_____ *The God of Indeterminacy.* University of Illinois Press, 1993.

_____ *The Spaces Between Birds: Mother/Daughter Poems 1967—1995.* Wesleyan University Press, 1996.

_____ *Edge Effect: Trails and Portrayals.* Wesleyan University Press, 1996.

_____ *Expectation Days.* University of Illinois Press, 2007.

Muske-Dukes, Carol. *Camouflage.* University of Pittsburgh Press, 1975.

_____ *Skylight.* Doubleday, 1981.

_____ *Wyndmere.* University of Pittsburgh Press, 1985.

_____ *Applause.* University of Pittsburgh Press, 1989.

_____ *Red Trousseau.* Viking/Penguin, 1993.

_____ *An Octave Above Thunder.* Penguin, 1997.

_____ *Sparrow.* Random House, 2003.

Rose, Wendy. *Hopi Roadrunner, Dancing.* Greenfield Review Press, 1973.

_____ *Builder Kachina: A Home-Going Cycle.* Blue Cloud Quarterly, 1979.

_____ *Lost Copper.* Malki Museum Press, 1980.

_____ *Long Division: A Tribal History.* Strawberry Press, 1981.

_____ *What Happened When the Hopi Hit New York.* Contact II Publications, 1982.

_____ *Halfbreed Chronicles.* West End Press, 1985.

_____ *Going to War with All My Relations: New and Selected Poems.* Northland Publishing, 1993.

_____ *Now Poof She Is Gone.* Firebrand Books, 1994.

_____ *Bone Dance.* University of Arizona Press, 1994.

_____ *Itch Like Crazy.* University of Arizona Press, 2002.

Ryan, Kay. *Dragon Acts to Dragon Ends.* Taylor Street Press, 1983.

_____ *Strangely Marked Metal.* Copper Beech Press, 1985.

_____ *Say Uncle.* Grove Press, 1991.

_____ *Flamingo Watching*. Copper Beech Press, 1994.

_____ *Elephant Rocks*. Grove Press, 1996.

_____ *The Niagara River*. Grove Press, 2005.

Salazar, Dixie. *Hotel Fresno*. Blue Moon Press, 1988.

_____ *Reincarnation of the Common Place*. Salmon Run Press, 1999.

_____ *Blood Mysteries*. University of Arizona Press, 2003.

_____ *Flamenco Hips and Red Mud Feet*. University of Arizona Press, 2010.

Shuck, Kim. *Smuggling Cherokee*. Greenfield Review Press, 2006.

Simon, Maurya. *The Enchanted Room*. Copper Canyon Press, 1986.

_____ *Days of Awe*. Copper Canyon Press, 1989.

_____ *Speaking in Tongues*. Gibbs Smith Books, 1990.

_____ *The Golden Labyrinth*. University of Missouri Press, 1995.

_____ *A Brief History of Punctuation*. Sutton Hoo Press, 2002.

_____ *Ghost Orchid*. Red Hen Press, 2004.

_____ *Weavers* (with artist Baila Goldenthal). Blackbird Press, 2005.

_____ *Cartographies*. Red Hen Press, 2008.

_____ *The Raindrop's Gospel: The Trials of St. Jerome & St. Paula*. Elixir Press, 2009.

Soto, Gary. *The Elements of San Joaquin*. University of Pittsburgh Press, 1977.

_____ *The Tale of Sunlight*. University of Pittsburgh Press, 1978.

_____ *Where Sparrows Work Hard*. University of Pittsburgh Press, 1981.

_____ *Black Hair*. University of Pittsburgh Press, 1985.

_____ *A Fire in My Hands*. Scholastic, 1990.

_____ *Who Will Know Us?* Chronicle Books, 1990.

_____ *Home Course in Religion*. Chronicle Books, 1991.

_____ *Neighborhood Odes*. Harcourt Brace, 1992.

_____ *New and Selected Poems*. Chronicle Books, 1995.

_____ *Canto Familiar*. Harcourt Brace, 1995.

_____ *Junior College*. Chronicle Books, 1997.

_____ *A Natural Man*. Chronicle Books, 1999.

_____ *Fearless Fernie*. G.P. Putnam's Sons, 2002.

_____ *One Kind of Faith*. Chronicle Books, 2003.

_____ *Worlds Apart: Traveling with Fernie and Me*. G.P. Putnam's Sons, 2005.

_____ *A Fire in My Hands*. (expanded edition) Harcourt, 2006.

_____ *A Simple Plan*. Chronicle Books, 2007.

_____ *Partly Cloudy: Poems of Love and Longing*. Harcourt, 2009.

_____ *Human Nature*. Tupelo Press, 2010.

St. John, David. *Hush*. Houghton Mifflin Company, 1976.

_____ *The Shore*. Houghton Mifflin Company, 1980.

_____ *No Heaven*. Houghton Mifflin Company, 1985.

_____ *Terraces of Rain: An Italian Sketchbook*. Recursos Books (Santa Fe Literary Arts Center), 1991.

_____ *Study for the World's Body: New and Selected Poems*. HarperCollins, 1994.

_____ *In the Pines: Lost Poems (1972—1997)*. White Pine Press, 1999.

_____ *The Red Leaves of Night*. HarperCollins, 1999.

_____ *Prism*. Arctos Press, 2002.

_____ *The Face: A Novella in Verse*. HarperCollins, 2004.

Terris, Susan. *Curved Space*. La Jolla Poets Press, 1998.

_____ *Fire is Favorable to the Dreamer*. Arctos Press, 2003.

_____ *Natural Defenses*. Marsh Hawk Press, 2004.

_____ *Contrariwise*. Time Being Books, 2008.

Thomas, Amber Flora. *Eye of Water*. University of Pittsburgh Press, 2005.

Thompson, Lynne. *Beg No Pardon*. Perugia Press, 2007.

Young, Al. *The Song Turning Back Into Itself*. Holt Rinehart Winston, 1971.

_____ *Geography of the Near Past*. Holt Rinehart Winston, 1976.

_____ *The Blues Don't Change*. Louisiana State University Press, 1982.

_____ *Heaven: Collected Poems 1956—1990*. Creative Arts Book Co., 1992.

_____ *The Sound of Dreams Remembered: Poems 1990—2000*. Creative Arts Book Co., 2006.

_____ *Coastal Nights and Inland Afternoons: Poems 2001—2006*. Angel City Press, 2006.

## COLORADO

Anderson, Peter. *First Church of Higher Elevations: Mountains, Prayer, and Presence*. Ghost Road Press, 2005.

Anstett, Aaron. *Sustenance*. New Rivers Press, 1997.
_____ *No Accident*. Backwaters Press, 2005.
_____ *Each Place the Body's*. Ghost Road Press, 2007.

Beachy-Quick, Dan. *North True South Bright*. Alice James Books, 2003.
_____ *Spell*. Ahsahta Press, 2003.
_____ *Mulberry*. Tupelo Press, 2006.
_____ *This Nest, Swift Passerine*. Tupelo Press, 2009.

Crow, Mary. *Woman Who Has Sprouted Wings: Poems by Contemporary Latin American Women Poets* (edited with translation). Latin American Literary Review Press, 1984 (rpt.1987).
_____ *Borders*. BOA Editions, 1989.
_____ *From the Country of Nevermore by Jorge Teillier* (translator). Wesleyan University Press, 1990.
_____ *Vertical Poetry: Recent Poems of Roberto Juarroz* (translator). White Pine Press, 1991.
_____ *I Have Tasted the Apple*. BOA Editions, 1996.
_____ *Engravings Torn from Insomnia by Olga Orozco* (translator). Boa Editions, 2002.
_____ *Vertical Poetry: Last Poems of Roberto Juarroz* (translator). White Pine Press, 2010.

Goodtimes, Art. *Embracing the Earth*. Homeward Press, Berkeley, 1984.
_____ *As If the World Really Mattered*. La Alameda Press, 2007.

Gordon, Noah Eli. *The Frequencies*. Tougher Disguises, 2003.
_____ *The Area of Sound Called the Subtone*. Ahsahta Press, 2004.
_____ *Inbox*. BlazeVOX Books, 2006.
_____ *A Fiddle Pulled from the Throat of a Sparrow*. New Issues, 2007.
_____ *Figures for a Darkroom Voice* (with Joshua Marie Wilkinson). Tarpaulin Sky Press, 2007.
_____ *Novel Pictorial Noise*. Harper Perennial, 2007.

Hilberry, Jane. *Body Painting*. Red Hen Press, 2005.
_____ *This Awkward Art: Poems by a Father and Daughter* (with Conrad Hilberry). Mayapple Press, 2009.

Hutchison, Joseph. *The Undersides of Leaves*. Wayland Press, 1985.
_____ *House of Mirrors*. James Andrews & Co., 1992.
_____ *Bed of Coals*. University of Colorado Press, 1995.
_____ *The Rain at Midnight*. Sherman Asher Publishing, 2000.

Irwin, Mark. *Against the Meanwhile (3 Elegies)*. Wesleyan University Press, 1989.
_____ *Quick, Now, Always*. BOA Editions, 1996.
_____ *White City*. BOA Editions, 2000.
_____ *Bright Hunger*. BOA Editions. 2004.
_____ *Tall If*. New Issues Press, 2008.

King, Robert. *Old Man Laughing*. Ghost Road Press, 2007.

Krysl, Marilyn. *Saying Things*. University of Nebraska Press, 1978.
_____ *More Palomino, Please, More Fuchsia*. Cleveland State Poetry Center, 1980.
_____ *Diana Lucifera*. Shameless Hussy Press, 1983.
_____ *What We Have to Live With*. Teal Press, 1989.
_____ *Midwife*. National League for Nursing, 1989.
_____ *Soulskin*. National League for Nursing, 1996.
_____ *Warscape With Lovers*. Cleveland State Poetry Center, 1997.
_____ *Swear the Burning Vow: New and Selected Poems*. Ghost Road Press, 2009.

Luna, Sheryl. *Pity the Drowned Horses*. University of Notre Dame Press, 2005.

Mason, David. *The Buried Houses*. Story Line Press, 1991.
_____ *The Country I Remember*. Story Line Press, 1996.
_____ *Arrivals*. Story Line Press, 2004.
_____ *Ludlow: A Verse Novel*. Red Hen Press, 2007.

Melendez, Maria. *How Long She'll Last in This World*. University of Arizona Press, 2006.
_____ *Flexible Bones*. University of Arizona Press, 2010.

Phillis, Randy. *A Man Explains His Posture*. Best Minds Press, 1994.
_____ *Kismet, Colorado*. Mellen Poetry Press, 2000.

Rogers, Pattiann. *The Expectations of Light*. Princeton University Press, 1981.
_____ *The Tattooed Lady in the Garden*. Wesleyan University Press, 1986.
_____ *Legendary Performance*. Ion Press, 1987.
_____ *Splitting and Binding*. Wesleyan University Press, 1989.
_____ *Geocentric*. Peregrine-Smith, l993.
_____ *Firekeeper: New and Selected Poems*. Milkweed Editions, l994.
_____ *Eating Bread and Honey*. Milkweed Editions, l997.
_____ *A Covenant of Seasons* (with artist Joellyn Duesberry). Hudson Hills Press, l998.
_____ *The Dream of the Marsh Wren, Writing as Reciprocal Creation*. Milkweed
   Editions, 1999.
_____ *Song of the World Becoming: New and Collected Poems,1981—2001*. Milkweed
   Editions, 2001.
_____ *Generations*. Penguin Group, 2004.
_____ *Firekeeper: Selected Poems* (revised and expanded edition). Milkweed Editions, 2005.
_____ *Wayfare*. Penguin Group, 2009.
Root, William Pitt. *The Storm and Other Poems*. Atheneum, 1969.
_____ *Striking the Dark Air for Music*. Atheneum, 1973.
_____ *Coot and Other Characters*. Confluence, 1977.
_____ *In the World's Common Grasses*. Moving Parts Press, 1981.
_____ *Reasons for Going It on Foot*. Atheneum, 1981.
_____ *Invisible Guests*. Confluence Press, 1984.
_____ *Faultdancing*. University of Pittsburgh, 1986.
_____ *Trace Elements from a Recurring Kingdom: The First Five Books of William Pitt Root*.
   Confluence Press, 1994.
_____ *The Storm and Other Poems*. Carnegie Mellon, 2006.
_____ *White Boots: New and Selected Poems of the West*. Carolina Wren Press, 2006.
_____ *Welcome Traveler, Selected Early Odes of Pablo Neruda*. Wings Press, 2010.
Saner, Reg. *Climbing into the Roots*. Harper & Row, 1976.
_____ *So This Is the Map*. Random House, 1981.
_____ *Essay on Air*. Ohio Review Books, 1984.
_____ *Red Letters*. Quarterly Review of Literature, 1989.
Tomlinson, Rawdon. *Touching the Dead*. Libra Press, 1979.
_____ *Deep Red*. University of Central Florida Press, 1995.
_____ *Geronimo After Kas-ki-yeh*. Louisiana State University Press, 2007.
Tremblay, Bill. *Crying in the Cheap Seats*. University of Massachusetts Press, 1971.
_____ *The Anarchist Heart*. New Rivers Press, 1977.
_____ *Home Front*. Lynx House Press, 1978.
_____ *Second Sun: New & Selected Poems*. L'Epervier Press, 1985.
_____ *Duhamel: Ideas of Order in Little Canada*. BOA Editions, 1986.
_____ *Rainstorm over the Alphabet*. Lynx House Press, 2001.
_____ *Shooting Script: Door of Fire*. Eastern Washington University Press, 2003.
Uschuk, Pamela. *Light from Dead Stars*. Full Count, 1981.
_____ *Without Birds, Without Flowers, Without Trees*. Flume Press, 1991.
_____ *Finding Peaches in the Desert*. Wings Press, 2000.
_____ *One-Legged Dancer*. Wings Press, 2002.
_____ *Scattered Risks*. Wings Press, 2005.
_____ *Heartbeats in Stones*. Codhill Press, 2005.
_____ *Crazy Love*. Wings Press, 2009.

## IDAHO

Gildner, Gary. *First Practice*. University of Pittsburgh Press, 1969.
_____ *Digging for Indians*. University of Pittsburgh Press, 1972.
_____ *Letters from Vicksburg*. Unicorn, 1977.
_____ *The Runner*. University of Pittsburgh Press, 1978.
_____ *Jabón*. Brietenbush, 1981.
_____ *Blue Like the Heavens*. University of Pittsburgh Press, 1984.

_____ *Clackamas*. Carnegie Mellon University Press, 1991.

_____ *The Bunker in the Parsley Field*. University of Iowa Press, 1997.

_____ *Cleaning a Rainbow*. BkMk Press, 2007.

Johnson, William. *Out of the Ruins*. Confluence Press, 2000.

McFarland, Ron. *Composting at Forty*. Confluence Press, 1984.

_____ *The Haunting Familiarity of Things*. Singular Speech Press, 1993.

_____ *Stranger in Town: New and Selected Poems*. Confluence Press, 2000.

Midge, Tiffany. *Outlaws, Renegades and Saints: Diary of a Mixed-Up Halfbreed*. Greenfield Review Press, 1994.

Raptosh, Diane. *Just West of Now*. Guernica Editions, 1992.

_____ *Labor Songs*. Guernica Editions, 1999.

_____ *Parents from a Different Alphabet*. Guernica Editions, 2008.

Wrigley, Robert. *The Sinking of Clay City*. Copper Canyon Press, 1979.

_____ *Moon in a Mason Jar*. University of Illinois Press, 1986.

_____ *What My Father Believed*. University of Illinois Press, 1991.

_____ *In the Bank of Beautiful Sins*. Penguin, 1995.

_____ *Reign of Snakes*. Penguin, 1999.

_____ *Lives of the Animals*. Penguin, 2003.

_____ *Earthly Meditations: New and Selected Poems*. Penguin, 2006.

## MONTANA

Alcosser, Sandra. *A Fish to Feed All Hunger*. University of Virginia Press, l986 (rpt. Ahsahta Press 1993, 2000).

_____ *Sleeping Inside the Glacier*. Brighton Press, 1997.

_____ *Except by Nature*. Graywolf Press, 1998.

_____ *A Woman Hit by a Meteor*. Brighton Press, 2001.

_____ *Glyphs*. Brighton Press, 2001.

_____ *The Blue Vein*. Brighton Press, 2006.

Allen, Minerva. *Like Spirits of the Past Trying to Break Out and Walk to the West*. Wowapi Books, 1974.

_____ *Spirits Rest*. Graphics Art, 1981.

_____ *Minerva Allen's Indian Cookbook*. Wowapi Books, 1988.

_____ *Campfire Stories of the Fort Belknap Community*. Fort Belknap Schools, 1980.

_____ *Winter Smoke Poetry*. M.A. Press, 1996.

Blunt, Judy. *Not Quite Stone*. Merriam Frontier Foundation (University of Montana),1991.

Cahoon, Heather. *Elk Thirst*. Merriam Frontier Foundation (University of Montana), 2005.

Charlo, Victor. *Good Enough*. Many Voices Press, 2008.

Dunsmore, Roger. *On The Road to Sleep Child Hotsprings*. Pulp Press, 1971.

_____ *Bood House*. Pulp Press, 1987.

_____ *Tiger Hill*. Camphorweed Press, 2005.

_____ *You're Just Dirt*. FootHills Publishing, 2010.

Gibbons, Mark. *Connemara Moonshine*. Camphorweed Press, 2002.

_____ *blue horizon*. Two Dogs Press, 2007.

_____ *War, Madness, & Love*. R & R Publishing, 2008.

_____ *Mauvaises Herbs (Weeds)*. PROPOS/2 Editions, 2009.

Greene, Jennifer. *What I Keep*. Greenfield Review Press, 1999.

Haaland, Tami. *Breath in Every Room*. Story Lines Press, 2001.

Jaeger, Lowell. *War on War*. Utah State University Press, 1988.

_____ *Hope Against Hope*. Utah State University Press, 1990.

_____ *Poems Across the Big Sky* (anthology). Many Voices Press, 2007.

_____ *Suddenly Out of a Long Sleep*. Arctos Press, 2009.

_____ *New Poets of the American West* (Anthology). Many Voices Press, 2010.

_____ *WE*. Main Street Rag Publishing, 2010.

Kwasny, Melissa. *The Archival Birds*. Bear Star Press, 2000.

_____ *Thistle*. Lost Horse Press, 2006.

_____ *Reading Novalis in Montana*. Milkweed Editions, 2008.

_____ *I Go to The Ruined Place* (Anthology). Lost Horse Press, 2009.

_____ *The Nine Senses*. Milkweed Editions, 2011.

Lahey, Ed. *The Blind Horses*. Montana Arts Council, 1979.

_____ *Apples Rolling On the Lawn*. Montana Writing Cooperative, 1999.

_____ *The Blind Horses and Still More Poems*. University of Montana, 2001.

_____ *Birds of a Feather: The Complete Poems of Ed Lahey*. Clark City Press, 2005.

_____ *The Thin Air Gang*. Clark City Press, 2007.

Pack, Robert. *The Irony of Joy*. Scribners, 1955.

_____ *A Stranger's Privilege*. MacMillan, 1959.

_____ *Guarded by Women*. Random House, 1963.

_____ *Selected Poems*. Chattoand Windus (UK), 1964.

_____ *Home from the Cemetery*. Rutgers University Press, 1969.

_____ *Keeping Watch*. Rutgers University Press, 1969.

_____ *Nothing But Light*. Rutgers University Press, 1973.

_____ *Waking to My Name: New and Selected Poems*. Johns Hopkins University Press, 1980.

_____ *Faces in a Single Tree: A Cycle of Dramatic Monologues*. David Godine Press, 1984.

_____ *Clayfield Rejoices, Clayfield Laments: A Sequence of Poems*. David Godine Press, 1987.

_____ *Fathering the Map: New and Selected Later Poems*. University of Chicago Press, 1993.

_____ *Minding the Sun*. University of Chicago Press, 1996.

_____ *Rounding It Out*. University of Chicago Press, 1999.

_____ *Composing Voices: A Cycle of Dramatic Monologues*. Lost Horse Press, 2007.

_____ *Elk in Winter*. University of Chicago Press, 2007.

_____ *Still Here, Still Now*. University of Chicago Press, 2009.

Pape, Greg. *Border Crossings*. University of Pittsburgh Press, 1978.

_____ *Black Branches*. University of Pittsburgh Press, 1984. (rpt. Carnegie Mellon University Press, 2005)

_____ *Storm Pattern*. University of Pittsburgh Press, 1992.

_____ *Sunflower Facing the Sun*. University of Iowa Press, 1992.

_____ *American Flamingo*. Southern Illinois University Press, 2005.

Pinet, Carolyn. *Poesies*. Presses de Villejuif, 1998.

Smoker, M. L. *Another Attempt at Rescue*. Hanging Loose Press, 2005.

_____ *I Go To The Ruined Place* (Anthology). Lost Horse Press, 2009.

Thomas, David E. *Fossil Fuel*. Montana Writers Cooperative, 1977.

_____ *Buck's Last Wreck*. Wild Variety Books, 1996.

_____ *The Hellgate Wind*. Camphorweed Press, 2004.

Zarzyski, Paul. *Call Me Lucky*. Confluence Press, 1981.

_____ *The Make-Up of Ice*. University of Georgia Press, 1984.

_____ *Tracks*. The Kutenai Press, 1989.

_____ *Roughstock Sonnets*. The Lowell Press, 1989.

_____ *The Garnet Moon*. Black Rock Press, 1990.

_____ *I Am Not A Cowboy*. Dry Crik Press, 1995.

_____ *All This Way for The Short Ride*. Museum of New Mexico Press, 1996.

_____ *Blue-Collar Light*. Red Wing Press, 1998.

_____ *Wolf Tracks on The Welcome Mat*. Oreana Books, 2003.

_____ *Flight*. The Heavy Duty Press, 2004.

_____ *51: 30 Poems, 20 Songs, 1 Self-Interview*. Bangtail Press, 2010.

## NEVADA

Cowee, Bill. *Bones Set Against the Drift*. Black Rock Press, 1998.

Griffin, Shaun. *Desert Wood, An Anthology of Nevada Poets* (editor). University of Nevada Press, Reno, 1991.

_____ *Torn by Light: Selected Poems of Joanne de Longchamps* (editor). University of Nevada Press, Reno, 1993.

_____ *Snowmelt*. Black Rock Press, 1994.

_____ *Death to Silence*: *Poems by Emma Sepúlveda* (translator). Arte Público Press, 1997.

_____ *Bathing in the River of Ashes*. University of Nevada Press, Reno, 1999.

_____ *Woodsmoke, Wind, and the Peregrine*. Black Rock Press, 2008.

Hussa, Linda. *Where the Wind Lives*. Peregrine Smith Books, 1994.

_____ *Ride the Silence*. Black Rock Press, 2001.

_____ *Blood Sister, I Am to These Fields*. Black Rock Press, 2001.
_____ *Tokens in an Indian Graveyard*. Black Rock Press, 2008.
Keelan, Claudia. *Refinery*. Cleveland State University Press, 1994.
_____ *The Secularist*. University of Georgia Press, 1997.
_____ *Utopic*. Alice James Books, 2000.
_____ *Of & Among There Was a Locus(t)*. Ahsahta Press, 2003.
_____ *The Devotion Field*. Alice James Books, 2004.
_____ *Missing Her*. New Issues Press, 2009.
Liu, Stephan. *Dream Journeys to China*. New World Press (Beijing, China), 1982.
_____ *My Father's Martial Art*. University of Nevada Press, 2000.
Louis, Adrian C. *The Indian Cheap Wine Séance*. Gray Flannel Press, 1974.
_____ *Muted War Drums*. Blue Cloud Abbey, 1977.
_____ *Sweets for the Dancing Bears*. Blue Cloud Abbey, 1979.
_____ *Fire Water World*. West End Press, 1989.
_____ *Among the Dog Eaters*. West End Press, 1992.
_____ *Days of Obsidian, Days of Grace*. Poetry Harbor, 1994.
_____ *Blood Thirsty Savages*. Time Being Books, 1994.
_____ *Vortex of Indian Fevers*. Northwestern University Press, 1995.
_____ *Ceremonies of the Damned*. University of Nevada Press, 1997.
_____ *Skull Dance*. Bull Thistle Press, 1998.
_____ *Ancient Acid Flashes Back*. University of Nevada Press, 2000.
_____ *Bone & Juice*. Northwestern University Press, 2001.
_____ *Evil Corn*. Ellis Press, 2004.
_____ *Logorrhea*. Northwestern University Press, 2006.
Nightingale, Steven. *Cartwheels: 33 Sonnets*. Black Rock Press, 2003.
_____ *The Planetary Tambourine: 99 Sonnets*. Black Rock Press, 2006.
_____ *Cinnamon Theologies: 99 Sonnets*. Black Rock Press, 2008.
_____ *The Light in Them Is Permanent: 99 Sonnets*. Black Rock Press, 2009.
northSun, nila. *diet pepsi & nacho cheese*. Duck Down Press, 1977.
_____ *Coffee, Dust Devils and Old Rodeo Bulls* (with Kirk Robertson). Duck Down Press, 1979.
_____ *small bones, little eyes* (with Jim Sagel). Duck Down Press, 1981.
_____ *a snake in her mouth: poems, 1974—1996*. West End Press, 1997.
_____ *love at gunpoint*. R. L Crow Publications, 2007.
_____ *whipped cream & sushi*. Raindog Press, 2008.
Pahmeier, Gailmarie. *The House on Breakaheart Road*. University of Nevada Press, 1998.
_____ *West of Snowball, Arkansas and Home*. Red Hen Press, 2010.
Short, Gary. *Theory of Twilight*. Ahsahta Press, 1994.
_____ *Flying Over Sonny Liston*. University of Nevada Press, 1996.
_____ *10 Moons and 13 Horses*. University of Nevada Press, 2004.

## NEW MEXICO

Baca, Jimmy Santiago. *Immigrants in Our Own Land*. Louisiana State University Press, 1979.
_____ *Swords of Darkness*. Mango Publications, 1981.
_____ *Poems Taken from My Yard*. Timberline Press, 1986.
_____ *Martín and Meditations on the South Valley*. New Directions, 1987.
_____ *Black Mesa Poems*. New Directions, 1989.
_____ *Immigrants in Our Own Land*. New Directions, 1990.
_____ *Set This Book on Fire*. Cedar Hill Publications, 1999.
_____ *Healing Earthquakes: A Love Story in Poems*. Grove Press, 2001.
_____ *C-Train and 13 Mexicans*. Grove Press, 2002.
_____ *Winter Poems Along the Rio Grande*. New Directions, 2004.
_____ *Spring Poems Along the Rio Grande*. New Directions, 2007.
_____ *Selected Poems of Jimmy Santiago Baca*. New Directions, 2009.
Barnes, Jim. *The Fish on Poteau Mountain*. Cedar Creek Press, 1980.
_____ *The American Book of the Dead*. University of Illinois Press, 1982.
_____ *A Season of Loss*. Purdue University Press, 1985.
_____ *La Plata Cantata*. Purdue University Press, 1989.

_____ *The Sawdust War*. University of Illinois Press, 1992.

_____ *Paris*. University of Illinois Press, 1997.

_____ *On a Wing of the Sun*. University of Illinois Press, 2001.

_____ *Visiting Picasso*. University of Illinois Press, 2007.

Broyles, Marianne. *The Red Window*. West End Press, 2008.

Davis, Jon. *Dangerous Amusements*. Ontario Review Press, 1987.

_____ *Scrimmage of Appetite*. University of Akron, 1995.

_____ *Preliminary Report*. Copper Canyon Press, 2010.

Harjo, Joy. *What Moon Drove Me to This?* I Read Books, 1979.

_____ *She Had Some Horses*. Thunder's Mouth Press, 1984  (rpt. W.W. Norton, 2008).

_____ *The Woman Who Fell from the Sky*. W.W. Norton, 1989.

_____ *In Mad Love and War*. Wesleyan University Press, 1990.

_____ *The Good Luck Cat*. Harcourt, 2000.

_____ *A Map to the Next World*. W.W. Norton, 2000.

_____ *How We Became Human: New and Selected Poems*. W.W. Norton, 2003.

Hoge, Phyllis. *Artichoke and Other Poems*. University of Hawai'i Press, 1969.

_____ *The Creation Frame*. University of Illinois Press, 1973.

_____ *The Serpent of the White Rose*. Petronium Press, 1975.

_____ *What the Land Gave*. QRL Poetry Series III, 1981.

_____ *The Ghosts of Who We Were*. University of Illinois Press, 1986.

_____ *Letters from Jian Hui and Other Poems*. Wildflower Press, 2001.

Logghe, Joan. *Twenty Years with the Same Man*. La Alameda Press, 1995.

_____ *Catch Our Breath: Writing from the Heart of AIDS* (anthology). Mariposa Publishing, 1996.

_____ *Sofia*. La Alameda Press, 1999.

_____ *Blessed Resistance*. Mariposa Publishing, 1999.

_____ *Rice*. Tres Chicas Books, 2005.

Moldaw, Carol. *Chalkmarks on Stone*. La Alameda Press, 1998.

_____ *Through the Window*. La Alameda Press, 2000.

_____ *The Lightning Field*. Oberlin College Press, 2003.

_____ *So Late, So Soon: New and Selected Poems*. Etruscan Press, 2010.

Pettit, Michael. *American Light*. University of Georgia Press, 1984.

_____ *Cardinal Points*. University of Iowa Press, 1988.

_____ *Riding for the Brand*. University of Oklahoma Press, 2006.

Romero, Leo. *Agua Negra*. Ahsahta Press, 1981.

_____ *Celso*. Arte Publico Press, 1985.

_____ *Going Home Away Indian*. Ahsahta Press, 1990.

_____ *Rita and Los Angeles*. Bilingual Review Press, 1995.

Shukman, Henry. *In Dr. No's Garden*. Random House (UK), 2002.

Sze, Arthur. *The Willow Wind*. Rainbow Zenith Press, 1972.

_____ *Two Ravens*. Tooth of Time Press, 1976.

_____ *Dazzled*. Floating Island Press, 1982.

_____ *River River*. Lost Roads Press, 1987.

_____ *Archipelago*. Copper Canyon Press, 1995.

_____ *The Redshifting Web: Poems 1970—1998*. Copper Canyon Press, 1998.

_____ *The Silk Dragon: Translations from the Chinese*. Copper Canyon Press, 2001.

_____ *Quipu*. Copper Canyon Press, 2005.

_____ *The Ginkgo Light*. Copper Canyon Press, 2009.

Thiel, Diane. *Echolocations*. Story Line Press, 2000.

_____ *Writing Your Rhythm*. Story Line Press, 2001.

_____ *The White Horse: A Colombian Journey*. Etruscan Press, 2004.

_____ *Resistance Fantasies*. Story Line Press, 2004.

_____ *American Fugue* (translator). Etruscan Press, 2008.

Vargas, Richard. *Mclife*. Main Street Rag Publishing Company, 2005.

_____ *American Jesus*. Tia Chucha Press, 2007.

Wurth, Erika. *Indian Trains*. West End Press, 2007.

Yazzie, Venaya. *Saad Alk'elchi': Navajo and English Children's Poetry*. New Mexico Arts Council, 2006.

Andrews, Ginger. *An Honest Answer.* Story Line Press, 1999.
_____ *Hurricane Sisters.* Story Line Press, 2004.
Axelrod, David. *Jerusalem of Grass.* Ahsahta, 1992.
_____ *The Kingdom at Hand.* Ice River Press, 1993.
_____ *The Chronicles of the Withering State.* Ice River Press, 2004.
_____ *Troubled Intimacies: A Life in the Interior West.* Oregon State University Press, 2004.
_____ *The Cartographer's Melancholy.* Eastern Washington University Press, 2005.
_____ *Departing by a Broken Gate.* Ice River Press, 2009.
Carlile, Henry. *The Rough Hewn Table.* University of Missouri Press, 1971.
_____ *Running Lights.* Dragon Gate Press, 1981.
_____ *Rain.* Carnegie Mellon University Press, 1994.
Dickman, Matthew. *All-American Poem.* Copper Canyon Press, 2008.
Drake, Barbara. *Love at the Egyptian Theatre.* Red Cedar Press, 1978.
_____ *What We Say to Strangers.* Breitenbush Press, 1986.
_____ *Driving One Hundred.* Windfall Press Books, 2009.
Glazer, Michele. *It Is Hard to Look at What We Came to Think We'd Come to See.* University of Pittsburgh Press, 1997.
_____ *Aggregate of Disturbances.* University of Iowa Press, 2004.
Hongo, Garrett. *Yellow Light.* Wesleyan University Press, 1982.
_____ *The River of Heaven.* Knopf, 1988 (rpt. 1996).
_____ *Coral Road.* Knopf, 2011.
Husted, Bette Lynch. *At This Distance.* Wordcraft of Oregon, 2010.
Inada, Lawson. *Before the War: Poems as They Happened.* Morrow, 1971.
_____ *Legends from Camp.* Coffee House Press, 1992.
_____ *Drawing the Line.* Coffee House Press, 1997.
Laux, Dorianne. *What We Carry.* BOA Editions, 1994.
_____ *Smoke.* BOA Editions, 2000.
_____ *Facts about the Moon.* W.W. Norton, 2005.
_____ *Awake.* Eastern Washington University Press, 2007.
_____ *The Book of Men.* W.W. Norton, 2011.
McDowell, Robert. *Quiet Money.* Henry Holt & Co., 1987.
_____ *The Diviners: A Book-length Poem.* Peterloo Poets (UK), 1995.
_____ *On Foot, In Flames.* University of Pittsburgh Press, 2002.
Reyes, Carlos. *The Shingle Weaver's Journal.* Lynx House, 1980.
_____ *Nightmarks.* Lynx House, 1990.
_____ *A Suitcase Full of Crows.* Bluestem Press, 1995.
_____ *At the Edge of the Western Wave.* Lost Horse Press, 2004.
_____ *The Book of Shadows: New and Selected Poems.* Lost Horse Press, 2009.
Rutsala, Vern. *The Window.* Wesleyan University Press, 1964.
_____ *Laments.* New Rivers Press, 1975.
_____ *The Journey Begins.* University of Georgia Press, 1976.
_____ *Paragraphs.* Wesleyan University Press, 1978.
_____ *Walking Home from the Icehouse.* Carnegie Mellon University Press, 1981.
_____ *Backtracking.* Story Line Press, 1985.
_____ *Ruined Cities.* Carnegie Mellon University Press, 1987.
_____ *Selected Poems.* Story Line Press, 1991.
_____ *Little-Known Sport.* University of Massachusetts Press, 1994.
_____ *The Moment's Equation.* Ashland Poetry Press, 2004.
_____ *A Handbook for Writers: New and Selected Poems.* White Pine Press, 2004.
_____ *How We Spent Our Time.* Akron University Press, 2006.
Scates, Maxine. *Toluca Street.* University of Pittsburgh Press, 1989.
_____ *Black Loam.* Cherry Grove Collections, 2005.
_____ *Undone.* New Issues Press, 2011.
Schott, Penelope Scambly. *The Perfect Mother.* Snake Nation Press, 1994.
_____ *Penelope: The Story of the Half-Scalped Woman.* University Press of Florida, 1999.
_____ *The Pest Maiden: A Story of Lobotomy.* Turning Point Press, 2004.

_____ *Baiting the Void*. Dream Horse Press, 2005.
_____ *May the Generations Die in the Right Order*. Main Street Rag Publishing, 2007.
_____ *A is for Anne: Mistress Hutchinson Disturbs the Commonwealth*. Turning Point Press, 2007.
_____ *Six Lips*.  Mayapple Press, 2010.
Sears, Peter. *Tour*. Breitenbush Books, 1987.
_____ *The Brink*. Gibbs-Smith, 1999.
_____ *Green Diver*. CW Books, 2009.
Skloot, Floyd. *Music Appreciation*. University Press of Florida, 1994.
_____ *The Evening Light*. Story Line Press, 2001.
_____ *The Fiddler's Trance*. Bucknell University Press, 2001.
_____ *Approximately Paradise*. Tupelo Press, 2005.
_____ *The End of Dreams*. Louisiana State University Press, 2006.
_____ *Selected Poems: 1970—2005*. Tupelo Press, 2008.
_____ *The Snow's Music*. Louisiana State University Press, 2008.
St. John, Primus. *Skin On the Earth*. Copper Canyon Press, 1975.
_____ *Love Is Not a Consolation: It Is a Light*. Carnegie Mellon University Press, 1982.
_____ *Dreamer*. Carnegie Mellon University Press, 1990.
_____ *From Here We Speak* (with Ingrid Wendt). Oregon State University Press, 1994.
_____ *Communion*. Copper Canyon Press, 1999.
Stafford, Kim. *A Gypsy's History of the World*. Copper Canyon Press, 1976.
_____ *The Granary*. Carnegie-Mellon University Press, 1982.
_____ *Places & Stories*. Carnegie-Mellon University Press, 1987.
_____ *A Thousand Friends of Rain*. Carnegie-Mellon University Press, 1998.
Staton, Patricia. *The Woman Who Cries Speaks*. Lost Horse Press, 2008.
Steele, Pamela. *Paper Bird*. Wordcraft of Oregon, 2007.
Steinman, Lisa. *Lost Poems*. Ithaca House, 1976.
_____ *Made in America: Science, Technology, and American Modernist Poets*. Yale University Press, 1987.
_____ *All That Comes to Light*. Arrowood Books, 1989.
_____ *A Book of Other Days*. Arrowood Books, 1993.
_____ *Masters of Repetition: Poetry, Culture, and Work*. St. Martin's Press, 1998.
_____ *Carslaw's Sequences*. University of Tampa Press, 2003.
_____ *Invitation to Poetry: The Pleasures of Studying Poetry and Poetics*. Blackwell, 2008.
Waterston, Ellen. *Between Desert Seasons*. Wordcraft of Oregon, 2008.
Wendt, Ingrid. *Moving the House*. BOA Editions, 1980.
_____ *Singing the Mozart Requiem*. Breitenbush Books, 1987.
_____ *The Angle of Sharpest Ascending*. Word Press, 2004.
_____ *Surgeonfish*. WordTech Editions, 2005.
Witte, John. *Loving the Days*. Wesleyan University Press, 1978.
_____ *The Hurtling*. Orchises Press, 2005.
_____ *Second Nature*. University of Washington Press, 2008.
Woody, Elizabeth. *Hand into Stone*. Contact II Publications, 1990.
_____ *Luminaries of the Humble*. University of Arizona Press, 1994.
_____ *Seven Hands, Seven Hearts: Prose and Poetry*. Eighth Mountain Press, 1994.

## UTAH

Anderson, Sandra. *At the Edge in White Robes*. Ghost Planet Press, 1978.
_____ *Jeanne Was Once a Player of Pianos*. Limberlost Press, 1998.
Carney, Rob. *Weather Report*. Somondoco Press, 2006.
_____ *Boasts, Toasts, and Ghosts*. Pinyon Press, 2003.
Christiansen, Elaine Wright. *At the Edges*. Utah State Poetry Society, 1990.
_____ *I Have Learned 5 Things*. Lake Shore Publishing, 1996.
Coles, Katharine. *The One Right Touch*. Ahsahta Press, 1992.
_____ *A History of the Garden*. University of Nevada Press, 1996.
_____ *The Golden Years of the Fourth Dimension*. University of Nevada Press, 2001.
_____ *Fault*. Red Hen Press, 2008.
Coulbrooke, Star. *Logan Canyon Blend*. Blue Scarab Press, 2003.

Johnson, Kimberly. *Leviathan with a Hook*. Persea Books, 2002.

_____ *A Metaphorical God*. Persea Books, 2008.

_____ *Virgil's Georgics: A Poem of the Land*. Penguin Classics, 2009.

Larsen, Lance. *Erasable Walls*. New Issues, 1998.

_____ *In All Their Animal Brilliance*. University of Tampa Press, 2005.

_____ *Backyard Alchemy*. University of Tampa Press, 2009.

Lee, David. *The Porcine Legacy*. Copper Canyon Press, 1974.

_____ *Driving and Drinking*. Copper Canyon Press, 1979.

_____ *The Porcine Canticles*. Copper Canyon Press, 1984.

_____ *Day's Work*. Copper Canyon Press, 1990.

_____ *My Town*. Copper Canyon Press, 1995.

_____ *Covenants* (with William Kloefkorn). Spoon River Poetry Press, 1996.

_____ *A Legacy of Shadows: Selected Poems*. Copper Canyon Press, 1999.

_____ *News From Down to the Cafe: New Poems*. Copper Canyon Press, 1999.

_____ *So Quietly the Earth*. Copper Canyon Press, 2004.

_____ *Stone   Wind   Water*. Black Rock Press, 2009.

Minich, Jan. *History of Drowning*. Owl Creek Press, 1990.

_____ *The Letters of Silver Dollar*. City Art, 2002.

Rekdal, Paisley. *The Night My Mother Met Bruce Lee*. Pantheon, 2000 ( rpt.Vintage Books, 2002).

_____ *A Crash of Rhinos*. University of Georgia Press, 2000.

_____ *Six Girls Without Pants*. Eastern Washington University Press, 2002.

_____ *The Invention of the Kaleidoscope*. University of Pittsburgh Press, 2007.

Sajé, Natasha. *Red Under the Skin*. University of Pittsburgh Press, 1994.

_____ *Bend*. Tupelo Press, 2000.

Sowder, Michael. *The Empty Boat*. Truman State University Press, 2004.

Takacs, Nancy. *Pale Blue Wings*. Limberlost Press, 2001.

_____ *Preserves,* City Art Press, 2004.

_____ *Juniper*. Limberlost Press, 2010.

Whitt, Laurelyn. *interstices*. Logan House Press, 2006.


## WASHINGTON


Alexie, Sherman. *The Business of Fancydancing*. Hanging Loose Press, 1992.

_____ *I Would Steal Horses*. Slipstream, 1992.

_____ *First Indian on the Moon*. Hanging Loose Press, 1993.

_____ *Old Shirts & New Skins*. American Indian Studies Center, University of California Los Angeles, 1993.

_____ *Water Flowing Home*. Limberlost Press, 1995.

_____ *The Summer of Black Widows*. Hanging Loose Press, 1996.

_____ *The Man Who Loves Salmon*. Limberlost Press, 1998.

_____ *One Stick Song*. Hanging Loose Press, 2000.

_____ *Dangerous Astronomy*. Limberlost Press, 2005.

_____ *Face*. Hanging Loose Press, 2009.

Balk, Christianne. *Bindweed*. Macmillan, 1986.

_____ *Desiring Flight*. Purdue University Press, 1995.

Benson, Boyd. *The Owl's Ear*. Lost Horse Press, 2007.

Bell, Marvin. *Things We Dreamt We Died For*. Stone Wall Press, 1966.

_____ *A Probable Volume of Dreams*. Atheneum, 1969.

_____ *The Escape into You*. Atheneum, 1971.

_____ *Residue of Song*. Atheneum, 1974.

_____ *Stars Which See, Stars Which Do Not See*. Atheneum, 1977.

_____ *These Green-Going-to-Yellow*. Atheneum, 1981.

_____ *Segues: A Correspondence in Poetry* (with William Stafford). David R. Godine, 1983.

_____ *Drawn by Stones, by Earth, by Things That Have Been in the Fire*. Atheneum, 1984.

_____ *New and Selected Poems*. Atheneum, 1987.

_____ *Iris of Creation*. Copper Canyon Press, 1990.

_____ *A Marvin Bell Reader: Selected Poetry and Prose*. Middlebury College Press/University Press of New England, 1994.

_____ *The Book of the Dead Man*. Copper Canyon Press, 1994.

_____ *Ardor: The Book of the Dead Man, Vol. 2*. Copper Canyon Press, 1997.

_____ *Wednesday: Selected Poems 1966—1997*. Salmon Publishing (Ireland),1998.

_____ *Poetry for a Midsummer's Night*. Seventy-Fourth Street Productions, 1998.

_____ *Nightworks: Poems 1962—2000*. Copper Canyon Press, 2000.

_____ *Rampant*. Copper Canyon Press, 2004.

_____ *Mars Being Red*. Copper Canyon Press, 2007.

_____ *7 Poets, 4 Days, 1 Book* [with Istvan Laszlo Geher (Hungary), Ksenia Golubovich (Russia), Simone Inguanez (Malta), Christopher Merrill, Tomaz Salamun (Slovenia), and Dean Young)]. Trinity University Press, 2009.

Bertolino, James. *Employed*. Ithaca House, 1972.

_____ *Making Space for Our Living*. Copper Canyon Press, 1975.

_____ *The Gestures*. Bonewhistle Press, 1975.

_____ *The Alleged Conception*. Granite Publications, 1976.

_____ *New & Selected Poems*. Carnegie Mellon University Press, 1978.

_____ *Precinct Kali & The Gertrude Spicer Story*. New Rivers Press, 1982.

_____ *First Credo*. Quarterly Review of Literature Award Series, 1986.

_____ *Snail River*. Quarterly Review of Literature Award Series, 1995.

_____ *Pocket Animals*. Egress Studio Press, 2002.

_____ *Finding Water, Holding Stone*. Cherry Grove Collections, 2009.

Braden, Allen. *A Wreath of Down and Drops of Blood*. University of Georgia Press, 2010.

Bradfield, Elizabeth. *Interpretive Work*. Arktoi Books/Red Hen Press, 2008.

_____ *Approaching Ice*. Persea Books, 2009.

Derry, Alice. *Stages of Twilight*. Breitenbush,1986.

_____ *Clearwater*. Blue Begonia Press, 1997.

_____ *Strangers to Their Courage*. Louisiana State University Press, 2001.

_____ *Tremolo*. Red Hen Press, 2011.

Flenniken, Kathleen. *Famous*. University of Nebraska Press, 2006.

Germain, Carmen. *These Things I Will Take with Me*. Cherry Grove Collections, 2008.

Green, Samuel. *Gillnets*. Cold Mountain Press, 1978.

_____ *Vertebrae*, Eastern Washington University Press, 1994.

_____ *The Grace of Necessity*. Carnegie Mellon University Press, 2008.

Halperin, Mark. *Backroads*. University of Pittsburgh Press, l976.

_____ *A Place Made Fast*. Copper Canyon Press, 1982.

_____ *The Measure of Islands*. Wesleyan University Press, l990.

_____ *Time as Distance*. New Issues Press, 2001.

_____ *Falling Through the Music*. Notre Dame University Press, 2007.

Hamill, Sam. *Only Companion: Japanese Poems*. Shambhala, 1992.

_____ *Narrow Road to the Interior & Other Writings of Basho*. Shambhala, 1996.

_____ *Gratitude*. BOA Editions, 1998.

_____ *Crossing the Yellow River:300 Poems from the Chinese*. BOA Editions, 2000.

_____ *Dumb Luck*. BOA Editions, 2001.

_____ *Almost Paradise: New & Selected Poems & Translations*. Shambhala, 2005.

_____ *Poetry of Zen*. Shambhala, 2005.

_____ *Tao Te Ching*. Shambhala, 2006.

_____ *Measured by Stone*. Curbstone Press, 2007.

Hashimoto, Sharon. *The Crane Wife*. Story Line Press, 2003.

Howell, Christopher. *The Crime of Luck*. Panache Books, 1977.

_____ *Why Shouldn't I?* L'Epervier Press, 1978.

_____ *Though Silence: The Ling Wei Texts* (1st Ed.). L'Epervier Press, 1981.

_____ *Sea Change*. L'Epervier Press, 1985.

_____ *Sweet Afton*. True Directions, 1991.

_____ *Memory and Heaven*. Eastern Washington University Press, 1996.

_____ *Though Silence: The Ling Wei Texts* (2nd Ed.). Lost Horse Press, 1999.

_____ *Just Waking*. Lost Horse Press, 2003.

_____ *Light's Ladder*. University of Washington Press, 2004.

_____ *Poems New & Selected*. University of Washington Press, 2010.

_____ *Gaze*. Milkweed Editions, 2010.

Lieberman, Kim-An. *Breaking the Map*. Blue Begonia Press, 2008.

Martin, Terry. *The Secret Language of Women*. Blue Begonia Press, 2006.

McNamara, Robert. *Second Messengers*. Wesleyan University Press, 1990.

_____ *The Body & the Day*. David Robert Books, 2007.

Niatum, Duane. *After the Death of an Elder Klallam*. Baleen Press, 1970.

_____ *Ascending Red Cedar Moon*. Harper and Row, 1974.

_____ *Digging Out the Roots*. Harper and Row, 1977.

_____ *Songs for the Harvester of Dreams*. University of Washington Press, 1981.

_____ *Drawings of the Song Animals*. Holy Cow Press, 1991.

_____ *The Crooked Beak of Love*. West End Press, 2000.

Partridge, Dixie. *Deer in the Haystacks*. Ahsahta Press, 1984.

_____ *Watermark*. Saturday Press, 1991.

Perillo, Lucia. *Dangerous Life*. Northeastern University Press, 1989.

_____ *The Body Mutinies*. Purdue University Press, 1996.

_____ *The Oldest Map with the Name America*. Random House, 1999.

_____ *Luck Is Luck*. Random House, 2005.

_____ *Inseminating the Elephant*. Copper Canyon Press, 2009.

Peter Pereira. *Saying the World*. Copper Canyon Press, 2003.

_____ *What's Written on the Body*. Copper Canyon Press, 2007.

Potts, Charles. *Blues from Thurston County*. Grande Ronde Review, 1966.

_____ *Burning Snake*. Presna de Lager, 1967.

_____ *Little Lord Shiva*. Noh Directions Press, 1969.

_____ *The Litmus Papers*. Gunrunner Press, 1969.

_____ *Blue up the Nile*. Quixote, 1972.

_____ *Waiting in Blood*. Rainbow Resin Press, 1973.

_____ *The Trancemigraçion of Menzu*. Empty Elevator Shaft, 1973.

_____ *The Golden Calf*. Litmus Inc., 1975.

_____ *Charlie Kiot*. Folk Frog Press, 1976.

_____ *Rocky Mountain Man*. The Smith, 1978.

_____ *A Rite to the Body*. Ghost Dance Press, 1989.

_____ *The Dictatorship of the Environment*. Druid Books, 1991.

_____ *100 Years in Idaho*. Tsunami Inc., 1996.

_____ *Lost River Mountain*. Blue Begonia Press, 1999.

_____ *Little Lord Shiva: The Berkeley Poems, 1968*. Glass Eye Books, 1999.

_____ *Angio Gram*. D Press, 2000.

_____ *Nature Lovers*. Pleasure Boat Studio, 2000.

_____ *Slash and Burn*. (with Robert McNealy) Blue Begonia Press, 2001.

_____ *Lucintite*. Butcher Shop Press, 2002.

_____ *Across the North Pacific*. Slough Press, 2002.

_____ *Compostrella/Starfield*. Time Barn Books, 2004.

_____ *Kiot: Selected Early Poems 1963-1977*. Blue Begonia Press, 2005.

_____ *The Portable Potts*. West End Press, 2005.

_____ *Inside Idaho*. West End Press, 2009.

Powell, Joseph. *Hard Earth*. March Street Press, 2010.

_____ *Getting There*. The Quarterly Review of Literature, 1997.

_____ *Winter Insomnia*. Arrowood Books, 1993.

_____ *Counting the Change*. The Quarterly Review of Literature, 1986.

Ransom, Bill. *Finding True North & Critter*. Copper Canyon Press, 1974.

_____ *Waving Arms at the Blind*. Copper Canyon Press, 1976.

_____ *The Jesus Incident* (with Frank Herbert). Putnam/Berkley, 1979.

_____ *The Single Man Looks at Winter*. Empty Bowl Press, 1982.

_____ *Learning the Ropes*. Utah State University Press, 1995.

_____ *The Woman and the War Baby*. Blue Begonia Press, 2008.

Rich, Susan. *The Cartographer's Tongue*. White Pine Press, 2000.

_____ *Cures Include Travel*. White Pine Press, 2006.

_____ *The Alchemist's Kitchen*. White Pine Press, 2010.

Skillman, Judith. *Worship of the Visible Spectrum*. Breitenbush Books, 1988.

_____ *Beethoven and the Birds*. Blue Begonia Press, 1996.

_____ *Storm*. Blue Begonia Press, 1998.

_____ *Sweetbrier*. Blue Begonia Working Signs Series, 2001.

_____ *Red Town*. Silverfish Review Press, 2001.

_____ *Circe's Island*. Silverfish Review Press, 2003.

_____ *Latticework*. David Robert Books, 2004.

_____ *Opalescence*. David Robert Books, 2005.

_____ *Coppelia, Certain Digressions*. David Robert Books, 2006.

_____ *Heat Lightning: New and Selected Poems 1986—2006*. Silverfish Review Press, 2006.

_____ *Prisoner of the Swifts*. Ahadada Books, 2009.

_____ *The Never*. Dream Horse Press, 2010.

Spence, Michael. *The Spine*. Purdue University Press, 1987.

_____ *Adam Chooses*. Rose Alley Press, 1998.

_____ *Crush Depth*. Truman State University Press, 2009.

Toledo, Eugenia. *Architecture of Absences*. Editorial Torremozas (Spain), 2006.

_____ *Time of Metals and Volcanoes*. Editorial 400 Elefantes (Nicaragua), 2007.

Wilcox, Finn. *Here among the Sacrificed*. Empty Bowl Press, 1984.

_____ *Working the Woods, Working the Sea: An Anthology of Northwest Writings*. Empty Bowl Press, 2008.

Wagoner, David. *Dry Sun, Dry Wind*. Indiana University Press, 1953.

_____ *A Place to Stand*. Indiana University Press, 1958.

_____ *Poems*. Portland Art Museum, 1959.

_____ *The Nesting Ground*. Indiana University Press, 1963.

_____ *Staying Alive*. Indiana University Press, 1966.

_____ *New and Selected Poems*. Indiana University Press, 1969.

_____ *Working Against Time*. Rapp & Whiting (UK) 1970.

_____ *Riverbed*. Indiana University Press, 1972.

_____ *Sleeping in the Woods*. Indiana University Press, 1974.

_____ *A Guide to Dungeness Spit*. Graywolf Press, 1975.

_____ *Traveling Light*. Graywolf Press, 1976.

_____ *Collected Poems 1956—1976*. Indiana University Press, 1976.

_____ *Who Shall Be the Sun?* Indiana University Press, 1978.

_____ *In Broken Country*. Little, Brown, 1979.

_____ *Landfall*. Little, Brown, 1981.

_____ *First Light*. Little, Brown, 1983.

_____ *Through the Forest: New and Selected Poems 1977—1987*. Atlantic Monthly Press, 1987.

_____ *Walt Whitman Bathing*. University of Illinois Press, 1996.

_____ *Traveling Light: Collected and New Poems*. University of Illinois Press, 1999.

_____ *The House of Song*. University of Illinois Press, 2002.

_____ *Good Morning and Good Night*. University of Illinois Press, 2005.

Wright, Carolyne. *Stealing the Children*. Ahsahta Press, 1992.

_____ *Premonitions of an Uneasy Guest*. Hardin-Simmons UP, 1983.

_____ *In Order to Talk with the Dead: Selected Poems of Jorge Teillier*. (translator) University of Texas Press, 1993.

_____ *The Game in Reverse: Poems by Taslima Nasrin* (Translator). George Braziller, Inc., 1995.

_____ *Another Spring, Darkness: Poems of Anuradha Mahapatra* (Translator). Calyx Books, 1996.

_____ *Seasons of Mangoes and Brainfire*. Eastern Washington University Press, 2000.

_____ *A Change of Maps*. Lost Horse Press, 2006.

_____ *Majestic Nights: Love Poems of Bengali Women* (Anthology, Translator). White Pine Press, 2008.

## WYOMING

Hix, H .L. *Perfect Hell*. Gibbs Smith, 1996.

_____ *Rational Numbers*. Truman State University Press, 2000.

_____ *Surely As Birds Fly*. Truman State University Press, 2002.

_____ *Shadows of Houses*. Etruscan Press, 2005.

_____ *Chromatic*. Etruscan Press, 2006.

_____ *God Bless: A Political/Poetic Discourse*. Etruscan Press, 2007.

_____ *Legible Heavens*. Etruscan Press, 2008.

Moore, Bo. *Parched: Poetry of Wyoming*. Dexa! Dog Books, 2008.

Northrup, Kate. *Back Through Interruption*. Kent State University Press, 2002.

_____ *Things Are Disappearing Here*. Persea Books, 2007.

Rea, Tom. *Man in a Rowboat*. Copper Canyon Press, 1977.

_____ *Smith and Other Poems*. Dooryard Press, 1985.

Romtvedt, David. *Moon* (illustrated by R. W. Scholes). Bieler Press, 1984.

_____ *How Many Horses*. Ion Books, 1988.

_____ *Yip, a Cowboy's Howl*. Holocene Books, 1991.

_____ *Crossing Wyoming*. White Pine Press, 1992.

_____ *A Flower Whose Name I Do Not Know*. Copper Canyon Press, 1992.

_____ *Certainty: Poems*. White Pine Press, 1996.

_____ *Deep West: A Literary Tour of Wyoming* (Anthology with co-editors Michael Shay and Linn Rounds). Pronghorn Press, 2003.

_____ *Some Church*. Milkweed Editions, 2005.

Roripaugh, Robert. *Learn to Love the Haze*. Spirit Mound Press, 1976 (rpt. High Plains Press, 1996).

_____ *The Ranch: Wyoming Poetry*. University of Wyoming, 2001.

Senior-Trask, Dawn. *Moonhorses and the Red Bull* (with B.J. Buckley). Pronghorn Press, 2006.

# Acknowledgments:

Addonizio, Kim. "Yes" and "In the Evening" published in *Lucifer at Starlight* (W.W. Norton, 2009). Copyright Kim Addonizio 2009. Reprinted with author's permission.

Aho, Margaret. "to be flanking the petiole" published in *Beloit Poetry Journal,* Vol. 59, No. 1 Fall, 2008.

Alcosser, Sandra. "Spittle Bug" and "Glory Monster" published in *Except by Nature* (Graywolf Press, 1998). Reprinted with author's permission.

Alexie, Sherman. "Wreck League" published in *River Styx* 80.

Andrews, Ginger. "Prayer" and "Rolls-Royce Dreams" published in *An Honest Answer* (Story Line Press, 1999). Reprinted with author's permission.

Anstett, Aaron. "Prayer Against Dying On Camera" published in *No Accident* (Backwaters Press, 2005). Reprinted with author's permission.

Anstett, Aaron. "Indeed I Was" published in *Each Place the Body's* (Ghost Road Press, 2007). Reprinted with author's permission.

Archila, William. "Blinking Lights" published in *Clackamas Literary Review,* 2009.

Atsitty, Tacey. "The waves and winds still know/ His voice who ruled them while He dwelt below" from "Be Still My Soul" by Katharina von Schlegel. Translated by Jane Borthwick.

Baca, Jimmy Santiago. "VIII" and "XXVI" published in *Selected Poems of Jimmy Santiago Baca* (New Directions, 2009). Copyright 2009 by Jimmy Santiago Baca. Reprinted by permission of New Directions Publishing Corp.

Bakken, Dick. "Going into Moonlight" published in *Ploughshares,* Vol. 16, No. 1, 1990.

Barnes, Jim. "Autobiography, Chapter 5" published in *Wing of the Sun* (University of Illinois Press, 2001). Reprinted with author's permission.

Barnes, Jim. "Paiute Ponies" published in *Visiting Picasso* (University of Illinois Press, 2007). Reprinted with author's permission.

Bass, Ellen. "Gate 22" published in *The Human Line*. Copyright 2007 by Ellen Bass. Reprinted with the permission of Copper Canyon Press. www.coppercanyonpress.org.

Bass, Ellen. "Ode to Dr. Ladd's Black Slit Skirt" published in *American Poetry Review*, January 2009.

Beachy-Quick, Dan. "Walking Through the Room" published in the *Virginia Quarterly Review*.

Bell, Marvin. "The Book of the Dead Man (The Northwest)" published in *Poetry Northwest*.

Bertolino, James. "Sun Worship" published in *Greatest Hits: 1965—2000* (Pudding House, 2000). Reprinted with author's permission.

Blunt, Judy. "Showdown" and " When Cowboys Cry" published in *Not Quite Stone*. Merriam Frontier Foundation (University of Montana, 1991). Reprinted with author's permission.

Blunt, Judy. "When Cowboys Cry" published in *Graining the Mare: The Poetry of Ranch Women*. Teresa Jordan, editor. (Peregrine/Gibbs Smith, 1994). Reprinted with author's permission.

Braden, Allen. "The Hemlock Tree" published in *The Georgia Review*.

Braden, Allen. "Grinding Grain" published in *North American Review*.

Bradfield, Elizabeth. "Multi-Use Area" published in *Interpretive Work* (Arktoi Books/Red Hen Press, 2008). Reprinted with author's permission.

Buckley, Christopher. "Off Shore" published in *Fall From Grace* (Bk Mk Press, University of Missouri Kansas City, 1998). Reprinted with author's permission.

Cahoon, Heather. "Rescue at L8000 Road" published in *Elk Thirst*. Merriam Frontier Foundation (University of Montana, 2005). Reprinted with author's permission.

Carlile, Henry. "Nature" published in *Poetry*.

Carter, Jefferson. "A Centaur" published in *Sentimental Blue* (Chax Press, 2007).

Chin, Marilyn. "Formosan Elegy" published in *Northwest Review*.

Chin, Marilyn. "Yam Gruel" published in *Harvard Review*.

Christiansen, Elaine Wright. "Inside" and "I Have Learned Five Things" published in *I Have Learned 5 Things* (Lake Shore Publishing, 1995). Reprinted with author's permission.

Cotter, Craig. "5/23/96," published in *Chopstix Numbers*. Copyright 2000 by Craig Cotter. Reprinted by permission of Ahsahta Press.

Coulbrooke, Star. "How I Stopped Selling Life Insurance" published in *Creosote,* Vol. 2, No. 1. Also in *Logan Canyon Blend* (Blue Scarab Press, 2003).

Crow, Mary. "Marfa, Texas" published in *Marginalia.*

Crow, Mary. "Saturday Matinee" and "Fault Finding" published in *I Have Tasted the Apple* (BOA Editions, 1996). Reprinted with author's permission.

Davis, Jon. "Loving Horses" published in *Ontario Review.* Also anthologized in *Cadence of Hooves: A Celebration of Horses* (Yarrow Mountain Press, 2008) and *The 2010 Poetry Calendar* (Alhambra Press, Belgium, 2009). Reprinted with author's permission.

Davis, Jon. "Horse in Shadow" published in the *Oregon Literary Review* (online). Also anthologized in *Cadence of Hooves: A Celebration of Horses* (Yarrow Mountain Press, 2008). Reprinted with author's permission.

Day, Lucille Lang. "710 Ashbury, 1967" published in *The Curvature of Blue* (Cervena Barva, 2009). Reprinted with author's permission.

Dickman, Matthew. "Some Days" published in *American Poetry Review.* Also published in *All-American Poem* (Copper Canyon Press, 2008). Reprinted with permission of Copper Canyon Press, www.coppercanyonpress.org

Dofflemyer, John. "I Owe My Soul" published in *Poems from Dry Creek* (Starhaven, 2008). Reprinted with author's permission.

Dowell, Theresa Chuc. "Names" published in *Babel Fruit,* 2009.

Drake, Barbara. "Driving One Hundred" published in *Left Bank #2*, Summer 1992. Also published in *Driving 100* (Windfall Press Books, 2009).

Dunsmore, Roger. "You're Just Dirt" published in *You're Just Dirt* (FootHills Press, 2010). Reprinted with author's permission.

Dunsmore, Roger. "A True War Story" published in *Drumlummon Views.*

Espinoza, John Olivares. "Aching Knees in Palm Springs" published in *The Date Fruit Elegies* (Bilingual Press, 2008).

Flenniken, Kathleen. "Whole-Body Counter, Marcus Whitman Elementary" and "Going Down" published in *The Iowa Review*, 2007.

Flenniken, Kathleen. "Herb Parker Feels Like Dancing" published in *Prairie Schooner*, 2008.

Fristad, Erin. "Advice to Female Deckhands" published in *StringTown,* No. 8.

Fristad, Erin. "What's Left" published in *Americas Review,* No. 14.

Germain, Carmen. "April, Seattle to Missoula" published in *Crab Creek Review*, 1999.

Gibbons, Mark. "Back Into Rock" published in *blue horizon* (Two Dogs Press, 2007). Reprinted with author's permission.

Gildner, Gary. "Spring Evenings" published in *The Georgia Review.*

Gildner, Gary. "The Wolverine" published in *The Bunker in the Parsley Fields* (University of Iowa Press, 1997). Reprinted with author's permission.

Gildner, Gary. "Cleaning the Rainbow" and "Ella" published in *Cleaning the Rainbow* (BkMk Press, 2007). Reprinted with author's permission.

Glazer, Michele. "To the Better View" published in *Gulf Coast,* No. 19, 2007.

González, Rafael Jesús. "A Una Anciana" published in *New Mexico Quarterly,* Vol. XXXI, No. 4, 1961.

Goodtimes, Art. "Skinning the Elk" published in *As If the World Really Mattered* (La Alameda Press, 2007). Reprinted with author's permission.

Green, Sam. "Grandmother Cleaning Rabbits" published in *Alaska Quarterly Review.*

Haaland, Tami. "Not Scientifically Verifiable" published in *Breath in Every Room* (Story Line Press, 2001). Reprinted with author's permission.

Haaland, Tami. "Liar" published in *5AM.*

Hales, Corrine Clegg. "Out of This Place" and "Covenant: Atomic Energy Commission, 1950s" published in *Separate Escapes* (Ashland Poetry Press, 2002). Reprinted with author's permission.

Halperin, Mark. "Fasting on Yom Kippur" published in *A Place Made Fast* (Copper Canyon Press, 1982). Reprinted with author's permission.

Halperin, Mark. "Accident" published in *Falling through the Music* (University of Notre Dame Press, 2007). Reprinted with author's permission.

Harjo, Joy. "Eagle Poem" and "Songline of Dawn" and "Perhaps the World Ends Here" and "Rainy Dawn" published in *How We Became Human: New and Selected Poems* (W.W. Norton, 2003). Reprinted with author's permission.

Hedge Coke, Allison. "Street Confetti" published in *Streetnotes Online Literary Magazine.*

Hashimoto, Sharon. "Because You Showed Me a Piece of Barbed Wire" and "Wonder Bread" published in *The Crane Wife* (Story Line Press, 2003). Reprinted with author's permission.

Hilberry, Jane. "The Moment" published in *The Hudson Review.* Also in *Body Painting* (Red Hen Press, 2005). Reprinted with author's permission.

Hirshfield, Jane. "First Light Edging Cirrus" published in *The Harvard Review.*

Hirshfield, Jane. "French Horn" published in *The New Yorker.*

Hirshfield, Jane. "Green Striped Melons" published in *The Alaska Quarterly Review.*

Hirshfield, Jane. "The Dark Hour" published in *Poetry Review* (UK).

Hix, H .L. "Spring" and "Summer" and "Fall" and "Winter" published in *Shadows of Houses* (Etruscan Press, 2005). Reprinted with author's permission.

Hogue, Cynthia. "That Wild Chance of Living (2001)" published in *The Salt River Review,* 2003. Also in *The Incognito Body* (Red Hen Press, 2006). Reprinted with author's permission.

Howell, Christopher. "Burning Bush" published in *Gettysburg Review*, 2005.

Howell, Christopher. "Greenhouse Sparks and Snow" published in *Southern Reveiw*, 2006.

Howell, Christopher. "Desperados" published in *Hubbub*, 2008.

Hussa, Linda. "The Weir" and "On a Clean, Cold Calving Night" and "Love Letters" published in *Blood Sister, I Am To These Fields* (Black Rock Press, 2001).

Hutchison, Joe. "Black River" published in *Poetry*, September 1993. Also in *The Rain at Midnight* (Sherman Asher Publishing, 2000). Reprinted with author's permission.

Hutchison, Joe. "From a Swaying Hammock" published in *Chatauqua Literary Journal*, Fall 2006.

Inman, Will. "The Bones that Humans Lacked" and "given names" published in *Leaps & Hope & Fury* (Howling Dog Press, 2008).

Inman, Will. "mesquite mother territory" and "To Catch the Truth" published in *I Read You Green, Mother* (Howling Dog Press, 2008)

Jaeger, Lowell. "My Neighbor" published in *Whitefish Review, Palo Alto Review*, and *Studio One.*

Jaeger, Lowell. "The Missionary" published in *StringTown.*

Jaeger, Lowell. "My Neighbor" and "The Missionary" and "Mother Said" published in *WE* (Main Street Rag Publishing, 2010).

Jaffe, Maggie. "Sign of the Times" published in *Flic(k)s: Poetic Interrogations of American Cinema* (Red Dragonfly Press, 2009). Reprinted with author's permission.

Johnson, Kimberly. "Pater Noster" published in *Leviathan with a Hook* (Persea Books, 2002). Reprinted with author's permission.

Johnson, Kimberly. "Voluptuary" published in *A Metaphorical God* (Persea Books, 2008). Reprinted with author's permission.

Johnson, William. "New Year's Eve" published in *Out of the Ruins* (Confluence Press, 2000). Reprinted with author's permission.

Keithley, George. "The Red Bluff Rodeo" published in *Song in a Strange Land* (George Braziller, 1974). Reprinted with author's permission.

King, Robert. "About Eight Minutes of Light in the Meadow" published in *Poetry,* Vol. CLXXVIII, No. 2, May 2001.

King, Robert. "Now" published in *Many Mountains Moving,* Vol. 8, No.1, 2007-2008.

Kowit, Steve. "Kiss" published in *The Dumbbell Nebula* (Roundhouse Press/Heyday Books, 2000). Reprinted with author's permission.

Krysl, Marilyn. "Sacrament: Central Bus Station" published in *Swear the Burning Vow: Selected and New Poems* (Ghost Road Press, 2009). Reprinted with author's permission.

Krysl, Marilyn. "Love, That Hugeness" and "Song of Some Ruins" published in *Prairie Schooner*, Vol. 82 No. 2, 2008.

Kwasny, Melissa. "Chokecherries" and "Iris" published in *Thistle* (Lost Horse Press, 2006). Reprinted with author's permission.

Lahey, Ed. "The Blind Horses" and "Gimp O'Leary's Ironworks" and "Inside Her" published in *Birds of a Feather* (Clark City Press, 2005). Reprinted with author's permission.

Lahey, Ed. "Moving" published in *Poems Across the Big Sky: An Anthology of Montana Poets.* (Many Voices Press, 2007). Reprinted with author's permission.

Larsen, Lance. "American" published in *Crab Orchard Review.*

Larsen, Lance. "Like a Wolf" published in *Nimrod.*

Lee, David. "Racehogs" and "The Tale of the Graveblaster" published in *The Porcine Canticles.* Copyright ©1984 by David Lee. Reprinted with permission of Copper Canyon Press, www.coppercanyonpress.org.

Levine, Philip. "Words on the Wind" published in *Georgia Review.*

Levine, Philip. "1934" published in *The New Yorker.*

Lieberman, Kim-An. "Translation" published in *CALYX,* 2002.

Lieberman, Kim-An. "Translation" and "Swallows Nesting" published in *Breaking the Map* (Blue Begonia Press, 2008). Reprinted with author's permission.

Liu, Stephen. "A Mid-July Invitation" published in *California Quarterly*, Winter 1977.

Louis, Adrian C. "In The Colony" published in *Chiron Review*, Spring 2008.

Louis, Adrian C. "Approximate Haiku, 1980" published in *Yellow Medicine Review*, Winter 2008.

Luna, Sheryl. "Los Almas" published in *Pity the Drowned Horses* (University of Notre Dame Press, 2005). Reprinted with author's permission.

McNamara, Robert. "Winter, Tulalip Shores" published in *Jeopardy.* Also in *The Body & the Day* (David Robert Books, 2007). Reprinted with author's permission.

Maio, Samuel. "South Central L.A." published in *New Mexico Humanities Review*. Also in *The Burning of Los Angeles* (Thomas Jefferson University Press, 1997). Reprinted with the author's permission.

Maio, Samuel. "Pleasanton Villanelle" published in *The Formalist,* Vol. 13, No 2, 2002.

Major, Clarence. "Photograph of a Gathering of People Waving" from *Waiting for Sweet Betty.* Copyright 2002 by Clarence Major. Reprinted with the permission of Copper Canyon Press, coppercanyonpress.org.

Major, Clarence. "The Doll Believers" from *Configurations*: *New and Selected Poems 1958—1998.* Copyright 1998 by Clarence Major. Reprinted with the permission of Copper Canyon Press, coppercanyonpress.org.

Manwaring, Marjorie. "Treasure" published in *Mirror Northwest* and *Northwind Anthology* 2005. Reprinted with author's permission.

Martin, Terry. "September Ripens and So Do We" published in *StringTown* 11.

Mason, David. "Fog Horns" published in *Poetry*, September 2004.

Mason, David. "Home Care" published in *Times Literary Supplement*, October 29, 2004.

McGriff, Michael. "Seasons between Night and Day" and "Buying and Selling" published in *Dismantling the Hills* (University of Pittsburgh Press, 2008). Reprinted with author's permission.

McPherson, Sandra. "Grouse" from *Expectation Days.* Copyright 2007 by Sandra McPherson. Used with permission of the poet and the University of Illinois Press.

McPherson, Sandra. "Phlox Diffusa," from *Edge Effect* (Wesleyan University Press, 1996). Copyright 1996 by Sandra McPherson and reprinted by permission of Wesleyan University Press.

Melendez, Maria. "Recipe" and "Backcountry, Emigrant Gap" published in *How Long She'll Last in This World.* (University of Arizona Press, 2006). Reprinted with author's permission.

Midge, Tiffany. "After Viewing the Holocaust Museum's Room of Shoes and a Gallery of Plains Indian Moccasins" published in *Cold Mountain Review,* Vol. 34, No.1, 2005.

Miller, Jane. "xii" excerpted from *Midnights* (Saturnalia Press, 2008). Reprinted with author's permission.

Moldaw, Carol. "Festina Lente" published in *Conjunctions.* Also published in *The Lightning Field* (Oberlin College Press, 2003). Reprinted with author's permission.

Moldaw, Carol. "Out of the West" published in *Ars Interpres.* Also published in *So Late, So Soon: New and Selected Poems* (Etruscan Press, 2010). Reprinted with author's permission.

Moore, Bo. "Forecast" published in *High Plains Register* Vol 14, 2004.

Muske-Dukes, Carol. "Condolence Note: Los Angeles" published in *Paris Review*.

Natal, Jim. "The Half-Life of Memory" published in *Memory and Rain* (Red Hen Press, 2009). Reprinted with author's permission.

Nevin, Sean. "Wildfire Triptych" and "The Carpenter Bee" published in *Oblivio Gate* (Southern Illinois University Press, 2008). Reprinted with author's permission.

Niatum, Duane. "A Tribute to Chief Joseph" published in *After the Death of an Elder Klallam* (Baleen Press, 1970). Reprinted with author's permission.

Niatum, Duane. "Digging Out the Roots" published in *Ascending Red Cedar Moon* (Harper and Row, 1970). Reprinted with author's permission.

Northrup, Kate. "Night Drive" published in *Raritan*.

Northrup, Kate. "Winter Prairie" published in *The Massachusetts Review,* Vol. XLVIII, No. 3, Fall 2007.

Pahmeier, Gailmarie. "Home Maintenance" published in *Mudfish* No. 10, 1997. Also published in *West of Snowball, Arkansas and Home* (Red Hen Press, 2010). Reprinted with author's permission.

Pape, Greg. "Storm Pattern" published in *Storm Pattern* (University of Pittsburgh Press, 1992). Reprinted with author's permission.

Partridge, Dixie. "About Stones" published in *The Georgia Review* Vol. 51 No 3, Fall 1997.

Partridge, Dixie. "Fish" published in *Writer's Forum,* Vol. 11, Fall 1985.

Pettit, Michael. "Driving Lesson" and "Sparrows of Española." published in *Cardinal Points.* (University of Iowa Press, 1988). Reprinted with author's permission.

Potts, Charles. "Starlight on the Trail" published in *Dry Crik Review*. Also published in *Maverick Western Verse* (Gibbs-Smith, 1994). Also published in *The Portable Potts* (West End Press, 2005). Also published in *Inside Idaho* (West End Press, 2009). Reprinted with author's permission.

Powell, Joseph. "Pecking Order" published in *Pontoon* VII.

Powell, Joseph. "The Apple-Heifer" published in *Colere*.

Ransom, Bill. "Shooting the Thief" published in *The Woman and the War Baby* (Blue Begonia Press, 2008). Reprinted with author's permission.

Raptosh, Diane. "Husband" published in *Fraglit: An Online Magazine of Fragmentary Writing,* No. 2, Spring 2008.

Ray, David. "Arizona Satori" published in *Arizona Illustrated,* December 2006.

Ray, David. "The Sleepers" and "Illegals" published in *When* (Howling Dog Press, 2007).

Rea, Tom. "The Black and the Dazzle" published in *Smith and Other Poems* (Dooryard Press, 1985). Reprinted with author's permission.

Red Elk, Lois. "Porcupine on the Highway" published in *Vermillion Literary Project* (University of South Dakota, 2001).

Rekdal, Paisley. "A Small, Soul-Colored Thing" published in *The Journal*.

Reyes, Carlos. "The Old West" published in *A Suitcase Full of Crows* (Bluestem, 1995).

Rich, Susan. "Mohamud at the Mosque" published in *Cures Include Travel* (White Pine Press, 2006). Reprinted with author's permission.

Rios, Alberto. "Border Lines" published in *Virginia Quarterly Review*.

Rios, Alberto. "Rabbits and Fire" published in *Quarterly West*.

Rogers, Pattiann. "For the Moral of the Story" published in *Wayfare* (Penguin, 2008). Reprinted with author's permission.

Rogers, Pattiann. "In General" published in *Generations* (Penguin, 2004). Reprinted with author's permission.

Romtvedt, David. "Bending Elbows" published in *Poetry East*.

Romtvedt, David. "Artificial Breeze" published in *Voicings from the High Country*.

Romtvedt, David. "Twenty-Five Vultures" published in *Some Church* (Milkweed Editions, 2005). Reprinted with author's permission.

Root, Jenny. "Money to Burn" published in *Windfall*, Spring 2009.

Root, William Pitt. "Craft" and "Crossing the Rez" published in *White Boots: New and Selected Poems of the West.* (Carolina Wren Press, 2006). Reprinted with author's permission.

Roripaugh, Robert. "The Old Horseshoer" published in *The Ranch:Wyoming Poetry* (University of Wyoming, 2001). Reprinted with author's permission.

Rutsala, Vern. "Speaking Her Lonely Greek" and "Prospectus for Visitors" published in *Ruined Cities* (Carnegie Mellon University Press, 1987). Also published in *Selected Poems* (Story Line Press, 1991). Reprinted with author's permission.

Ryan, Kay. "Cirque" and "Dew" and "How Birds Sing" published in *Elephant Rocks* (Grove Press, 1996). Reprinted with author's permission.

Safford, June Billings. "The Vet Said She May Have Been Thirty" published in *Manzanita, Poetry and Prose of the Mother Lode, Sierra,* Vol. 4.

Sajé, Natasha. "Reading Henry Fowler's *Modern English Usage* in Salt Lake City in November" published in *Kenyon Review.* Also in *Bend* (Tupelo Press, 2000). Reprinted with author's permission.

Saner, Reg. "Alpine Forget-Me-Nots" published in *On Earth,* Vol. 23 ,No. 4, Winter 2002.

Saner, Reg. "North of Wupatki" published in *Poetry,* CLXIII, No. 6, March 1994.

Scates, Maxine. "What Do We Know and When Do We Know It?" published in *Virginia Quarterly Review*, 2008.

Scates, Maxine. "What I Wanted to Say" published in *The American Poetry Review.*

Schott, Penelope. "In This Time of War" and "April, Again" published in *Georgia Review.*

Schott, Penelope. "In This Time of War" published in *May the Generations Die in the Right Order* (Main Street Rag Publishing, 2007). Reprinted with author's permission.

Schott, Penelope. "April, Again" published in *Baiting the Void* (Dream Horse Press, 2005).

Sears, Peter. "Plane Down in Moriches Bay" published in *The Brink* (Gibbs Smith, 2000).

Seiferle, Rebecca. "Apache Tears" and "Ghost Riders in the Sky" from *Wild Tongue.* Copyright 2007 by Rebecca Seiferle. Reprinted with permission of Copper Canyon Press, www.coppercanyonpress.org.

Sheffield, Derek. "A Good Fish" published in *Poetry.*

Short, Gary. "Test" published in *Theory of Twilight* (Ahsahta Press, 1994). Reprinted with author's permission.

Short, Gary. "Teaching Poetry to 3rd Graders" and "Magpies in the Graveyard" appeared in *10 Moons and 13 Horse.* (University of Nevada Press, 2004).

Shukman, Henry. "The Airport Shuttle" published in *London Review of Books*, July 2006.

Shukman, Henry. "Step" published in *In Dr. No's Garden* (Random House, 2002). Reprinted with author's permission.

Shultz, Jeffrey. "J. Learns the Difference between Poverty and Having No Money" published in *Poetry* February 2008.

Silko, Leslie. "How to Hunt Buffalo" published in *People's Tribune* (Chicago), 1998.

Simon, Maurya. "Waste Management" and "Keeping Track" published in *Cartographies* (Red Hen Press, 2008). Reprinted with author's permission.

Skillman, Judith. "Used" published in *Latticework* (David Robert Books, 2004). Reprinted with author's permission.

Skloot, Floyd. "Dowsing for Joy" published in *Selected Poems: 1970—2005* (Tupelo Press, 2008). Reprinted with author's permission.

Soto, Gary. "Anniversary Poem" and "Romance at the River Bend Called Three Rocks" and "Short Lives" published in *Human Nature* (Tupelo Press, 2010). Copyright 2010 Gary Soto. Reprinted with author's permission.

Sowder, Michael. "The Lost Verse" published in *The Empty Boat* (Truman State University Press, 2004). Reprinted with author's permission.

Speer, Laurel. "Buffalo Stones" published in *Times of Sorrow, Times of Grace: Writings by Women of the Great Plains* (The Backwater Press, 2002).

Speer, Laurel. "Candyman" published in *Sin* (Geryon Press, 1990). Reprinted with author's permission.

Spence, Michael. "The Bus Driver's Threnody" published in *The Hopkins Review*, 2008.

Spence, Michael. "And Don't Forget the Fruit" published in *The North American Review*, 2008.

Stafford, Kim. "Beside the Road While Our Nation Is at War" published in *Café Review*.

Stafford, Kim. "Louise" published in *Oregon Quarterly*. Also in *A Thousand Friends of Rain*. (Carnegie Mellon University Press, 1998). Reprinted with author's permission.

Staton, Patricia. "Walking After Dinner" published in *Mid-American Review*. Also in *The Pushcart Prize XXIX*.

Steele, Pamela. "Hands" and "Geography" published in *Talking River Review,* 2007.

St. John, David. "Los Angeles, 1954" published in *Study for the World's Body: New and Selected Poems* (HarperCollins, 1994). Reprinted with author's permission.

St. John, Primus. "The Sniper" and "Water Carrier" and "The Marathon" and "Yellow Sweet Clover" published in *Skin on the Earth*. Copper Canyon Press, 1975. Reprinted with permission of Copper Canyon Press, www.coppercanyonpress.org

Sze, Arthur. "Looking Back" and "Quailia" from *Ginkgo Light*. Copyright 2009 by Arthur Sze. Reprinted with permission of Copper Canyon Press, www.coppercanyonpress.org.

Terris, Susan. "Undercut" published in *Wind*.

Tiffany, Georgia. "Trouble With Kindness" published in *Poems and Plays,* No. 17-18, Spring 2008.

Thiel, Diane. "Wild Horses, Placitas" published in *Resistance Fantasies* (Story Line Press, 2004). Reprinted with author's permission.

Thiel, Diane. "At the Mailbox" published in *Echolocations* (Story Line Press, 2000).

Thomas, Amber Flora. "Swarm" published in *PMS: PoemMemoirStory*, Spring 2008.

Thomas, David E. "The Ten Thousand Things" published in *Buck's Last Wreck* (Wild Variety Books, 1996). Reprinted with author's permission.

Thompson, Lynne. "Soar" published in *Beg No Pardon* (Perugia Press, 2007). Reprinted with author's permission.

Tomlinson, Rawdon. "Flying With Father" published in *New Letters*.

Tomlinson, Rawdon. "Deep Red" published in *Deep Red* (University of Florida Press, 1995). Reprinted with author's permission.

Uschuk, Pamela. "Loving the Outlaw" published in *Without Birds, Without Flowers, Without Trees* (Flume Press, 1990). Reprinted with author's permission.

Uschuk, Pamela. "Finding Peaches in the Desert" published in *Finding Peaches in the Desert* (Wings Press, 2000). Reprinted with author's permission.

Vargas, Richard. "laid off" and "ancestor" and "baby brother's blues" and "race war" published in *Mclife*. (Main Street Rag Pulishing, 2005). Reprinted with author's permission.

Waggener, Miles. "Direction" published in *Phoenix Suites* (The Word Works, 2003). Reprinted with author's permission.

Wagoner, David. "Panic" and "Pleasant Dreams" published in *Margie: The American Journal of Poetry,* Vol 7, 2008.

Walker, Nicole. "Canister and Turkey Vulture" published in *Ploughshares,* Vol. 29 No. 4, 2003.

Waterston, Ellen. "Painted Shut" published in *High Desert Journal*.

Waterston, Ellen. "Spring Calver" published in *West Wind Review.*

Waterston, Ellen. "Painted Shut" and "Spring Calver" and "Drought Dirge" published in *Between Desert Seasons* (Wordcraft of Oregon, 2008). Reprinted with author's permission.

Wendt, Ingrid. "Benediction" published in *Prairie Schooner*, 2007.

White, Mike. "The Bowling Alley's Giant Neon Pin" published in *Poetry East*.

White, Mike. "Go Around" published in *Western Humanities Review.*

White, Mike. "Basho, Glimpsed" published in *Rattle.*

Whitt, Laurelyn. "Aftershocks" first published as "Everything" in the *Palo Alto Review,* Vol. XV, No.1, 2006.

Whitt, Laurelyn. "Deertime: Spanish Fork Canyon" published in *interstices* (Logan House Press, 2006). Reprinted with author's permission.

Wilcox, Finn. "Women" published in *Lessons Learned: Love Poems* (Tangram Press, 2008).

Wilkins, Joe. "Then I Packed You up the Ridge Like a Brother on My Back" and "Highway" published in *The Southern Review.*

Witte, John. "Truck" published in *Second Nature* (University of Washington Press, 2008). Reprinted with author's permission.

Wöhrmann, Deborah. "The Rocking Chair" published in *The Salal Review.*

Wright, Carolyne. "After the Explosion of Mount St. Helens, The Retiring Grade-School Teacher Goes for a Long Walk through the Wheatlands" published in *Ploughshares.* Also published in *A Change of Maps* (Lost Horse Press, 2006).

Wrigley, Robert. "Progress" published in *BigCityLit.com.*

Wrigley, Robert. "Misunderstanding" published in *Café Solo.*

Wrigley, Robert. "The Other World" published in *Earthly Meditations: New and Selected Poems* (Penguin Books, 2006). Reprinted with author's permission.

Woody, Elizabeth. "Flight" published in *Frontiers: A Journal of Women Studies.* Vol. 23 No. 2, 2002.

Young, Al. "Process" Copyright 1992 by Al Young, published in *Heaven: Poems 1956—1990,* (Creative Arts Book Co., 1992). Reprinted with permission of the author.

Young, Al. "American Time" Copyright 1992 by Al Young, published in *Heaven: Poems 1956—1990,* (Creative Arts Book Co., 1992). Reprinted with permission of the author.

Young, Al. "Dawn at Oakland Airport" Copyright 2001 and 2006 published in *Coastal Nights and Inland Afternoons: Poems 2001—2006* (Angel City Press, 2006). Reprinted with permission of the author.

Zeller, Maya. "Tire Hut" published in *Poet Lore,* Vol. 2, No. 3/4.

Zeller, Maya. "Facing" published in *New Ohio Review*, 2010.

## Photo Credits:

Aho, Margaret: photo by Sadie Babits.
Alcosser, Sandra: photo by Philip Meachling.
Alexie, Sherman: photo by Rex Rystedt
Anstett, Aaron: photo by Jake Adam York
Atsitty, Tacey: photo by Dorothy Grandbois.
Axelrod, David: photo by Ezra Axelrod.
Bakken, Dick: photo by Richard Byrd.
Bell, Marvin: photo by John Campbell.
Broyles, Marianne: photo by Diane Fields.
Carlile, Henry: photo by Genevieve Long.
Chin, Marilyn: photo by Don Romero.
Coles, Katharine: photo by Kent Miles.
Day, Lucille Lang: photo by Paul Csicsery.
Dunsmore, Roger: photo by Kent Ord.
Goodtimes, Art: photo by Kit Hedman.
González, Rafael José: photo by Peter St. John.
Green, Samuel: photo by Sean McDowell.
Haaland, Tami: photo by Robert Osler.
HedgeCoke, A. A.: photo by Travis HedgeCoke.
Hirshfield, Jane: photo by Nick Rosza.
Hix, H. L.: photo by Nancy M. Stuart.
Hogue, Cynthia: photo by Sylvain Gallais.
Hongo, Garrett: photo by Michael Pettit.
Inada, Lawson Fusao: photo by Michael Green.
Jaeger, Lowell: photo by Sally Johnson.
Jay, James: photo by Thor Nelson.
Lahey, Ed: photo by Roger Dunsmore.
Laux, Dorianne: photo by John Campbell.
Levine, Philip: photo by Geoffrey Berliner.
Minich, Jan: photo by Ian Minich.
Ortiz, Simon: photo by David Burckhalter.
Palacio, Melinda: photo by Nell Campbell.
Pereira, Peter: photo by Tom Collicot.
Potts, Charles: photo by Terri Silverman.
Rattee, Michael: photo by Hannelore Rattee.
Red Elk, Lois: photo by D.L. Minawmish.
Rogers, Pattiann: photo by John R. Rogers.
Rose, Wendy: photo by Arthur Murate.
Ryan, Kay: photo by Christina Koci Hernandez
Sajé, Natasha: photo by David Baddley.
Smoker, M. L.:photo by M. Stella McRoberts.
Skloot, Floyd: photo by Beverly Hallberg.
St. John, Primus: photo by Henry Carlile.
Takacs, Nancy: photo by Ian Minich.
Thomas, David: photo by Anne Kilcup.
Uschuck, Pam: photo by William Pitt Root.
Waterston, Ellen: photo by Carol Sternkopf.
Wilkins, Joe: photo by Liz Wynne.
Wrigley, Robert: photo by Matt Valentine.
Zarzyski, Paul: photo by Kevin Martini-Fuller.
Zeller, Maya: photo by Christopher Zeller.

## To Purchase Books by Poets in This Anthology:

Ahsahta Press                 http://ahsahtapress.boisestate.edu
Boise State University, 1910 University Drive, Boise, ID 83725-1525

Alice James Books             www.alicejamesbooks.org
238 Main Street, Farmington, ME 04938

Arctos Press                 www.arctospress.com
P.O. Box 401 Sausalito, CA

Ashland Poetry Press           http://static.ashland.edu/aupoetry/
401 College Avenue, Ashland University, Ashland, OH 44805-3700

The Backwaters Press           www.thebackwaterspress.com
3502 North 52nd St., Omaha, NE 68104-3506

Barrow Street Press            www.barrowstreet.org
P.O. Box 1831, New York, NY 10156

Bilingual Press               http://www.asu.edu/brp/
P.O. Box 875303, Tempe, AZ 85287-5303

BkMk Press                 http://web2.umkc.edu/bkmk/
University of Missouri Kansas City, 5101 Rockhill Rd., Kansas City, MO 64110

Black Rock Press             www.blackrockpress.org
University of Nevada, Reno, Reno, NV 89557-0044

Blue Begonia Press           www.bluebegoniapress.com
225 S. 15th Ave, Yakima, WA 98902

BOA Editions                http://boaeditions.org
250 N. Goodman St., Suite 306, Rochester, NY 14607

Brighton Press               www.ebrightonarts.com
5433 Linda Vista Road, Suite B, San Diego, CA 92110

Carnegie-Mellon University Press     www.cmu.edu/universitypress/
5032 Forbes Ave., Pittsburgh, PA 15289-1021

Carolina Wren Press           www.carolinawrenpress.org
120 Morris Street, Durham, NC 27701

Cervena Barva Press          www.cervenabarvapress.com
P.O. Box 440357, W. Somerville, MA 02144-3222

Cleveland State University Press      www.csuohio.edu/poetrycenter/
2121 Euclid Ave., RT 1841, Cleveland, OH 44115-2214

Coffee House Press           www.coffeehousepress.org
79 Thirteenth Ave. NE, Suite 110, Minneapolis, MN 55413

Confluence Press            www.confluencepress.com
1705 9th St., Lewiston, ID 83501

Copper Canyon Press          www.coppercanyonpress.org
P.O. Box 271, Port Townsend, WA 98368

David Robert Books                          www.davidrobertbooks.com
P.O. Box 541106, Cincinnati, OH  45254-1106

Dream Horse Press                           http://home.comcast.net/~jpdancingbear/dhp.html
P.O. Box 2080, Aptos, CA  95001-2080

Eastern Washington University Press         www.ewu.edu/ewupress
534 E. Spokane Falls Blvd. Suite 203, Spokane, WA  99202

Etruscan Press                              www.etruscanpress.org
84 West South Street, Wilkes-Barr, PA  18766

The Foothills Press                         www.foothillspress.com
2425 N. Chelton Road, Colorado Springs, CO  80909

Ghost Road Press                            www.ghostroadpress.com
820 S. Monaco Pkwy #288, Denver, CO  80224

Graywolf Press                              www.graywolfpress.org
250 Third Avenue North, Suite 600, Minneapolis, MN  55401

Grove Press                                 www.groveatlantic.com/grove/default.htm
841 Broadway, 4th Floor, New York, NY  10003

Hanging Loose Press                         www.hangingloosepress.com
231 Wyckoff Street, Brooklyn, NY  11217

HarperCollins                               www.harpercollins.com
10 East 53rd Street, New York, NY  10022

Helicon Nine Editions                       www.heliconnine.com
P.O. Box 22412, Kansas City, MO  64113

Indiana University Press                    www.iupress.indiana.edu
601 North Morton Street, Bloomington, IN  47404-3797

Kent State University Press                 http://upress.kent.edu/
307 Lowry Hall, Kent, OH  44242

Knopf Publishers                            http://knopf.knopfdoubleday.com/
knopfpublicity@randomhouse.com

La Alameda Press                            www.laalamedapress.com
9636 Guadalupe Trail NW, Albuquerque, NM  87114

Logan House Press                           http://www.loganhousepress.com/
205 ½ South Douglas, Wayne, NE  68787

Lost Horse Press                            www.losthorsepress.org
105 Lost Horse Lane, Sandpoint, ID  83864

Louisiana State University Press            www.lsu.edu/lsupress/
3990 West Lakeshore Drive, Baton Rouge, LA  70808

Main Street Rag Publishing Company          www.mainstreetrag.com
P.O. Box 690100, Charlotte, NC  28227-7001

Many Voices Press                           www.fvcc.edu
Flathead Valley Community College, 777 Grandview Drive, Kalispell, MT 59901

Marsh Hawk Press                                www.marshhawkpress.org
P.O. Box 206, East Rockaway, NY  11518-0206

Milkweed Editions                               www.milkweed.org
1011 Washington Avenue South, Suite 300, Open Book, Minneapolis, MN  55415

New Directions Publishing Corp.                 www.ndpublishing.com
80 Eighth Ave, New York, NY  10011

New Issues Press                                www.wmich.edu/newissues/
1903 W. Michigan Ave., Kalamazoo, MI  49008-5463

Oregon State University Press                   http://oregonstate.edu/dept/press/
121 The Valley Library, Corvallis, OR  97331

Penguin Group                                   http://us.penguingroup.com/
375 Hudson Street, New York, NY  10014

Persea Books                                    www.perseabooks.com
853 Broadway, Suite 601, New York, NY  10003

Perugia Press                                   www.perugiapress.com
P.O. Box 60364, Florence, MA  01062

Red Hen Press                                   www.redhen.org
70 N. El Molino Ave., Pasadena, CA 91101

Red Dragonfly Press                             www.reddragonflypress.org
307 Oxford Street, Northfield, MN  55057

Sarabande Books                                 www.sarabandebooks.org
2234 Dundee Road, Suite 200, Louisville, KY  40205

Saturnalia Books                                www.saturnaliabooks.com
105 Woodside Road, Ardmore, PA  19003

Shambhala Publications                          www.shambhala.com
P.O. Box 308, Boston, MA  02117

Sheep Meadow Press                              www.sheepmeadowpress.com
P.O. Box 1345, Riverdale, NY  10471

Southern Illinois University Press              www.siupress.com
1915 University Press Drive, SIUC Mail Code 6806, Carbondale, IL  62901

Timberline Press                                www.timberlinepress.com
6281 Red Bud, Fulton, MO  65251

Truman State University Press                   http://tsup.truman.edu/
100 East Normal Avenue, Kirksville, MO  63501-4221

Tupelo Press                                    www.tupelopress.org
The Eclipse Mill, Loft 305, P.O. Box 1767, North Adams, MA  01247

University of Akron Press                       www.uakron.edu/uapress
30 Amberwood Parkway, Ashland, OH  44805

University of Arizona Press                     www.uapress.arizona.edu
355 S. Euclid Ave., Suite 103, Tucson, AZ  85719

University of Chicago Press
1427 E. 60th Street, Chicago, IL 60637

www.press.uchicago.edu

University of Florida Press
15 NW 15th Street, Gainesville, FL 32611

www.upf.com

University of Georgia Press
330 Research Drive, Athens, GA 30602-4901

www.ugapress.org

University of Illinois Press
1325 South Oak Street, Champaign, IL 61820-6903

www.press.uillinois.edu

University of Iowa Press
119 W. Park Road, 100 Kuhl House, Iowa City, IA 52242-1000

www.uipress.uiowa.edu/

University of Massachusetts Press
P.O. Box 429, Amherst, MA 01004

www.umass.edu/umpress

University of Nebraska Press
1111 Lincoln Mall, Lincoln, NE 68588-0630

www.nebraskapress.unl.edu

University of Nevada Press
Morrill Hall Mail Stop 0166, Reno, NV 89557-0166

www.unpress.nevada.edu

University of New Mexico Press
1312 Basehart Rd. SE, Albuquerque, NM 87106-4363

www.unmpress.com

University of Notre Dame Press
310 Flanner Hall, Notre Dame, IN 46556

http://undpress.nd.edu/

University of Oklahoma Press
2800 Venture Drive, Norman, OK 73069-8216

www.oupress.com

University of Pittsburgh Press
Eureka Building, Fifth Floor, 3400 Forbes Ave, Pittsburgh, PA 15260

www.upress.pitt.edu

University of Tampa Press
401 W. Kennedy Blvd., Tampa, FL 33606

http://utpress.ut.edu/

University of Texas Press
P.O. Box 7819, Austin, TX 78722

www.utexas.edu/utpress/

University of Washington Press
P.O. Box 50096, Seattle, WA 98145-5096

www.washington.edu/uwpress/

Utah State University Press
7800 Old Main Hill, Logan, UT 84322

www.usu.edu/usupress/

Wesleyan University Press
215 Long Lane, Middletown, CT 06459

www.wesleyan.edu/wespress/

West End Press
P.O. Box 27334, Albuquerque, NM 87125

http://westendpress.org/

White Pine Press
P.O. Box 236, Buffalo, NY 14201

www.whitepine.org

Wings Press
627 E. Guenther, San Antonio, TX 78210-1134

www.wingspress.com

Wordcraft of Oregon, LLC                    www.wordcraftoforegon.com
P.O. Box 3235, La Grande, OR  97850

The Word Works                             www.wordworksdc.com
P.O. Box 42164, Washington, DC  20015

W. W. Norton & Company, Inc., New York, NY.    www.wwnorton.com
500 Fifth Avenue, New York, NY  10110


# Some Poetry Sites on the Internet


http://writersalmanac.publicradio.org/archive.php
Garrison Keillor reads a poem every day and  comments on writers.

www.poems.com
Poetry Daily. A poem posted each day.

www.versedaily.org
Posts a new poem every day.

www.loc.gov/poetry/180
A poem for each day of the school year selected by Billy Collins, former U.S. Poet Laureate.

www.poetryfoundation.org
Many links to poetry sites. Access to *Poetry* Magazine

www.poets.org
The website of the Academy of American Poets. Links to many poets and poems.

www.theotherpages.org/poems
Links to many poems.

www.bartleby.com/verse
Books of poetry.

www.serv.com/Lucious/PLG.index.html
Links to many poetry sites.

www/heydays.ws
An anthology of poems about being young and growing up.

# Index of Authors and Poem Titles